BEAUTIFUL FABLES

Beautiful Fables

Self-consciousness in Italian Narrative from Manzoni to Calvino

GREGORY L. LUCENTE

THE JOHNS HOPKINS UNIVERSITY PRESS
Baltimore and London

For Robert Penn Warren and David Hayman

This book has been brought to publication with the generous assistance of the Andrew W. Mellon Foundation.

© 1986 The Johns Hopkins University Press
All rights reserved
Printed in the United States of America

The Johns Hopkins University Press
701 West 40th Street
Baltimore, Maryland 21211
The Johns Hopkins Press Ltd., London

The paper used in this publication meets the minimum requirements of American National Standard for Information Sciences—Permanence of Paper for Printed Library Materials, ANSI Z39.48-1984.

Library of Congress Cataloging-in-Publication Data
Lucente, Gregory L.
Beautiful fables: self-consciousness in Italian narrative from Manzoni to Calvino.
Bibliography: p.
Includes index.
1. Italian fiction—20th century—History and criticism
2. Italian fiction—19th century—History and criticism.   I. Title.
PQ4174.L8   1986   853'.009   86-7373
ISBN 0-8018-3331-0 (alk. paper)

Sheherazade

Il mio sposo celeste
(padrone dei miei respiri)
benigno ritarda per me
la sentenza mortale:
perché fra le tante spose
io sola, unica io,
so con bellissime fiabe
consolare la notte.

Non è mio pregio, ma del cielo
che mi fece fantastica
se degna io sono della grazia.

E voi, non portatemi invidia,
né, dispettosi, lasciate
queste veglie felici
pei vostri inanimati sonni.

A voi diletto, a me speranza
rechi l'Oscura.

My heavenly husband (the lord of my breath) benignly postpones for me
the mortal sentence: because only I, among all the brides,
I alone know how, with beautiful fables, to console the night.
If I am worthy of grace, it is not my doing but that of heaven,
which gave me my inspiration. And you, do not envy me, or, obstinate,
abandon the happiness of these wakeful hours for your inanimate sleep.
For you, may the Darkness bring delight, for me, hope.

Elsa Morante, *Alibi*

Contents

Acknowledgments ix

Introduction. Literary Self-consciousness: History, Ideology, Genre, Mode, and History Again 1

1. The Uses and the Ends of Discourse in *I Promessi Sposi*: Witnessing the Rebirth of History's Truth 26

2. "What's in a name?": Symbolic Meaning and the Play of Narrative Perspective in Verga's "Rosso Malpelo" 68

3. Dossi and D'Annunzio: Artists' Self-portraits 98
   Dossi's *Vita di Alberto Pisani*: "Whom do you love?" or Alberto Pisani's "Love Story" 99
   D'Annunzio's *Il fuoco*: Portrait of the Artist as Superman 106

4. "Non conclude": Narrative Self-consciousness and the Voice of Creation in Pirandello's *Il fu Mattia Pascal* and *Uno, nessuno e centomila* 116

5. The Genre of Literary Confession and the Mode of Psychological Realism: The Self-consciousness of *Zeno* 156

6. Silone and Neorealism 177
   Signs and History in Silone's *Vino e pane*: The Dilemma of Social Change 177
   Postilla on Neorealism 194

7. Lampedusa's *Il Gattopardo*: Figure and Temporality in a Historical Novel 196

8. System, Time, Writing, and Reading in Gadda's *La cognizione del dolore:* The Impossibility of Saying "I" 222

9. History and the Trial of Poetry: Everyday Life in Morante's *La Storia* 246

10. Self-conscious Artifacts: Calvino's Fictions 266

    Il sentiero dei nidi di ragno: The World and Its Narration 267

    Signs and Science in *Le Cosmicomiche: Fantascienza* as Satire 276

    Se una notte d'inverno un viaggiatore: Or, You Can't Judge a Book by Its Title 287

11. Continuations: Samonà, Manganelli, Eco, and Considerations on Postmodernism 301

    Carmelo Samonà.   In the Grotto of the Psyche 302

    Giorgio Manganelli.   The World of the Word: Fool's Truth 312

    Umberto Eco.   Interpretation without End: The Word of the World 322

Conclusion. Who, How, and Why 329

Notes 335

Index 381

Acknowledgments

It is impossible to acknowledge all of the people who have contributed to the shaping of this study. The project has been too long in the making, and remaking, for that. To compound the problem, during its course its author has become constantly more adept at gathering, refashioning, and, *faute de mieux*, simply stealing the many different sorts of material that contribute to the composition of a study such as this, with the result that the list of those who should be mentioned is undoubtedly longer than even he knows. It would, however, be the most unforgivable form of ingratitude not to thank by name at least the following: Charles Singleton, Sam Weber, Eduardo Saccone, Harry Sieber, Olga Ragusa, Ezio Raimondi, René Girard, Dick Macksey, John Irwin, Alicia Borinsky, Jeffrey Mehlman, Eduardo González, Frank Romer, Solange Guénoun, Rainer Nägele, Piero Aragno, Bob Rodini, Mario Trovato, Pier Massimo Forni, Ronnie Terpening, Jane Warth, Clare Godt, James Mandrell, Jane Tylus, Deanna Shemek, and Craig Frisch.

I am also grateful to the students in my seminars in the novel at Loyola University of Chicago and at Johns Hopkins; and I owe special thanks to Mary Jane Hall, who managed to interpret and transcribe all of those strange scratchings which in time became this book.

Early versions of portions of this study appeared in *MLN*, *Italica*, *NOVEL*, *Forum Italicum*, and *Criticism*. I would like to thank the publishers of those journals for permission to reprint here. Research for this book was supported in part by grants from the National Endowment for the Humanities and from the Fulbright Commission, for which I am deeply grateful.

INTRODUCTION

Literary Self-consciousness

History, Ideology, Genre, Mode, and History Again

I

The temptation to begin a study of literary self-consciousness in a self-conscious manner is a strong one, but in the interest of clarity it should probably be avoided, at least for the moment. The topic is no stranger to recent American criticism and theory, although it has usually made its appearance in an indirect way (with a few important exceptions to be discussed shortly), in the midst of, or at times on the margins of, discussions about something else. Such characteristic presentation by indirection and allusion indicates not only that the subject is so widespread and important as to be immediately recognizable but also that it remains a thorny issue for American criticism, one with which even those who are obliged to mention it feel some degree of uneasiness and uncertainty.

This sort of indirect acknowledgment has been the case in several of the more distinguished literary studies of the past six or seven years. Patricia Drechsel Tobin discusses the future of the novel in terms of the shift from the untroubled consciousness of nineteenth-century positivist historicism to the "crisis" of twentieth-century man, a shift that is linked within the conceptual framework of her argument to postmodern culture's self-consciousness of its own state of temporal belatedness (*Time and the Novel: The Genealogical Imperative* [Princeton: Princeton University Press, 1978], 192–93). Alvin B. Kernan pushes literary self-consciousness in a general sense back to the nineteenth-century Romantics and then traces the notion forward through the modern novel to the works of Bellow, Nabokov, and Mailer. He does so with the more or less explicit assumption that the profound opposition, beginning in the early nineteenth century, between the poet and the society in which he lives and writes is once again shifting its terrain, though, to be sure, not in any simple or easily predictable fashion (*The Imaginary Library: An Essay in Literature and Society,* Princeton Essays in Literature [Princeton: Princeton University Press, 1982], esp. 7–8, 148–49, 170–75).

Similar versions of this historical model underlie a great many works of modern American criticism. The basic paradigm begins with the engendering of the artist's self-consciousness by the separation between the individual author and society in the late Enlightenment and early nineteenth century, continues through a period of rapprochement in the midand late nineteenth century as evidenced by the work of the European realists, leads to another major break and to a marked increase in the delights of self-display in the era of modernism (as embodied, for Kernan, in "the art of the surrealists, of Picasso, of Borges, Robbe-Grillet, Pynchon, Pinter and many others," 170–71), and then closes with the problematization of self-consciousness as such in the postmodern works of our own times (treated by Tobin as the currently widespread undermining of narrative genealogies and the concomitant textual "wager on surface," 192–213). But even though the principal characteristics of this historical formula are easily recognizable in a large number of literary studies, the topic of self-consciousness remains secondary in almost all of them.[1]

One recently published book that does treat self-consciousness in a more direct, though still sporadic, fashion—one that any overview of the topic is bound to consider sooner or later—is Gerald Graff's *Literature against Itself: Literary Ideas in Modern Society* (Chicago: University of Chicago Press, 1979). Graff's discussion includes the current critical and theoretical treatments of self-consciousness as well as various examples drawn from contemporary fiction. In Graff's sustained denunciation of the critical/theoretical "vanguard" of American and, in part, European letters, the critical analyses and the literary manifestations of self-consciousness fare no better than the other aspects of the vanguard's supposedly "anti-representational" aesthetic (6). Graff shares the historical paradigm outlined previously in terms of the development of self-consciousness (a paradigm that he restates, however, in notably precise fashion with reference to Lukács's *Theory of the Novel*). But rather than elucidating or attempting to explain in detail the values and procedures of either the contemporary literature of self-consciousness or the critical approaches that have dealt with it at greatest length (such as Russian Formalism, Saussurean structuralism, poststructuralism, or deconstruction), Graff launches a frontal attack on what he sees as the whole "antimimetic" *équipe*. Graff's intent, quite obviously, is not so much to engage his opponents in dialogue as to reject them root and branch. One of the principal objects of Graff's scorn—and in the context of Graff's account of the present malaise in humanist education and culture it is not hard to understand the reasons for his choice—is the work of J. Hillis Miller.

Graff regards Miller's work as emblematic of the anti-referential aesthetic shared by such critics and theorists as Jacques Derrida, Geoffrey Hartman, Paul de Man, and, though less centrally for Graff's argument, Jacques Lacan. The critical procedure that Graff describes—in which Miller takes texts from the classical realism of nineteenth-century fiction and separates their internal structures of meaning, which for Miller are created by linguistic interrelation and difference, from any notion of external reference, such as either the illusions of mimesis or the "mirroring of reality" (19–20, 174–79, 201–2)—has been an important aspect of Miller's work for well over a decade.[2] But Miller's approach, consisting first in the division of meaning from reference and then in the valorization of the former to the detriment, if not the total denial, of the latter, as carried forth in a series of essays and longer studies over this entire period, has been infinitely more complex than Graff makes it sound. It should also be borne in mind that particularly at first Miller was arguing against a way of reading realistic fiction—as though there existed a one-to-one correspondence between the literary text and external reality—which in spite, or perhaps because, of its naiveté and simplicity was so deeply entrenched in American academe and criticism that neither Miller nor anyone else could possibly have threatened its dominance in any but the most ethereal regions of literary theoretics. Indeed, the effect of Miller's work of these past years has not been the overthrow and certainly not the extinction of this naively positivistic way of treating realistic narratives but merely the establishment of a beachhead for his type of deconstructive practice within the broader realm of American realist criticism. In part, Miller has been able to gain this position, as Jonathan Culler has noted, precisely because of his ability to calm the waters of critical turmoil even as he set about introducing such concepts as meaning without external reference and the primacy of fiction's often contradictory self-knowledge as expressed through the text's "linguistic moment" (concepts that according to Culler have been "tamed" through their passage from European philosophical and rhetorical theory to American interpretive practice, at least by comparison with the work of Derrida and of the other Continental *maîtres* of deconstruction).[3]

Such taming aside, the most important aspect of Miller's approach for our present purposes, one that has also been pointed out by Graff and Culler, is Miller's contention that all great literary works come to terms in some way with their own fictionality, which means that they all thematize the basic undecidability between the figural and the referential functions of their language.[4] That this contention may or may not be true seems obvious; the proposition would, in any event, have to be investigated case by case, a procedure that, however definitive, would require not only an encyclopedic library but also an encyclopedic critic or more likely school of critics. Yet whether or not Miller is right—and my guess on this point is that he is probably more right than wrong—the real danger of this approach lies elsewhere. Even assuming that all great works not only contain but also display their knowledge of their own contingency and, in the terminology of deconstruction, of their ultimate undecidability, the task is not, it seems to me, to stop either with that assertion or with the demonstration of its accuracy, since to find both self-knowledge and expression of that knowledge everywhere is merely to trivialize each of them. Rather than locating similarities that endlessly reconfirm this sort of proposition, a goal that seems more fruitful is to account for the extraordinary differences that any group of major narratives demonstrate both in the weight given to their self-consciousness and in their means of expressing it. What I am suggesting, of course, is an investigation along historical lines, one necessarily concerned with technique as well as theme and with divergences as well as likenesses. Although Miller's work on narrative has shown little interest in this sort of approach, it is probably the one manner of proceeding that picks up the recent proposals made by Charles Altieri and others for the reintroduction of the notion of historical context into humanist discourse even as it gives the lie to Graff's significant, if stridently voiced, objections, since the historical context of the expression of self-consciousness thus becomes itself the very locus of humanist investigation.[5] At the same time, such an approach provides a needed corrective to those overly zealous adepts of self-reflection who would, for one bucketful of water, declare the trickle a torrent.

There have been, it is true, several notable strains of literary criticism that treat self-consciousness as the object, at least *in potentia*, of genuine historical inquiry. Ironically enough, one of them, that of the Russian Formalists, led eventually to the ahistorical approach of the Parisian structuralists. Nevertheless, the Formalists' notions of *ostranenie*, or defamiliarization, is one way of approaching the major shifts in literary presentation over time, as the individual writer attempts to make the linguistic form of his literary representation new and different and thereby draws attention to that form as specifically poetic (bringing to mind Jakobson's concept of the poetic "function" as well as that of "literariness"). If this process of defamiliarization is carried out openly, as in the Formalists' English darling, *Tristram Shandy*, it can indeed contribute to the effects of literary self-consciousness. The general notion of historical progression and poetic differentiation, furthermore, calls forth assessments of the history of literary form as diverse as those of Frye's ever more "realistic" (i.e., more skeptical and more knowledgeable) progression of modes to Bloom's endless anxieties of influence; but in the context of the historical understanding of self-consciousness, the companion of choice, to be read with and against the works of the Russian Formalists, is not the work of any Anglo-American critic but rather the influential oeuvre of another Eastern European scholar, Georg Lukács.

Lukács has been one of the critics most directly responsible for the propagation of the sort of historical paradigm of literary self-consciousness sketched earlier. Rather than a history of literary *forms* as such, however, the focus of his mature work (that is, after his early and openly Hegelian *Theory of the Novel*) was on the history of the literary expression of *ideologies*. Despite the fact that as Lukács's aesthetic thought developed he occasionally cast his discussions in terms of such seemingly technical concerns as "narrate or describe," objective versus subjective time, narrative perspective, stream of consciousness, and broadly evaluative as opposed to densely detailed description, his underlying interests were almost always in thematics and particularly in the themes of social morality. Within Lukács's methodology, conscious and imaginative ideological evaluation of social reality—as in the classical realism of Balzac, the critical realism of Thomas Mann, and some of the contemporary works of social realism—is seen as propadeutically enriching and therefore good, whereas strictly *literary* self-consciousness, or consciousness of the status of the work itself *qua* fiction—as in Kafka, Joyce, Benn, and Beckett—indicates a refusal to come to grips with external reality and is therefore condemned as both misleading and dangerous. Despite Lukács's occasionally laudatory comments regarding the aesthetic and the aims of social realism (in its attempt to restore the epic unity of subject and object lost in the contemporary novel in the West), his writings regularly demonstrate greatest sympathy neither for the unimaginatively programmatic works of current Russian fiction nor for the obfuscating ones of bourgeois modernism, also termed "anti-realism," but rather for novels that fall in the intervening category of "critical realism." For Lukács, these are works that at one and the same time represent *and* criticize the world of everyday life.

This odd combination of idealist aesthetic evaluation (reminiscent of Plato's *Republic*) and Marxian polemic makes sense if viewed as deriving from one central system of thought, acknowledged though in large part repudiated by Lukács: Hegelian idealism.[6] In Hegelian philosophy, the telos of knowledge, for the absolute, transcendent Spirit as well as for the individual consciousness, is self-consciousness, which, like the maxim "know thyself," is both the end and the rebeginning of the ongoing development of intelligent life. Through the constant process of identity, negation (or the experience of contradiction and therefore of otherness), and reincorporation of difference into the growing dialectic of self-knowledge, the individual subject becomes a knowledgeable social entity in a system of relations that can be construed as civil society. As absolute Spirit strives for self-consciousness in and through history, moreover, each epoch has a particular, temporally situated spirit of its own, which will then be transcended through contradiction by, and conflict with, its antithesis. The Spirit embodied sensibly in works of art—in which Spirit, individual, and society all come together—reflects this zeitgeist and this struggle. The progression of art within and across periods, moreover, inevitably moves toward increasing self-consciousness, which means toward unity with the Spirit along with knowledge of that unity (the result of which will eventually be the "death" of art as superfluous, in its ultimate transcendence by purer modes of expression). In terms of literary genres, the modern novel (with Goethe as the prime example) is thus the prosaic reflection and expression of the subjective freedom of the new bourgeois age of Christianity in its approach toward the objective truth of the Spirit.

The split of both the Russian Formalists and Lukács from Hegelian idealism is instructive. The Formalists retained the concepts of the essence and the progression of works of art but found that essence and that progression within artistic form itself (for which they were roundly upbraided by Trotsky, Bukharin, and others for having limited both art's meaning and its social power).[7] Lukács, on the other hand, severed the essence of art from connection with the Spirit and relocated it in the representation of material society. Increasing self-consciousness, then, was still the primary attribute of human development, but for Lukács, as opposed to Hegel, self-consciousness did not reside in any sort of idealist conception of increasing knowledge of, and unity with, a transcendent source of meaning. Instead, it resided in the (at best) knowledgeable or (at worst) obfuscating expression of the ideological valuations of social life itself.

The results of Lukács's retention of the Hegelian frame, in which *philosophical* self-consciousness is at once the result and the very ground of knowledge, along with his specifically materialist recentering of the concept's locus in social life, is especially clear in his treatment of alienation. For Lukács, modern man's alienation, his estrangement from society and from society's modes of economic production, is the central fact of life both for the artist and for society at large. Yet, alienation appears in the works of bourgeois modernism not as part of a critique but as a symptom. This accounts to some extent for the procedures of such modernist writers as Kafka, Joyce, and Benn, who, according to Lukács, both indulge in the illusions of subjective time and pile detail upon detail in descriptive passages without ever gaining a true perspective on the objective social import of what they are describing. In the West, only the writers of critical realism, such as Mann and Moravia, have actually described alienation and criticized it at the same time, in consciously knowledgeable investigations of modern self-consciousness itself. As distinct from the Formalists, then, Lukács disparages the modern development of *literary* self-consciousness to the exact extent that it impedes, in his view of the modern novel, the all important treatment of *social* self-consciousness.

It is not difficult to grasp the differences in literary, social, and philosophical interests between, on the one hand, Lukács's position regarding self-consciousness and, on the other, those both of Miller's deconstruction and of the happily positivistic "realist" stance of more traditional American criticism. It should be added at least in passing, however, that as far as Lukács is concerned, there is no reason, except for the virulent political polemics of the period between 1930 and the 1950s, why he could not have seen that literary self-consciousness should itself be studied (rather than rejected *in toto*) as an authentic object of aesthetic inquiry and social analysis, since such was in fact the practice during that period of European writers and critics as diverse as Moravia, Sartre, Benjamin, and Adorno. In recent years, the center of studies of literary self-consciousness in Europe has shifted to France. But despite the influence of such post-Hegelians as Sartre and others in the early postwar period, the major

French treatments of self-consciousness in the 1970s were not concerned so much with questions of art and society as with questions of art within art, or what is currently termed the *mise en abyme*.

The mise en abyme in literature is the duplication of theme on the level of character and action (or vice versa), the effect of which is an endlessly repeated formal and thematic doubling, as in a perfectly situated series of mirrors. French letters has been taken with this type of effect since Hugo and Gide (in whose journals the term first appeared), though structuralism did a great deal to rekindle interest in it, often invoking examples not only from Gide (*Les Faux Monnayeurs*) but also from Renaissance portraiture (Van Eyck, Memling, Velázquez) and from the *nouveau roman*. The major treatments of the mise en abyme include studies by Jean Ricardou, Lucien Dällenbach, and Mieke Bal, as well as special issues of two serials, *Romanica Gandensia* and *Texte*.[8]

The most useful of these works in the present context is Lucien Dällenbach's, in which he is careful to distinguish the interrelation between three types of reflection (simple, infinite, and aporistic) and three corresponding *degrees* of analogy between the text's mise en abyme and the reflected object (that is: a similar work, or "similitude"; an apparent double of the work, or "mimeticism"; and the work itself, or "identity").[9] But regardless of the technical dexterity of all these studies, the topic itself has remained an extremely limited one within the broader outlines of self-consciousness, one that has almost never broached or even acknowledged social questions or social contexts. These treatments, moreover, have tended to be oddly mechanistic, doubtless due to their descent from structuralism's flirtation with "science," so that their assessment of such favored authors as Robbe-Grillet and Borges takes the form of a rationalist game in which the most unsettling aspects of the mise en abyme in particular, and of literary self-reflection in general, are either quickly passed over or easily contained.

In this respect, then, these writers share a symptomatic tendency in their reading of a variety of authors on the topic of self-consciousness, one that can be linked, for example, to a passage from Borges taken up by almost all of the studies of the mise en abyme at one point or another (as well as by the prime mover of this type of investigation, Gérard Genette.).[10] The passage comes at the conclusion of Borges' "Partial Magic in the *Quixote*," following the well-known discussion of Josiah Royce's worldly map within the map:

Why does it disturb us that the map be included in the map and the thousand and one nights in the book of the *Thousand and One Nights*? Why does it disturb us that Don Quixote be a reader of the *Quixote* and Hamlet a spectator of *Hamlet*? I believe I have found the reason: these inversions suggest that if the characters of a fictional work can be readers or spectators, we, its readers or spectators, can be fictitious. In 1833, Carlyle observed that the history of the universe is an infinite sacred book that all men write and read and try to understand, and in which they are also written.[11]

The problem discussed here by Borges, the disturbing aspect (for the reader) of the potential inversion between the reader and the written text, between the real and the fictitious, could be treated purely as a logical one and, as such, could even be transformed into an algorithmic notation and be diagrammed. The affirmation of the concluding sentence, despite its metaphysical grandeur, could be treated the same way. But in neither case would the really disturbing feature of self-consciousness—which, despite Borges' many commentators *en abyme,* is not the fear of inversion but rather the anxiety *inherent* in self-consciousness itself—be given anything but short shrift.

Unfortunately, the major treatments of literary self-consciousness in English do better in this regard only on occasion, notwithstanding the fact that the English term includes anxiety as one of its meanings. The first of these books, Robert Alter's groundbreaking study of self-consciousness in the novel, takes its title from the essay by Borges quoted above: *Partial Magic: The Novel as a Self-Conscious Genre* (Berkeley and Los Angeles: University of California Press, 1975). This study was followed by two others, both of which, as distinct from the works in English mentioned earlier, take the various aspects of literary self-consciousness as their primary topic: Linda Hutcheon's *Narcissistic Narrative: The Metafictional Paradox,* Library of the *Canadian Review of Comparative Literature,* 5 (Waterloo, Ontario: Wilfrid Laurier University Press, 1980; rpt. New York and London: Methuen, 1984), and Bruce Kawin's *The Mind of the Novel: Reflexive Fiction and the Ineffable* (Princeton: Princeton University Press, 1982). To differing degrees, all three of these books reflect the approaches considered so far, whether such approaches be traditionally humanist in the

American sense, deconstructive, formalist, historical, or concerned with the mise en abyme.

Alter's book, owing in part to its comparatively early publication date and in part to its concern for establishing a dialogue within the mainstream of traditional Anglo-American criticism, is the least *à la page* in terms of modern European approaches (despite mention of Roland Barthes and an opening reference to Benjamin's conception of the contemporary artist's plight and the diminishment of "aura" as formulated in the essay on "The Work of Art in the Age of Mechanical Reproduction").[12] Throughout his study, Alter's primary intent is not so much to treat self-consciousness *in* the novel as to single out and describe novels *of* self-consciousness. In other words, as his title indicates, Alter is interested in self-conscious modes of novelistic presentation only as they become so thoroughgoing and dominant as to constitute a genre. He states the criteria for this subgenre of the novel in his book's preface: "A self-conscious novel, briefly, is a novel that systematically flaunts its own condition of artifice and that by so doing probes into the problematic relationship between the real-seeming artifice and reality" (x). It is not enough, therefore, in terms of the categories of Alter's study, for a novelist merely to represent a labyrinthian world in a skillfully labyrinthian way (such as occurs, for instance, in Conrad's *Lord Jim* and Ford Madox Ford's *The Good Soldier*). In explaining why John Fowles' *French Lieutenant's Woman* is a self-conscious novel whereas *Lord Jim* and *The Good Soldier* are not, Alter expands on the notion of ostentatious and systematic "flaunting" that was already present in his initial definition: "This [self-conscious] novelist . . . pointedly asks us to watch how he makes his novel, what is involved technically and theoretically in the making, as the novel unfolds" (xiii). After narrowing the range of interest by introducing the further criterion of seriousness (a novel that is merely a "self-indulgent game" may well be self-conscious, but that in itself does not make it an important novel and thus worthy of discussion), Alter goes on to list "the four major self-conscious novelists of the first great age of the novel [roughly 1600–1800]," Cervantes, Fielding, Sterne, and Diderot. These authors then constitute the subjects of the first sections of his book, followed by chapters on the supposed "eclipse" of self-consciousness in the Victorian era, the revival of self-consciousness in the period of modernism, Nabokov's fictional worlds, and the hyper-self-conscious narrative of the postwar period.

Alter's study thus extends the borders of the usual historical paradigm back into the seventeenth and eighteenth centuries to include what are by now the two more or less universally acknowledged cornerstones of the self-conscious novel in the West, *Don Quixote* and *Tristram Shandy*. Within the context of American criticism, Alter's work therefore runs counter to such treatments as Graff's, not only because he tends to value self-consciousness itself but also because he posits a historical line of interest in, and manifestation of, self-consciousness that begins prior not only to the contemporary novel but also to the Romantics. At the same time, however, he does so without succumbing to the allure of those critics who manage to find self-consciousness, in one form or another, just about everywhere. It is true that Alter's argument does demonstrate a few obvious failings, some of them self-imposed. Even though Alter's comments on the nineteenth-century novel generally and on Balzac in particular follow the series of criteria laid out in his preface, it still seems odd to claim that Balzac's commentary on book production in *La Comédie humaine* and Thackeray's pointedly orchestrated use of highly stylized literary language in *Vanity Fair* are not self-conscious merely because such effects are discontinuous or because they fall more comfortably within the general sphere of literary representation than do similar effects in works by Gide or Fielding.[13]

Alter's most notable insights occur in his treatment of the earlier literary examples in his study; yet he is also sensible in his discussion of the extraordinary proliferation of self-conscious novels in the fiction of the past few decades. In this sense, his book provides the background for Linda Hutcheon's work on contemporary American and European "metafiction," as she duly acknowledges in the introduction to *Narcissistic Narrative*. But in spite of the cogency of Hutcheon's practical treatments of current self-conscious narratives and her continuation, and often extremely perceptive refinement, of the work of such American commentators as Alter, Ihab Hassan, Robert Scholes, and William H. Gass, her major contribution seems, to me at least, to lie elsewhere.[14] The most stimulating and in many respects the most useful sections of Hutcheon's discussion are those theoretical passages in which her aim is, first, to come to terms with the various interactions of what she regards as the two major paradoxical tendencies of modern fiction—outward communication and internal self-involvement—and, second, to formulate a general typology not of genres but of metafictional modes.

Hutcheon begins by rejecting what she regards as Alter's dialectic of "art" and "life," of artistic "consciousness" and "the world" (4). For her methodology, she proposes a twofold version of mimesis: first, "mimesis of product," in which, generally speaking, fiction attempts to re-present the characteristics of the external world, and second, "mimesis of process," in which fiction takes its own internal creation for its subject (4–5). Novelistic self-consciousness, or what she terms more narrowly "auto-representation" as embodied in the "narcissism" of contemporary metafiction, is not, therefore, an unruly stepchild but rather a logical historical result of the centuries-old trend from mimesis of product to that of process.[15] Her revision and extension of Alter's work is thus, in her words, an attempt to retain Alter's perception that the novel changes dialectically, "but in literary as well as ontological terms" (5). As is obvious throughout her discussion, moreover, Hutcheon is intent on refuting those who have asserted that metafictional narrative is "sterile, that it has nothing to do with 'life'" (5); and in regard to this issue her treatment—as far as it can go, given the boundaries she draws—is consistently illuminating, even though her attention to such topics as alienation and the social context of literature is scant.

Hutcheon divides metafictional narcissism into two modes, diegetic and linguistic, which are each further subdivided into the overt (including such obviously self-conscious phenomena as the mise en abyme) and the covert. The primary distinction, between diegetic and linguistic modes, depends on whether the text in question is principally concerned with its operation as narrative, that is, as an ongoing story, or with its status as language, that is, as a linguistic construct. The secondary distinction within each category has to do with degrees of openness and constancy. All of these distinctions are instructive and useful, especially that between narrative ("diegetic") and linguistic self-consciousness, even though they slight the all-important effects—so dear to practitioners of deconstruction—of narrative's self-reflective consciousness of its epistemological status *as* fiction and even though they tend to lose the clarity of their outlines in the course of Hutcheon's often intricate explications of specific metafictional texts. The blurring is also true in regard to her handling of the additional notions of thematization and actualization, around which (combined with the varying degrees of freedom on the part of the reader) she organizes her conclusion. This concluding discussion, replete with chart, takes her all the way from the novel's "parodic" origins and Romantic self-consciousness up to the *Tel Quel* group and the "limits of the novel genre" (154).

Hutcheon's concern for theoretical rigor (which, again, yields results that are important even though, or perhaps because, not always thoroughly convincing) is part and parcel of her desire to introduce to an English-speaking audience such influential Continental theories of literary self-consciousness and auto-referentiality as those of Ricardou, Dällenbach, and Barthes and, at the same time, to refine them through critical practice. Hutcheon's study, therefore, updates both American and European approaches by means of her readings of metafiction from such various literatures as French, Italian, English, American, and Latin American. However, despite the fact that the European interest in self-consciousness originally grew out of the intellectual context with which Hutcheon is most comfortable (structuralism and both Sartrean and post-Heideggerian, or Derridean, philosophical speculation), current French theory, after the works of the three authors mentioned above, has taken another turn. While not abandoning the type of inquiry that culminated in the interest in auto-referentiality and the mise en abyme, more recent theorists like François Récanati have extended the investigation of self-consciousness along the lines of Anglo-American ordinary language philosophy (in *La Transparence et l'énonciation: Pour introduire à la pragmatique* [Paris: Seuil, 1979]).

Récanati adopts the terminology and some, though hardly all, of the interests of various recent schools of the philosophy of language to distinguish (following Quine) between transparent and opaque language.[16] Briefly, transparent language is language that functions as a glass through which discourse indicates its referents directly. In theory at least, this is the language of referentiality and unproblematic communication. Opaque language, on the other hand, is language that impedes the progression of meaning from discourse to things or ideas and thus draws attention to itself rather than to any external referent. Récanati traces assessments of these practical problems of language back through Austin's speech act theory to conceptions of the sign in the philosophy of Port-Royal and even in Descartes. But Récanati's most interesting contribution is his understanding that both of these aspects of language are operative *at the same time* in discourse. (He reaches this conclusion by following the nineteenth-century theories of Franz Brentano concerning the subject-object relation in reflexive mental acts and by adopting certain postulates of recent ordinary language philosophy, though in a historical rather than a merely formalistic vein.)[17]

In literary terms, therefore, even though the language of realism would seem to be (or, better, to strive to be) transparent and that of metafiction opaque, each type of literature demonstrates significant attributes of both transparency and opacity. As in Hutcheon's theory of modes, but primarily on a linguistic rather than a literary plane, Récanati's work on the supposed "transparency" of discourse posits a constant tug-of-war, in every respect, between language's referential functions and its tendency toward reflexivity and self-involvement. This is more, it should be added, than merely a distinction between literal and figural (or between unembellished and rhetorical) language, since the play of transparency and opacity is operative *in praxis,* although with markedly different emphases, on every level of every sort of discourse.

The continuous give-and-take between representation of the external world and absorption in the linguistic medium of discourse is also one of the topics (though conceived in a very different sense and presented in different terminology) of Kawin's *Mind of the Novel.* Like the critics mentioned previously who write in the Anglo-American critical tradition, Kawin sees self-consciousness as a problem of both literary form and literary history with particular relevance to current fiction, although it should be noted that both his comments on form and meaning and his elaboration of historical paradigms are imaginatively heterodox rather than being in any way conventional.[18] Kawin begins his detailed discussion of literary texts with Melville and continues through the modernists up to the works of contemporary French, American, and Latin American writers. The predominantly philosophical nature of his discussion, which treats reflexive fiction as the metaphorical embodiment of mind approaching the limits of the mysteries of human consciousness and therefore pointing toward the "ineffable," provides ample room for such theorists as Hegel, Heidegger, Derrida, and Lacan, and even for such writers as Carlos Castaneda (whose works receive extended attention) and Mary Daly (whose *Gyn/Ecology* serves as both the beginning and the end in Kawin's concluding treatment of feminism and sexual roles in current fiction).

In the course of his discussion, Kawin makes several telling distinctions. One of these has to do with the difference between reflexivity and self-consciousness (a distinction also made by Hutcheon, who comments further that covertly self-aware "narcissistic" texts are self-reflective without necessarily being self-conscious, 7). For Kawin, a reflexive text is one that "is set, as it were, between facing mirrors" so that "its world doubles back on itself, often generating in the reader a paradoxical impression of *limited* being" (16, my italics). Self-consciousness, on the other hand, is a matter not only of reflexivity but also of knowledge. The term thus suggests, at least in Kawin's view, a higher order of apprehension, "as if on some level the text 'knows' that it is a text" (16). Kawin goes on to say that between the two terms, reflexivity is the more general one. But the distinction he draws seems to be less than complete, since—Kawin's appeal to the experience of the reader aside—in practice, even the smallest dose of literary self-reflection implies a degree of self-knowledge. Nonetheless, whether or not Kawin's description of the difference between the terms "self-conscious" (the term usually used in the present study as the more accurate one for most literary texts) and "reflexive" is in the end felicitous, it does lead to a further distinction that is helpful indeed, that between "authorial" and "systemic" self-consciousness. The general distinction that Kawin draws is between literary self-awareness which is identifiable as the attitude of the author (Alter's prime concern, according to Kawin) and that which is presented as "an inherent property of the 'autonomous' text." Although Kawin's definitions are often fraught with theoretical peril and tend, as he freely admits, to break down in practice, the tripartite typology to which these distinctions give rise is nevertheless suggestive. For Kawin, a reflexive novel such as García Márquez's *One Hundred Years of Solitude* can be distinguished, on the one hand, from such authorially self-conscious works as Joyce's *Ulysses* and Pope's *Dunciad* and, on the other, from such systemically self-conscious texts as Beckett's *The Unnamable* and Faulkner's *As I Lay Dying*. Other works—Borges' essays, for example,—demonstrate authorial and systemic self-consciousness by turns, while at least one, the *Quixote*, is neatly divided, being authorially self-conscious in its first half and systemically so in its second.

Throughout Kawin's discussion, it is apparent that he regards systemically self-conscious texts, and particularly those in which narrative frames constantly push against one another, as the most thoroughgoing in the expression of their self-knowledge. In general terms, this type of self-consciousness goes hand in hand, according to Kawin, with the text's sense of its own limits, which arises when literature's drive to "confront or describe the ineffable—any ineffable" is necessarily frustrated (21). This notion of a negation that leads to self-awareness through awareness of the self *as* other has a venerable tradition in the dualistic philosophy of reflection (from Kant through Hegel, Freud, Heidegger, and Sartre to Lacan's theory of the "mirror stage" in human development), and it does Kawin credit that he handles the subject in a lively yet, on the whole, consistent manner both in his theoretical passages and in his readings of specific novels.

But this dualist path is not, of course, the only choice available. One theorist whom Kawin does not mention is René Girard. This lacuna is especially regrettable since many of Kawin's most interesting arguments, such as those dealing with the tensions between expanding narrative frames, are reminiscent of Girard's comments (particularly those on mimetic desire in Proust, but also on Cervantes, Stendhal, and Dostoevsky) in his early work on the novel, *Deceit, Desire, and the Novel: Self and Other in Literary Structure* (trans. Yvonne Freccero [Baltimore: Johns Hopkins Press, 1965]). For Kawin, these tensions arise from fiction's attention to its medium and from the paradox of narrative language aiming toward the wholeness, being, unity that both precedes and follows it but that it can never quite attain, no matter how much it wants to or how hard it tries. In *The Mind of the Novel* these tensions are portrayed as leading eventually to the sort of literary self-consciousness that Kawin regards most highly, the systemic, "which is one of the most elegant and successful means of actually resolving the problem, manifesting an identity it cannot in any case explain" (142). Although Kawin is suggestive on this point, it must be said that the next question—whether this "identity" or unity is a source not just of mystery but also of philosophical and social *mystification*—remains outside the purview of his treatment, and this neglect limits the utility of his study in terms of social, if not of literary, investigation.

The conception of the novel set forth in *Deceit, Desire, and the Novel* is as stimulating as it is original. For Girard, the primary characteristics of the novel, as opposed to the romance, are mediation and the *revelation* (or, for Kawin, "manifestation") of mediation. The "triangular" nondualistic desire proper to the novel, in which characters desire an object only because of and through the desire of the other, is thus itself the object of novelistic discourse. This is an advance—indeed a change not so much in degree as in kind—over the normally dualistic theories of the philosophies of reflection discussed by Kawin. It is true that Girard is not principally concerned with self-consciousness as such. But at times in his treatment of Proust—who constructs Marcel as the other through the temporal distance between the narrating "I" and the narrated "I"—Girard comes very close to casting his argument in terms of a self-conscious play of revelation and concealment that is operative not so much on the level of narrator-as-character as on that of narrator-as-voice (297–98).

This basic view of novelistic self-consciousness moves the question from one of self-knowledge (as for Miller and in part for Alter) or even of dualistic self-reflection as such (as for Dällenbach and Hutcheon) to one of both of these *plus* desire: that is, plus imitation, repression, deferral, and endless mediation. That the dynamic representation of desires, reversals, and progressively *internalized* mediations drawing Girard's attention can be seen, at least in certain instances, to be a function of narrative *voice* returns our discussion to the level of discourse, as with Récanati's study, but now to literary, and more specifically novelistic, discourse.[19] The dynamism of Girard's view of the novel, moreover, is similar in significant respects to Kawin's, though Kawin's interest in novelistic discourse as at once the voice and the mediation of desire is even less clear than Girard's. Literary self-consciousness would seem to be an extraordinarily fertile ground for Girardian analysis, but Girard has not, unfortunately, pursued the topic with any consistency in his later work. Moreover, in spite of the fact that one of his followers, Eric Gans, has recently treated the topic of linguistic consciousness at considerable length, the implications of Gans's work, if any, for the study of self-consciousness in *literary* texts remain, at least for the moment, undeveloped.[20]

II

Throughout the studies considered thus far, two basic issues recur with particular regularity. Although they may seem unrelated, their ties are both more intimate and more intricate than might at first be supposed. One of these is the question of genre as distinguished from mode, and the other is that of historical as opposed to ahistorical approaches. The distinction between mode and genre is in a sense a technical problem of literary form and focus and may therefore appear ahistorical. But in the end this is not the case. Almost every study of self-consciousness per se that we have discussed has been concerned with self-conscious fiction as a *genre* of narrative. This concern is clearest in Alter's work, but it is present in one shape or another almost everywhere else, too. This is true whether the key term is literary "self-consciousness" (as for Graff as well as, often, for his "anti-representational" and on occasion outspokenly antihistorical antagonists) or whether it is replaced by some other master term, such as "modernist" or "postmodernist" ideology, the *mise en abyme*, "reflexivity," "metafiction," and the like. Even within the context of Hutcheon's interest in presentational *modes*, furthermore, these modes are considered only when they are dominant aspects of a delimited genre of texts (i.e., "narcissistic" metafiction).[21] As we have seen, these genre studies are not necessarily ahistorical. On occasion, as for Alter's "other great tradition" (that of the self-conscious novel) and for Kawin's study, this type of approach does in fact lead to a genuine historical treatment of generic development, usually beginning with Cervantes, continuing through Sterne and Diderot, and ending with the *nouveau roman* and such contemporary American and Latin American authors as Barth, Barthelme, Pynchon, Borges, and García Márquez.

There is nothing inherently mistaken about such a view of literature and literary history, in which narratives are extracted from their literary and cultural environments and examined together because of their one salient similarity, with little or no regard for their more immediate literary traditions or for the extraliterary conditions of their conception, production, and reception. But it is important to see that this type of literary "history"—history conceived of more as a game of hop, skip, and jump around the Western world than as a dynamic, dialectical, yet continuous process—is not the only way in which to understand the development of literary self-consciousness. The generic histories we have been considering, whether truncated or full, avant-garde or traditional, are in fact histories of the narrative *of* self-consciousness. The present study therefore parts company with these others because of its focus on the workings and on the history of self-consciousness *in* narrative. The discontinuous history of generic progression thus gives over to the more consistent, though also more complex, history of narrative modes of self-conscious presentation in modern fiction.

What this interest means in practical terms is that the most apposite texts for my purposes are often those in which, owing both to historical and to more narrowly literary reasons, self-consciousness is an important factor but not a dominant one. My analysis will thus eventually have to deal not only with the techniques of self-conscious presentation but also with the weight that self-consciousness carries in individual texts as well as with the variations in emphasis (often striking) within and between diverse authors' work as literary, cultural, and social history unfolds. Perhaps not surprisingly, it is precisely those narratives in which self-consciousness is not so thoroughgoing as to function either in an ostentatious or in a constant manner (i.e., those in which the mode of self-conscious presentation does not constitute a genre) that tell us most about literary self-consciousness as a historical phenomenon. Indeed, one prerequisite for assessing the present rage for self-consciousness (in criticism and in fiction, as noted by critics as diverse as Tobin, Kernan, Graff, Gans, and Christine Brooke-Rose) is an account of the history of narrative self-consciousness beginning with and moving through periods in which the novel was not a remarkably self-conscious conscious genre.

The goal of this investigation is thus a reconsideration of the theoretical and critical findings discussed up to now both insofar as they concern matters of literary technique and as they attempt to construct cultural paradigms and historical genealogies. Within its boundaries, consideration of presentational mode, epistemological concern, and literary history—in other words, all the most impressive and most instructive aspects of the studies we have been considering, both in their strengths and in their weaknesses—forms the basis for a discussion that is aimed at technique as well as at meaning and in which the category of history, however uncertain and as yet imperfectly defined, serves as the rich tapestry over which the effects of self-consciousness play themselves out.

Beyond considerations of literary technique, some of the recurrent interests of this study—in particular, those that often draw the focus of literary self-consciousness itself—are easier to list than to define, at least for the moment. These topics include such uneasy relationships as those between textual meaning and authorial intention (involving questions of critical understanding and authorial will), between literary representation and veracity (involving questions of literary imitation and authenticity, artistic fidelity, and the powers and limits of fictional discourse), and between literary communication as a private and as a social phenomenon. Other recurrent topics, regarding the textual operations and attributes of self-consciousness, are, if finally no less tricky, at least easier to characterize, especially those concerning the ways in which literary self-consciousness can be distinguished in any given work.

By "literary self-consciousness," then, I mean the text's self-reflexive knowledge of its status as fiction and of its literary techniques and procedures as both narrative and narration, as both the tale and its telling. At this point it is important to add that what I intend here by "knowledge" has more to do with awareness than it does with complete understanding. More often than not, the narrative's self-conscious effects serve to turn its discourse into hide-and-seek rather than to create a closed or stable system of knowledge. In other words (as the nonspecialized use of the term "self-conscious" in English suggests) mystification and doubt, fully as much as comprehension, play major roles in literary self-consciousness. In narrative fiction, such self-reflexive awareness may be expressed directly or indirectly in various ways: either by the narrator (through open commentary and/or through irony); by the characters; through thematic development in conjunction with the progression of narrative events; through such appended matter as introductions, prefaces, postscripts, and the like; or through any amalgam of the above. Hutcheon's distinctions between linguistic and diegetic self-consciousness and between overt and covert modes of expression are undoubtedly useful. But at the same time it is important to see, first, that these categories usually overlap in the texts we will be considering and, second, that the crucial question of narrative's consciousness of itself *as* fiction, and as imitation both of the world and of other discourse, tends to spread across and finally to dominate all such heuristic divisions.

Certain of the texts under consideration, especially the more recent ones, display literary self-consciousness on almost every page, whereas others, such as those from the various schools of nineteenth- and twentieth-century realism, manifest their self-consciousness much less directly, though not necessarily less importantly. In all cases, however, as in Récanati's schemas (which are derived from eighteenth- and nineteenth-century German and French philosophies but which, with even greater profit in the sense of social signification, could also have been gleaned from Vico), attentive examination of literary self-consciousness demonstrates the inadequacy of any neatly drawn representational/nonrepresentational or transparent/opaque opposition in the language of fiction. In other words, what has often in the past (and again as recently as Graff's study) been regarded as a case of "either/or" is in fact one of "both/and." Nonetheless, it does not follow that all fictional narratives are equally or even similarly self-conscious in terms of emphasis or meaning, and this is part of the reason for the interest in historical progression within the discussion that follows.

The principal texts to be considered are narratives by Manzoni, Verga, Dossi, D'Annunzio, Pirandello, Svevo, Silone and the neorealists, Lampedusa, Gadda, Morante, Calvino, Samonà, Manganelli, and Eco. With the exceptions of the chapter on Verga and part of the chapter on Calvino (and with the necessary caveat in regard to Manganelli), all of the texts to be considered are novels. Doubtless, other novelists or other works (or even other literary genres) could have been selected, but these choices, in addition to being a matter of personal taste, seemed the most workable and most appropriate both for their literary and historical stature and for their relevance to the theoretical issues at stake. The restriction of this sequence to Italian novels, moreover, has a rationale that is at once theoretical and practical. For reasons stated earlier, I am not interested here in plucking novels from various national traditions in order to pursue the study of a literary genre or subgenre. That type of work on the self-conscious novel has been done, and it does not seem to me that we need more of it just now. In terms of self-consciousness *in* narrative, to repeat, the only way to chart real historical changes, rather than those that merely reconfirm a priori paradigms and preconceived notions (however fanciful or engaging) of literary genealogies, is to move forward along and within the lines of literary and, more broadly speaking, cultural tradition. True, this could be done over the entire spectrum of narrative fiction in the West, but such a study is well beyond not only the capacities of this writer but also, most likely, the patience of any reader, not to mention the benevolence of any publishing house.

Besides the need to limit the national and literary boundaries of investigation so as to gauge specific historical shifts, there is a further reason why this study concentrates solely on Italian literature. Despite the wide-ranging importance of this topic in recent American and European criticism, there has been, as yet, almost no critical discussion of self-consciousness in Italian narrative beyond occasional commentary by Giacomo Debenedetti, Salvatore Battaglia, Ezio Raimondi, and a very few others. Indeed, Italian lacks even a critical vocabulary of its own to deal with the issues involved. The one book of Italian criticism that has treated the problem in an extensive fashion, by Mario Perniola, is occupied not with Italian literature but with French, American, and English novelists.[22] The blame for this neglect can be laid in part to chance, no doubt, but it also derives from the still pervasive influence of Crocean aesthetics, which would consider literary self-consciousness as a topic of at best secondary interest and a history of self-consciousness as an outright anathema. At the same time, the combination of literary *and* social analysis adopted here—a combination necessitated by the basic questions of worldly representation that recur throughout these narratives—is, if not entirely new in Italian criticism, an approach of recent development, roughly since the post-1968 revaluation of Verga's *verismo* and the mid-1970s discussions of the nature of representation in novels as diverse as Manzoni's *I Promessi Sposi* and Morante's *La Storia*. Thus, the intent of this study, both in its overall theoretical slant and in its recurrent critical concerns, is to fill a perplexing lacuna in Italian criticism and, in so doing, to right a wrong in sore need of redress.

A historical approach is singularly illuminating in a study of this sort, since it is when things change, in a practical as well as in a Hegelian sense, that the subject turns back on itself and begins to question its own status, taking the self as both the subject and the object of inquiry and, at least in that regard, actually constituting the self *as* an entity. Within narrative, whether this inquiry amidst shifting codes of signification intensifies, fizzles, or grows to develop offshoots of its own varies from author to author and from book to book. If it does go somewhere, whether it leads to questions about the nature of meaning (arbitrary or motivated, worldly or transcendent), about artistic form (free or determined, innovative or conventional), or about both, depends in part on the individual artist, in part on the literary tradition in which change occurs, and in part on the extraliterary cultural and social environment. In the history of Italian narrative, there is no doubt that self-consciousness has been a significant aspect of literary expression at least since Dante and Boccaccio.[23] Nonetheless, restricting the scope of investigation to the nineteenth and twentieth centuries has two definite advantages. First, it limits the focus to the genre of the novel (with the few exceptions mentioned earlier); and second, it keeps discussion to the modern period, and in Italy this means the period in which there has been a consciously unified literary tradition on a national rather than merely a local scale, a historical tradition within which it thus makes sense to speak of both consistency and change.

It would not be right to bring these introductory remarks to a close without commenting more precisely on what this study is and is not. It is not in any sense a theoretical grammar of self-consciousness, nor, at the opposite extreme, is it a *complete* history of the subject as found in all Italian narrative from 1800 to the present. The first of these is already available, albeit in limited versions, in some of the French and Anglo-American works discussed earlier (though again, the real value of the theories elaborated therein can be affirmed or denied only as they are put to the test in close relation to specific narratives). The second would be either so voluminous as to daunt the most enthusiastic of readers or so mechanical as to induce slumber rather than to inspire critical engagement. Furthermore, even within the survey of narratives singled out for analysis and discussion, self-consciousness is not the only topic to be pursued here. Literary self-consciousness does indeed serve as the center of the discussion that follows, as the issue around which the individual chapters and the study as a whole are organized; but it is also used as a means of broaching other subjects that are germane and illuminating for each narrative taken on its own terms. This study's aim, then, even at its inception, is twofold—to furnish the material for a history of self-consciousness as it occurs in a series of major Italian narratives over roughly the last two hundred years and, by using this issue as a springboard, to give more or less detailed readings of each of the texts at hand. Ultimately, this combination of theoretical interest and critical concern, within the frame of two centuries of Italian cultural and social history, should provide a way of approaching the fundamental question around which studies of literary self-consciousness continue to hover: not just who speaks and how, but also why.

III

This study begins with the author of *I Promessi Sposi*, the writer who, after Dante and Boccaccio, did the most to codify the language of fictional narrative in Italy. But it could also have begun with one of the novelists preceding Manzoni—Ugo Foscolo, for example, or even the Abate Chiari (1711–85). Several of Pietro Chiari's sentimental narratives are not without interest in this context, especially as the memorialistic "confessions" of socially elevated *female* narrators; yet for all his literary energies, Chiari remains a minor writer of the mid-eighteenth century, little more than a footnote to the great tradition of the Italian novel in the subsequent era.

Foscolo is, to put it mildly, of an entirely different stripe. His most important narrative, *Le ultime lettere di Jacopo Ortis* (1798–1802; *Last Letters of Jacopo Ortis*) is in many respects the first major novel in modern Italian literature. If a study of literary self-consciousness were to include a detailed discussion of *Jacopo Ortis*, it would have to find a way to come to terms with the novel's relation to at least the more prominent of its forebears, Richardson's *Pamela*, Rousseau's *Nouvelle Héloïse*, and the work on which *Ortis* is methodically patterned in terms of its epistolary organization, its sentimentality (with the addition of the passion of patriotism to that of love), its characters, and even its plot, Goethe's *Werther*. Since the language of the letters in *Jacopo Ortis* is considerably less precious than that of the Italian "novels of sentiment" of the previous era, moreover, Foscolo's text demonstrates a linguistic concern that, very generally speaking, foreshadows Manzoni's thoroughgoing renovation of the language of Italian narrative. Careful consideration of these two topics, however, would direct the course of inquiry not so much forward into the major strains of Italian fiction in the nineteenth century as backward into the eighteenth, and, at the same time, outside of Italy altogether, into the language and traditions of the novel in England, France, and Germany.

But in spite of the fact that this temporal and national orientation would carry the discussion well outside the borders already set, the primary reason for not dealing at greater length with *Le ultime lettere di Jacopo Ortis* is a different one. The reason, quite simply, is that, in terms of literary self-consciousness, the turbid, melodramatic *Jacopo Ortis* is by no means the most significant of Foscolo's fictional texts. *That* text is in fact not a novel at all but the deceptively lucid, essayistic epilogue concluding Foscolo's translation of Sterne's *A Sentimental Journey through France and Italy* (1768), published in 1813 under the title *Viaggio sentimentale di Yorick lungo la Francia e l'Italia*, with the attribution "traduzione di Didimo Chierico" and a salutation ("Didimo Chierico A' Lettori Salute") supposedly penned by the "translator."

Foscolo's epilogue (designated "Notizia intorno a Didimo Chierico," or "Notice concerning Didimo Chierico"), purports to be a sketch of the translator, who, sometime after sending the manuscript containing the translation and other texts to the editor (yet another of Foscolo's screens, this, too, evocative of eighteenth-century fiction and of Foscolo's own *Jacopo Ortis*), seemingly vanished without a trace.[24] The description in the "Notizia" of Didimo's assiduous studies and intellectual habits makes him sound uncannily like a hybrid of Yorick/Sterne and Foscolo himself; it ends, in a manner reminiscent of Sterne's own fictional practices throughout *Tristram Shandy* and in parts of *A Sentimental Journey*, by echoing the conclusion of the text that it follows. The story in Foscolo's "Notizia" is as fancifully peculiar as anything in Sterne's original. Before taking off for parts unknown, Didimo had presented an aged priest with a copy of the text to be used for his epitaph, which the priest has in turn consigned to the editor and which is then reproduced at the end of the "Notizia" just as Yorick/Sterne's "actual" epitaph had been at the conclusion of *A Sentimental Journey*. Foscolo/Didimo's "Notizia" thus reveals the internally triadic organization of self-consciously novelistic discourse (in which the self as subject reflects on the self as object only *in* and *through* the existence of the other, be this the "editor," the "translator," the narrator, the reader, another character, another text, or all of these) that had remained unclear in the segmentation of editor/character/reader throughout the persistently Romantic *Jacopo Ortis*. Despite the fact that Foscolo is only the translator of Sterne's text, he therefore manages to have the last word, or perhaps it would be more accurate to say that, literally, Didimo does.

By virtue both of its wittily ironic self-involvement and of the multiply specular relationship that it establishes with Sterne's narrative (which is itself an implicit commentary on, and parody of, the travel books and the sentimental novels that were staples of eighteenth-century European literature), Foscolo's appended "Notizia intorno a Didimo Chierico" is an intriguing example of literary self-consciousness. It reflects back not only on Foscolo and on Sterne but also on the collaborative play of identity and difference inherent in literary editing and in literary translation, both of which were markedly on the rise in turn-of-the-century European publishing. It does so, moreover, in a way that is complex enough so that no dualistic model of reflection is adequate to contain it. That the "Notizia" is not as richly rewarding either in a literary or in a cultural sense as Manzoni's pre-Risorgimento historical novel, Verga's postunification *verismo*, D'Annunzio's fin de siècle decadence, the modernist narratives of Pirandello's *umoristi* (who nonetheless bear a striking resemblance to Foscolo's Didimo), or, indeed, any of the more recent works that will follow here, is due in large part to the very limitations of the form in which the "Notizia" is cast, as a secondary pendant rather than as a full narrative text in its own right. Therefore, even though it is not to be the object of extended attention, it does furnish what is to come with a historically fitting, if all too briefly acknowledged, point of departure.

ONE

The Uses and the Ends of Discourse in I Promessi Sposi

Witnessing the Rebirth of History's Truth

> *Se le lettere dovessero aver per fine di divertire quella classe d'uomini che non fa quasi altro che divertirsi, sarebbero la più frivola, la più servile, l'ultima delle professioni. E vi confesso che troverei qualche cosa di più ragionevole, di più umano, e di più degno nelle occupazioni di un montambanco che in una fiera trattiene con sue storie una folla di contadini: costui almeno può aver fatti passare qualche momenti gaj a quelli che vivono di stenti e di malinconie; ed è qualche cosa.*
>
> If the end of literature were to amuse that class of mankind that does little else but seek amusement, it would be the most frivolous, the most servile, the very last of all professions. And I have to confess that I would find something more reasonable, more human, and more worthy in the activities of a mountebank whose stories entertain the crowd at a country fair: maybe he at least has given a few moments of pleasure to those who live in poverty and sorrow; and that is something.
>
> Fermo e Lucia, II, 1

Questions of language, particularly of its worldly use and abuse, are of major concern in Manzoni's *I Promessi Sposi (The Betrothed)*.[1] These questions begin with the book's introduction and continue, though in constantly varying forms and contexts, throughout the novel. In the introduction, Manzoni's narrator states his reasons for reworking the story, which he claims to have found in an anonymous seventeenth-century manuscript, and begins to explain the procedures he has adopted for revising its language. Although toward the end of the introduction the narrator makes an oblique reference to himself as an "author," the guise he assumes actually combines the attributes of two traditional roles, that of the dutiful editor, common to eighteenth-century fiction from Defoe, Richardson, and Laclos to Goethe and Foscolo, and that of the historical novel's more actively creative writer, such as found in the contemporary and highly influential books of Sir Walter Scott.

The introduction opens with a passage supposedly copied verbatim from the scratched and faded original, which the narrator had intended to transcribe from first to last, word for word. But after a page or so the narrator breaks off the transcription of the autograph and gives vent to his doubts about the entire project. As the narrator laments, and as the language of the opening passage amply demonstrates, the original is so full of elaborate conceits, Lombard idioms, incorrect Italian, arbitrary grammar, poorly articulated sentences, Spanish elegance, and inappropriate rhetoric that, even transcribed, no one would ever endure the toil of reading it. Regardless of all of the narrator's efforts at transcription, therefore, the story would remain unread and unknown—in short, useless.

The narrator finds this situation distressing for a single reason: the story itself is too beautiful to lose. Therefore, in order to salvage it from the oblivion of unread texts, he proposes what he has already done—that is, to rework the original, leaving the events and their sequence as they stand while changing what he at first terms the manuscript's "language" ("dicitura") and later its "style" ("stile"). In regard to the obvious problem of what sort of language or style to adopt instead, the narrator admits that at one point he had actually considered furnishing an account of each and every change along with the logic behind it, but by the time that he began putting the explanations together, he realized that they would have made up another book all by themselves. He accordingly refuses the temptation to explain himself at such length, and he seems content to let the matter rest there, without further clarification beyond the inferences to be drawn from his introductory comments and the evidence of the narrative itself. He excuses this omission by saying that, along with the fact that one book at a time seems quite enough, "un libro impiegato a giustificarne un altro, anzi lo stile d'un altro, potrebbe parer cosa ridicola" (6; "a book written to justify another book, not to mention the style of another book, might seem rather ridiculous," xiv).

Manzoni's work on the novel extended over a period of many years and included several thorough revisions. Both in the unpublished draft of *Fermo e Lucia* (1821–23) and in the first edition of *I Promessi Sposi* (1827), the device of the "found" manuscript and its reworking may have been little more than a literary conceit—though one of a different sort from those of the text's "anonymous" original—just a convenient and currently fashionable way to get the story going, insignificant in itself and of little direct relation to the narrative that follows. But by the appearance of the novel's definitive revision of 1840, it was clear that Manzoni's intent in the language of the novel as a whole was not only to display his editorial footwork but also to provide a viable standard for modern Italian narrative on a national scale. The thoroughly revised language of the 1840 edition, based on Manzoni's years of research into the idiom of *lingua toscana*, was therefore meant as a unifying model for Italian letters, one that could be read and understood by the great preponderance of Italy's still limited but growing readership.

The novel's self-reflexive introduction, in which the narrator first broaches the subject of language and style and then renounces further explanation except to offer the narrative itself as its own justification, might initially seem to preclude any subsequent thoroughgoing consideration of the issues of language in the text. But, as might be expected, given Manzoni's fascination with language and his unflagging interest in both linguistic and aesthetic theory, this is not the case. As the story develops, it becomes increasingly apparent that questions of language are not only central to the narrative's style but are also a part of the story's subject matter. After the openly self-conscious introduction, these issues, which involve linguistic mastery as well as linguistic hierarchy, are clearest in the text's treatment of the official state edicts, in Renzo's linguistic education, in the story of Fra Cristoforo's conversion and his encounter with Don Rodrigo, in the massive effects of the plague, and, finally, in the narrator's overall relation to the product of his own discourse in terms of worldly meaning and worldly use. In the end, no account of the narrative's organization and meaning is complete without coming to terms with the ways in which the novel presents and attempts to resolve these questions.

The first clear sign that the narrative's concern with language is going to continue past the introduction and into the story itself is the presentation in chapter 1 of the government edicts, the language and style of which recall the circumlocutory and affectedly "elegant" discourse of the anonymous manuscript quoted at the introduction's beginning. The *gride*, in this case dealing with the vagabonds and *bravi* of seventeenth-century Lombardy, are indeed examples of the inflated rhetoric that Manzoni regularly associates with the upper strata of the dominant Spanish hierarchy. But along with Manzoni's ongoing critique of social behavior, and the stamp of historical authority that the proclamations lend to the novel's own discourse, the *gride* also give Manzoni a way of broaching one of his favorite topics, the relationship between discourse and worldly action:

> Quelle gride, ripubblicate e rinforzate di governo in governo, non servivano ad altro che ad attestare ampollosamente l'impotenza de' loro autori; o, se producevan qualche effetto immediato, era principalmente d'aggiunger molte vessazioni a quelle che i pacifici e i deboli già soffrivano da' perturbatori, e d'accrescer le violenze e l'astuzia di questi. L'impunità era organizzata, e aveva radici che le gride non toccavano, o non potevano smovere. Tali eran gli asili, tali i privilegi d'alcune classi, in parte riconosciuti dalla forza legale, in parte tollerati con astioso silenzio, o impugnati con vane proteste, ma sostenuti in fatto e difesi da quelle classi, con attività d'interesse, e con gelosia di puntiglio. Ora, quest'impunità minacciata e insultata, ma non distrutta dalle gride, doveva naturalmente, a ogni minaccia, e a ogni insulto, adoperar nuovi sforzi e nuove invenzioni, per conservarsi. Così accadeva in effetto. (16–17)

> Those proclamations published and republished by government after government, only served as pompous attestations to the impotence of their authors; or, if they had an immediate effect, it was principally to add further vexations to those that the peaceful and weak already suffered at the hands of the iniquitous, and to increase the latter's violence and cunning. Impunity was organized, and it had roots that the proclamations did not touch or could not move. Such were the sanctuaries and privileges of certain classes, partly recognized by the legal authorities, partly tolerated in resentful silence, or contested by vain protests, but upheld by deed and defended by those classes with active interest and jealous punctilio. Now, this impunity, threatened and insulted by the proclamations but not destroyed, with every threat and with every insult naturally had to make new efforts and find new ways to preserve itself. This was in fact what happened. (9–10)

The intention of the narrator's commentary on the *gride* is, of course, to account for the continuing corruption and abuse by powerful, though supposedly outlawed or legally restricted, segments of local society. This and contiguous passages thus help to explain how and why the basic mechanism of the narrative—the blocking of Renzo and Lucia's marriage at the capricious whim of Don Rodrigo in his competition with his cousin Attilio—can have occurred at all. Indeed, the passage goes on to describe the hapless state of the peaceful and unprotected ordinary man ("l'uomo bonario"), who is, ironically, subject both to the arbitrarily enforced rules of the official law and to the unofficial but no less real illegal harrassment on the part of the outlaws.

But there is a complementary set of thematics at work in this explanation that, in the long run, is equally telling in *I Promessi Sposi*. These thematics, like those in the introduction, deal with questions of language and utility. What, after all, do the high-flown, often repeated, and elaborately elegant edicts represent if not the "impotence" of their authors? Their meaning seems directed outward, into the world of everyday activity. But in another sense their meaning is reflected back inward, to show the ineffectiveness of their authors' endeavors; and *this* meaning is only underscored by their endless repetition. What, therefore, is the worldly effect of these edicts if not precisely the opposite of that which, at least in practical terms, is intended? The lesson, in this very hierarchical and complexly ordered society, is especially obvious despite—or perhaps because of—the well-known ironic detachment with which Manzoni's narrator views it: pompous show goes hand in hand with worldly failure. At best, such overbearing pomposity will end as it began, in vapid rhetoric and "vain protests." At worst, it will result in the opposite of what is hoped. This is a difficult lesson to learn, since it involves aspects of style in regard both to discourse and to other forms of human behavior; but as the narrator is already aware (indeed as is demonstrated in the very revisions of his text) and as Renzo must eventually realize too, this lesson is crucial for anyone who seeks to get along, and possibly even to do well, in human society.

It is the narrator's assessment of the *gride*, both in their rhetorical complexity and their worldly ineffectiveness, that ties the thematics of this first chapter to those of the exchange in chapter 3 between Renzo and the devilishly tricky lawyer, popularly known as Dr. Azzeccagarbugli, and that thus leads to the scene of Renzo's first great failure in the lessons of discourse as presented in the novel. Renzo goes to consult Azzeccagarbugli at Agnese's instigation and with his hopes high. Both because of Don Rodrigo's interest in Lucia and Don Abbondio's personal shortcomings, Renzo and Lucia are in stormy seas, with their wedding and their happiness in jeopardy, and Renzo knows it. Yet, given the unpleasant situation, Renzo has done all right for himself up to this point. By his directness and the strength of his will, he has forced the necessary information out of

Don Abbondio, cutting through the haze of the timorous priest's obfuscations and "latinorum," and together with Agnese and the less than enthusiastic Lucia, he has decided on the next step to be taken. But unlike Don Abbondio, who is still within the social realm of Renzo's everyday life in the village, the once important Azzeccagarbugli is a figure from another social sphere altogether.[2] In this respect, therefore, the scene between Renzo and Azzeccagarbugli foreshadows Renzo's experiences in Milan after the bread riot, where he is again notably out of his element.

As Manzoni makes clear in the scene between Renzo and the lawyer, the passport that permits passage from one level of society toward the next (though without destroying either the hierarchical levels themselves or the privileges that they protect) is language. Azzeccagarbugli, of course, knows this from the start. His particular professional talent is the use of language to defend his clients from the apparent intent of the law. He does this, as his epithet of "Quibbleweaver" suggests (a name so thoroughly associated with the man's essence that Agnese can no longer recall what his real name is), by turning the language of the law away from its worldly referents and then directing it back into a maze of discourse, so that its worldly, legal sense is nothing more than a conundrum, null and void, and his clients, no matter how miscreant, can go scot free.

When Renzo first enters the lawyer's studio and asks to have a word in confidence, Azzeccagarbugli makes everything seem simple: "'Son qui,' rispose il dottore: 'parlate. . . . Ditemi il fatto come sta'" (44; "'Here I am,' replied the doctor: 'go ahead and speak. . . . Tell me the facts as they are,'" 35). But there is a problem that is greater than either of them, at least for the moment, realizes. As Renzo himself admits: "Lei m'ha da scusare: noi altri poveri non sappiamo parlar bene" (44; "You'll have to excuse me: poor folk like us don't know how to speak very well, 35). Renzo finally manages to mention the threats made to the priest and the unfulfilled matrimony, at which point Azzeccagarbugli takes over.

Throughout the lawyer's subsequent comments and his reading of the *gride* that treat forcible interference with marriage, Renzo remains so thoroughly immersed in the "words" themselves (which he is convinced will aid him but which he can read only "un pochino," or "a little") that it never occurs to him that the lawyer has taken him for a bravo in need of a shrewd defense instead of a poor silk-worker in search of justice. When the truth finally comes out—that Azzeccagarbugli has gotten things exactly reversed—the lawyer has a simple explanation. According to Azzeccagarbugli, the fault is Renzo's because he, along with all those of his class, is ignorant of the uses of language in the world: "Diavolo! . . . Che pasticci mi fate? Tant'è; siete tutti così: possibile che non sappiate dirle chiare le cose?" (49; "Devil take it! . . . What kind of a mess have you got me in? It's always this way; you're all the same: how is it possible that you never know how to say things clearly?" 40). Now that Azzeccagarbugli has given Renzo a moment to talk, Renzo tells him the rest of the story, stressing that in fact he did make Don Abbondio "speak clearly" ("io l'ho fatto parlar chiaro") and then coming out with the name of Don Rodrigo. This is quite enough for Azzeccagarbugli, who washes his hands of the entire matter. The lawyer's only advice to Renzo is to leave people of his station alone. If Renzo really wants to tell his story, he should tell it among his equals, who do not know any better than he does how to measure their words.

At this turn of events, Renzo seems intent on justifying himself, but the lawyer, obviously concerned for his own interests now that the name of Don Rodrigo has been mentioned, cuts his ex-client off and shoves Renzo toward the door, insisting to the astounded servant that she return Renzo's capons, since he wants nothing from Renzo or, indeed, anything whatever to do with him. Before pushing Renzo out of his studio, however, Azzeccagarbugli—more from anger and frustration than anything else— gives him one last piece of advice that will turn out to be of special significance in the development both of Renzo's character and of Manzoni's narrative in general: "*Imparate a parlare:* non si viene a sorprender così un galantuomo" (50, my italics; "*Learn to speak* [properly]: and don't come surprising a gentleman in this way," 40, my italics).

The importance of language is emphasized in the exchange between Renzo and the hapless Azzeccagarbugli by the narrator's insistent repetition of the word "parola," which resounds like a tattoo throughout the scene. It is true that Azzeccagarbugli's type of discourse is not intended in any sense as a model for Renzo to follow, that, because of the lawyer's present condition and his linguistic chicanery, he is actually, as Giorgio De Rienzo has pointed out, a champion of the word who is now "decaduto (e avvilito)" ("fallen [and degraded]").[3] Nevertheless, Azzeccagarbugli's climactic exhortation does provide a clear beginning (after Don Abbondio's Latinate preface) to Renzo's *Bildungsroman* in the world of language.[4] Renzo's real education has to wait, however, until after he, Lucia, and Agnese, with the assistance of Fra Cristoforo, have fled to Monza and then split up, and Renzo has arrived, on his own and dejected, in the turbulent atmosphere of Milan.

Following the bread riot, with its heady mixture of confusion, scuffling, and camaraderie and its odd linguistic amalgam of Italian and Spanish, Renzo, having taken a moment to catch his breath, begins to make a speech. The narrator's attitude toward this and Renzo's subsequent behavior in Milan has already been suggested in chapter 11, just prior to the narrator's self-conscious comparison of his own narrative practice with that of a child herding animals, losing sight of one here and there only to go fetch it and bring it back into the pen after its day's romp, like so many characters in the narrator's telling of the present story (202; 177). What the narrator says about Renzo in chapter 11 is that no matter how adept Azzeccagarbugli might have proved at serving Don Rodrigo's ends and eliminating Renzo from the picture once and for all, Renzo himself was turning out to be an even better servant. Renzo simply is not yet competent to act profitably on his own in the broader world of society. It is important to see, moreover, the critical role that language plays in Renzo's worldly ineptitude. Almost everything of note that happens to Renzo in this section of the story in Milan—including the events to which he will later refer in his final summary of the lessons he has learned—occurs through the medium of discourse. This is not to say that in Manzoni's view discourse itself is somehow superior to other worldly endeavor, but only that there is no action or interaction among human beings that is completely outside of it or that does not depend on it in some fashion or other, which is why language is one thing that Renzo must learn to use if he is to learn others, one key to the kingdom of social wisdom and success.

The following scene at the Inn of the Luna Piena, framed by the hustle and bustle of the crowd and presented through the narrator's juggling of various perspectives all at once, is one of the most astutely organized and precisely sketched in all of Manzoni's narrative.[5] The action of this scene proves to be crucial, moreover, for Renzo's progressive education in the ways of discourse and in the limits of social behavior. After a brief introduction, the narrator frames the scene with the thoughts of the innkeeper, who immediately recognizes Renzo's companion and wonders whether Renzo himself is "hound or hare," hunter or prey. Renzo orders wine and stew, and at the innkeeper's apology for the lack of bread, he produces the third and last of his supply of rolls, raising it high to show the crowd and shouting (amidst a gentle narrative irony over which he has no control) "Ecco il pane della provvidenza!" (246; "Here is the bread of Providence!" 218). With the approval of his companions and the encouragement of one in particular ("Viva il pane a buon mercato!"; "Hurrah for cheap bread!"), Renzo goes on to give his thumbnail sketch of the ideal economic program: "'A buon mercato?' disse Renzo: 'gratis et amore'" ("'Cheap?' said Renzo: *'gratis et amore'*").

In the course of this pronouncement, the narrator demonstrates Renzo's inability, at this point in the narrative, to formulate and express clear ideas either about his own situation or about that of others. This failing was already apparent in his high-flown pronouncements and exhortations before meeting his "guide"; and as occurs with regularity throughout the first half of the novel, Manzoni again makes use of lexical indicators to shade Renzo's limitations. During Renzo's encounter with Don Abbondio, one of Renzo's primary objections had been to the priest's resorting to the linguistic trickery of Latin (a language that, as Manzoni suggests on several occasions in the story, was not understood by the general populace). Moreover, while still at the inn, Renzo complains obliquely about Don Abbondio's linguistic subterfuge and openly about Ferrer's "qualche parolina in latino" (255; "few words in Latin," 225), which Renzo attempts to repeat in his own wine-addled discourse ("*siés baraòs trapolorum*"), thus reflecting both Ferrer's Spanish and Don Abbondio's "*latinorum.*" But to state his economic program, Renzo himself has resorted to the Latinate formula "*gratis et amore.*"

Such logical inconsistency within Renzo's behavior would not be disturbing in and of itself, but as Renzo continues, the inconsistencies mount. Indeed, it is obvious to the innkeeper and perhaps to others present as well that Renzo is not only a hare, but also (as the narrator already suggested in his comments on Don Rodrigo's schemes in chapter 11) one that is doing everything possible to get caught. Renzo, of course, knows nothing of this, and therein lies both his foolishness and his weakness. Earlier, in the street, he thought he had spoken "con un po' di politica, per non dire in pubblico i fatti miei" (244; "with a bit of politic, so as not to talk about my personal affairs in public," 216). But at the Inn of Luna Piena, where he is not only urged on by the crowd but also animated by the wine, Renzo lets himself go, as though he were indeed inspired by the Full Moon, and he does so at precisely the wrong moment.

On Renzo's behalf, several points should be remembered: first, that he is still nursing resentment for the injustice of his separation from Lucia; second, that he is in fact a "montanaro" (mountaineer—i.e., an unsophisticated country boy) on his own in the big city; and third, that his adversary, in this game of which Renzo is still totally unaware, is both powerful and highly skilled. The presentation of Ambrogio Fusella is one of those instances in which Manzoni's gift for the creation of memorably detailed minor characters is particularly evident. The inkeeper demonstrates his understanding of Fusella's authority both by his fears, expressed in the narrator's report of the man's thoughts, and in the explanation of his behavior toward Renzo (for which, when demonstrated *too* directly in his discourse, the innkeeper is quickly reproved). The narrator's denomination of Fusella as a character proceeds by means of a sort of deflected irony that plays off the ignorance of "il nostro Renzo," or "our Renzo," but without attenuating the narrator's, or by extension the reader's, sympathy for Renzo as a character. Fusella goes from "la guida," or guide (repeated later from the innkeeper's perspective), and "lo sconosciuto," or stranger (again repeated, though negated, in relation to the innkeeper's perceptions), to "l'amico," or friend. This last appellation is used by the narrator at the moment of Fusella's departure, after he has obtained the information desired and has refused Renzo's drunken offer of further libations. As if the irony of this shift in terminology were not sufficient, the term is one that Renzo himself had adopted earlier ("'Bravi amici!' disse," 249; "'Good friends!' he said," 220) and one that is then immediately repeated in Renzo's own discourse, when he laments the departure of the "galantuomo" for whom he had poured another glass of wine, "proprio da amico" (253; "just like a friend," 223). Again, this sort of semantic sequence attests to the precision with which Manzoni grades his presentation of even minor characters and events; and in this case it also demonstrates the semantic irony with which he underscores the ironic organization of the entire scene (though such semantic drift is by no means always ironic, as is shown by the narrator's careful transitions in chapter 8's denomination of Renzo, Lucia, and Agnese as "fuggiaschi" [fugitives] to "viaggiatori" [travelers], and only at the end, after taking leave of Fra Cristoforo and after Lucia's well-known "Addio, monti," to "pellegrini" [pilgrims]).

In the scene at the Inn of the Luna Piena, Fusella's task is as precise as it is tricky: to find out Renzo's name without arousing either Renzo's suspicions or the ill will of the inn's other customers. After Renzo's assertion of his legal expertise (probably a result of his single disastrous experience with Azzeccagarbugli) and his refusal to give his name and province of origin despite the innkeeper's dutiful citation of the appropriate *gride* under the agent's watchful gaze, Renzo's "guide" is constrained to hold his tongue and wait for his loquacious prey to set his own trap, in which Renzo is quick to oblige. Having thanked his guide and the others who have helped him to avoid the innkeeper's pen, ink, and paper, Renzo once again, as in his earlier speech in the street, assumes the attitude of a preacher ("mettendosi di nuovo in attitudine di predicatore") and decries those who rule the world and who always want to make writing enter into everything: "Sempre la penna per aria! Grande smania che hanno que' signori d'adoprar la penna!"(250; "Always brandishing a pen! A great mania those gentry have for using the pen!" 220–21). One of the gamblers nearby makes a joke of this, saying that once "que' signori" have finished eating their geese, they have to find something to do with all those quills. Here Renzo responds in kind, and the narrator, in an important aside to which we will return shortly, comments on Renzo's reply. But the matter is more serious than either the gambler's initial jest or Renzo's jocular response, and Renzo continues along the same line he had taken previously to lament the close association between writing and power and the use of writing to subject the unlettered: "Ma la ragione giusta la dirò io . . . : è perché la penna la tengon loro: e così, le parole che dicon loro, volan via, e spariscono; le parole che dice un povero figliuolo, stanno attenti bene, e presto presto le infilzan per aria, con quella penna, e te le inchiodano sulla carta, per servirsene, a tempo e luogo" ("But I'll tell you the real reason . . . : it's because they're the ones who hold the pen: and so the words that they say fly off and vanish into thin air; but they're very careful about the words that a poor chap says, and quick as a flash they impale them with that pen and nail them down on paper, to use them as they wish, at the right time and place"). Renzo's lament leads to his complaints about the treacheries of Latin and then once more to the day's affairs, all of which were conducted "in volgare," or the common speech of the local populace, and all, Renzo notes, without recourse to pen, ink, and paper. This brings Renzo back to his expectations for the following day, and he thereby gives the guileful agent, who up to now has listened in silence, the opening he needs.

The program Fusella outlines for the rectification of the pricing and distribution of bread depends, first, on pen, ink, and paper and, second, on the gathering up of all the names of those involved, as the narrator emphasizes in an aside. But, as the narrator also points out, Renzo, "invaghito del progetto" ("carried away by the project") does not notice any of that, and he falls for the ruse without hesitation when asked to participate in a trial run, giving not only his name but also the details of his marital status. With this, the "guide" has obtained exactly what he wanted, and he departs posthaste—in fact so abruptly that Renzo is left talking to himself, apparently loudly enough that the serving boy thinks

Renzo is addressing him rather than the agent's undrained glass (which Renzo then downs in one gulp). When the waiter responds to Renzo, saying he has understood ("Ho inteso"), Renzo seems bemused but not surprised, since he still believes, despite all the lessons of his own experience, that when reasons are just ("giuste"), every reasonable person will understand and agree. For Renzo at this point, when language is used in the service of justice and truth, it is or should be transparent, that is, significant but secondary: expression is only a necessary means to a much more important end. Ironically, the more he drinks the more he demonstrates the failures of this belief, since he cannot find the words to finish his well-meant but poorly formed sentences.

The narrator handles the description of the entire scene by distancing himself from its presentation both through the use of such screens as the innkeeper and even Fusella and through direct addresses to the reader. As Renzo drinks more and more, the narrator recounts less and less. Early in the scene, during the exchange over the official registration of guests at the inn, Renzo downs his third glass of wine, and the narrator, after reporting that fact, adds: "E d'ora in poi ho paura che non li potremo più contare" (248; "and I am afraid that we shall be unable to count them anymore from now on," 219). Later on, just after Fusella's departure and Renzo's oblique exchange with the waiter, the narrator again interrupts the course of his description in order both to provide extra information not discernible from the present scene and to explain the rationale for the gaps in representation that are to follow:

> Qui è necessario tutto l'amore, che portiamo alla verità, per farci proseguire fedelmente un racconto di così poco onore a un personaggio tanto principale, si potrebbe quasi dire al primo uomo della nostra storia. Per questa stessa ragione d'imparzialità, dobbiamo però anche avvertire ch'era la prima volta, che a Renzo avvenisse un caso simile: e appunto questo suo non esser uso a stravizi fu cagione in gran parte che il primo gli riuscisse così fatale. Que' pochi bicchieri che aveva buttati giù da principio . . . gli diedero subito alla testa: a un bevitore un po' esercitato non avrebbero fatto altro che levargli la sete. Su questo il nostro anonimo fa una osservazione, che noi ripeteremo: e conti quel che può contare. Le abitudini temperate e oneste, dice, recano anche questo vantaggio, che, quanto più sono inveterate e radicate in un uomo, tanto più facilmente, appena appena se n'allontani,

se ne risente subito; dimodoché se ne ricorda poi per un pezzo; e anche uno sproposito gli serve di scola. . . .

Noi riferiremo soltanto alcune delle moltissime parole che [Renzo] mandò fuori, in quella sciagurata sera: le molte più che tralasciamo, disdirebbero troppo; perché, non solo non hanno senso, ma non fanno vista d'averlo: condizione necessaria in un libro stampato. (253–54)

Here all our love of truth is necessary to make us proceed faithfully with a narrative that does so little credit to a character of such importance that he might almost be called the hero [*literally*: leading man] of our story. But for the same reason of impartiality, we must also state that this was the first time such a thing had happened to Renzo: and it was his very inexperience in such excesses that made this first one of his turn out so fatally. Those few glasses that he had tossed down at the start . . . went immediately to his head: to an experienced drinker they would have done nothing more than slake his thirst. On this point our anonymous chronicler makes an observation which we will repeat for what it is worth. Temperate and honest habits, he says, also have this advantage, that the more they are settled and rooted in a man, the more sensitive he is to even the slightest departure from them; so that he remembers it for some time afterwards; and even a folly becomes a useful lesson to him. . . .

We will record only a few of the vast number of words that [Renzo] sent forth in that disastrous evening: the many that we leave out would be too inappropriate because not only do they not make sense, they do not even make a pretense of any: a necessary condition for a printed book. (223–24)

Manzoni's narrator thus excuses Renzo's behavior (and quietly asks the reader's complicity) by saying not only that this is Renzo's first indulgence in such excess but also that Renzo will learn from it; and what he will learn, in his passage from inexperience to maturity, will be the value of honesty and temperance and the dangers of excessive behavior of any sort. At the same time, the narrator reaffirms his own love of truth and his commitment to representational fidelity (in following the anonymous manuscript's story if not its style), even though he later qualifies this commitment, within his own narrative intended for publication, by subordinating representational fidelity to sense. This valuation in regard to narrative practice is of the same sort that the narrator and, perhaps surprisingly, even the author of the anonymous original make in regard to Renzo's social behavior: it is important to act in the world and to believe in something that is worthy of action, but it is equally important to exercise restraint in all endeavors or chaos will reign in terms of both literary representation and worldly comportment. This attitude toward behavior also recalls the narrator's initial goal in redoing the anonymous manuscript, that is, to rid it of linguistic excesses, thereby making it readable and pleasant so that its story can be followed and understood. The lesson for Manzoni's narrator as well as for the narrative's "leading man" is clear: following one's beliefs and even acting on one's impulses can be a benefit and a virtue, but only as they are subordinated to a higher value, that of making sense (and although exactly what *this* value is subordinate to is not yet apparent in Manzoni's text, it will become much more so by the story's end).

If, however, this dual appeal to both behavioral and linguistic discretion in worldly action as well as in worldly representation seems too limited—indeed, entirely too sober in view of Renzo's extraordinary spirit and Manzoni's strikingly rich text—it must be remembered that these comments on narrative and linguistic aims and practices are not the only self-consciously literary notations in this portion of the narrative. The other commentary in this vein, produced by Renzo before his fall into drunkenness and explained by the narrator in the aside mentioned previously, comes earlier in the chapter, following the gambler's joke about the geese and the quills. Renzo responds to the gambler's witticism with a significant remark: "'To', 'disse Renzo: 'è un poeta costui. Ce n'è anche qui de' poeti: già ne nasce per tutto. N'ho una vena anch'io, e qualche volta ne dico delle curiose . . . ma quando le cose vanno bene'" (250; "'Ooh!' said Renzo: 'he's a poet, that fellow. So you've got poets here, too. They're cropping up everywhere nowadays. I have a vein, too, and sometimes I say some curious things . . . but that's when everything is going well,'" 221). The narrator explains Renzo's words with the pretense of clarifying the key term's local usage:

Per capire questa baggianata del povero Renzo, bisogna sapere che, presso il volgo di Milano, e del contado ancora più, poeta non significa già, come per tutti i galantuomini, un sacro ingegno, un abitator di Pindo, un allievo delle Muse; vuol dire un cervello bizzarro e un po' balzano, che, ne' discorsi e ne' fatti, abbia più dell'arguto e del singolare che del ragionevole. Tanto quel guastamestieri del volgo è ardito a manomettere le parole, e a far dir loro le cose più lontane dal loro legittimo significato! Perché, vi domando io, cosa ci ha che fare poeta con cervello balzano?

To understand this foolishness of poor Renzo's, it is necessary to know that among the commoners in Milan, and even more so in the countryside nearby, "poet" does not signify at all, as it does for every gentleman, a sacred genius, an inhabitant of Pindus, a pupil of the Muses; it means a person with a mind that is peculiar and a bit crazy, and who, in his speech and in his deeds, demonstrates more wit and oddity than reasonableness. What an impertinent interference it is of commoners to tamper with words and to make them mean things that are at the furthest extreme from their legitimate sense. Because, I ask you, what does being a poet have to do with having a mind that's a bit crazy?

As is often true of Manzoni's irony in the novel, this passage is equally as interesting for what it omits as for what it says. It is clear that Renzo's tongue has long since been loosened by the exuberance of the day's events and that his head is light from the wine, and it is also obvious that Renzo's reply is meant as a facetious feint. In both of these respects, it is a "baggianata," or, roughly, a piece of nonsense. But the narrator's explanation of the term, or indeed his reason for explaining it at all, is far from straightforward. The importance of the quality of behavior in regard to both speech and other forms of action ("ne' discorsi e ne' fatti") is a theme that, as we have seen, runs throughout the entire chapter, so *that* part of the narrator's commentary seems clear enough. But neither of the two definitions of "poet" that the narrator offers—either the supposedly correct one, cast in the erudite, neoclassical frame of the gentlemanly allusion to Pindus and the Muses, or the popular meaning of "poet" as a term designating an irrational oddball—seems entirely acceptable to the narrator. The first is treated ironically through its inflation; the second, through its vulgarity and illegitimacy. Therefore, the next step, rather than the outright rejection of the populace's wisdom as contained in language, is the questioning of this wisdom without offering any real solution, as though maybe there were some truth, though not the whole truth, in the popular conception of the poet as a singular, exceptionally imaginative individual. Finally, rather than affirming or denying either sense of the word or taking any sort of definite stance on the question—Classical as well as Shakespearean and Romantic—of the relation between poetry and irrationality, the narrator lets the whole matter drop with a question of his own.

Although this approach differs from the narrator's later explicit explanation of his representational procedure in regard to Renzo's drunken discourse, the technique of placing two positions on an issue side by side and then withdrawing from any definitive solution (often weighting the second over the first by means of a question that seems merely rhetorical) recurs throughout Manzoni's text, beginning with his prepublication consideration of stylistic questions as described in the introduction and running all the way to Renzo's and Lucia's closing evaluations of the meaning of their experience. At the inn, the weight seems to fall on the imagination as significant in its own right even if it *is* peculiar and even if, in excess, it too is doubtless either hazardous or repugnant, or both. Renzo's depiction of himself as something of a poet (though only in better times) thus joins the other indications of the close relation between the narrator and his character; and it tempers the narrator's sober judgment of Renzo's follies even as Renzo indulges in the excesses for which he will have to pay but from which, eventually, he will learn. That the narrator himself is implicated in this assessment of human discourse and behavior is important, therefore, since this self-reflexive implication demonstrates the ties of sympathy between the narrator and his "primo uomo" at the same time that it reinforces the narrative bond between action and discourse and again underscores the continuing thematics of excess and restraint in both areas. But however significant the narrator's excursus is, it must also be remembered that, at least at this point, the narrator's reaction to the questions he raises is neither affirmation nor denial but instead clever, ironic withdrawal.

Consequent to what the authorities have learned from their informants, the notary and his bailiffs arrive at the inn early the following morning to take Renzo into custody. At first it may seem that the change in Renzo's attitude from the night before—from acceptance and unquestioning fellowship to skepticism and recalcitrance—is simply the result of his sobriety, the usual feelings and reactions of the "morning after." But as is typical of the multilayered depth of Manzoni's narrative technique, there is no single logical or psychological explanation for Renzo's sudden enlightenment. Part of his learning has, however, already been explained by the narrator in the lengthy excursus dealing with the limitations of the text's fidelity to complete representation and with the moral effects that extreme behavior has on normally reserved individuals. Within the narrator's earlier scheme of things, therefore, Renzo's awakening into the light (however grim) of knowledge can be explained by his excesses of the previous evening, the very same excesses, in fact, that have got him into the straits in which he now finds himself.

This combination of psychological notation—broadly stated and then subtly developed without further narratorial commentary—and implicit literary "explanation" (in terms of the topos of the reawakening into moral knowledge) is most clearly demonstrated, as is again customary in Manzoni's representationally oriented aesthetics, in the character's deeds. At first Renzo can do little except to watch, look, and think (269; 237). This is the same behavior that, in a later context, is extolled by Manzoni as the exemplary conduct of human beings, who all too often, by separating speech from those other aspects of intelligent behavior and by being too quick to leap to language, manage only to make themselves lamentable rather than admirable (543; 486). As distinct from Renzo's earlier reactions in Milan, his behavior now shows that he no longer indiscriminately believes whatever he hears ("Però, di tante belle parole Renzo, non ne credette una," 271; "But of all these fine words Renzo did not believe a single one," 239). When Renzo sees and recognizes others who might help him approaching him and his captors on the street, he signals to them by moving his head and coughing; and when the right moment comes, he seizes the opportunity that fortune has provided and states his case in both practical and moral terms: "'Se non m'aiuto ora, pensò, mio danno.' E subito alzò la voce: 'figliuoli! mi menano in prigione, perché ieri ho gridato: pane e giustizia. Non ho fatto nulla; son galantuomo: aiutatemi, non m'abbandonate, figliuoli!'" (273; "'If I don't help myself now,' he thought, 'it's all the worse for me.' And he raised his voice at once: 'Friends! They're taking me off to prison because yesterday I cried: bread and justice. I haven't done anything; I am an honest citizen. Help me, friends, don't abandon me!'" 241). So Renzo has begun to learn the importance and utility of language, and he demonstrates what he has learned by using discourse (including body language) in action. His words are skillfully framed, and they play once again on that trickiest of terms, "galantuomo."[6] He seizes the moment and speaks, and shortly thereafter is free.

In the narrative organization of these central chapters (14–16), the efficacy of the concluding harangue at least in part makes up for the foolishness of the introductory one as well as the discursive errors in between.

If there is any doubt as to what Renzo has learned in Milan, it is quickly dispelled by his behavior at the inn in Gorgonzola, where the way in which he conducts himself reaffirms his newly acquired wisdom in the uses of discourse. As the Milanese merchant begins to relate his version of the story of the previous day's events, in which Renzo figures as a dangerous provocateur, Renzo listens "zitto e attento" (284; "silent and attentive," 252), paying closer attention than any of the others in the audience while carefully concealing his interest. Along with this cautious, in part fear-driven behavior, he also refrains from the sort of alcoholic indulgence of the evening before—although he does not refuse wine altogether, as he had meanwhile at the rustic inn—and now remains content with a half liter of "vino sincero" ("good wine"). Even when the merchant's story becomes most animated and the reactionary slant of his opinions most obvious, Renzo, despite all his perfectly natural desires to flee, continues to sit quietly and restrain himself (as Fusella had done at the Luna Piena and as Fra Cristoforo had also done during another meal). Finally, when Renzo sees the opportunity to depart without giving rise to suspicion, he pays the innkeeper and leaves "senza far altri discorsi" (289; "without saying another word," 257), thereby conducting himself in a manner completely different from that of the previous evening in Milan. Renzo has thus begun to learn not only how to use language (though this is just a beginning and nothing more) but also how to refrain from linguistic excess in the interest of his own well-being, and his behavior at the inn in Gorgonzola aptly attests to this knowledge.

In this case, of course, Renzo's silence has nothing to do with acquiescence. His fury at the merchant's tale is reflected, however, not in public discourse but in his thoughts to himself as he heads away from the inn towards the Adda. After mentally berating the merchant for the inaccuracies of his report, Renzo concludes with an internally voiced imperative, again directed to the merchant, that both binds Renzo's linguistic experiences together into a consistent process of learning and recalls the beginning of that very process: "E imparate a parlare un'altra volta; principalmente quando si tratta del prossimo" (291; "And learn to speak properly another time, especially when it's a question of a fellow human being," 260). From a beginning pupil, Renzo has, at least in the context of *this* moment, become the master.

At the end of this chapter, there is a codicil to the entire lesson that extends from Renzo's entry into Milan to his arrival at his cousin Bortolo's in the territory of Bergamo in chapter 17. Bortolo, after praising the *bergamasco* lawyer who has made such an impression in Venice and done so much for his fellows in Bergamo precisely because he "knows how to speak" (304; 271), cautions Renzo that, if he wants to stay and work in the silk industry nearby, there is a local linguistic oddity that he must learn to accept, however repugnant it may be to him at first. This is the *bergamasco* habit of referring to anyone from the territory of Milan as a "baggiano," or fool. Renzo's reply, that he is ready to live with this less than complimentary epithet, pleases Bortolo at the same time that it indicates another stage on the way to Renzo's understanding of the ways and the deformations of language in the world. The term itself casts back, furthermore, to the narrator's description of Renzo's own "baggianata" concerning poets at the inn in Milan, and it also casts forth to the novel's conclusion. The narrative is not done, therefore, either with this epithet or with the process of linguistic education signaled by the repetition of the verb *imparare*. But before reviewing where these terms lead within the story, we must double back to trace the development of another set of concerns that are also of crucial significance both within Azzeccagarbugli's initial command and within the order of language itself, those of hierarchy.

In *I Promessi Sposi* hierarchy is important to language both in an external and in an internal sense. Externally, the forms of language correspond to the already hierarchical ordering of society: each class, and each local division within a given class, has its own regular way of expressing meaning in discourse. Internally, language depends on the ordered priorities of hierarchy for its articulation and so for the production of its meaning. These two aspects of linguistic hierarchy—social and grammatical—are already apparent in the novel's introduction, in the narrator's reflection on the *gride,* and in Azzeccagarbugli's discussion with Renzo concerning the laws and their meaning; but they are presented with special force in the story of Fra Cristoforo's conversion and change of appellation in chapter 4 and in the scene of his encounter with Don Rodrigo in chapter 6, in each of which questions of hierarchy assume the primary focus of the narrative.

The bitter yet codified exchange of insults and the subsequent altercation that leads to Fra Cristoforo's conversion (via the death of his faithful servant and that of his opponent) arises from a question of the rules of courtesy governing relations between Lodovico's class (the upper bourgeoisie) and that of the irascible young nobleman whom he meets on the street.[7] The basic question—which set of rules to follow when two equally artificial laws contradict one another—is fairly clear-cut. Lodovico claims the right of passage on the street according to the rule of physical position (his right shoulder is adjacent to the wall), whereas the nobleman claims the right of class, which, according to him, has priority over all other kinds of rules. In fact, however, the encounter is due as much to the pettiness and the overbearing pride of both parties as to the contradictions within the laws of conduct, and the dispute is finally resolved not by intricate interpretation but by the violence that cuts through and thus renders mute all artificial questions of hierarchy and privilege.

The narrator's condemnation of the arbitrariness of the social codes, as well as of the heartfelt enmity that such rules can lead men to harbor even for those whom they do not know, is apparent both from the narrator's open commentary and from his one attempt to explain, if not to excuse, Lodovico's murderous reaction at the sight of his faithful servant dying at his feet: "A quella vista, Lodovico, *come fuor di sé*, cacciò la sua [spada] nel ventre del feritore, il quale cadde moribondo, quasi a un punto col povero Cristoforo" (62, my italics; "At this sight, Lodovico, *beside himself*, plunged his own [sword] into the vitals of the nobleman, who fell dying, almost at the same moment as poor Cristoforo," 51, my italics). After the encounter, the nobleman's bravoes flee in total disorder, while Lodovico, mortified at the result of his own act, follows the voice of the onlookers and enters the refuge of a Capuchin church. For the moment, it seems as though the breaking of the order of social and legal hierarchy can only be atoned by recourse to the further rules of that same hierarchy, which in this case means submission to the vengeance of the nobleman's family. That this does not happen in the narrative is not so much a denial of the importance of hierarchy as an affirmation of the guiding principles by which hierarchies *should* be ordered. In other words, Manzoni's polemic, which underlies the action of Fra Cristoforo's background story as well as that of the entire narrative, is not directed *against* the hierarchical ordering of the rules of human society but rather *toward* the knowledgeable readjustment of such hierarchies along the lines of revealed Christian truth.[8]

This assertion of the Christian ethos as the solution to problems of social as well as individual morality is particularly forceful in the story of Fra Cristoforo's conversion and in the scene of his pardon. These are the third and fourth sections of the sketch of his background (the first being the description of his needlessly self-tormenting father and the second being the encounter and the fatal swordplay on the street). That Lodovico is guided into the Capuchin church by the words of the onlookers ("queste parole") and that one of the central aspects of his subsequent conversion is his change of name demonstrate Manzoni's attention to, and respect for, the worldly powers of language in the course of Fra Cristoforo's experiences immediately following the slaying. But the importance of discourse is still more pointed in the story's last section. Even the slain nobleman's brother thinks of the whole matter of Fra Cristoforo's request for public forgiveness as a beautifully fitting conclusion to this sad but soon to be completed family tale, "una bella pagina nella storia della famiglia" (67; "a fine page in the family history," 55). But the "narrative" in which Fra Cristoforo is a key figure takes an unexpected turn. The Capuchin's expression and his demeanor literally speak for themselves ("disser chiaro"), and they do so with such force that they have the startling effect of calming the hostility of the crowd and of drawing the familial onlookers over to the repentant friar's side. Their sympathy in and of itself is not enough, however, since Fra Cristoforo wants to hear their pardon expressed, and thus confirmed, in speech: "Oh! s'io potessi sentire dalla sua bocca questa parola, perdono!" (68; "Oh! if only I could hear that word from your lips—pardon!" 57). Of course, Fra Cristoforo does hear the requested word from the nobleman and hears it confirmed by the joyous chorus of all the onlookers.

This turn of events furnishes the polemical climax to the thematic progression of this segment of the narrative, which has moved through careful gradations of character motivation—psychologicial, social, and moral—to end with an affirmation of the predominance of the *religious* values of repentence and forgiveness. That this entire scene is framed by means of a skillful twist on the story of the return of the prodigal son (a story openly referred to in chapter 23 in regard to the repentence of the Unnamed) only attests to Manzoni's versatility in utilizing traditional literary and moral motifs to heighten the effects of his text's religious themes. By the end of the scene of Fra Cristoforo's pardon, the friar is ready to set out on his own "journey" ("viaggio") and, by extension, to guide others on their journeys as both the servant of Christ and the figure of Saint Christopher.

But before the narrator's self-conscious reinsertion of Fra Cristoforo into the story of Renzo and Lucia at the end of chapter 4, with Agnese and Lucia's traditional though heartfelt greeting ("Oh padre Cristoforo!

The Rebirth of History's Truth

sia benedetto"; "Oh, Fra Cristoforo! Bless you!"), the narrative provides one last notation concerning Fra Cristoforo's character, this, too, presented in terms of language. After remarking that, even though Fra Cristoforo's language was habitually restrained, the narrator adds that whenever questions of justice or truth were involved, he would again show his old fire, albeit modified by the solemnity gained from years of preaching. This constant battle between the vigorous force of Fra Cristoforo's spirit and the counterbalance of his willful self-control, which is always directed by higher motives and inspiration, gives both the character's behavior and his language a remarkable turn. But not only is his language distinctive, he is himself, in his psychological makeup and in his behavior, *like* the dynamics of language. In one of the novel's passages that indicates how deeply Manzoni felt about language and how thoroughly he had considered its relation to the broader scope of human endeavor, the narrator caps his introduction to Fra Cristoforo by borrowing the comparison of one of the Capuchin's fellows, who knew him well and who had likened him to the most energetic components of discourse itself:

> Un suo confratello ed amico, che lo conosceva bene, l'aveva una volta paragonato a quelle parole troppo espressive nella loro forma naturale, che alcuni, anche ben educati, pronunziano, quando la passione trabocca, smozzicate, con qualche lettera mutata; parole che, in quel travisamento, fanno però ricordare della loro energia primitiva. (70–71)

> One of his fellow friars and friends, who knew him well, once compared him to those words that are too strong in their natural form, and that certain people, even well educated ones, pronounce when carried away by passion in a jumbled way, with a letter or two changed; words that, even in such a disguise, remind one of their primitive energy. (59)

This view of both men and language as caught in a constant give-and-take between undying passion and overriding control—a view which has roots in Enlightenment philosophies of man as well as in more traditionally Christian thought—is confirmed, in regard to Fra Cristoforo, during the dinner at Don Rodrigo's palace in the next chapter. When Fra Cristoforo is asked to offer his opinion concerning the treatment or mistreatment of messengers (a role in which, unbeknownst to his questioners, he now finds himself), he tries to avoid the question first by feigning ignorance and then by circumnavigating the issue. Pressed further, Fra Cristoforo takes a moment for a word with himself in private ("una parolina in segreto a sé medesimo"). His counsel of self-restraint in the service of those he is trying to protect is at once admirable and instructive: "Queste vengono a te; ma ricordati, frate, che non sei qui per te, e che tutto ciò che tocca te solo, non entra nel conto" (82; "They are trying to get at you; but remember, friar, that you are not here on your own behalf and that everything that touches you alone is outside of the matter at hand," 69).

At the same time that this passage reaffirms the earlier description of Fra Cristoforo as a walking amalgam of primitive energy and self-restraint, it also demonstrates in action that Fra Cristoforo has already learned what the narrator and perhaps Lucia know about language and what Renzo in the end will learn too: that often it is better not to speak at all than to speak too openly or rashly. The passage also shows Fra Cristoforo's ability to subordinate his actions within a hierarchy of values, which means his ability to discern the difference between sanctioned use and mere utility. The question for Fra Cristoforo, here and elsewhere in the text, is not only what will work, but what will work within the graded system of values in which he believes and according to which he conducts himself. This and similar passages explain why Manzoni could be in favor of worldly use as a value in and of itself *within* a sanctioned system even while he remained adamantly opposed to utilitarianism as such or to any notion of morality based on the common perception of happiness, an opposition which he eventually explained at length in his additions to the 1855 version of *La morale cattolica*.[9]

Manzoni's two-pronged polemic *for* worldly use within a hierarchically ordered set of values and *against* either disuse or incorrectly ordered hierarchies runs throughout the novel (accompanied and complicated by his concern not only for "doing good" but also against "doing evil"); and the polemic recurs with special historical significance at the novel's conclusion, when it appears as both a moral and a social doctrine without losing any of the power of its religious thrust. This same thematic concern for the use of language as worldly action, moreover, is again central to the "colloquium" between Fra Cristoforo and Don Rodrigo that begins the subsequent chapter. The scene of this exchange recapitulates the thematics and in part the action of the encounter between Fra Cristoforo (then Lodovico) and the arrogant nobleman of two chapters earlier. In terms of the metaphorical parallels of narrative scenes, the effect of this encounter is as though Fra Cristoforo had learned everything he now holds dear in that prior exchange and Don Rodrigo, by contrast, had learned nothing. Don Rodrigo unwittingly contributes to this comparison by intensifying his previous allusions during dinner to Fra Cristoforo's earlier life and by now referring to Fra Cristoforo's conversion and his current office in a way that an arrogant nobleman would in addressing an overreaching plebeian: "Escimi di tra' piedi, villano temerario, poltrone incappucciato. . . . Villano rincivilito!" (91–92; "Get out from beneath my feet, you impudent peasant, you sluggard in a Capuchin cowl. . . . You presumptuously civilized peasant!" 78).

Initially, Fra Cristoforo had hoped for the best (notwithstanding Don Rodrigo's coolness and his abrupt way of speaking, which tell the friar to weigh his words and to hurry up [88; 75]), since he knows that Don Rodrigo has the power to put an end to Renzo and Lucia's suffering by means of a single decisive word ("Una parola di lei può far tutto," 90; "A word from you can settle everything," 77). But in reaction to Don Rodrigo's refusal to acknowledge either his own worldly transgressions or his duty to the higher authority of Christian morals, along with the nobleman's continued insistence on the unquestionable rights granted him by the established social hierarchy, Fra Cristoforo loses both his patience and his temper. The friar now gives voice to his feelings in a way that he had so studiously avoided during the exchange at dinner, when the question had regarded *him* rather than those for whom he was petitioning; and in his anger he makes one of the most concise and memorable predictions in the narrative, that the day of judgment will arrive for Don Rodrigo, ready or not ("Verrà un giorno," 91; 78).[10]

In the face of this "promise," Don Rodrigo's rage overcomes his momentary astonishment, and he finds his tongue, abandoning definitively the *Lei* of hierarchical equality and adopting the *tu* in his address to the friar (in a distinction reminiscent of the play of *tu* and *voi* between Agnese, Renzo, and Lucia at the beginning of chapter 3). In the course of this outburst, the nobleman uses a phrase that both recalls Azzeccagarbugli's admonition to Renzo (while perhaps suggesting that Azzeccagarbugli, who is also present at the dinner, has mentioned Renzo's visit to Don Rodrigo) and foreshadows Renzo's own process of linguistic education:

"Villano rincivilito!" proseguì don Rodrigo: "tu tratti da par tuo. Ma ringrazia il saio che ti copre codeste spalle di mascalzone, e ti salva dalle carezze che si fanno a' tuoi pari, per insegnar loro a parlare. Esci con le tue gambe, per questa volta; e la vedremo." (92)

"You presumptuously civilized peasant!" went on Don Rodrigo. "You dare treat me as an equal. But you can thank the cassock that covers your rascally shoulders for saving you from the strokes that the likes of you get in order to teach them to speak properly. You can leave on your own legs this time; and then we'll see about it." (78)

This working out of hierarchies, both inside and outside of language, and between almost all of the major characters as well as many of the minor ones, is characteristic of an extraordinary variety of the novel's elements.[11] It is emphasized again, for example, in the meeting in chapter 19 between Don Rodrigo's supporter, the powerful *conte zio* (who, in the game of hierarchies, regards Don Rodrigo as a nobleman in the world but as a mere boy before his betters), and Fra Cristoforo's superior, the Capuchin *padre provinciale*. But despite the nearly endless series of embedded hierarchies that the novel sets forth in these early chapters and then elaborates as the story progresses, the most interesting ramification of the violent postprandial exchange between Fra Cristoforo and Don Rodrigo is the eventual reversal of the hierarchy that Don Rodrigo asserts and the affirmation of the one that Fra Cristoforo suggests, this effected, too, in and through speech itself.

This reversal—actually a series of reversals involving Fra Cristoforo's upbraiding of Renzo and Renzo's pardoning of Don Rodrigo—is intimately associated with the term *benedire,* or "to bless," which follows a long and complex path throughout the narrative leading all the way to the plague, as has recently been pointed out by Giorgio Ficara.[12] In regard to Renzo's sentiments and actions, the two crucial uses of the term occur at the end of chapter 35 and at the beginning of chapter 36. At the conclusion of chapter 35, Fra Cristoforo reveals to Renzo the ghastly sight of the once all-powerful but now cadaverous Don Rodrigo. Fra Cristoforo refuses to judge the significance of the frightful condition of Renzo's nemesis ("Può esser gastigo, può esser misericordia," 619; "It may be punishment, it may be mercy," 555) and asks only that Renzo offer his forgiveness in the spirit of Christian humility and love.

Just as the request for human "pardon" (again linked to God's "blessing") casts back to Fra Cristoforo's own experience before the family of the nobleman he had slain in mindless rage (66, 68; 55, 57), so the request for blessing, as action in language (*bene/dire*), casts forward to the beginning of the next chapter, in which the preacher, Padre Felice, exhorts his listeners to bless God actively and repeatedly, in no matter what circumstances they find themselves and despite the awful trials of the plague, since there is always a reason in everything God ordains even though mankind may not be able to see it (622; 558). Padre Felice goes on to interpret the meaning of the pestilence (in his view, those few who have been "chosen" to live through it will be more grateful to God for the gift of life and more mindful of him and helpful to their fellows), and it is true that his words carry a great deal of weight as one of the voices of organized Christianity. But it must be remembered that his is only one assertion among many in the text as to the plague's meaning; Don Abbondio, for example, sees it as a sort of divinely ordained housecleaning ("una scopa," 660; 593), whereas Fra Cristoforo, as we have seen, declines to offer any definitive interpretation of its meaning, at least in specific cases. What is indisputably clear in regard to the plague's effects on worldly institutions, however, is that its arrival creates disorder and chaos, breaking down both the bonds between individuals and the overall hierarchies on which the previous social order had depended.[13]

The description of the confusion, terror, and chaos caused by the plague is especially powerful and incisive in chapter 34, in which, after two-thirds of the populace of Milan has died, those left alive amidst the gruesome revelry of the *monatti* are said to be afflicted by fears (both reasonable and unreasonable), isolated from one another, and utterly without concern for the usual habits of personal comportment ("negletta e trasandata ogni persona," 594; "neglected and disorderly every person," 532). That this natural disaster comes along with the emissaries of another that is man-made (the plague was brought into Italy by the foreign soldiers) extends the novel's image of the origins of chaos to cover all the realms of worldly activity. In chapter 31, moreover, one of the first institutions portrayed as being affected by the plague—perhaps not unexpectedly, given the novel's habitual concerns—is language itself. As in the novel's initial discussions of the *gride*, Manzoni again concentrates on the use and abuse of language in the state's official pronouncements. After generalizing on the all-too-common examples of gradually increasing errors in the history of human expression, in which words and ideas often do not coincide in any transparent fashion, Manzoni's narrator concludes, in a passage mentioned earlier in the context of Renzo's escape, by offering first a "method" of proceeding that demonstrates his confidence in regard to human potential and then a lament that shows his pessimism in regard to human practice:

> In principio dunque, non peste, assolutamente no, per nessun conto: proibito anche di proferire il vocabolo. Poi, febbri pestilenziali: l'idea s'ammette per isbieco in un aggettivo. Poi, non vera peste; vale a dire peste sì, ma in un certo senso; non peste proprio, ma una cosa alla quale non si sa trovare un altro nome. Finalmente, peste senza dubbio, e senza contrasto: ma già ci s'è attaccata un'altra idea, l'idea del venefizio e del malefizio, la quale altera e confonde l'idea espressa dalla parola che non si può più mandare indietro.
> Non è, credo, necessario d'esser molto versato nella storia dell'idee e delle parole, per vedere che molte hanno fatto un simil corso. Per grazie del cielo, che non sono molte quelle d'una tal sorte, e d'una tal importanza, e che conquistino la loro evidenza a un tal prezzo, e alle quali si possano attaccare accessòri d'un tal genere. Si potrebbe però, tanto nelle cose piccole, come nelle grandi, evitare, in gran parte, quel corso così lungo e così storto, prendendo il metodo proposto da tanto tempo, d'osservare, ascoltare, paragonare, pensare, prima di parlare.
> Ma parlare, questa cosa così sola, e talmente più facile di tutte quell'altre insieme, che anche noi, dico noi uomini in generale, siamo un po' da compatire. (542–43)

At first, then, it was not the plague, absolutely not, on no account: the very mention of the word was forbidden. Then it was pestilential fever: the idea was admitted obliquely in the adjective. Then it was not the true plague; that is to say, it was plague, but only in a certain sense; not real plague, but something for which no other name could be found. Finally, it was plague beyond any doubt or contradiction. But already another idea—the idea of poison and spells—had become attached to it, which altered and confused the idea that was expressed by the word that could no longer be suppressed.

It is not, I think, necessary to be deeply versed in the history of words and ideas to see that many others have followed a similar course. Thank heaven that there are not many examples of such a sort, and of such importance, which conquer their evidence at such a price and to which accessories of such a character can be attached. But, in great as well as little things, this lengthy and crooked path could be avoided, in large measure, by following the long established method of observing, listening, comparing, and thinking before speaking.

But speaking is, all by itself, so much easier than all the others put together that we, too—I say we humans in general—are a little to be pitied. (486)

The damage done to language by man's reaction to the plague is not different in kind from that which periodically afflicts, and progressively contaminates, the relationship between words and ideas, though it is far more severe. Indeed, the temptation to use language too freely, and so to abuse its true meaning and propriety, is one that is shared even by the narrator, as part of the human condition ("anche noi, dico noi uomini in generale"; "we, too—I say we humans in general"). It is probably a simplification to say that, with the passing of the plague, language as well as everything else in the novel is put right again, and that in fact all is far better than before. Nevertheless, something of the sort is the case, because this is, of course, the general motion of Manzoni's *commedia*. The absolution of Lucia from her vow, which Fra Cristoforo, as the worldly instrument of God's *word* (637; 572), accomplishes by placing one good alongside another and choosing between them in the Christian system of values, is a part of this process, as had been Renzo's pardoning of Don Rodrigo. It is also true that, after the passing of the plague and the completion of Renzo and Lucia's union, many of the linguistic practices that earlier had presented difficulties are now acceptable as an aspect of the new order of things. Don Abbondio's Latin, now "honest, sacrosanct" rather than guileful, is no longer offensive to Renzo (663; 595), and even the references to Lucia in Bergamo as "quella bella baggiana" are taken for honest admiration (as the narrator remarks approvingly, "L'epiteto faceva passare il sostantivo," 671; "The epithet made the noun pass muster," 603).

But despite the temptation to view the plague primarily as a terrifying yet arbitrarily conceived and introduced *deus ex machina*, as an important yet mechanical device that intervenes from outside the story to remove all difficulties and set everything straight, the plague's role in the story should not be taken lightly. It does in fact serve the function of a dark though effective *toccasana*, as Manzoni's text, at its conclusion, does not hesitate to point out in a wide variety of contexts, from the arrival in Lecco of Don Rodrigo's beneficent successor, to the joy of Renzo and Lucia's wedding, and even to their setting up shop at the silk mill in Bergamo left suddenly vacant because the previous owner was carried off by the catastrophe. But in terms of its symbolic value in the narrative, the plague is also much more than such an assessment might indicate. Rather than being an external phenomenon in relation to the thematic development of the novel, the plague is part and parcel of a cluster of themes that have been inextricably present since the very beginning of the story (and fairly obvious since the violent deaths in chapter 4 and the initially humorous but later deeply serious moral, social, and physical confusion of the attempted but thwarted trickeries in the village in chapter 8).

The primary components of this narrative cluster are, first, various forms of reciprocal violence and, second, the lengthy process of decay that leads to chaos and then to sacrifice before it culminates in the reinstitution of a newly sanctified order. That this process plays itself out on the level of language as well as on those of other social, moral, and religious institutions demonstrates the all-encompassing nature of these Girardian thematics in Manzoni's text.[14] The wager voiced between Don Rodrigo and Attilio, his "colleague" and at the same time his rival in libertinism and bullying (78; 65), also shows the power of mimetic desire within Manzoni's story. That is, Don Rodrigo desires Lucia in large measure because he perceives that Attilio desires her, and Don Rodrigo perseveres in his otherwise unlikely plot because of his pride and his concern for his reputation, which is to say, his concern for the way in which others perceive him. Don Rodrigo thus demonstrates the sort of melodramatically active and profane desire that is the other side of the narrator's own benignly chaste (i.e., idealistically Romantic) though only slightly less obvious feelings for Lucia (256; 226). The disconcerting hubris of Don Rodrigo's attitude toward Attilio's death, moreover, quickly turns him into the uncanny double of all the plague's other victims, thus extending his role past that of an individual villain into that of the communal scapegoat, at once the embodiment and the carrier of all that is evil in regard to both cruelty and sexual transgression. In Girardian terms, therefore, it is not a coincidence that Don Rodrigo shows the unmistakable signs of the plague immediately after his evening of wine and his hubristic mock eulogy for his dead cousin.[15] The Unnamed, of course, would have been the prime candidate for this part, especially after the abduction of Lucia and his symbolic usurpation of Don Rodrigo's role, however temporary, in relation to her. But the Unnamed's conversion short-circuits such a fate. It also, surprisingly enough, indicates the eventual turn of the narrative's entire representation of society away from the corrupted order of chivalry—Spanish, petty, and thoroughly decadent, the type of social order in which the unrestrained treachery of Don Rodrigo, a mediocre man yet one inhabited by the devil (309; 275), could not only exist but also dominate—and toward the newly (re)established power and authority of traditional Christian values.[16]

Although within this narrative development the lecherous and occasionally bibulous Don Rodrigo cannot be saved, his position as scapegoat is thereby altered in a crucial way, since, after Don Rodrigo's dream, the narrative openly and consistently treats him both as villain and as victim (in contrast to his other double in treachery, the equally unfaithful Griso, who contracts the plague from him and dies almost at once). The story accomplishes this alteration, moreover, through the offices of the one character who is probably too good for this or any other world and yet who cannot really die (except to be resurrected), Fra Cristoforo. The novel thus plainly demonstrates the mechanism of the scapegoat, but without doing away with the ingrained need for a victim in the procedure of ritual cleansing. The lesson of Christian pardon and love is reaffirmed even as the worldly existence of evil and the necessity of combatting it are left unquestioned. It is important to see, therefore, that what Renzo and Lucia learn from the entire arc of their experience and are free to express after the plague has first reunited them and then passed, is not a group of lessons adduced by the narrator at the story's conclusion like a handful of morals plucked from the body of the story and tacked onto its conclusion at the last minute. Rather, they represent the lessons embedded in the entire process of decadence, violence, and reestablished (though inherently precarious) hierarchical order that has been an integral part of the narrative's subject matter, in its representation of all levels of society, from the very start.

But what exactly do Renzo and Lucia learn from their "adventures," or, better yet, what are we as readers intended to make of what they say they have learned? Lucia, of course, understands a great deal more than her husband and, despite her unusually quiet nature, speaks the crucial lesson at the narrative's conclusion. But prior to that, Renzo relates what he has learned. The narrator's report of Renzo's recapitulation of his own story and his account of what he has gained from it follows two paragraphs of description of the young couple's current circumstances. According to this passage, Renzo's business is going extremely well ("d'incanto"), and he and Lucia, as new arrivals in the region of Bergamo, have been granted a special exemption from the local taxes ("Per i nostri fu una nuova cuccagna," 672; "For our couple, this was a new land of Cockaigne," 603). Before a year of marriage has ended they have a baby girl, named, not surprisingly, for the Virgin, and thereafter follow others of both sexes, all of whom, Renzo decides, must learn to read and write, "dicendo che, giacché la c'era questa birberia, dovevano almeno profittarne anche loro" ("saying that since this trickery existed, they ought at least to profit from it themselves, too"). At the end of the narrator's telescoped description of the couple's present life, Renzo gets to his list of individual lessons:

> "Ho imparato . . . a non mettermi ne' tumulti: ho imparato a non predicare in piazza: ho imparato a guardare con chi parlo: ho imparato a non alzar troppo il gomito: ho imparato a non tenere in mano il martello delle porte, quando c'è lì d'intorno gente che ha la testa calda: ho imparato a non attaccarmi un campanello al piede, prima d'aver pensato quel che possa nascere." E cent'altre cose.

> "I've learned . . . not to get into riots: I've learned not to make speeches [preach] in the streets: I've learned to pay attention to the people with whom I'm talking: I've learned not to bend my elbow too much: I've learned not to grab ahold of door-knockers when there are hot-headed people about: I've learned not to fasten a bell to my feet before thinking of the consequences." And a hundred other things.

All of these individual lessons (regardless of Renzo's notable and continuing limitations) derive primarily from what is, for Renzo, the story's germinating center, made up of his experiences in Milan in the novel's middle chapters. The *ritornello* of "ho imparato," however, along with its connection to the acts of discourse (making speeches and paying attention to those with whom one speaks), ties this concluding litany to the entire process of linguistic and social education that begins, in regard to Renzo, with the exhortation from Azzeccagarbugli to learn to speak properly, and in regard to the novel as a whole, with the narrator's explanation of his linguistic aims and procedures in the story's introduction. In both cases, though in different ways, the goal of this process has been the attainment of the ability to *use* language and other forms of behavior to make one's way in the world of men, in what is now a symbolically and literally purged society.

It is this concluding chapter's valorization of social and economic activities in a specifically Christian world that ties this underlying polemic of use to the thematics of decadence, disorder, destruction, and reorder mentioned earlier. The plot of the novel, at least along its main lines, can be stated without much difficulty. The marriage of a young couple is blocked by a powerful nobleman, and as a result the prospective bride and groom go through a separation and a series of trials. In the end, they are reunited in the midst of the worldly catastrophe that eliminates their nemesis and that, with the concomitant intervention of their journey's guide to remove the last encumbrances, leaves them free to become man and wife. In terms of the novel's thematics, however, matters are somewhat more complicated. What is initially blocked is not just any union of two people, but the sacred wedding of man to wife on which the entire worldly cycle of Christian propagation and productivity depends. In this sense, Don Rodrigo is far more than a frustrated, self-indulgent, *spagnolesco* Don Juan, acting out his role in a story that he has chosen by mistake. Rather, he is literally an *agent* of the devil (however minor), since by his action he hinders the entire worldly basis of the Church's teaching and its replenishment. The narrative's condemnation of Don Rodrigo's fall into the endless chain of mimetic desire, which is the basis of the hierarchical but, in a Christian view, incorrectly ordered code of chivalry, is especially severe precisely because, in this instance, that fall threatens to bring down with it the most basic edifice of Christian society.

Nonetheless, even though Manzoni sees that the hierarchy of the chivalric code, particularly as interpreted by such adepts as Don Attilio, Don Rodrigo, and their companions (with Don Ferrante and his useless magic thrown in for good measure), is on its face thoroughly mistaken and, at least in potential, evil, Manzoni also sees that without hierarchy, without some sort of established order and authority, language and even society itself, as pure disorder, are not just impossible but also unthinkable. There must, therefore, be a difference between acceptable hierarchies and unacceptable ones. Manzoni's text conceives of and portrays this difference in two main ways. First, it presents the representatives of the Christian order visibly at work *within* the worldly system of values and actions; Fra Cristoforo and his hierarchically more authoritative comrade-in-arms, Cardinal Borromeo, are unquestionable, if not always unquestioned, forces for good. At the same time, it posits their diabolic counterparts as just that: devils so corrupt that at their extreme they are not only outside all acceptable limits of behavior, like Don Rodrigo and Attilio, but even, symbolically, outside the institution of language itself (the Unnamed).

The second, and even more fundamental, way in which the narrative draws the difference between these two systems is by implicitly contrasting their sources of meaning and so their claims to truth. The source of life's meaning for Don Rodrigo and his compatriots, like that of all their deeds, always remains *within* their worldly system. If there is any question concerning interpretation or judgment, no matter how pointed or how abstruse, that question will itself only grow out of and feed back into the worldly code (as at the dinner at Don Rodrigo's palace during which Fra Cristoforo is so discomforted). For the Christian system, however, even though truth is evidenced in the world, it neither begins nor ends there. In other words, Manzoni's view of Christianity, as an idealist system of action and belief with the worldly revelation of divine truth as its mainstay, posits a source of meaning the effects of which are immanent in the world but the essence of which remains outside of worldly endeavor, as the unseen force moving the visible wheels of earthly life. A character such as Don Ferrante can feel the attraction of this idealist argument and can even try to respond to it, but so long as that response remains caught in the web of superstition, and therefore of error, it will lead nowhere, either within the world or without.

This, then, is the second difference between the two hierarchies, in the end a far more significant one than the perhaps more easily grasped distinctions between individual characters. The earlier hierarchy is in and of itself helpless and hopeless since, like the never-ending mimetic doubling and rivalry to which it gives rise, it has no guarantee of value or truth outside its own outlines. (In this regard it is similar to the utilitarianism Manzoni also condemned.) By contrast, the Christian hierarchy, including even such apparently minor aspects of it as the ecclesiastical titles discussed offhandedly at the conclusion of the narrative, is not only workable but finally also true, despite its all too common worldly failings; it maintains this truth because its source of meaning is not worldly but transcendent and thus both timeless and unimpeachable. Owing to the overall certainty of the Christian system, moreover (a certainty guaranteed by the system's transcendent source), its internal workings can be far more flexible than the arbitrary and seemingly fixed rules of systems such as the chivalric code that have *only* their rules as guarantees of their validity and that therefore foster interminable rounds of interpretation, the results of which seem utterly certain until they are overthrown by equally certain contradictions, and so forth and so on. The flexibility inherent in the Christian ethos, once the intention of the individuals in question is assured, explains, for example, why Fra Cristoforo can accept the kindly old servant's eavesdropping at Don Rodrigo's palace (even though the narrator feels obliged to suspend judgment in the matter), and it offers another more general explanation of why the Capuchin feels he can release Lucia from her vow with such certitude, even after her promise to Renzo.

Manzoni's term for this combination of guaranteed transcendent truth and worldly effect, the term also used in previous and contemporary religious treatises, is divine Providence. Providence is the force that no one can really see (which is why Lucia, in reciting what she has learned, cautions against both the neatness and, as indicated by Renzo's apparent certainty, the underlying hubris of her husband's litany). In spite of its invisibility, however, everyone experiences Providence's effects all the time, whether or not in a conscious fashion, and no one can escape it (which is why Fra Cristoforo can promise with such conviction that "a day will come" for Don Rodrigo). Still, it would be a mistake to conclude, as many readers have been led to since the novel's publication, that Manzoni's argument is purely an idealist one, with no direct material application beyond that suggested at the novel's end as the value of the constancy of faith in all worldly affairs. There is, indeed, a material root to Manzoni's overtly Christian novel, one that anchors it in its own time even more securely than in the historical period it purports to represent. That root, as Carlo Salinari suggested perhaps too forthrightly but on the whole convincingly, is not only religious but also economic and social, not oriented only toward the Church but also toward that other burgeoning hierarchy of early-nineteenth-century Italian life, the new and rising preunification bourgeoisie.[17]

This historical interest gives Manzoni's depiction of the decadent, backward-looking nobility, occupied with questions of chivalry and feudal obligation perhaps appropriate to an earlier age but now thoroughly out of place, a pointedly contemporary cast. Although Manzoni was himself a member of the social, intellectual and, to an extent, the financial elite, he viewed the present and future of society with a constant eye to the burgeoning energies of the middle classes. It is true that Renzo and Lucia are depicted first, in the introduction's sample of the anonymous autograph, as "gente meccaniche," or common laborers, and later, by Don Rodrigo, in chapter 11, as "gente di nessuno," or nobody's people; but by the end of the narrative they are well on their way to being *bons bourgeois* (in a town-centered rather than in a village-based or a rural world). At the conclusion they find themselves with a shop and children who will learn to read and write and who will *profit* by that ability, and they are also endowed with the economic hopes and concerns characteristic of the growing class of northern Italian tradesmen and merchants, hopes and concerns that would produce by Manzoni's own era a middle class interested in both independence and national unity. This class orientation, furthermore, is one of the historical reasons why, despite the occasional claims made for Manzoni's novel regarding the national scope of its language and its moral interests, *I Promessi Sposi* remains a distinctly northern Italian story, written in Manzoni's version of the "ideal" language of the northern bourgeoisie, with a historical frame including characters, events, and social aspirations many of which would have been either noticeably out of place or utterly incomprehensible in the south even two centuries afterward.

Manzoni's mixture of Christian and bourgeois values is especially telling in regard to the narrative's valorization of worldly use. Use, within the limits of reason and therefore without unnecessary or ill-advised risk (as Renzo's concluding litany clearly counsels), is not so much an ecclesiastically Christian as a bourgeois value, a value of the marketplace rather than one of either the chapel or the cloister. That Manzoni's narrative, however, frames its valuation of use in such heavily dominant Christian terms lends an extraordinary weight to what would otherwise be merely an incipient bourgeois polemic. He thus permits the non-Christian but highly marketable values of pride and self-interest, from which Renzo never entirely escapes, to exist within a Christian frame by counterbalancing Renzo's concluding remarks with Lucia's more perspicacious ones and thus leaving the real problems of ajudication up to the transcendent offices of Providence itself. This narrative sleight of hand, which is reminiscent of Vico's treatment of an analogous problem—that of the relation between divine intention and man's free will (or, in other terms, objective religious truth and free subjective consciousness)—is characteristic of Manzoni's incorporation of specific character traits and motivations within a system that, on its face, would not necessarily countenance or even contain them.[18] Although economic "cuccagna" and Christian fulfillment are not logically interdependent either in terms of activity or aspiration, at the end of the novel they exist in an inextricable relationship for the young couple because both are part of Manzoni's assessment of human good; or in still different terms, as Salinari and others have perceived, they are both part of Manzoni's ideological evaluation of the path of human history.[19]

The implications of Providence's effects on the course of this history, as presented at the story's conclusion, are especially telling for each individual. Since one cannot hope to know the motions of Providence, even the most cautious and innocent conduct is insufficient to guarantee a secure and trouble-free life (as Renzo and Lucia conclude together and as the narrator offers as "il sugo di tutta la storia"; "the juice of the whole tale"). Therefore, the best one can do is to maintain faith in God and pursue one's activities, or, as the narrator claims the anonymous original puts it, "far bene," rather than to seek immediate comfort, or "star bene." The felicitous result of such behavior will be that one will in fact gain even greater comfort and success thereby, or "star meglio." This concluding praise of meaningful and productive activity within the givens of the Christian ethos corresponds to the narrator's broad yet elliptically stated economic theories (generally based on usefulness) expressed here and there throughout the novel.[20] It joins, moreover, with the story's earlier portrayals of the utility of language to demonstrate the completion of the novel's presentation and assessment of what De Rienzo describes, in terminology reminiscent of both Pindar and Kant, as the worldly "realm of the possible," with linguistic knowledge as the realm's means of access and bourgeois activity as its (now sanctioned) path of development.

This is not to say, of course, that the bourgeoisie is always portrayed in a positive light. But whenever such characters are presented in a less than positive manner in the story, what is depicted as negative is an attribute that is not necessarily tied to their economic activities as such. This is the case, for example, in the narrative's treatment of the merchant of Gorgonzola's slanderous gossip and in the memorable depiction of the psychological torment of Fra Cristoforo's father, who became unjustly ashamed of his prior activities as a vendor amidst a world of buyers, a function viewed by the narrator as a necessary one given the economic conditions of everyday life. What is constantly seen as positive in the text, on the other hand, is the drive to produce and exchange in the world of day-to-day society, as long as that drive is channeled within the proper system of values. The narrative's ideological perspective thus unites the underlying values and energies of the bourgeoisie with those of Christian truth and, in the process, frames Manzoni's text as the nineteenth-century tract that it is, from the narrator's opening apologetics, through the tale of intrigue, adventure, and cataclysm, and at last to the fulfilled wishes of the suddenly foreshortened happy ending.

This ideological slant of Manzoni's narrative can be seen in all of the aspects of the novel that we have considered thus far. But these individual aspects of the narrative, when taken separately, do not represent the only ways in which Manzoni's novel demonstrates its valuation of Christian use in the world of the marketplace. Indeed, the entire text, in the form of Manzoni's product as a writer, fits into this same framework of ideological valuation. In order to see how this is so, and why literary self-consciousness plays such a crucial if circumspect role in this process, it is necessary to return once more to the novel's introduction.

When Manzoni's narrator changes his mind about giving up on the project of reproducing the anonymous manuscript and decides instead to retain the story while reworking its style, he offers, as we have mentioned, one reason for doing so: the story is a beautiful one. Linked to the notion of beauty is another that should be stressed, and once again it is that of use. What Manzoni's narrator laments is precisely that such a beautiful story will not be read, that it will remain unexperienced and unknown: "Nell'atto però di chiudere lo scartafaccio, per riporlo, mi sapeva male che una storia così bella dovesse rimanersi tuttavia sconosciuta" (5; "But in the act of closing up the notebook to put it away, I felt a pang of regret that so beautiful a story should nonetheless remain unknown," xiii). What Manzoni finally produces, of course, is not just the story but the story's entire underlying polemic in regard to the priority of Christian faith and activity in the world of men. His activity as a writer thus participates in that same polemic, while the useful product of his labors enters the world in a direct, practical way.

Manzoni's feeling that this would be the case—that once published his book would take on a practical life of its own (and would therefore be free to instruct or displease or even, as the narrator himself says at the conclusion, bore its readers)—is confirmed by Manzoni's continued preoccupation with the book's contents, which did not end with the 1840 revision but, rather, persisted and intensified for decades afterwards. Within the novel, as we have seen in various contexts, Manzoni's concern for selecting the most apposite manner of framing and presenting his story, in order to make it both readable and effective, is evident in the many self-reflexive comments on the often competing claims of artistic representation and historical fact concerning both character and event. But it is important to see, too, that the self-consciousness of Manzoni's story extends far beyond his interest in the techniques of presentation as such. Rather, the self-conscious reworking of language and style in *I Promessi Sposi* goes right to the heart of what it means to write a historical novel and to publish one for the consumption, edification, and pleasure of its readership (the first among whom was, of course, the author himself).

This dual aspect of narrative discourse—its being written and its being read—is pointedly underscored by the illustrations that Gonin provided (as always, in close collaboration with Manzoni) for the opening and closing of the novel's introduction, the first of which shows a man seated at a desk in a cap and robe following a text with his index finger as though to transcribe it word for word, whereas the second shows a man relaxing in an easy chair in his library, with the wastebasket full and a manuscript in his hand, seemingly completed, since the single discernible word on the page is "Fine," or "End." In the course of the introduction, however, as well as in the course of the narrative from its beginning to its conclusion—at which point the narrator refers to himself not as the one who wrote the oddly yet pointedly "anonymous" story but as "chi l'ha raccomodata" ("the one who repaired it")—Manzoni's narrative persona is neither that of an author nor of a reader but instead that of an intermediary, or, in the subtle "rettorica discreta" of the introduction, a sort of midwife; "Ma quando io avrò durata l'eroica fatica di trascriver questa storia . . . *e l'avrò data*, come si suol dire, *alla luce*, si troverà poi chi duri la fatica di leggerla?" ("But when I have endured the heroic effort of transcribing this story . . . *and have brought it into the world*, as the saying goes, will anyone be found who can endure the effort of reading it?" [my italics]).

This self-consciously adopted guise of a midwife to whom has fallen the task of bringing the story of the young couple into the world is in one sense a literary cliché, as the narrator himself demurs ("si suol dire"), a commonplace of the historical novel.[21] But in this instance the ruse has much deeper roots, both aesthetic and religious. As Manzoni's various reflections on the aesthetics of narrative fiction attest (though with markedly differing measures of optimism and pessimism during different periods of his life), in his view the historical novel attempts to unite the effects of two distinct sorts of writing, poetry, broadly defined, and history. Traditionally, this sort of distinction might have led to a further one, that, roughly speaking, between creating and reporting. But in regard to *I Promessi Sposi* this was not Manzoni's concept. For Manzoni, history already contained the evidence of divine Providence, and so of the *one* Creator, in its course, however difficult or even impossible to discern this evidence might be.[22] The writer's goal, as Olga Ragusa has pointed out in regard to Manzoni's Romantic aesthetic theories, was not to create but to find the suitable object to *re*-create.[23] The writer's distinctive imaginative skill lay both in conceiving of that object and in imitating it in the most effective, verisimilar manner possible. If he could succeed in getting his representation of "history" right (i.e., both imaginatively effective *and* seemingly transparent), then that representation would contain, and at the same time bear witness to, the immanent signs of truth, of meaning, with which the Creator had already endowed the world's story. This is the theoretical reason why language and style are so important to Manzoni as a Christian author. As an artistic product, moreover, a Christian historical *novel* would serve its end in a form that was not only instructive but also pleasurable, not only meaningful in a moral and religious sense but also satisfying in an aesthetic sense, even an eloquently Ambrosian one.

The religious and the aesthetic tenets of Manzoni as a novelist and as a Christian devout, as a man having experienced both the power of fictional discourse *and* the mystery of revelation, thus unite in *I Promessi Sposi* to define the legerdemain at the center of the writer's task, as the specially gifted intermediary between God's creation and man's understanding and between the story of the world's characters and events and the reader's experiencing of that (re)told story. The opportunity offered to the reader of Manzoni's novel by its midwife is thus nothing less than bearing witness to the rebirth not just of history but, more to the point, of history's truth. The exceptional ambition of his project, and the responsibility he felt for it, suggest some of the reasons for Manzoni's agonizing over the novel both before and after its publication. In a lighter vein, the epigraph cited here, included in *Fermo e Lucia* but then excised as too extensively explanatory and digressive to fit within the representational aesthetic of the published novel, indicates the extent of Manzoni's preoccupation with the question of *how,* and by *whom,* his book would be received and used or misused in the world of nineteenth-century Italian society (or not used at all, as the narrator's comments at the conclusion of chapter 22 suggest in regard to Cardinal Borromeo's unread and virtually unknown works).

At the same time, the thoroughgoing nature of the novel's representational aesthetic, with its religious as well as its artistic rationales, explains in large part why, after the introduction, the tale usually turns back on its telling only in secondary ways, like the habitual broaching but then stylized curtailment of such topics as fictional representation and the status and fortunes of books in the world of the present as well as in the historical past.[24] Other potentially self-conscious topics are also handled with a large measure of narrative discretion; these include the presentation of the three most carefully described collections of books (the private library of Don Ferrante the "letterato," the information in which turns out to be utterly useless when it comes to the plague; the books of popular wisdom and entertainment in the collection of the humble but literate village tailor; and Cardinal Borromeo's Ambrosian Library, the quality and, as the narrator is at pains to insist, the usefulness of which make it one of the few idealized worldly institutions in Manzoni's text).[25] In the published versions of the novel, moreover, this same restraint is generally evident in Manzoni's self-reflexive commentaries on authors and their audience, including Manzoni's actual readership, as well as in his invitations to his readers, or at times his challenges, to fill in the novel's gaps in representation (which remain brief *boutades* rather than the harangues or the extended excurses of *Fermo e Lucia*).

Besides the narrator's often discussed self-distancing and thus self-protective Romantic irony, which permits him to take the story at hand as the object as well as the subject of his discourse, the primary exception to this narrative suppression of self-conscious effects is, of course, the lengthy and many-faceted treatment of language itself. This interest in language concentrates on the narrator and on Renzo, but it also includes Fra Cristoforo, Don Rodrigo, Lucia, and eventually almost every other major character. It must be remembered, however, that except for the question of the choice of style, in which both the entire narrative and its narration are framed, Manzoni's examination of the use and abuse of language, and so of the medium of his own activity as an author, is portrayed as an integral part of worldly endeavor and so falls well within the bounds of the historical novel's representational aesthetic. Therefore, despite the commitment to representation announced in the introduction and generally adhered to in the text, language and its use in the world can continue to rank among the novel's primary topics, not only for its characters but also for its author.[26]

There is, however, a further example of literary self-consciousness that is striking both in its openness and in the aura of skepticism surrounding it. The passage in question is a lengthy explanation in chapter 27. It picks up the thread of the narrator's various earlier references to books and writing (and particularly the discussions of Renzo the "poet" and of the requirements of intelligibility for printed books in chapter 14). In chapter 27, the narrator's commentary begins with consideration of the inevitable gaps between intention, literary reproduction, and meaning in the letters written and interpreted by the "letterati" for Agnese and Renzo. The "letterato," similar to Manzoni's narrator in relation to the story's anonymous manuscript, is not content merely to copy out whatever he is told but feels obliged both to put whatever it is in literary form and to improve on it. These remarks would not be so obviously disturbing if they did not go on to include a self-consciously pointed discussion of *published* authors. Such writers—explicitly including Manzoni himself—are in fact prey to the same pitfalls in the relationship between words, things, and human understanding and are thus victims of the same problems in the praxis of writing: "Con tutto ciò, al letterato suddetto non gli riesce sempre di dire tutto quel che vorrebbe; qualche volta gli accade di dire tutt'altro: accade anche a noi altri, che scriviamo per la stampa" (464; "For all that, the aforesaid man of letters does not always succeed in saying everything that he would like; at times it happens that he says something completely different: it even happens to those of us who write for publication," 413). That this process of error and confusion is then seen to extend past writing to reading and interpretation (including, in this instance, Renzo's fury with the "lettore interprete," or "reader and interpreter") confirms our earlier consideration of Manzoni's concerns for his book as a meaningful product in the world of everyday communication at the same time as it casts those concerns in a remarkably uncertain and troubled light.

Once again, part of this uncertainty stems from Manzoni's concept of communication not only in terms of logic but also in terms of religious truth. Within Manzoni's religious system, language's relation to its referents may not, finally, be accidental or arbitrary (the question occupying the story's anonymous chronicler at the very point at which Manzoni's narrator breaks off his transcription); nevertheless, man cannot *know* the precise nature of the motivation between names and things, signs and referents, since *that* knowledge is restricted to the barred realm of Providence's source. Sometimes, as in "Lucia," the relation may seem to be clear by divine intention, or, as in "Cristoforo," it may appear meaningful both beyond and also within human design; but usually understanding, and in all cases complete certainty, is reserved to one realm alone.

This abdication of final authority on the part of the worldly author helps to account for the fact that *I Promessi Sposi*, even when it is self-conscious, is most often not overly disturbed or disturbing in that regard. Like the organizing effects of Romantic irony itself, moreover, this abdication makes the narrative into a seemingly closed system, though one in which closure is raised to the second power, wherein resides the will of the true Author. But at the same time it is essential to see that this abdication, this very lack of certainty, cuts both ways, since it returns to disrupt Manzoni's text to such a degree that no amount of self-conscious apologetics can finally resolve the continuing doubts about not just the use but also the ends of novelistic discourse. Given this impasse, all that man can do—as is affirmed by the narrator, Fra Cristoforo, and eventually even Renzo (whose offspring would now in theory be able to read about and thus to follow their forebear's lesson in Manzoni's book)—is to learn to use language, despite all its inherent difficulties and pitfalls, as well and therefore as effectively as possible. As far as the novel is concerned, this ability, within the limits of mankind's intellectual and moral capacities and his social opportunities, can help to furnish the keys to the kingdom of this world, if not the next. At the narrative's conclusion, as for Manzoni himself through the entire novel, this turns out to be no small prize and no meager responsibility, either for the story's characters, striving to live and communicate in their world, or for Manzoni in his.

TWO

"What's in a name?"

Symbolic Meaning and the Play of Narrative Perspective in Verga's "Rosso Malpelo"

> A fugitive and a vagabond shalt thou be in the earth. . . .
> And the Lord set a mark upon Cain.
> Genesis 4:12, 15

> La porta della casa era chiusa, ed ei non aveva altro che le scarpe di suo padre appese al chiodo; perciò gli commettevano sempre i lavori più pericolosi, e le imprese più arrischiate.
>
> The house was closed up, and he didn't have anything but his father's shoes hanging from a nail; that's why they always gave him the most dangerous jobs, and the riskiest undertakings.
> "Rosso Malpelo"

The vogue of the historical novel lasted in Italy well past mid-century, as witnessed by the massive narrative of Ippolito Nievo, among those of many lesser known writers. In the first decade of the second half of the century, moreover, there arose another distinctive literary school, the northern *Scapigliatura*, to which we shall return. Yet without question the single great literary movement in the early era of Italian unification, both in terms of aesthetic theory and literary accomplishment, was that of *verismo*, or literary realism.

The aesthetics of verismo, as formulated by Luigi Capuana and by Giovanni Verga (most notably in the dedicatory epistle introducing "L'amante di Gramigna" and in the preface to *I Malavoglia*), should logically have precluded self-consciousness, since the author's stated task was to present the story in the most objective manner possible, as a "fatto diverso," or roughly a "slice of life," which, in Verga's words, would "seem to have made itself."[1] In a fashion reminiscent of the procedures of French naturalism but contrary to those of Manzoni's actively involved translator and editor, verismo's narrator was thus to be an observer and, at least momentarily, *only* that, watching from life's sidelines in order to report what he saw as accurately and as dispassionately as possible. Because of this programmatic concern for representational transparency, any tendency toward opacity, any instance of the story's losing sight of its goal of worldly representation and turning back on *itself* as an object of inquiry, should thus have been banned from the narrative proper (though not necessarily from prefaces, introductions, and the like); and to a degree that is genuinely impressive, this ban was actually adhered to in Verga's most effective realist narratives of the 1870s and 1880s. In his major short stories and novels, however, the very success of verismo's objectivist aesthetic brought with it a perhaps unexpected series of literary results that are as intricate as they are illuminating. Even though it should be borne in mind that *literary* self-consciousness is a secondary issue in Verga's narrative practice, it is equally important to see that its effects on *social* representation are significant indeed. In other words, literary self-consciousness figures in Verga's realist texts not through openly stated self-interest but rather by means of the narratives' repressed yet all-powerful social polemics, which are expressed in the texts only through indirection and silence.

The story "Rosso Malpelo," from *Vita dei campi* (1880), is particularly well suited to the examination of self-consciousness in Verga's work. This is true for a pair of reasons: first, because the story is in large part *about* the ways in which language means and the ways in which symbolic meanings play themselves out in the events and "stories" of everyday life; and second, because the novella was of distinctive import both for *Vita dei campi* and for the overall development of Verga's realist oeuvre.[2] In fact, the treatment of self-consciousness in "Rosso Malpelo"—in its systematic effacement from the narrative surface only to reappear at the story's most basic levels—anticipates the handling of similar issues in Verga's two major realist novels, *I Malavoglia* (1881) and *Mastro-don Gesualdo* (1888–89), at the same time as it echoes the effects of other stories in *Vita dei campi*, in particular "Jeli il pastore" and "La Lupa."[3]

As in most of Verga's short stories conceived and written according to the tenets of verismo, the events of the novella are not difficult to summarize. After a brief introduction to Malpelo (by way of an explanation of his proverb-inspired nickname and a cursory sketch of his uniformly evil character), the narrator describes the event that shapes the entire narrative, the death of Malpelo's father in the local quarry. The middle sections of the story relate Malpelo's sadistic behavior towards the animals and the other children working in the mine as well as towards just about everything and everyone else, himself included. Eventually, the story's focus narrows to Malpelo's sadomasochistic relationship with Ranocchio ("Frog"), the boy who is obliged to come to the quarry to work after suffering a broken leg in a fall and thus being unable to continue as a bricklayer's helper. The story's conclusion, following Ranocchio's illness and death, relates how and, so it seems, why Malpelo meets his own destiny, when he disappears alone into the mine one day never to be heard from again.

If the plot of the story is simple, however, the perspective from which it is told and the effects that this perspective generates are decidedly complex. Although the narrative itself seems uniform and straightforward, there are actually three fairly distinct perspectives from which the characters and the events of the story are presented. The first of these is that of the local populace, in whose attitudes and opinions, at least in appearance, the narrator shares; the second, which often coincides with the first—on occasion in remarkably disconcerting ways—is that of Malpelo himself; and the third, which is at once the most subtle and the most pervasive, must for the moment remain uncharacterized, if not to say mysterious, since it assumes a clear identity only after the other two have been considered in some detail. Within the narrative these three perspectives are always linked, inasmuch as they all take the same series of characters and events as their objects. But despite their entwinement in practice, they can be traced schematically through the story, at least for analytical purposes, along separate lines.

The narrative opens with an explanation of Malpelo's nickname, the motivation for which is offered by the seemingly objective narrator as common knowledge among the local populace:[4]

> Malpelo si chiamava così perché aveva i capelli rossi; ed aveva i capelli rossi perché era un ragazzo malizioso e cattivo, che prometteva di riescire un fior di birbone. Sicché tutti alla cava della rena rossa lo chiamavano Malpelo; e persino sua madre col sentirgli dir sempre a quel modo aveva quasi dimenticato il suo nome di battesimo.

He was called Malpelo because he had red hair; and he had red hair because he was a mean and bad boy, who promised to turn into a first-rate scoundrel. So everybody at the red-sand quarry called him Malpelo; and even his mother, having always heard him called by that name, had almost forgotten his real one [*literally*: his baptismal name].

This view of Malpelo, which, as this introductory passage notes, is held even by his mother, seems fairly direct. Indeed, since the nickname is a proverb (in Sicilian, "russu malupilu"), it carries its own explanation with it: red hair, at least in this part of Sicily, is a sign of evil. The name thus characterizes Malpelo and reaffirms the local judgment of his character at one and the same time. The unity of this process of naming and judgment, which will eventually require further comment, is seemingly airtight, as is also suggested by the impenetrable circularity of the opening passage's series of explicatives, "perché . . . perché . . . sicché."

The uniformity of Malpelo's evil is thus seen as absolute rather than contingent. The local populace's view of him is, of course, reinforced by what it considers his evil deeds, but the communal estimation of his character does not in any sense *derive* from his behavior, since it is not so much his comportment that is evil but instead his very essence (as is regularly repeated in the story, "è *malpelo*"—"he is *malpelo*"). Following the logic of this perspective (though running contrary to what would otherwise be normal expectations for the affective relations between mother and child), Malpelo's mother is perfectly justified in never caressing her son, since he never caresses her; and the workers in the quarry as well as the owner are equally right to beat and abuse the boy, since in their eyes, stated brutally but accurately, he deserves everything he gets. It is in part this extraordinary unity of evil that makes Malpelo into a local legend even before his disappearance and thus provides the mine's popular designation as "la cava di Malpelo" ("Malpelo's quarry"). But in spite of the narrative's portrayal of Malpelo's evil character as innate and therefore timeless if not static, there does occur a central event in time, one portrayed in the early part of the narrative, that intensifies the attitude with which the workers and even the "padrone" ("boss") regard the boy. That event, as suggested earlier, is the death of Malpelo's father.

Mastro Misciu (a diminutive of "Domenico") contracts to use his wagon to remove a pillar of sand, which is calculated by sight to come to thirty-five or forty cart loads but which in reality amounts to much more. The simple economic motivation of Malpelo's father for taking on the extra work even though everyone can see the extreme danger of this particular job is clear from his mumblings as he labors away at his task, heedless of the taunts of his fellow workers who are heading for their rest: "E intanto borbottava: 'Questo è per il pane! Questo pel vino! Questo per la gonnella di Nunziata!' e così andava facendo il conto del come avrebbe speso i denari del suo *appalto*—il cottimante!" (175; "And meanwhile he muttered: 'This is for the bread! This for the wine! This for Nunziata's dress!' And so he went on figuring how he'd spend the money from his contract—the contract worker!" 67). Of course, Mastro Misciu never does get to spend the money, since the pillar caves in and Mastro Misciu, caught in the avalanche of red sand, dies what the others in the mine term "la morte del sorcio" ("the death of a rat").

It is of interest that Malpelo's father is called not only Mastro Misciu but also Mastro Misciu Bestia and even Mastro Bestia. It is clear that this name is pejorative, but it is uncertain in the text exactly why Malpelo's father deserves it. True, even though he owns a cart, which may set him apart from many of his fellows, he also seems to be characteristically hapless at ordering his own affairs, as the "magro affare" ("poor bargain") of the contract that leads to his death amply demonstrates. So it is possible that the reaction of his fellow workers is simply one of diffidence or jealousy turned to disdain. But, insofar as can be discerned from the few indications in the text, the animosity of his fellows does not really seem to stem so much either from Mastro Misciu's position or his gullability as from his passivity: "Ei, povero diavolaccio, lasciava dire e si contentava di buscarsi il pane colle sue braccia, invece di menarle addosso ai compagni, e attaccar brighe" (174; "The poor devil let them talk, and all he wanted was to earn his bread with his hands instead of raising them against his companions and starting fights," 66–67). In other words, Misciu Bestia is in a dog-eat-dog world and refuses to fight back; in this world, his refusal gains him not the respect but instead the contempt of his fellows, who regard him as "l'asino da basto di tutta la cava" ("the pack animal of the whole quarry") and treat him accordingly.

When framed within this perspective, the reaction of the engineer in charge of the quarry to the news of Mastro Bestia's death is at least partially understandable. Word of the tragedy arrives while the engineer is at the theater, attending a Saturday evening performance. Since he is a devotee of the stage and "non avrebbe cambiato la sua poltrona con un trono" ("wouldn't have changed his seat for a throne"), he is less than pleased to be bothered with the news of an event which had occurred several hours earlier and about which he can seemingly do nothing. He does leave the performance in order to go examine the site, and in fact, nothing can be done. Mastro Bestia's "deal" was so bad that there was at least a week's worth of material to be removed, and every bit of it had caved in on him. Meanwhile, before all of the workers have gone off, Malpelo is noticed digging in the sand like a wild animal, his torn nails hanging from his bloody hands, foam at his mouth, and his eyes suddenly glassy in the light of the workers' lamp. In the end they have to drag him away like a mad dog. The response of the workers to the sight of Malpelo is probably to be expected: his presence merely reaffirms the luck of the wicked, since if he had not been "Malpelo," he would not have escaped so easily.

In the following days, not surprisingly, Malpelo reacts to the death of his father in a much deeper and also in a much more noticeable way than any of the others. When Malpelo's mother brings Malpelo back to work in the mine (for purely economic reasons), Malpelo behaves worse than ever, at least in the eyes of the other workers, as though he intended not only to pick up where his outcast father had left off but also to revel in the satanic state of his anathema. Malpelo's reactions manifest themselves in several forms. Besides beating the animals without pity (saying "Così creperai più presto!"; "This way you'll die sooner!") and being unmercifully cruel to the other children, he curses both the boss, who gave the dangerous and undervalued contract to his father, and the Cripple ("lo Sciancato") who laughed at his father's death ("È stato lui, per trentacinque tarì! . . . E anche lui! e si metteva a ridere! Io l'ho udito, quella sera!"; "He's the one, for thirty-five tarì! . . . And him too! And he laughed! I heard him that night!"). In short, as though it were a matter of pride, Malpelo causes as much trouble as possible—and he does so to such an extent that whenever something bad happens, the others, well aware of his nature, know without hesitation who is to be blamed and, consequently, to be punished (177; 70).

It is clear, from the absoluteness of various passages describing Malpelo's evil, that despite several allusions to Malpelo's being possessed by the devil after the death of his father, the local populace does not truly regard this as a case of possession. Their world (unlike Manzoni's, for example, in which moral exorcism is a reality and conversion and rehabilitation are always possible) is one in which evil actually exists as the *essence* of certain individuals. Although, through the narrator, the local people at times adopt the terminology of possession, as though Malpelo's behavior were the result of another force or being entering his body from without and contaminating his behavior, their fundamental belief, neatly encapsulated in the proverb of the story's title, is that Malpelo is not a neutral or even a potentially good figure temporarily in the service of evil but the very embodiment of wickedness itself. Similar to La Lupa (in terms of the unity of her passion) but distinct from say, either l'Innominato or Don Rodrigo, Rosso Malpelo is, in the eyes of his fellows, a totally unified character from first to last, evil and only that through and through.

The unity of Malpelo's nature and behavior is especially clear-cut in the way the others view his relationship with Ranocchio, the unfortunate boy to whom Malpelo attaches himself, according to the narrator, "per un raffinamento di malignità" (177; "out of a refined malice," 71). From the perspective of the others, it appears that Malpelo establishes this relationship merely for the joy of playing the tyrant. If it is also true that Malpelo occasionally gives his food to Ranocchio, the narrator has no doubt that he does this out of pride and because, like his father before him, he is "avvezzo a tutto" (used to everything); and indeed, he is used to going hungry in part because of his earlier rejection of food and in part because the boss cuts his rations as punishment for his evil ways. The one thing that no one is sure of, however, is whether Malpelo's constant wickedness, extending even to his acceptance of punishment in instances when he is not guilty, is the result of savageness or timidity, of wicked pride or desperate resignation ("di bieco orgoglio o di disperata rassegnazione"). What is certain—as Ranocchio's health deteriorates and his relationship with Malpelo becomes even closer, until Malpelo says it would be better for Ranocchio to die than for him to suffer as he does—is that the owner feels some responsibility for Ranocchio's well-being and therefore says that Malpelo should be watched carefully, since he is a dangerous character: "E il padrone diceva che Malpelo era capace di schiacciargli il capo a quel ragazzo, e bisognava sorvegliarlo" (187; "The boss said Malpelo was capable of smashing the boy's head in, and he'd have to be watched," 83).

In the course of the middle portion of the story, Mastro Misciu's body is found, along with his tools and clothing. After the driver carts off the body—this time neither sand nor animal but baptized flesh—Malpelo inherits his father's almost new fustian pants and his shoes, which, on Sunday, the boy shines and slips on, gazing at them for hours on end, "rimugginando chi sa quali idee in quel cervellaccio" (183; "brooding over god knows what ideas in that warped brain of his," 78). In the end, even Malpelo's reaction to his inheritance confirms the local view of him as a misfit, since instead of selling the pickaxe and hoe, the handles of which have been left incomparably smooth and shiny by the action of his father's hands, he proceeds to use them himself despite the fact that they are far too heavy for a boy of his age. As the narrator exclaims, again reflecting the choral voice of the local populace, "Ei possedeva delle idee strane, Malpelo!" ("He had some strange ideas, that Malpelo!").

Although Malpelo's mother and sister both leave for other parts, Malpelo stays on to work in the mine, regardless of the fact that the work underground is to some so unpleasant that (according to the escaped convict) prison, by comparison, is paradise. Since Malpelo is all alone, effectively without father, mother, or responsibilities, and since he is anything but the apple of the boss's eye, he is regularly assigned the most dangerous tasks, including the one that finally leads to his disappearance and to the lively anxieties of the other boys, who are afraid to see the ghost of their nemesis reappear: "Così si persero persin le ossa di Malpelo, e i ragazzi della cava abbassano la voce quando parlano di lui nel sotterraneo, ché hanno paura di vederselo comparire dinanzi, coi capelli rossi e gli occhiacci grigi" (189; "So even Malpelo's bones were lost, and the boys of the quarry lower their voices when they speak of him in the underground gallery, for they are afraid of seeing him appear before them, with his red hair and awful grey eyes," 85).

Malpelo's view of all this, of both the events and the characters of his "story," diverges noticeably from the view of the others in several important ways. These differences are most apparent, first, in his relationship with his father, and, second, subsequent to Mastro Misciu's death, in the development of Malpelo's relationship with Ranocchio. The narrative's initial reference to the relationship between father and son comes in the form of an explanation of the miners' "carità," or "charity," in keeping Malpelo on, which is done specifically "perché Mastro Misciu, suo padre, era morto nella cava" ("because Mastro Misciu, his father, had died in the mine"). For the moment at least, this reference puts an end to the talk of charity, and the next paragraph describes the relationship between the two in a somewhat different and clearer light, since Malpelo is now presented as internalizing the abuses suffered by Mastro Misciu at the hands of the other workers: "Malpelo faceva un visaccio come se quelle soperchierie cascassero sulle sue spalle" (174; "Malpelo would make a face as if those abuses fell on his own shoulders," 67).

The psychological effects of this process of identification and internalization—which, in the economy typical of Verga's narrative practice throughout *Vita dei campi*, is presented only once, but in the imperfect tense and therefore meant to be construed as occurring gradually over a period of time—are telling indeed. It should be borne in mind, however, that the identification itself is not perfect, that the internalization of the position and experience of the father includes, for Malpelo, not only aspects of repetition, or of sameness, but also of difference. Indeed, the very miners who see him associated with his father also distinguish him from Mastro Misciu, in a sense that is at least in appearance to Malpelo's detriment: "E così piccolo com'era aveva di quelle occhiate che facevano dire agli altri: 'Va' là, che tu non ci morrai nel tuo letto, come tuo padre'" ("and small as he was, he had such a look in his eyes that made the others say: 'Go on, you won't die in your bed like your father'"). Shortly thereafter in the story, Mastro Misciu evinces a similar play of identification and differentiation in regard to his son, but this time in Malpelo's favor. Mastro Misciu feels unquestionable affection for Malpelo ("Il padre che gli voleva bene . . ."; "His father, who loved him . . ."); but because of this very affection he is also solicitous of his son's welfare and does not want Malpelo to get too close to the most dangerous work, which is not to be Malpelo's but Mastro Misciu's alone ("Tirati indietro! . . . Sta attento! Sta attento se cascano dall'alto dei sassolini o della rena grossa"; "Get back! . . . Watch out! Watch out if you see any stones or heavy sand fall from above").

These distinctions can be taken, then, in the first instance as negative and in the second as positive. Nevertheless, in terms of the thematic organization of the entire story, what is crucial to see is that each of these portrayals of identification and distinction is simply the other side of the same coin viewed from a different angle. Therefore, merely retracing these linked parallels and contrasts, in and of themselves, does nothing to lead past the illusory symbolic unity of psychological and social representation that such similarities and distinctions both reflect and foster within the story. Nonetheless, the bond of affection between father and son does constitute one of the most significant aspects of the narrative, since its understanding is central to the process of interpretation that the text itself invites and that will eventually show the way out of this seemingly closed circle of representation and evaluation.

The affection between Malpelo and Mastro Misciu, both in its depth and in its constancy, provides an implicit argument against the view of Malpelo as an unfeeling, inhuman monster. This bond is given extra strength by the narrative depiction of Master Misciu as a provider who, though concerned for all of the members of his family, enjoys a special relationship with his son, since Malpelo accompanies him and assists him in his work. After the catastrophe in the quarry, the narrative creates a potentially sympathetic view of Malpelo by continuing its dramatic depiction of the boy's attachment to his father (in Malpelo's frenzied attempts to dig through the sand with his bare hands) even as it portrays the condemnatory view of him held by the other workers. The workers' reactions to the details of the torn fingernails and the bloody hands that again symbolically unite father and son serve to reinforce this same effect—here, in narrative sympathy created through unjustifiably massive condemnation, something like an observer's natural reaction to seeing someone kill a fly with a hammer—since lo Sciancato emphasizes the parallel between the boy and the father as though it were not part of a tragedy but instead part of a cruel joke (182; 77).

The relationship between father and son lives on, of course, in Malpelo's memory and sentiments long after Mastro Misciu's death, but it does so in the key of bitterness. Along with his cursing of lo Sciancato and the *padrone*, this bitterness is apparent in the way Malpelo recalls his father's situation and laments the treachery of the other workers as well as that of the sand itself:

> Lavorando di piccone o di zappa poi menava le mani con accanimento, a mo' di uno che l'avesse con la rena, e batteva e ribatteva coi denti stretti, e con quegli *ah! ah!* che aveva suo padre. "La rena è traditora," diceva a Ranocchio sottovoce; "somiglia a tutti gli altri, che se sei più debole ti pestano la faccia, e se sei più forte, o siete in molti, come fa lo Sciancato, allora si lascia vincere. Mio padre la batteva sempre, ed egli non batteva altro che la rena, perciò lo chiamavano Bestia, e la rena se lo mangiò a tradimento, perché era più forte di lui." (178–79)

> Working with pick or hoe, he swung his arms furiously, like one who had something against the sand, and he struck and struck with clenched teeth, and with the *ah! ah!* of his father. "The sand's a traitor," he would say to Ranocchio in a whisper; "it's like all the others, who'll smash your face if you're weaker, but if you're stronger, or with a group, like the Cripple, then it'll give in. My father used to strike the sand all the time, and he struck nothing but the sand, that's why they called him the Jackass,

and the sand set its trap and ate him up, because it was stronger than he was." (72)

In this key passage Malpelo expresses the basic lessons to be learned in this post-Darwinian world: first, strength resides either in individual force or in numbers; and second, the strong survive by devouring the weak. Malpelo passes the lessons of his education on to Ranocchio by making Ranocchio his pupil. The preferred manner of instruction combines both lecture and example. Malpelo thus treats Ranocchio in the way that, in this world, the strong characteristically treat the objects of their aggression, by beating him and denouncing him as "bestia" in a fashion similar to that adopted by the other workers when dealing first with Mastro Misciu and then with Malpelo himself. Over the course of his teachings, Malpelo demonstrates, moreover, not only what he has learned but also that he has advanced well beyond his father, since Misciu Bestia, in his Christ-like combination of goodness and passivity, had regularly refused to fight back.[5] The tools and clothes that Malpelo inherits from his father—and that Vittorio Spinazzola has perceptively termed the sacred objects of his cult—symbolize the son's assumption of Mastro Misciu's identity even as they again attest to the differences between originator and offspring.[6] Malpelo uses the tools out of pride as well as reverence. Indeed, this prideful stubbornness, along with Malpelo's aggression, distinguishes him both from his idol (whose caresses he first experiences and then recalls with the distortion born of reverence) *and* from his pupil, since Ranocchio never gets the hang of acting like Malpelo, no matter how hard Malpelo tries to inculcate his lessons. Ranocchio remains first to last a "femminuccia," or roughly, a "little girl," notwithstanding Malpelo's attempts to teach him the importance of asserting himself and fighting back ("Bestia! Bestia sei! Se non ti senti l'animo di difenderti da me che non ti voglio male, vuol dire che ti lascerai pestare il viso da questo e da quello! . . . Così, come ti cuocerà il dolore delle busse, imparerai a darne anche tu!"; "Jackass! A jackass, that's what you are! If you're not game enough to defend yourself from the one who doesn't have anything against you, you'll let just anybody smash your face! . . . If you feel how blows hurt, you'll learn to give some yourself!"). When Malpelo sees his efforts at pedagogy come to naught, he despairs of refashioning Ranocchio in his own image; but at the same time, Malpelo takes a certain pride in his own resignation and in his strength, which he uses to assist his weaker companion.

It is interesting in this regard to consider the deterioration of Ranocchio's health. Although it is probable that Malpelo's blows, and especially the one that results in Ranocchio's spitting up blood, aggravate Ranocchio's illness, it is unlikely that Malpelo actually causes the malady, since its symptoms seem to predate their relationship. But whatever the exact cause of Ranocchio's condition (most likely consumption), it is clear that the boy's illness contributes to both Malpelo's disgust with and his concern for his weaker companion, and so to the dual aura of guilt and aggression that surrounds the sadomasochistic intimacy between the two boys. What makes this odd relationship possible is, of course, Malpelo's narcissism, his pride and self-aggrandizement, in strict combination with his internalization of the common judgment of his character, resulting paradoxically in his disproportionate self-hatred. Ranocchio fits into the first part of this psychic *iter* in that Malpelo draws the "Frog" close to himself as a fellow outcast, as a companion in vituperation and mistreatment; and the sick boy fits into the second part in the way that Malpelo treats him, giving him the same sorts of blows that Malpelo gives the grey donkey and that the other workers (in a figurative sense) and the sand (in a literal sense) had given his father, that other "bestia."

This is not to say, strangely enough, that Malpelo is cruel to the boy, as appears to be the case to the boss and to the other workers. Indeed, from Malpelo's perspective, he is actually being more than considerate, as Spinazzola has painstakingly demonstrated.[7] Malpelo, besides trying to teach Ranocchio the lessons of life, not only gives the boy his clothes when Ranocchio's malady intensifies, but he also takes money from his own weekly pay (as he had never done before, despite his sister's suspicions) in order to provide his weaker companion with wine and warm food.

It is also true, of course, that even in this instance Malpelo does not succumb completely to the sway of affection. He had been totally overcome by emotion once, when his reaction to his father's disappearance turned him into a "mad dog" digging in the sand, intent on finding the object of his affection and only on that, but he never again cedes completely to the powers of affect. Now that he has learned the cold, worldly rule of reason he does not forget it: "Ecco come vanno le cose!" (184; "That's how things go!" 79). Malpelo knows the ways of destiny and that it is useless to fight against them. He watches incredulously as Ranocchio's mother grieves for her dying son because he knows that, like the grey donkey, Ranocchio would be better off never to have been born at all if he has to suffer as he does. The boy is weak, and therefore he will die: life is as simple as that. At the same time, Malpelo takes pride in what he knows to be his own strength: "Egli invece era stato sano e robusto, ed era *malpelo*" (187; "He instead had always been healthy and strong, and he was *malpelo*," 83). So there are certain advantages to being "malpelo" in this world of Darwinian *bellum,* where the only law that finally holds sway is that of the seemingly logical destiny of internecine violence. Oddly enough, however, life's ultimate rule is the one that Malpelo, in what Sergio Campailla terms his *"furor* pedagogico," can teach but cannot change, can know but cannot thereby escape, since before it, he, too, is helpless: "Ecco come vanno le cose."[8]

This dual knowledge, of the laws of the world and of his place in it, shapes Malpelo's view of his relation to others in a fundamental way. Although he takes pride in his strength and resilience, he is also resigned to being the outcast, because he *is* "malpelo": "Sapendo che era *malpelo.* . . . 'Sono *malpelo!*' . . . ed era *malpelo*" (177, 179, 187; "Knowing he was *malpelo.* . . . 'I'm *malpelo!*' . . . and he was *malpelo,*" 70, 73, 83). This knowledge of his essence combines with Malpelo's acceptance of his position in the world of work, an acceptance that is reminiscent of certain passages in *I Malavoglia.* Laboring in the quarry was the occupation of his father and the role into which Malpelo was born (181; 75). Even if he would have preferred to work above ground, like Ranocchio prior to his accident, such a preference is immaterial. Malpelo thus embraces his occupation and all its trappings of death and darkness with the same fervor that he shows in accepting his own nature, rejecting even the light of the moon and feeling an affinity for the owl that screeches on the *sciara* when it longs to be underground with the dead: "'Per noi che siamo fatti per vivere sotterra, pensava Malpelo, ci dovrebbe essere buio sempre e dappertutto'" (185; "'For us who are made [i.e., born] to live underground,' thought Malpelo, 'it should always be dark, everywhere,'" 80).

Although Ranocchio, as Malpelo's less than perfect pupil, never gets used to the darkness and continues to fear its creatures, Malpelo has no fear, except in one instance, when the first of Mastro Misciu's shoes is found. Otherwise, Malpelo is both resigned to his role and proud of it, thus demonstrating the insufficiency of the others' views in judging his attitude. In other words, Malpelo's character is not formed by either pride or resignation but by both. Therefore, even though his pride might naturally lead to revolt, his resignation guarantees that such rebellion will occur only *within* the system of beliefs and practices that the others share and that Malpelo himself has accepted, just as he has accepted the place assigned to him within their world even though that place is coded as one of marginality and aberration.

This portrayal of graded differences in perception within a carefully delimited arena of overall similarity is shaded by Verga in various ways. One of the most precise of these is the narrator's use of a term with two possible, and in part contradictory, interpretations. When this effect occurs in a single word, as is often the case, it is evocative of Bakhtin's discussion of the many degrees of the "double-voiced" word. Once again, however, the effects of Verga's narrative techniques are not just dual but actively polyphonic, since the two ways of regarding the semantics of any individual lexical item in the narrative eventually imply the existence of yet another point of view (to be considered shortly) that extends beyond the perspectives of either the local populace or Malpelo himself. A good example of this technique, which initially appears to be built on a single opposition, occurs in a passage immediately following one that we have already discussed when dealing with Malpelo's willingness, after the death of his father, to receive blows in his mulelike stubbornness: "Cogli altri ragazzi poi era addirittura crudele, e sembrava che si volesse vendicare sui deboli di tutto il male che *s'immaginava* gli avessero fatto, a lui e al suo babbo" (177, my italics; "With the other boys he was downright cruel, and it seemed that he wanted to take vengeance on the weak for all the wrongs he *imagined* the others had done to him and his father," 70, my italics).

This brief passage, which may at first seem direct and concrete but which in fact consists of speculation built on speculation, contains a series of terms that invite multiple interpretation. It is doubtless true that the other boys in the mine consider Malpelo "cruel," since he does not hesitate to strike them when he can; but from his perspective this behavior is both natural and appropriate for the simple reason that, in the world as it is, the others hit him too. The clause following the narrator's opening affirmation of Malpelo's cruelty gives rise first to speculation as to why Malpelo is so pitilessly aggressive ("sembrava che si volesse vendicare"; "it seemed that he wanted to take vengeance") and then to an implicit contradiction of Malpelo's perception of the injustice of his and his father's treatment at the hands of the others ("di tutto il male che *s'immaginava* . . . avessero fatto"; "for all the wrongs he *imagined* the others had done"). The parallel in verbal construction—imperfect indicatives leading to imperfect subjunctives—thus forms a contrast in meaning, since the first pairing is intended to affirm the validity of the narrator's speculation whereas the second is meant, at least on the surface, to deny the validity of Malpelo's memories and attitudes. The separation of Malpelo from the others in his inward withdrawal is underscored, moreover, by the use of the reflexive form of the verb, *s'immaginava*.

The narrator's adoption of the pronominal *gli* for *loro*, technically "him" for "them," followed at once by the clarification of the reference ("a lui e al suo babbo"; "to him and his father") provides the flavor of common speech at the same time that it suggests the closeness of the ties between Malpelo and his father, who at this point are linked together in their victimage in a solitary word. Beyond demonstrating the extraordinary narrative economy for which Verga is justly renowned, this particular example of pronominal concentration emphasizes that Malpelo has internalized not only certain aspects of his father's character but also all the evil done to him by the others. The emotional ties between father and son are also suggested, moreover, by the use of the term *babbo*, or roughly "dad," which here as elsewhere emphasizes Malpelo's affective point of view. Both of the key terms in the second half of the passage, *s'immaginava* and *babbo*, thus reaffirm the differences in perspective between Malpelo and the rest of the workers even as, on a superficial level, they support the view of the others and condemn that of Malpelo. This sort of semantic multiplicity, in which two views coexist uncomfortably in one word, regularly corresponds in its *effect* in this novella to Verga's extensive use of the *style indirect libre* throughout such contemporary narratives as "Cavalleria rusticana" and *I Malavoglia*, in which the narrator's perspective mixes with those of certain characters much more closely (and much more sympathetically) than is the case here. The reason for the predominance of this particular technique here in creating the play of perspective that is a hallmark of Verghian narrative is that in "Rosso Malpelo" the narrator remains, at least in appearance, thoroughly unsympathetic to and therefore external to Malpelo's point of view.

At times this sort of effect is not so much a question of semantics as one of worldly reference within a narrowly encompassed natural and cultural setting. The narrator's reference to the "povere lucertole" (180; "poor lizards," 74) that are the objects of Malpelo's stones, for example, demonstrates the extremity of the local antipathy for Malpelo, since it is inconceivable, given the usual children's pastimes in this culture, either that anyone else would be condemned for throwing stones at lizards or that lizards themselves would be the objects of sympathy ("le quali non gli avevano fatto nulla"; "which hadn't done anything to him"). This same contrast in perspective is heightened by the narrator's lack of concern for Malpelo when he is mistreated by the others and thus constrained to wander in solitude along the deserted pathways; and it is again present in the depiction of Malpelo's treatment by both his sister and his mother, as I have already mentioned. In terms of verismo's realist aesthetic, the narrative's condemnation of Malpelo is, therefore, semiologically extensive, including myriad types of signs, from words themselves to natural and even human "signifiers."

The totality of this condemnation both derives from and in turn contributes to the novella's extraordinarily thorough symbolic consistency, which remains unbroken by the marked variance in perspectives between Malpelo and the others because Malpelo himself is subsumed within the established system of social and economic relations regardless of his limited rebellion. This consistency can be traced through practically every aspect of the story, from scene, character, and imagery to plot itself. The story's color imagery—signaled first by the story's title—is of particular centrality, since it links together many seemingly disparate elements of the narrative's organization. Malpelo, of course, is red in almost everything from his name to his freckles, to his bleeding hands, and to the sand that covers him. In terms of popular belief, his red hair is the color of Judas' and, through Judas, the sign of Cain.[9] The quarry itself, needless to say, is also red, so distinctively so that it is referred to as "la cava della rena rossa," or the red-sand quarry (and, popularly, as "la cava dei Malpelo," or Malpelo's quarry).

In the text of 1880, furthermore, there was another notable occurrence of the word for red, in the name of the well-known actor Ernesto Rossi, who was playing the part of Hamlet on the fateful evening of Mastro Misciu's accident. This reference to local history was deleted in the version revised by Verga for the deluxe edition of 1897, although whether this deletion was made because Verga felt that the reference was too extraneous and journalistic to be significant (as Giovanni Cecchetti believes) or, on the contrary, because Verga felt that the *symbolic* conjuncture of this further occurrence of redness strained the realist aesthetics of verismo, is impossible to ascertain beyond doubt.[10] Nonetheless, the obviously overdetermined color imagery embedded in the name of the actor, combined with the novella's second dominant color, the blackness traditionally associated with the play's eponymous character, suggests a question that the criticism of Verga's novella has never considered, beyond the obvious analogy between Mastro Misciu's "burial" and Ophelia's interment. Given the otherwise striking coherence of the story's imagery and allusions, the real question is, Why *Hamlet?*

Although the reference to the play may seem in fact too "literary" and too symbolically obvious to fit easily within the supposed randomness of verismo's programmatic objectivity, the relation between Shakespeare's tragedy and the story recounted in the novella is nonetheless both pertinent and instructive. What is *Hamlet* about, after all, but the attempts of a melancholic and justly bereaved son to come to terms with, and if possible to avenge, the murder of his father? The sort of sexual intrigue apparent in the play is, of course, only briefly suggested in the novella by the remarriage of Mastro Misciu's widow. But, as we shall see, the judgment of the forces that permit the initial death to occur and that contribute to the breaking up of the family as a unit is, if anything, even more severe in Verga's Sicilian novella (though here presented on a much more limited scale) than it is in Shakespeare's portrayal of the tragedy of Danish history. The ritual, almost supernatural aura of the death and its aftermath is apparent in both works and is perhaps heightened in a very general sense in Verga's story by the choice of names for Mastro Bestia, since Misciu, as a diminutive for Domenico (and accompanied by the eventual notation "baptized flesh") may serve to recall the original Christian sacrifice. In any case, the identification of the son with the father is evident in each story through constant verbal allusions as well as psychological development (and, in Shakespeare, through the repetition of naming itself: Hamlet/Hamlet). The willfulness of both characters is obvious, moreover, as is their shared skepticism regarding the value of life itself. But what is significantly different—with a significance of special import for Verga—is the end to which that willfulness ultimately leads. Hamlet and presumably Malpelo meet their deaths at the conclusion of their stories, but Hamlet's demise is in part a stepping-stone to a new order, whereas Malpelo, in death as in life, remains within the dominant social order, and his disappearance therefore leads only to the circularity of his own ghostly and potentially horrifying return. In other words, in Verga's view of Sicilian history, as opposed to Shakespeare's vision of the "righted" future of the Danish monarchy, there simply was no Fortinbras, no direct way of moving outside of the given system. At this crucial point, then, the parallels between the two pensive and reclusive loners, with their heads full of "idee strane," Rossi/Amleto and Rosso Malpelo, come to an end.

The third color with an important symbolic function in the story is gray. In the middle sections of the narrative this color is most obviously associated with the gray donkey, "il *grigio*," the death of which incites Malpelo's laments about the cruelty of life and his grim commentary on the advantages of never having been born at all. The most gruesome detail in the description of the dead animal is that of its eyes, which in life seemed to beg from exhaustion, "Non più! non più!" (184; "No more! No more!" 79), but which now in death no longer suffer even when the dogs empty out the sockets with their teeth.

In terms of the novella's skein of color imagery, this macabre association of grayness with the eyes of death serves, of course, as preparation for the story's conclusion. Malpelo's eyes are designated by the pejorative "occhiacci" several times in the story and are described in various ways, but they are not actually depicted in regard to their color until the story's conclusion, when the other boys are said to live in fear of his sudden appearance out of the darkness. This revelation adds to the climactic effects of the last words of the narrative's extended final period at the same time that it closes the circle of narrative symbolism in terms of both color imagery and meaning: "coi capelli rossi e gli occhiaci grigi" ("with his red hair and awful grey eyes"). The grayness of Malpelo's eyes and the redness of his hair are here mentioned directly as the signs by which the others recognize both Malpelo's physical being and his character. By this time the redness of Malpelo's hair merely reaffirms once more the truth of the novella's initial proverb, whereas the gray eyes link Malpelo to the dead mule, another victim of both the mine and the miners, and, indeed, more than either of these, of life itself. The mention of the "bones" at the beginning of the passage reinforces the connection with the *grigio*, the bones of which, "spolpate . . .[e] sgangherate" ("stripped . . . [and] jumbled"), are the object of Malpelo's melancholy contemplation after the death of Ranocchio. Of course, the reference to Malpelo's "lost bones"—an important circumstance in a culture that puts great emphasis on Christian burial—also recalls the other death with which Malpelo's fate is regularly compared and contrasted in the story, that of Mastro Misciu. The narrator's concluding shift into the present tense when describing the other boys' behavior and their continuing fears adds both the techniques of popular storytelling and the apparent immediacy of everyday life to what has now become not just the story but also the constantly retold legend of Malpelo. The boys' worry—that their speech will actually invoke Malpelo to return from beyond to torment his previous victims as well as his previous oppressors—closes the story's system of symbolism even as it seems to leave the narrative with an open ending. At the conclusion, this very openness, when considered in the light of the relations between oppressor and oppressed as presented explicitly within the narrative, is itself illusory, since the basic network of aggression and victimization remains unchanged despite the possibility of Malpelo's supernatural reappearance. Indeed, in terms of *that* network, his return would only reaffirm the now transcendent truth of his character, which the others already know far too well.

This concluding paragraph, with its mixture of fact and imagination, is preceded by an explanation as to why Malpelo is regularly chosen for dangerous ventures (the others have families and responsibilities and so would not risk their lives for all the gold in the world) and by an allusion, from Malpelo's perspective, to the miner who was lost in the underground caverns years before and who still wanders in the dark crying for help, to no avail. The explanation extends Malpelo's earlier account of why the boss sends him farther than the others—they are simply afraid to go (184; 80)—while the allusion repeats Malpelo's retelling of the same startling story of the lost miner to Ranocchio (a story that echoes Malpelo's earlier, more personal comments on lost miners sought desperately by their children) just before Malpelo's initial mention of his underground explorations (181–82, 184; 76, 80).

Like the novella's color imagery, these repetitions serve to emphasize the effects of overall narrative unity; but, as usual, Verga also uses the emphasis lent by repetition to the story of the lost miner in another way. It is peculiar that, in a novella set in and around a mine, with the workers as the narrative's principal characters, the actual term for miner, *minatore,* appears so rarely. The word is used three times in the version of 1880 and only twice in the 1897 revision, in the two allusions just referred to, each time from Malpelo's perspective and each time in reference to the lost miner wandering for years in the underground cave. Given the context of the dark "labyrinth" of the quarry's underground passageways, it is not difficult to see that the narrative adopts the term so sparingly in order to point up the orthographic similarity of the lost miner's chthonic double: *minatore/minotauro.*[11]

The underlying myth of the minotaur, with its admixture of sacrifice and terror, serves to extend the pre-Christian symbolism of the story's carefully chosen nature imagery. At the same time, it confirms the transitional *and* transcendent essence of Malpelo's character, since, as the figure most recently subsumed within the continually revitalized myth, Malpelo takes his place as the new if malevolent *genius loci,* a being that has a definite place of its own but that is no longer limited to any single temporal or physiological sphere, either animal or human, natural or cultural. The logic of Malpelo's role and behavior, like that of his dog-eat-dog surroundings, thus extends to all aspects of Verga's depiction of life in the mine. Now, notwithstanding the owner's feelings in the matter, the cave really *is* Malpelo's, and once inside it, the other boys act accordingly: "la cava di Malpelo." The myth thus reinforces the story's man/beast imagery even while it expands the range of this imagery's meaning. Unlike such other transitional narrative elements as the *sciara* (above ground but melancholy and desolate), the meekly Christian figure of "Mastro/Bestia," and even Malpelo himself as son/dog/wolf (180; 74), at the story's conclusion Malpelo does not so much move back and forth across possible distinctions as transcend them: his gray eyes are therefore not really a sign of the union of black and white, death and life, but rather a sign of his transcendence of the opposition itself. By moving past the temporal and physical boundaries of both nature and culture, the conclusion of the story reaffirms the potency and the universality of Malpelo's role and of his character, which are now *super*natural.

The novella's portrayal of the local belief in superstition, like its adoption of nicknames for proper names and of locally common animal imagery (which includes the manner of Mastro Misciu's demise in the "death of a rat" and even the "traitor sand" perceived as a part of animate nature), serves the ends of verismo's realism through the seemingly accurate depiction of the customs and beliefs of the Sicilian populace. At the same time, these realist effects combine with the story's color imagery and its portrayal of character to reinforce the extreme consistency of the novella's *symbolic* organization. This consistency is perhaps most obvious in the plot itself, which simply reaffirms both the initial description of Malpelo as an outcast and the miners' prediction of his fate. Indeed, the apparent closure of the story's symbolic *and* realistic presentation in terms of plotting as well as imagery, character, and background myth is in many respects nothing more than a confirmation of the story's title, with the result that Rosso Malpelo seems at the end merely to demonstrate the truth that, for the local populace, has been contained within his name all along. The relation between physical characteristics and moral character, between the signs of physical appearance and the evidence of worldly values and behavior, is thus seen, in this case, as motivated and absolute rather than as casual or contingent. In formulaic terms, Malpelo's story both starts and finishes with this single overriding truth, as what at first seems the oddity of his name is justified by the proof of his narrative: Rosso Malpelo equals "rosso malpelo."

Again, this sort of narrative coherence is possible because of Malpelo's acceptance of the role that the others assign to him. This acceptance is, of course, part of Malpelo's identification with his father, but even at the story's conclusion the process of differentiation as well as similarity continues. Like his father, Malpelo meets his end in the mine, "ma in modo diverso" (188; "but in a different way," 85). One of the most obvious differences is that Malpelo's bones really are lost in the mine, along with his spirit, and (like those of the lost miner) they remain so, whereas Mastro Misciu's body was eventually discovered and removed, presumably for proper Christian burial. But another important aspect of this difference is Malpelo's willful complicity in his own destiny, as though he actually *chooses* that which befell Mastro Misciu through no design of his own. This aspect of will, which is already at work in Malpelo's pride, should not be exaggerated, however, since it is important only within the context of his resignation to his role and to the tasks that the owner gives him.

This odd combination of pride and resignation helps us to ascertain just what that role is. Both in his own eyes and in the view of the others Malpelo is the scapegoat, the carrier of all that is evil, and the one that is to be sacrificed through banishment and/or death if society itself is to remain healthy and strong.[12] In the eyes of the others, he is a version of the traditional scapegoat-criminal, "torvo, ringhioso, e selvatico" (173; "surly, snarling, and wild," 66), no better than, and in essence no different from, the criminals who end up in jail and die there, which is the fate incorrectly predicted for Malpelo by lo Sciancato just before the story's conclusion (188; 85). But in Malpelo's own experience he is another sort of scapegoat, not the victim-criminal (from whom he is clearly distinguished in the narrative's penultimate section, *pace* lo Sciancato) but the victim-king, proud of his role and of his strength as the prince of darkness: "Sono *malpelo!*" In this regard, even though Malpelo remains within the system of moral and cultural relations determined by the local society, his end reaffirms *his* view of his role, through his dominion over his true realm in a way that, both realistically and symbolically, includes natural, cultural, and now supernatural supremacy.

As can be seen from the novella's remarkable economy of event, the coherence of the story derives in large part from the centrality of Mastro Misciu's death. It is also clear that for Malpelo the trauma of this event triggers his identification with his lost father and leads to his intolerable behavior.[13] Malpelo's subsequent condition—as a child brought back to work in the mine by his widowed mother, who cannot afford to do without his salary but who abandons him when she finds another husband—effectively turns Malpelo into an orphan, laboring fourteen hours a day (179; 73) and suffering the abuse of the other workers and the "sassate," or stones, hurled by the other children. Nonetheless, for the reasons we have already discussed, there is simply no pity for his plight either on the part of the others or on the part of Malpelo himself. As in "La Lupa," this extraordinary unity of the narrative perception of the character's situation—a perception in which the narrator, the local populace, and to a certain extent even the major character all share—depends on the suppression of the contingency of temporal development in favor of the absoluteness of atemporal truth: from this perspective, as we have seen, Malpelo is evil, period; he always has been and always will be. As distinct from "La Lupa," however, there is another point of view in "Rosso Malpelo" that serves to break apart the apparent narrative unity created by the essential agreement of the two perspectives considered thus far.

This third perspective is inherently disruptive (even though it does not interfere with the symbolic unity of the story's imagery) because it accords neither with the local populace's view nor with Malpelo's.[14] One of the principal mechanisms of its presentation, furthermore, is already in operation, however subtly, as early as the novella's introductory period: "Malpelo si chiamava così *perché* aveva i capelli rossi; ed aveva i capelli rossi *perché* era un ragazzo malizioso e cattivo, che prometteva di riescire un fior di birbone" ("He was called Malpelo *because* he had red hair; and he had red hair *because* he was a mean and bad boy, who promised to turn into a first-rate scoundrel"). Rather than explaining the "why" of the purported relationship between Malpelo's nickname, the color of his hair, and his character, the opening repetition "because . . . because" merely reaffirms the local populace's superstition as embodied in the proverb.[15] The paragraph proceeds immediately with another explanation, with "sicché" ("so") used to account for the unanimity of the workers in calling "Malpelo" by that name; and the paragraph concludes the strange syllogism by adding Malpelo's mother to the like-minded coterie ("persino sua madre"; "even his mother") and explaining that she had almost forgotten his baptismal name since she had always ("sempre") heard him called "Malpelo" and only that.

This chain of explicatives that explain nothing, followed by the totality of the agreement of the local populace as well as the absoluteness of the temporal frame, provides a way for Verga's narrative to question the presuppositions of what it describes even as the description itself continues to stand as an accurate representation of local life and attitudes. At the beginning of the paragraph, there are simply too many *becauses* for the text not to pose, though in a different way, the supposedly unasked question: why? At the end, the unanimity and the totality of the judgment regarding Malpelo only *reinforces* the initial doubt. In subtly questioning the motivation underlying the relation between naming and character, signs and referents, the narrative breaks the unity of its own presentation by putting in doubt not the fact but the logical and moral status of the local populace's beliefs and practices.

Throughout the story the text's explicatives continue to raise as many questions as they answer.[16] At the same time, other techniques we have already considered, such as the multilayering of perspectives either within a single description of characters in reaction to their environment or at times within a single word, also have the effect not just of creating a duality of perspective (the populace as a whole and Malpelo) but of establishing a further point of view that remains persistently external to the logic of either of the other two. The novella's depiction of personal relations, furthermore, has this same disconcerting effect, beginning with the odd lack of warmth on the part of Malpelo's mother and his sister, continuing with the genuine emotional bond that exists between "babbo" and son, and culminating with the regard that Malpelo, at least on occasion, shows for Ranocchio. These latter relations stand out by contrast, moreover, on account of the total lack of emotional warmth among any of the other characters in the story.

The result of these discrepancies between what the others construe to be the nature of human motivation and action and what the narrative actually demonstrates it to be is the creation of a constant narrative distance. This distance is the reason the narrative can present the life of the characters in and around the mine objectively—just as it is—and can at the same time both sketch and criticize the two major perspectives that come together *within* that seemingly objective presentation. Because of the representational slant of verismo's aesthetic, this criticism remains implicit rather than overt, proceeding by means of contradictions that are merely intimated rather than stated, or indeed at times by what is left unsaid altogether, in a fashion that brings to mind the roughly contemporary experimentation with the arrangement of point of view in short fiction by writers like Flaubert, Maupassant, Tolstoi, James, and Joyce. Nonetheless, the fact that Verga's critique proceeds by indirection does not indicate at all that the novella's criticism is either intermittent or halfhearted. If anything, the critique that Verga presents in "Rosso Malpelo" is even more thoroughgoing and more resolute than is the local populace's condemnation of the novella's eponymous central figure.

At whom, or perhaps better, at *what* is Verga's critique directed? We can begin to answer this question first by adopting the text's third perspective to reconsider some of the major elements of the narrative and then by determining which ones can be regarded as negative. When Mastro Misciu makes the contract for the removal of the sand, it is clear that he does so in order to gain extra income. But it is also clear that the deal that the boss has made is a good one, considering the "mountain" of sand to be removed. Verga knew the mechanics and the finances of local mine operations both from his own observations and from the descriptions in the Franchetti-Sonnino official inquest into the region published in 1877, as Romano Luperini has been able to demonstrate in some detail.[17] Generally speaking, Verga's description of such a transaction was, therefore, both informed and accurate. At the story's conclusion, moreover, when Malpelo is sent on his final exploration, the boss's economic motivation for the speculative and potentially dangerous project is again beyond question: "Se la cosa era vera, si sarebbe risparmiata una buona metà di mano d'opera nel cavar fuori la rena" (188; "If it was true, a good half of the labor of taking out the sand could be saved," 85). This is the type of behavior—risking the lives of human beings in order to turn a profit—that Malpelo himself condemns when he curses the boss. If the text included these condemnatory details and only these, the point would be fairly obvious: industrial capitalists are heartless, inhuman cutthroats. This condemnation could be extended fairly easily to include the engineer's initial reaction to the news of Mastro Misciu's death. But it is significant that when Malpelo curses the boss, this curse is paired with another. The second object of Malpelo's invective is neither an owner nor a boss of any official sort, but the representative of the collective in the mine, lo Sciancato.

It should be obvious, then, that the object of Verga's criticism is not any single representative of capitalist desire but instead the entire network of human relations created by capitalism and by the kind of pitiless competition among men that this sort of desire both fosters and sustains. The breadth of Verga's critique is especially apparent when the two economic and social institutions that suffer most directly in the story are considered: the working unit and the family. For Verga, as for Padron 'Ntoni in his famous five-finger metaphor for family life, these institutions are ideally one and the same. At the beginning of the novella, this ideal is represented *in nuce* in the working relationship between father and son. Mastro Misciu's own departure from his proper sphere via his entry into the maze of capitalist venture ("e così andava facendo il conto del come avrebbe speso i denari del suo *appalto*—il cottimante!"; "and so he went on figuring how he'd spend the money from his contract—the contract worker!") can perhaps be excused by the fact that he intends to use the money to sustain his family, or, as he puts it, for the bread, the wine, and Nunziata's dress. But, as is also the case in Padron 'Ntoni's contract for the lupins in *I Malavoglia*—that deal, too, made with a similar end in mind—the force of capitalist desire is, at least symbolically, far stronger than any individual or any single family unit; and both Padron 'Ntoni and Mastro Misciu, as heads of their families, pay for their error in judgment in a way that is not only symbolic but also real. In the long run, the result of Mastro Misciu's venture extends beyond his own death to include the symbolic demise of his family as well. "Comare Santa" abandons the traditional Christian meaning of her name and takes a new husband in another town, leaving Malpelo by himself with his memories of his father and closing up, both in a symbolic and a real sense, the family home.

Again and again in Verga's realist narratives of the 1870s and 1880s this sort of total condemnation can be seen at work. It is true that in "Rosso Malpelo" there is a specific spur to Verga's narrative interests, due to the growing concern for the abuses of child labor in the course of the rising industrialization in late-nineteenth-century Italy.[18] But it is also obvious that Verga's condemnation of the economic system that makes such social abuses possible is not limited exclusively to the relations between the children and those responsbile for the operation of the mine. Indeed, the evidence of the twisted, destructive force that contaminates all of the relations in the story shows up in an extraordinary variety of ways and contexts.

Malpelo demonstrates that he, too, has internalized the lessons of the marketplace by his amazement that Ranocchio's mother carries on as though her son were one of those who made ten *lire* a week rather than a sickly cripple who no longer even earns his keep ("da due mesi ei non guadagnava nemmeno quel che si mangiava," 187; "for two months he hadn't even earned what he had eaten," 83) and of whom the owner gladly washes his hands. After Ranocchio's death, nonetheless, Malpelo is certain that the boy's mother will learn to dry her tears and put aside the memories of her son, just as Malpelo's mother had forgotten about Mastro Misciu and left Malpelo to fend for himself. Despite the technical closeness to Malpelo's perspective that is evident in much of the later narrative, therefore, these and similar passages demonstrate that Malpelo is not some sort of anticapitalist hero, fighting the good fight for the tradition of the family and for the value of labor as an activity in its own right, but rather, that he too is now caught up in the same corrupted web of relations as are all the rest.

That the workers are more than willing to have Malpelo go on such dangerous explorations is one of the many indications that the collective in the mine is just as tainted as is its nastiest member, lo Sciancato. Although "the Cripple's" affliction furnishes an exact physical analogue to the story's other cripple, Ranocchio, lo Sciancato suffers in a way that differentiates his handicap from the boy's. In symbolic terms, lo Sciancato's malady emblematizes the damage to affective relations that systems organized solely around the powers of capitalist competition and profit regularly cause. To see another, more direct Verghian treatment of this type of real malaise with symbolic overtones, one need only turn to the sickness eating away at Mastro-don Gesualdo and the concomitant deterioration of his emotional life. I do not mean to imply, of course, that Verga was in any sense in favor of the socialist Left. Because of Verga's belief in the strength and the values of the familial unit, he had no more use for socialism than for industrial capitalism. Nor does Verga's critique mean that lo Sciancato, as a single character, is any more strictly an embodiment of either socialist treachery or of capitalist desire than Malpelo or Malpelo's mother or sister or any of the other workers *qua* individuals. As Malpelo notes, lo Sciancato's characteristic procedure is to find security and strength in groups, not in personal financial success. The point, however, is that the collective itself, without the guiding ideals of the family or of familial warmth to protect it, is just as contaminated as the larger system into which it fits.[19]

In terms of the story, this system has perverted the values and skewed the perspectives of every individual and every unit making up the narrative fabric—from the owner to the miners to Malpelo's family to Malpelo himself—with the sole pitiful exceptions of Ranocchio and his mother, who still believe in filial duty and piety (185; 81). But this very belief is treated by Malpelo—and rightly so, given the context of the story's characters and events outside of Ranocchio's household—as a sign not of Ranocchio's wisdom but of his gullability, since in this world, that is, Malpelo's world, such values simply do not belong. That Malpelo denigrates Ranocchio in bitterly antifeminine terminology, moreover, further demonstrates the complete undermining of the Verghian ideal of manhood and of the relationship of love and respect between mother and son, brother and sister, that the dominant system has caused (cf. 179; 72).

Even this cursory treatment of the novella's underlying social polemic suggests the role that social Darwinism played in Verga's view of the world. But it is also important to see that this aspect of Verga's thought does not by any means tell the whole story. True, Verga believed that the world of men, outside of the family unit, was just as deeply and viciously competitive as that of nature, and in this regard his views differed significantly from the more optimistic social theories of the Enlightenment and the early Romantics. Far from guaranteeing and protecting civilized life, any sort of "social contract," for Verga, merely put a more pleasant face on what continued to be a world of hierarchically ordered and officially sanctioned greed, exploitation, and destruction. Nonetheless, Verga, unlike most late-nineteenth-century inheritors of Darwinian thought, did not seem to believe that the world *had* to be that way. He could see that nineteenth-century industrial capitalism, with its myths of profit and progress, was a path that led to an inferno of heartless violence rather than to worldly salvation. But he also saw that time does go forward, that man's world is one of change and contingency rather than absolute fixity; and it is this perception that permits his subtle unmasking of the local Sicilian belief in the atemporal absoluteness of the powers of such characters as la Lupa and the "malarnese" ("useless implement") that is Malpelo. At the same time, Verga conceived of an ideal social and economic unit and an alternative set of values that went with it, centered on the cherished familial *focolare*. But within his fictional narrative he saw no way, despite this ideal and the motion of time, to achieve the world in which that ideal could and would thrive. What he did see, and what the aesthetics of verismo required him to portray if not to approve, was the sort of cruel everyday logic that resulted in the utter destruction of the familial unit and that permitted the scapegoating of a traumatized orphan and the exploitation of his labor even to the point of ending his life on account of a potential for minor profit: "La porta della casa era chiusa, ed ei non aveva altro che le scarpe di suo padre appese al chiodo; perciò gli commettevano sempre i lavori più pericolosi, e le imprese più arrischiate" ("The house was closed up, and he didn't have anything but his father's shoes hanging from a nail; that's why they always gave him the most dangerous jobs, and the riskiest undertakings").

Whether the golden age of warmth and respect based on familial unity and familial labor ever really existed or not is a question that remains outside the representational aesthetic of Verga's realist narratives. Indeed, in the 1897 version of the story, even the passage just quoted was trimmed back to eliminate the unnecessarily repetitive and overly polemical details (though the explicative *perciò*, "that's why," was merely replaced by *sicché*, "so"). Nevertheless, given Verga's views of economic and social life in nineteenth-century Sicily as portrayed in so many of his other generally contemporaneous games of narrative exclusion, the displacement of Mastro Misciu's family and the exploitation of its unprotected offspring should not surprise us. The only freedom left to Malpelo within this world is to use his will to choose his own end and thus to reaffirm his destiny rather than having it forced on him. Such are the narrowly circumscribed boundaries within which the ordinary laborer must remain if he is to continue to pursue what, for Verga, was the one absolute value in life, energetic human labor (as is indicated in obverse fashion by the story's reference to the "avvocato," or lawyer, who pays for his security by being cut off from both physical activity and physical production).

In the end, it is beyond question that Malpelo is society's scapegoat in his own view as well as in that of all the others left alive at the story's conclusion. By his victimization, the local society can reaffirm the truth of its order and continue as it is. It is also true, moreover, that Verga's polemical critique of this situation is effaced from the surface of the text (even more meticulously so in the 1897 revision than in the earlier versions). But significantly enough, at the base of Verga's own representation of everyday life in the mines of mid-nineteenth-century Sicily, the real scapegoat is not Malpelo. As is demonstrated by the ruthless totality of Verga's critique, that scapegoat is what Verga perceived—and what the text's third and most complete perspective regards—as the condition that belongs to neither man nor beast alone but rather is made up of the worst of both: in Verga's view, the *real* minotaur, the present historical situation itself.

If this overall perspective seems to be a particularly severe and pessimistic one, so be it. Such was Verga's view both of Italy's historical moment and of history's progression, and such was the view expressed at the deepest levels of his most realistic works. This characteristic portrayal of suffering and exclusion can, of course, be said to reflect indirectly Verga's perception of the fate of his own class in postunification Italy (a perception in certain respects confirmed by the Franchetti-Sonnino inquest), in which the established southern landowners were in effect excluded from the future of Italian social and political life in favor of the incipiently industrial northern bourgeoisie.[20] In other words, what Manzoni had seen as a positive future for Italy turned out, in Verga's texts written by a southern landowner after the unification, to be a just as polemically represented disaster. Whereas Renzo's experience led him into the bourgeois world and, at least in his hopes, into its future, Rosso Malpelo's education led him out of it. In certain respects, this general perspective can also be linked, though even less directly and considerably less securely, to Verga's view of the artist's fate in bourgeois European society, as the powerless, solitary, yet (as Luperini comments) "clairvoyant" individual, resigned yet proudly ironic and specially privileged in his own worldly estrangement.[21] This is, of course, the attitude to which D'Annunzio will eventually react so forcefully, retaining the artist's privilege of insight while attempting a return into society through social leadership.

Because of the dual subject matter of "Rosso Malpelo"—first, the relation between naming and destiny, whether construed as between symbolic, proverbially expressed wisdom and actual fact, linguistic signs and worldly referents, or more generally between the truth of language and that of life; and second, the motivation, if any, underlying that relation, whether its source be fate, society, or individual intent—this novella is, *in potentia*, the most self-conscious moment in Verga's great realist production of the 1870s and 1880s. That the story's self-consciousness is programmatically banished from the surface of verismo's ideologically "objective" representation (only to reappear in the guise of a basic yet implicit question) reconfirms the thoroughgoing nature of Verga's realist procedures *and* his text's refusal to offer solutions to the problems that, through its play of narrative perspective, it both presents and criticizes. Despite this lack of solution, yet in another sense because of it, Verga's narrative sets forth with extraordinary prescience many of the difficulties regarding the individual in relation to society, human will in relation to human destiny, and representational fidelity in relation to unrepresented yet expressed truth that inform not only the fin de siècle novels of D'Annunzio and the self-reflexive fiction of Pirandello and Svevo but also much of the narrative of our more recent writers. In "Rosso Malpelo" as elsewhere,

Verga viewed contemporary life with a gaze from the past. But his fiction regularly foresaw both the region's and the nation's future, in this instance by posing a seemingly innocuous yet multilayered symbolic *and* real question and then following that question's logic persistently to its end, however bitter: What's in a name?

THREE

Dossi and D'Annunzio

Artists' Self-portraits

The *Künstlerroman*, or artist's portrait, is one of the principal subgenres of nineteenth- and early-twentieth-century narrative. Taken together, Carlo Dossi's *Vita di Alberto Pisani* (1870; *Life of Alberto Pisani*) and Gabriele D'Annunzio's *Il fuoco* (1900; *The Flame*) are two different but instructive examples of the *Künstlerroman* in Italy. Although both novels are undeniably distinctive, each has a special relation to a collection of other contemporary literary works: Dossi's to the writings of the school of which he was a member, the *Scapigliatura*, and D'Annunzio's to the fin de siècle novels and plays of European decadence in general.

It should be said at the outset that these two novels are in many respects remarkably dissimilar. Each is a love story of sorts, and each emphasizes the expressive subjectivity of its obviously exceptional central figure (in sharp contrast to the supposedly objectivist aesthetics of the historical movement intervening between them, verismo), and in these respects both novels continue the central preoccupations of the Romantics and of Verga's highly elegant preverismo narratives. However, Dossi's novel does so in the mode of thematic and formal disruption, whereas D'Annunzio's narrative regularly strives for aesthetic unity and closure. Of course, neither book actually attains these ends, which is one of the reasons why pairing them in terms of their aims and their limitations, as well as their similarities and contrasts, is useful. Indeed, when viewed in historical terms, the formal and thematic revolt that Dossi and the Scapigliatura attempted to carry out in the 1860s and 1870s was in some ways rechanneled and in others closed off in D'Annunzio's turn-of-the-century works. In other words, even though the novels of Dossi and of D'Annunzio demonstrate many similar concerns, the two authors regarded those concerns in markedly different fashions. Since the works of the Scapigliatura and of Italian decadence have important social as well as literary aspects, furthermore, it will eventually be necessary to consider both Dossi's and D'Annunzio's novels in their different relations not just to their literary tradition but also to their social environment.

Dossi's *Vita di Alberto Pisani*: "Whom do you love?" or Alberto Pisani's "Love Story"

The term *Scapigliatura* was coined in 1862 by Carlo Righetti (who published under the anagrammatic pseudonym Cletto Arrighi) as the Italian equivalent to the French *bohème*. Almost exclusively a northern phenomenon, overseen by the *pater familias* Giuseppe Rovani, the Scapigliatura was the first important movement in literature and the other arts in the period of Italian unification. Dossi's linguistic experiments and his parodic scrambling of literary genres and narrative perspectives, along with his engaging and at times confusing *umorismo*, have made his works among the most salient and enduring examples of the movement's narrative endeavors.[1] Dossi's interest in the philosophy of relativism reflects the general aura of disillusionment following the fervent hopes of the Risorgimento and the initial period of unification, and his stories regularly evince his distaste (typical of the rest of the Scapigliatura as well) for the narrow outlook, sensibilities, and morals of the Italian bourgeoisie. His adoption of Lombard and occasionally Tuscan orthographic forms and expressions, moreover, demonstrates his concern for the local languages and customs of the peninsula. But none of this made Dossi into either a populist or a political revolutionary. (He did in fact serve the government in various ambassadorial capacities and was for a time Francesco Crispi's secretary.) If anything, Dossi's social beliefs and literary practices merely confirmed his individualist eccentricity and his estrangement in relation to what the Scapigliatura regarded as the colorless mass of northern bourgeois society.

This peculiar mixture of radical and conservative thought and attitudes, including equal doses of erudition and provincialism framed within Dossi's characteristically patriarchal misogyny, shows up clearly in his narratives and in his voluminous *zibaldone* published posthumously in 1964. Although Dossi's fortunes have risen notably in recent years, there is no question but that his stature as a writer remains well below that of Verga or D'Annunzio. Nonetheless, Dossi's narrative cycle of adolescent, youthful, and finally adult romance is both historically enlightening and aesthetically fascinating in its own right. This cycle includes three major works, *L'altrieri: Nero su bianco* (1868; *The Day before Yesterday: Black on White*), *La vita di Alberto Pisani*, and *La desinenza in A* (1878; *Ending in A*).[2] The first two of these take as their subjects the development of a boy and then a young man in his relations with his family and his acquaintances, including friendships, jealousies, petty infatuations, and finally young love, whereas the last book (part of the *Ritratti umani*, or *Human Portraits*), treats these same themes in what is now a fully adult world. While the topic of the relations between the sexes is fairly constant, the manner in which it is represented grows increasingly complicated, beginning with straightforward if sprightly representation, continuing through the typically Dossian pastiche (one of the more obvious reasons for Carlo Emilio Gadda's well-known admiration), and leading eventually to the complex intermixing of genres, both narrative and theatrical ones. By the end of *La desinenza in A*, confusions of genre are joined by discussions of confusions of gender (especially in "Il fèmmino," 226–28), all tinged with Dossi's misogyny and evincing his characteristic fascination with *dandysmo* and grotesquerie. The farrago of this novel's generic presentation is complemented by the increasingly strident tones of umorismo, though here, as distinct from the two earlier books, the effects tend more toward the caustic tones of satire than toward the milder ones of irony.

The narrative experiment of *La vita di Alberto Pisani* is less radical, and considerably subtler, than that of *La desinenza in A*. Although Dossi was still quite young (only twenty-one) in the year that his second novel was published, his judgment and his wit were already keen enough so that his portrait of Alberto's youthful studies and desires, and, finally, of his one great love, is both masterfully shaded and cleverly distanced. Dossi's language resonates with the Tuscan/Lombard lesson of Manzoni as well as with the lively Milanese influences of Carlo Porta's verse. The book's dedication to Cletto Arrighi, who also turns up as one of the apostrophied interlocutors in the course of the narration, provides the narrative with the imprimatur of the Scapigliatura from its opening stages (which actually commence with what is numbered as chapter 4 and the protagonist's maturity rather than with his subsequently depicted childhood, chapters 1–3).

It is true that the protagonist of Dossi's *Künstlerroman* is as occupied with questions of moral philosophy as with fiction or aesthetics, but in this instance such distinctions are more misleading than helpful. This is so because the book actually falls in the line of European sentimental novels of romance that feature the development of youths who are primarily sensitive, emotional, and bookish and only secondarily "artists" as such (of which Foscolo's *Jacopo Ortis* is the great Italian model). To say that Dossi's book follows in this tradition, however, is true only by half, since his novel not only utilizes the tradition's conventions but also parodies them. At the same time, *La vita di Alberto Pisani* parodies another characteristic of these narratives, the "heroic" aspect of the autobiographical novel, as Francesca Tancini has shown.[3] To view this in another light, the sorts of narrative conventions that D'Annunzio's novels of artist-heroes go so far to reaffirm are precisely the ones that Dossi's *Vita* attempts to break apart. Dossi's novel also shares in part another of D'Annunzio's narrative traits, that of establishing an extremely close tie between the persona of the book's author and its central character, evident here in Dossi's selection of names for his protagonist, since the Lombard author's full name was in fact Alberto Carlo Pisani Dossi. Even in this regard, however, Dossi and D'Annunzio are not only similar but also different, since Dossi established this relationship not merely to reaffirm it but also to question it within his text, as occurs, for example, in the umorista's self-identifying authorial address to his female readers (58–59).

From the beginning sections of the narrative on, the extreme significance of literature and of the powers of the literary imagination are primary among the story's recurrent themes. References to books and examples of stories abound, including the stories told to Alberto by his grandmother, which, on occasion, are so affecting as to make the child relive them in his dreams (21). Alberto's studiousness, appropriate to the young *gentiluomo lombardo,* is also obvious, and his preferences for certain authors over others, as well as his concern for the proper format and binding of his favorite books, are staples of the narrative. It quickly becomes clear not only that Alberto is interested in books at the expense of worldly experience but also that his bookish studies are more in the nature of an obsession than a mere interest, that, indeed, books are almost all he knows (157; cf. 140). Along with these thematic concerns, the *form* of the narrative is also obtrusively bookish, with the inserted stories breaking up the narration and then connecting back into the story in uncannily disconcerting ways, so that the epistemological status of the overall story and the relation between it and the inserted stories (linked by the character and eventually by the authorial hand of Alberto) is placed repeatedly in question.

But the crucial importance that writing is to have in the narrative in terms of its plot as well as its thematics and its formal presentation is not apparent until roughly midway through the novel, following Alberto's initial reactions to the beautiful young Claudia, at which point the love story and the *Künstlerroman* come together in a striking manner. This occurs at the beginning of chapter 8, when Alberto, having decided that what he desires from Claudia is indeed *"perfetto amore"* (*"perfect love"*), also decides that there is one ideal means of achieving it: "Un mezzo? Scrìvere un libro; giùgnersi a lei in ispìrito" (71; "A means? Write a book; join himself to her spiritually"). That Alberto's intentions are not, in fact, quite so spiritually pure as this initial formulation might imply becomes obvious before too long, but for the moment Alberto has his first task squarely before him: to channel his energies and his talents into the creation of the work that will win Claudia's love.

As is probably not surprising, given what the narrator describes in an excess of nationalistic semideprecation as Alberto's typically Italian traits of indecision and self-doubt (in short, his umorista's tension-filled inertia), Alberto's task turns out to be considerably more difficult than it may at first seem. After a series of abortive attempts, however, Alberto does at last get started, and in eight months of work in an especially conducive setting he produces the manuscript of a book, entitled "Le due morali" (101; "The Two Kinds of Morality"). The narrator specifies that Alberto's project is not an autobiography ("Al diàvolo le autobiografie!"; "To the devil with autobiographies!") but a novel, which is to say, a work in which connotation and interpretation count for at least as much as the autobiography's usual self-serving autodescription and its seemingly authoritative assertions of univocal meaning. In order to demonstrate straightaway the manner in which Alberto's work fits this description, the narrator first excuses himself with the reader for skipping the standard narrative portrayal of the *process* of Alberto's writing ("a scrìverne io, troppo mi annojerei per riuscire a piacervi"; "in writing about it, I would be too bored myself to succeed in providing you with any pleasure") and then reproduces samples of the *product* of Alberto's labors. These all have to do with the same sorts of interpersonal and interfamilial (here, also dangerously *intra*familial) relationships as does the narrative of *La vita di Alberto Pisani*, and they manifest the same alternation of perspective that is characteristic of Dossi's frame story as well as the same distinctive mixture of melodrama, illicit desire, grotesquerie, and once in a while even slapstick. Language, too, in its function as both the bearer of meaning and the agent of meaning's concealment, is as much the object of attention in the inserted stories as in the narrative frame. Indeed, in one of the early samples portraying an English lesson, the pedagogically and thematically apposite practice question, "Whom do you love?" has a humorously potent double meaning not only for the young female instructor and the male student but also for the disgruntled father who is looking on (113).

The question of who loves whom—along with the influential part that language plays in the formulation and the determination of this question itself—recurs, of course, when Dossi's narrative returns to the life of Alberto. Once Alberto has arrived back in town, he receives the printed copy of his book, which dismays him immediately for its typographical errors and subsequently for its development of ideas and its style, but which nevertheless, as he learns shortly thereafter from his friend Enrico, may actually have served its purpose after all. According to Enrico, Claudia claims to have loved the book (which, in spite of its odd authorial pseudonym, she has found out is really Alberto's). In Enrico's presence, moreover, she has spoken out on Alberto's behalf against his critic (an overbearing, prudish Marchesa), defending Alberto like a paladin and then discussing him as though he were more a saint than an ordinary man (148–49).

Alberto is flabbergasted by such news but also delighted with what he regards as his good fortune ("O amico! . . . Gli è un caso sì strano! miracoloso!" 149; "Oh, my friend! . . . This luck is so strange! miraculous!"). Later on, despite his characteristic inertia and his eventual panic, Alberto finally arrives—by means of Enrico's good offices, not to mention his repeated prodding—at the appointed meeting with Donna Claudia. But here the story takes a thoroughly unexpected turn. Alberto and his companion cannot see the object of the young lover's desires since, as an old woman announces peremptorily to the two visitors, "Donna Claudia è morta" (151; "Donna Claudia is dead").

Although Alberto cannot bring his beloved back to life, he does manage, with the help of a financial consideration, to get the gravedigger to deposit the corpse, not at its proper site, but at the "casa del mago," or the same "magician's house" where Alberto had written his book. The following scene, which concludes the narrative, is nothing short of bizarre. It incorporates conventional elements of both Romantic and gothic literature as well as a pastiche of those same conventions (which is to say, among other things, that the text's reference to the beloved's specifically camellia-like pallor is not gratuitous). The result is both a repetition of late-eighteenth- and nineteenth-century literary traditions and a clever play on them, in which Alberto, with his literature-saturated spirit and intellect, is, to put it mildly, deadly serious, whereas the narrative itself is serious only by half, since the other half of its discourse constitutes a thoroughgoing literary parody, as Roberto Bigazzi has perceived.[4] Inside the house Alberto stands gazing at the body, in hopes of seeing some sign of life, some indication that the union is still possible. He rips open the corpse's clothing and puts his hand to the beloved's chest, searching for a sign of life, the beat of her heart, but in fact only discovering a locket, which he immediately takes to be confirmation that, even if she were to come back to life, she would live not for him but for another. In a fit of romantic jealousy, Alberto pulls his pistol from his pocket and reduces the metal case to smithereens, then turns the weapon on himself. As the pistol falls into a (romantically appropriate) basket of roses, Alberto falls, too, "sul *desiato corpo* di lei, morto" (157; "on her *body, so fervently longed for,* dead").

Again, the narrative's resort to rarefied literary language in this concluding description ("desiato corpo," emphasized through italicization) is not a matter of happenstance. Whereas Alberto's highly theatrical, sentimental plot of uncertainty and longing—which leads to his version, however macabre, of the "love/death"—is at its end irremediably closed, Dossi's text itself is not nearly so conclusive as its character's "life." Even at its seemingly dramatic conclusion, the narrative's insistently literary language and imagery point, slyly as well as self-consciously, to its pastiche. This is not to say that the relation between the story and its main character is always one of irony—far from it—or that the narrative's wit is single-mindedly focused throughout either to the advantage or the disadvantage of any one character. Indeed, even characters who are generally portrayed in a sympathetic light are on occasion the objects of subtle correction. (To take just one example, Paolino's seemingly precise, popular image of the "calamai"—or, literally, "inkwells"—for the circles under Alberto's eyes at the opening of chapter 14 suggests not the servant's usual understanding of Alberto's situation but in this case his ignorance, since Alberto's "inkwells" result not so much from studying or writing as from his sleepless lovesickness, reported by him in piquant Milanese: "Ma se fui tutta notte in stondèra!" ["But if I spent the whole night wandering around!"].) The novel's cleverly shifting multiple perspective, along with its exceptionally fragmentary presentation and its linguistic dexterity, ties its self-consciously literary pastiche both to the effects of earlier umoristi (to the Foscolo of "Didimo Chierico" or even to Ariosto or Pulci) and, perhaps more notably, to those of twentieth-century modernist narrative (to Gadda, for example, who is the most common point of reference in the criticism of Dossi's works, as well as to the later Svevo or to Pirandello).[5] At the same time, however, the literary objects of Dossi's parodies—the heroic autobiography and the Romantic love story—also keep *La vita di Alberto Pisani* rooted in its own century, even if in rebellion.

Because Dossi's revolt is a matter of moral assumptions as well as literary and linguistic traditions—that is, because his barbs are regularly aimed at social behavior as such behavior is portrayed in literary discourse—it is impossible to say that his highly idiosyncratic "revolution" is merely a matter of style, even style conceived of in its broadest sense to include formal organization, as in the comments of Elio Gioanola.[6] Dossi's interest in the conventions and the authority of social comportment as well as in those of literary style and the standard expressive procedures of bourgeois literary representation (including mistaking literature for life) go hand in hand both in his novels and in his diaries. The questions of style—in both a social and an artistic sense—also infiltrated Dossi's nonliterary occupations and preoccupations, his diplomatic career and his eccentric decoration and furnishing of his northern villas; and his questioning of authority extended past bourgeois literature and culture to include the traditional authority of the Church (apparent in *La vita di Alberto Pisani* in the narrator's description of the faithful actively engaged in competing for the attention of the unresponsive diety, "il sordomuto eterno" [143; "the eternal deaf-mute"]).[7]

Whereas the title of Alberto Pisani's book points towards Dossi's belief that "morality" constitutes a duality, in the opposition of the official ethics of accepted, or conventional, behavior to the real morality of everyday life, it is also clear from Dossi's narratives that in terms of both social behavior and literary creation this sort of duality quickly breaks up further into the most peculiar sorts of multiplicity. Whether Dossi's attitude evinces as much an aristocratic nostalgia for the long-lost wholeness of prebourgeois culture as a delight in the contemporary joys of antibourgeois rebellion and fragmentation is a question that has no single answer. However, this fundamental set of interests—in artistic and sexual experience, in literary and social authority, and in the openness and/or closure of the work of art—does serve to link Dossi's work to that of D'Annunzio, whose ideas in regard to these interests, coming as they do toward the end rather than in the middle of nearly a half-century of Italian unification, diverge from Dossi's in ways that are at once incisive and mutually illuminating.

D'Annunzio's *Il fuoco*: Portrait of the Artist as Superman

The picture of the writer that emerges from D'Annunzio's major novels is one of the author as an all-knowing and potentially all-powerful creator, the voice of the myth-inspired soul as well as of the imagination of his people. That D'Annunzio's novels are extremely self-conscious in a literary/autobiographical sense is fairly obvious, owing primarily to his ostentatious re-creation of his own life as an author in his art. What is even more fascinating, however, given the social climate of the early twentieth century in Italy as well as elsewhere in Europe, is that the self-consciousness of his fiction is directed at questions that are not only aesthetic but also political, at issues that have to do not just with creation as vision and imagination but also with creation as power.

Certain of these interests are also apparent in other turn-of-the-century novelists—the works of Antonio Fogazzaro come immediately to mind—but this combination is presented more openly and indeed more aggressively in D'Annunzio's novels than in those of any other writer of the period, and perhaps than in those of any other writer in modern Italy either before or since.[8] The interweaving of sensuality, sentiment, and creativity so central to D'Annunzio's polemical association of sexuality with poetic expression was no doubt part of the reason for the extraordinary success of his works, and especially of his theater, throughout Europe.[9] But another aspect of D'Annunzio's popularity, in his Late Romantic mixture of high art, *midcult*, and *masscult*, was his constant reworking of the myths of specifically artistic worldly potency, which is to say his attempt at reframing the poetic tradition in terms of the poetic reality of the present, and then in extrapolating from these, if only by suggestion, the poetic and political hopes of the Italian future.

The major novels of D'Annunzio's early and middle period—*Il piacere* (1889; *The Child of Pleasure*), *Trionfo della morte* (1894; *Triumph of Death*), *Le vergini delle rocce* (1896; *The Virgins of the Rocks*), and *Il fuoco* (1900; *The Flame*)—all focus on the actions and attitudes of central artist-intellectuals.[10] D'Annunzio was keenly aware both of his position at the end of a century of active aesthetic inquiry in Europe and of his potential for reaching a broad European audience, and he took care to endow each of his protagonists with a suitably developed artistic theory. Sharing aesthetic perceptions with Mallarmé and even with the later Oscar Wilde, D'Annunzio and his characters believe not so much in the separation of art from life as in the triumph of art over life: "Arte è vita."[11] For D'Annunzio, however, unlike his symbolist contemporaries in France, this was a way of focusing the Italian literary *and* political tradition through the central figure of the specially gifted and therefore authoritative artist.

D'Annunzio's fiction leading up to *Il fuoco* takes form in the elaboration of typically D'Annunzian native energy placed in elegant settings and consciously infused with mythic backgrounds. In each novel the thematic content of myth serves as an organizational determinant for the narrative and as a means of portraying the artist-hero as both artistic and social seer. To be sure, the myth in question is never taken up as a single unity, nor is there a clear one-to-one correspondence between the original mythic elements and the elements of the narrative at hand. But the mythic shadings are present and functional, however scattered, and ultimately combine to produce the effect of intermittent allegory. In D'Annunzio's work, this allegorical process does not represent the repetition of a mythic tale in modern form, as may be found in Flaubert or in Goethe, for example. Rather, it develops as a compendium of hints and oblique references gesturing with increasing strength toward a body of texts outside the narrative and only partially subsumed into it. Instead of direct retelling, D'Annunzio's method thus represents the gradual *re-creation* of myth through this selective renewal of allegorical materials. That D'Annunzio's narrative regards these subtexts in the positive light of reaffirmation rather than in that of questioning or of humor attests to the literary and philosophical differences between his allegorical procedures and Dossi's parodic ones.

The allegorical elements receive their fullest development in *Il fuoco*, as Stelio Èffrena, the mature poet-hero and author of the play *Persephone*, combines with the beautiful but doomed "dark" one, "la Foscarina," also called "Perdita," or the "lost" one. The plot of the novel, which is set in Venice, traces Stelio's preparations for his projected triumph as a playwright at the "Teatro d'Apollo" under construction on the Janiculum in Rome. This parallels the achievement of the Germanic laureate of the previous age, Richard Wagner (whose funeral cortege in Venice closes the narrative) and the establishment of the Festspielhaus in Bayreuth. Stelio's love affair with the tragic actress la Foscarina forms the second element in the plot, and the motifs of sensual and artistic fulfillment, at times complementary, at times contradictory, serve as counterpoint throughout the narrative. Indeed, it might be said that in this novel the lyrical depiction of the characters' sensations and reactions *is* the plot, since sensual characterization and aesthetic discussion (in the forms of dialogue and Stelio's address in the Sala del Maggior Consiglio) are far more important in the narrative than is action. Each of the major figures has a subordinate in aesthetic appreciation, Daniele Glàuro and Donatella Arvale. In terms of autobiographical reference, it should be recalled that Stelio and la Foscarina reflected the widely publicized liaison between D'Annunzio and Eleonora Duse (Venetian by birth), who had occupied neighboring villas in Settignano during the period of the novel's composition. The intimate revelations within the narrative were not lost on a fin de siècle public eager for titillation, and *Il fuoco* was a *succès de scandale* both inside and outside of Italy.

The characterization of Stelio is built around a series of lyrical moments of illumination involving profound emotional feeling and unexpected insight, all leading up to Stelio's departure from la Foscarina and the projected journey to Rome. Near the midpoint of *Il fuoco*, Stelio recalls the moment of inspiration for his current work, which occurred in front of what was believed at the time to be the tomb of the Atreidae in Mycenae. He relates his visit and the significance that his illumination holds for the new poetry to his fellow in aesthetic inquiry, Daniele Glàuro: "Bisognerebbe, Daniele, che il mito si rinnovasse perché ci fosse dato di creare l'arte nuova. . . . Come ti comunicherò la vita e il mistero infinitamente fluido che ho dentro di me?" (714–16; "It is necessary, Daniele, that the myth be renewed in order for us to create the new art. . . . How can I communicate to you the life and the infinitely fluid mystery that I have inside of me?"). The discussion involves elements not only of the fall of Troy, the Aeschylean trilogy, and the story of Perseus, but also of Christian sacrament, this, too, subordinated to the unifying structure of mythic reference.

In a major passage later in the narrative, Stelio separates himself from la Foscarina within his fancied version of the Daedalean labyrinth, within which, by his will and his imagination, he renews the world of myth:[12]

> Carponi egli s'era insinuato nel cespuglio, a capo scoperto. Sentiva sotto i ginocchi le foglie macere, il musco molle. E come egli respirava nei rami e palpitava in essi e aveva tutti i sensi presi da quel piacere, la comunione della sua vita con la vita arborea

si fece più stretta e l'incanto della sua imaginazione rinnovò in quel viluppo di vie dubbie l'industria del primo fabbro di ali, il mito del mostro nato da Pasifae e dal Toro, la favola attica di Teseo in Creta. Tutto quel mondo si fece reale per lui. Sotto la sera purpurea d'autunno egli si trasfigurava, secondo gli istinti del suo sangue e i ricordi del suo intelletto, in una di quelle forme ancípiti tra bestiali e divine, in uno di quei genii agresti la cui gola era gonfia delle glandule stesse che pendono dal collo delle capre. Una salacità ilare gli suggeriva atti e gesti strani, sorprese, insidie. (776–77)

He had crept into the hedge on all fours, his head bare. Beneath his knees he could feel the damp leaves, the soft moss. And as he breathed amid the branches and felt his heart beat among them and felt all his senses taken by that pleasure, the communion of his life with the life of arboreal nature became immediate, and the enchantment of his imagination renewed in that tangle of uncertain paths the industry of the first creator of wings, the myth of the monster born from Pasiphaë and the Bull, the Attic fable of Theseus on Crete. That whole world became real for him. Under the purple evening of autumn, he transfigured himself, according to the instincts of his blood and the memories of his intellect, into one of those ambiguous forms between the bestial and the divine, one of those agrarian deities whose throat was swollen with the same glands that hang from the neck of goats. An exuberant salaciousness prompted him to think of strange acts and gestures, surprises, snares.

This is the novel's clearest reference to the Cretan labyrinth, but it is by no means unique, as Stelio's continual allusions to Theseus and Ariadne readily demonstrate. Moreover, the topic of bestial divinity, associated with sexual and artistic creativity, appears early in part 1, "L'Epifania del fuoco" ("The Epiphany of the Flame"), in the form of the Centaurs, which serve as Pindaric emblems for all inspired creation and particularly for the art of the Venetian Renaissance, from Giorgione to Tintoretto: "'I Centauri conobbero la virtù del vino soave come il miele.' . . . E nelle loro [i.e., dei pittori] creature più belle il battito violento dei loro polsi sembra persistere a traverso i secoli come il ritmo stesso dell'arte veneziana" (613–14; "'The Centaurs knew the virtue of wine as sweet as honey.' . . . And in their [i.e., the painters'] most beautiful figures the violent beat of their pulses persists across the centuries as the very rhythm of Venetian art"). The combined imagery of the environment as phenomenal labyrinth and the mind of the creator as mysterious maze is also echoed in the novel's second part, as Stelio walks the pathways beside the Venetian canals, at first penetrating into the city "alla ventura" ("by chance"), but then "quasi per istinto" ("as though by instinct") wandering toward a vague yet constant goal: "verso una casa lontana che di tratto in tratto gli appariva come nel guizzo d'un lampo animata da un'attesa profonda" (713; "toward a distant house that from time to time appeared to him, as if in a flash of lightning, to be animated by a profound expectation").

D'Annunzio's blend of psychological and physical imagery is instructive here. As in the scene at Stra within the labyrinth of Stelio-Theseus's fancy, the poet's perambulations about the city serve to subsume the material environment within the myth-obsessed consciousness of the main character. The centrality of the creating ego gives rise on the level of aesthetic perception to Croce's often quoted tag for D'Annunzio as a "dilettante di sensazioni," or "dilettante of the senses," whereas the fluidity of the technique has led Giorgio Luti to describe the progression of D'Annunzio's major fiction as the "processo distruttivo della sintassi narrativa" ("process of destroying narrative syntax").[13] Especially in the first part of *Il fuoco*, moreover, these rapid and unannounced shifts in temporal and spatial setting as well as in mode of presentation (dialogue, extended monologue, direct "quotation" of thought) all contribute to the fluidity of the narration in a manner that is distinctively new in Italian fiction.

This is not to say, however, that D'Annunzio's texts appear disordered or confusing. D'Annunzio's allusions are constantly shifting, but in contrast to the effects of Dossi's novels, for example, here the allusions are regularly created and *controlled* by the character who occupies the narrative's dominant position, as is evident in both the Theseus-Ariadne scene and the allusion to the Centaurs. Since the external referent is always potentially explicable in strict relation to a unified set of signs within the text, this is a process of allegoresis rather than true symbol formation. Stelio consciously elicits both awe and trust, and all the references to mythic or formally artistic elements arrayed at the periphery of the narrative are clearly subordinated to this central consciousness. In this way, both the Orphically allusive title of part 2 ("L'impero del silenzio"; "The

Empire of Silence") and that of the projected "Melagrano," or "Pomegranate," trilogy help to build a closed system with the fictional author of *Persephone* at its center. This same effect may be seen in operation within D'Annunzio's various works based on the myths of such other intellectual heroes and victims as Icarus and Ulysses.

Throughout *Il fuoco* the rhythmically recurrent mythic references contribute to the sustained harmony of allegorical vision toward which the narrative strives. The result, in fictional as well as autobiographical terms, is the consciously conceived allegory of the self. Again, this process involves la Foscarina as well as Stelio, in fictional parallel with the D'Annunzio-Duse relationship. Stelio Èffrena is permitted to play a Roman Orestes to the dying Wagner's Germanic Agamemnon, but the work to arise from the new Latin order, *La vittoria dell'uomo* (*The Victory of Man*, announced first within the narrative, 821, and then in an addendum, 861) was not to be Stelio's but *D'Annunzio's* own.[14]

Though it is important to see the striving for artist-centered unity in D'Annunzio's work, it is equally essential to note that D'Annunzio's "armonia" is itself accomplished only as a semiwillful accommodation with a prior perception of loss. The implications of this give-and-take are curious but noteworthy. Success in artistic expression is never quite allowed to coincide with sexual fulfillment. This is one reason for the alternating sentiments of joy, melancholia, and sexual enmity that pervade D'Annunzio's fiction. Beginning with the novella of the Duca d'Ofena and continuing through the *Trionfo della morte* and *Il fuoco*, D'Annunzian narrative takes as its basic organizational determinants myths of failure in the world and/or separation in love: Siegfried-Brunhild, Tristan-Isolde, Theseus-Ariadne, Orpheus-Eurydice. Throughout the later sections of *Il fuoco*, la Foscarina expresses her knowledge of inevitable doom through repeated evocation of time lost: "È tardi" ("It is late").[15] Her emotional relationship with Stelio is framed, furthermore, in this same perspective of destined failure: "Chi ama teme" (684; "Whoever loves, fears"). Indeed, it is only in response to the previous perception of worldly failure that Stelio's conscious striving toward an exterior set of artificially ordered signs arises, as he substitutes the willfully controlled duration of self-allegorization for the physical separation from his dismayed companion in the scene of the labyrinth at Stra. The narrative ends, moreover, not with mutual fulfillment but with separation. Through the central character, the surface of the D'Annunzian text attempts to mask the knowledge of failure residing at its core, becoming, with Stelio's final departure, a full and energetically valorized allegory of Orpheus's *loss*. In this way the D'Annunzian narrative may be seen as the affirmation of the self in relation not just to success but also to threatened adversity. D'Annunzio's artistic harmony thus becomes a unity to the second degree, an attempted isolation of the fictional subject in continual flight from the full recognition of predetermined loss. As Carlo Salinari has said of D'Annunzio's fiction, "Il suo motivo vero è la sconfitta" ("His true theme is defeat").[16] Shorn of its mask, the misapprehension hidden at the core of D'Annunzio's narrative appears as the accommodation it is, the willed striving for the apparent stability of allegory against the external and *real* worldly threat of disordered and uncontrollable flux.

From this perspective D'Annunzio assumes the pivotal position as Italian narrative enters the twentieth century, twisting yet at the same time completing the unfinished line of Verga's "vinti" and preceding the openly fractured personalities of Pirandello's narrative and drama. In biographical terms D'Annunzio's life furnishes analogues of this same process. It was not as a secure member of the aristocracy that he conceived the elegant settings of the novels and designed the assertive opulence of La Capponcina and Il Vittoriale, but as the self-conscious son of a middle-class *pescarese* bankrupt. In this regard, perhaps the most telling memory of D'Annunzio's early years was the protracted jeering of his fellow students upon his first recitation at the Collegio Cicognini in Prato, during which he erred not in grammar but in pronunciation, with his unmistakably provincial (and, worse, *meridionale*) accent. D'Annunzio's characteristically extreme reactions, expressed in terms of the seemingly unqualified reassertion of the Romantic ego, show through in all his major works. In his maturity, D'Annunzio, resembling the heroes of his later fictions, would participate in the world of men only if he could reign supreme, as is indicated both by his self-imposed exile in France (1910–15) and by the otherwise inexplicable episode at Fiume (1919–20), in which D'Annunzio caused an international crisis by not only taking over the city but actually running it for over a year with his irredentist brigade before having to relinquish it under fire.

The characteristically D'Annunzian affirmation of strength in strict relation to the underlying fear of both temporal progression and the conflictual presence of others occurs in each of the interconnected spheres of poetic fame and of love. In either realm the affirmations in *Il fuoco* seem, at first blush, to be without reservation; but on closer examination, it is clear that Stelio's powers are not absolute, that they depend on others and on the challenges that others provide for his poetic as well as his sexual "victories." This type of underlying competition is suggested at the novel's conclusion as Stelio moves with Wagner's funeral procession amidst the symbols of the "lauri latini," or "Latin laurels," toward "la collina bàvara ancóra sopita nel gelo; mentre i tronchi insigni mettevano già i nuovi germogli nella luce di Roma, al romorio delle sorgenti nascoste" (861; "the Bavarian slope, still drowsy in the ice; while the illustrious trunks were already putting forth new shoots in the light of Rome, amidst the murmur of hidden springs"). In terms of sexual competition, Stelio's need to see himself as a part of a progression of lovers is even clearer: "Egli doveva vedere pur sempre l'ombra di altri uomini su la sua carezza e da quell'ombra sentire pur sempre incitato l'instinto di ferocia bestiale che si celava in fondo alla sua sensualità possente" (703; "He needed always to perceive the shadows of other men under his caress and, by means of those shadows, to feel the incitement of his instinctive, bestial ferocity that lay concealed at the base of his powerful sensuality"). Again, even though this appears to be purely a position of strength, a sort of instinctively aggressive one-upsmanship, it does so only by dissimulating the characteristic vulnerability which is the other side of the D'Annunzian coin and from which D'Annunzio's heroes never completely escape, even in—or, better, particularly in—those relationships in which they seem so potent:

> Ella [la Foscarina] supplicava, bianca e tenue come la piuma di cigno che correva intorno alle sue spalle nude e al suo petto palpitante. Ella pareva disciogliersi dalla sua potenza, divenir lieve e debole, vestirsi d'una sua segreta anima tenera, così facile a essere uccisa, a esser distrutta, immolata senza sangue.
> . . . Gli parve di non riconoscerla più, di avere dinanzi a sé una creatura ignota, infinitamente umile e dolorosa, priva d'ogni forza. . . . un piccolo essere inoffensivo e solo.
> "*Perdonatemi!*" (667–68, my italics)

She [la Foscarina] supplicated him, white and slender as the swansdown that ran across her bare shoulders and her throbbing chest. She seemed to dissolve from his power, to become light and weak, to cover herself with a secret, tender soul, so easy to be killed, to be destroyed, to be bloodlessly immolated.
. . . It seemed to him that he no longer recognized her, that

he had before him an unknown creature, infinitely humble and sorrowful, deprived of any force whatever. . . . a little being, harmless and alone.

"*Forgive me!*" (my italics)

It is true that D'Annunzio's lush, often extravagant prose is designed to portray his novels' heroes in the attitude of literary and social triumph, such as in the culminating poetic exhortation at the end of "L'Epifania del fuoco" (elements of which run through the text) describing Stelio's goal and his artist's right of eminent domain, both of which are immediately reaffirmed through the narrator's intervention: "Gli parve che tutto il mistero di quella bellezza gli chiedesse l'atto trionfale. Si sentì capace di compierlo. 'Creare con gioia!' . . . *E il mondo era suo*" (681, my italics; "It seemed to him that all of the mystery of that beauty required the triumphal act from him. He felt capable of performing it. 'Create with joy!' *And the world was his*," my italics).[17] But even here, amid the strongest textual assertion of the artist's power and authority, it must be remembered that such affirmations occur in a text riddled with implicit doubts.

In contrast to the cleverly parodic works of the Scapigliatura, which aim toward the breaking of prior literary conventions and toward internal disruption, and in contrast to the polemical randomness of verismo's aesthetic, D'Annunzio's allegorical decadence thus appears as a willful affirmation of unity, but of a unity that is itself illusory. This is the strength as well as the weakness of the D'Annunzian hero, who attempts to give order and meaning to the world by passing the poetic tradition through the will and the imagination of the specially gifted individual re-creator, exactly the obverse of Dossi's attempts at parodic dissolution. Yet, because this very unity now perceives itself as suspect, as based on a prior perception of loss, it can speak only in the increasingly affirmative tones of a condition that is in certain respects negative though still highly valued. Nonetheless, D'Annunzio's allegorical labyrinth cannot easily lead its isolated subject back into the contradictions of the world. The only possible source of stability resides in the creating ego of the Romantic poet-*vates*, and even that unity is seen as doomed. In this way D'Annunzio's self-proclaimed turn-of-the-century hero becomes, in Fredric Jameson's terms, a "post-individual" subject who finally refuses to acknowledge either the present nature of the material world of the bourgeoisie in fin de siècle Italy or his position in that world.[18] Both historically and structurally, the novels of D'Annunzio's mature years thus arise at the affirmation of a vision of life already perceived as past, as "decadent." At the same time, of course, their aspirations parallel and to an extent predict the grand view of the Italian future reflected in the disastrous delusions of political empire that began in Italy in the nineteenth century but that did not die out entirely until the fall of Mussolini and of Fascism. Again, in contrast to Dossi's general practice, D'Annunzio included suggestions of his political concerns—however aestheticized these may have been (in this regard similar to the Futurists)—in his fiction as well as in his nonliterary works. He did so in part, as is evident in *Il fuoco*, because he believed that the artist's role was not so much to observe or even to prod society as to lead it.

The extraordinary degree of artistic self-reflexivity of *Il fuoco*, in which the narrator not only describes but repeatedly lauds the central artist-hero, does not necessarily make for D'Annunzio's most engaging or most successful narrative (a position usually reserved by critics for *Forse che sì* or, on occasion for *Il piacere* or *Trionfo della morte*); nor does it even begin to suggest the rarely acknowledged variety of D'Annunzian prose, which extends from his early forays into verismo via his violent *abruzzesi* short stories, through his cycle of elegant, artist-centered novels, to the psychological internalization of the narrative voice in *Notturno*, and finally to the self-centered and disconcertingly ironized notations of his writer's "book of memory" (all of which serve only to highlight the essential precariousness of the superman's stance), entitled *Cento e cento e cento e cento pagine del libro segreto di Gabriele D'Annunzio tentato di morire* (1935; *Hundreds and Hundreds and Hundreds and Hundreds of Pages of the Private Book of Gabriele D'Annunzio Tempted by Death*). But *Il fuoco* does represent the highest moment of D'Annunzio's self-consciously focused artist-narrative, the point in his work at which the interests as well as the profound afflictions of literary, sexual, and sociopolitical potency come together most clearly and most insistently in the myth-inspired figure of the seer, the artist, the superman: Stelio Èffrena/Gabriele D'Annunzio.

FOUR

"Non conclude"

Narrative Self-consciousness and the Voice of Creation in Pirandello's *Il fu Mattia Pascal* and *Uno, nessuno e centomila*

> . . . *l'aliénation paranoïaque qui date du virage du je spéculaire en je social.*
> . . . the paranoid alienation that dates from the shift from the specular I to the social I.
>
> Jacques Lacan, "Le stade du miroir comme formateur de la fonction du Je"

Pirandello's major works constitute a departure, in many respects a radical one, from much of the literary tradition preceding him.[1] This novelty can be seen in the content of his works as well as in their form. Gramsci, with his usual perspicacity, understood that by introducing the dialectics of contemporary philosophy into literary discourse, Pirandello called into question, at the level of everyday life, the very foundations of the standard Italian "aristotelico-cattolico" concept of supposedly "objective" reality. For Gramsci, moreover, Pirandellian subjectivism put in doubt the validity of the "positivist humanism" underlying many of the literary products of later-nineteenth-century verismo, with their traditionally "borghese e piccolo borghese" ideological slant.[2] Although Gramsci's main concern in his treatment of Pirandello was with the Italian theater, much the same could be said for Pirandello's short stories and novels, especially the later ones. The analytical skepticism of Pirandello's views, which tended to expose if not to destroy the existing structures of both normative social behavior and the literary representation of life, made his works seem strikingly different from anything that his public in Italy, and to a certain extent in the rest of Western Europe and the United States, had been used to. But at the same time, his works were not completely new, nor could they be.

Pirandello's first mature novel, *Il fu Mattia Pascal* (1904), begins and ends in the patently bookish setting of a library. This fictional library brings to mind several others that are at least as well known: Don Ferrante's private collection and Cardinal Borromeo's Ambrosian Library in *I Promessi Sposi*, and the all-inclusive and all-consuming libraries of Borges' stories and essays. If the humorously self-reflexive frame-setting of Pirandello's chaotic "biblioteca Boccamazza" is not yet an indication of the subjectivist bibliomania of such later writers as Borges, Gadda, and Calvino, it nonetheless points toward a constellation of contemporary concerns clearly divergent from those at work in Manzoni's historically "objective" and respectfully laudatory treatment of Cardinal Borromeo's trustworthy collection of volumes or even in his ultimately ironic portrayal of Don Ferrante's cherished tomes. Like more recent novels of the avant-garde in Europe and America, Pirandello's works show a deep-rooted interest in such modernist topics as the dissolution of the individual subject, the problematic nature and status of language, and the epistemological validity of communication itself. At the same time, his early novels continue to demonstrate their derivation from conventional nineteenth-century assumptions of character formation and plotting. Furthermore, Pirandello's fictions remained dependent on such models despite the fact that by the publication of *Uno, nessuno e centomila* (1925–26) this dependence had begun to manifest itself in a deeply negative sense. As this late *romanzo a tesi* demonstrates, even though Pirandello did not leave his literary predecessors totally behind, by the end of his novelistic production he was no longer concerned so much with refurbishing or even revitalizing earlier literary, psychological, and philosophical conventions as with relentlessly "decomposing" them in a new way.

The issue of narrative self-consciousness is central to this line of development in Pirandello's novels. The process of decomposition and recreation, with its attendant successes and failures, figures with growing self-awareness in *Il fu Mattia Pascal* and *Uno, nessuno e centomila*. Indeed, in a progressively forthright manner, these two narratives actually take this process as their primary topic. This is not to say, however, that these novels are about the construction of fictions in either a self-satisfied or a statically self-reflexive fashion. Rather, with increasing insistence, they are about the complex *search* for a way to create a valid and workable "character" in the contemporary world. Their real subject, then, is the *endeavor* to find new methods of investigation and a new understanding of that world, not the endeavor's goal as such. Therefore, the question of whether or not this quest for "fictional" validity is itself ultimately successful in terms of art and/or life is one that, although pertinent, must await consideration of a different set of questions: what exactly is Pirandello trying to get at in these novels, and why does whatever it is seem at once so original and so urgent?[3]

After *Il fu Mattia Pascal*'s anecdotal, chatty, and on occasion whimsical beginnings ("Premessa" and "Premessa seconda [filosofica] a mo' di scusa"; "Preface" and "Second Preface [Philosophical] by Way of Excuse"), the novel gives the background of Mattia's early life along the lines of seemingly conventional, even naturalistic narrative procedure.[4] A brief history of the Pascal family and its fortunes and misfortunes is deftly sketched, as is other background material: the education of Mattia and his brother Berto under the eye of an eccentric tutor, nicknamed "Pinzone"; the financial chicanery of the stereotypically untrustworthy family manager, Batta Malagna; the various social options open to Mattia's mother once she is widowed; and the sexual exploits of Mattia's youth (the general configurations of which later furnish the plot for one of Pirandello's most successful and least troubled comedies, *Liolà* [1916]).

It would be misleading, certainly, to put too much stress on the representational nature of these early sections. Even at this point, Pirandello's approach is far from single-minded. Since the novel is narrated in the first person, the disruptive, mocking, and often self-deprecatory tone of the character-narrator, who has already experienced and therefore learned from the events of the entire story, is continuously present, with the result that even the simplest description of character and event is shot through with the cleverness and the witty skepticism of the "mature" (in this sense, literally "late") Mattia Pascal. This same tone, moreover, serves to complicate and at times almost to eclipse the outlines of the overall anecdote, which, in other hands, could have seemed just another version, though with a special concluding twist, of the story of the man who died and then returned to this world from beyond with the uncanny knowledge of his own "death." But despite these contrastive tonal effects, the main line of this section of the narrative follows more or less directly the path of Mattia's development vis-à-vis his family and his early acquaintances.

The section devoted to background material comes to a close as Mattia, at his mother's anxious behest ("preghiere"), agrees to make an honest woman of Romilda Dondi, one of the young ladies with whom he has had relations (353; 32). Unfortunately, along with Mattia's new bride comes her own widowed mother, "Marianna Dondi, vedova Pescatore," who is subsequently referred to as "la strega," or "the witch."[5] Primarily for financial reasons—those common to more or less the entire *piccola borghesia* of the period—all four characters, the newlyweds and the two widows, end up living under the same roof. It does not take long before the tensions among them have grown to such a degree that an explosion is inevitable. The climactic scene of communal outburst is prepared for and described, up to a point, in the relatively straightforward manner of realistic fiction. There is a preliminary "tempest" (357–59; 35–36), but the real eruption occurs two days later, when Mattia's Aunt Scolastica comes to save his overly submissive mother from the clutches of the widow Pescatore. Although the "vedova Pescatore" is indeed a "strega," she is no match for Mattia's extraordinarily energetic and aggressive aunt. Scolastica enters the home and proceeds directly to Mattia's mother; at first Aunt Scolastica pays no heed whatever to the widow Pescatore, who is busy making bread, kneading the dough and slamming it down rhythmically on the bread-board in defiant response to Scolastica's exhortations addressed to Mattia's mother. A moment later the widow Pescatore, apparently not satisfied with such oblique gestures of defiance, goes to get the rolling pin and lays it down beside her. This threat sets off the explosion. Aunt Scolastica springs to her feet and orders Mattia's mother to get her things together and start on her way. As the narrator himself has commented earlier, the entire scene deserves presentation on the stage (359; 37). But the culminating confrontation is especially noteworthy and results in the widow Pescatore standing alone with a head full of dough. In terms of Pirandello's thematic concerns, the scene's coda is even more telling:

> Quel che seguì fu per me solo. La vedova Pescatore, ruggendo dalla rabbia, si strappò la pasta dalla faccia, dai capelli tutti appiastricciati, e venne a buttarla in faccia a me, che ridevo, ridevo in una specie di convulsione; m'afferrò la barba, mi sgraffiò tutto; poi, come impazzita, si buttò per terra e cominciò a strapparsi le vesti addosso, a rotolarsi, a rotolarsi, frenetica, sul pavimento; mia moglie intanto (*sit venia verbo*) receva di là, tra acutissime strida, mentr'io:
> "Le gambe! le gambe!" gridavo alla vedova Pescatore per terra. "Non mi mostrate le gambe, per carità!" (360)

> The next scene was just for me. The widow Pescatore, roaring with anger, ripped the dough from her face, from her sticky hair, and threw it at me, while I laughed in a kind of convulsive hilar-

ity. She seized my beard, scratched me all over. Then, as if she had gone mad, she threw herself on the floor and began to tear off her clothes, rolling over and over frantically on the tiles. Meanwhile in the other room, my wife (*sit venia verbo*) was retching amid piercing screams, as I shouted at the widow Pescatore on the floor: "Your legs! Your legs! Don't show me your legs, for heaven's sake!" (38)

The opening part of the encounter is built around a typically Pirandellian confrontation, in which a tyrant (in this case the widow Pescatore), due to circumstances beyond his or her control, is suddenly laid low and thus becomes the underdog. In this respect the last part of the scene is typical, too, since even though a revised hierarchy of sorts has been established, its outlines are far from stable. This Pirandellian instability is important despite the fact that the comic effects of the scene's coda—with its farcical joke on the vanity of the arbitrarily fixed forms of social comportment ("Non mi mostrate le gambe, per carità!"; "Don't show me your legs, for heaven's sake!")—tend to obscure the overall inconclusiveness of the situation as far as Mattia is concerned. The uncertainty of Mattia's predicament is made abundantly clear in the subsequent section of the chapter, but before consideration of Mattia's future, the text provides a series of crucial notations as Mattia reflects on his reactions of the previous moment and on the present state of affairs:

> Posso dire che da allora ho fatto il gusto a ridere di tutte le mie sciagure e d'ogni mio tormento. Mi vidi, in quell'istante, attore d'una tragedia che più buffa non si sarebbe potuta immaginare: mia madre, scappata via, così, con quella matta; mia moglie, di là, che . . . lasciamola stare!; Marianna Pescatore lì per terra; e io, io che non avevo più pane, quel che si dice pane, per il giorno appresso, io con la barba tutta impastocchiata, il viso sgraffiato, grondante non sapevo ancora se di sangue o di lagrime, per il troppo ridere. Andai ad accertarmene allo specchio. Erano lagrime; ma ero anche sgraffiato bene. Ah quel mio occhio, in quel momento, quanto mi piacque! Per disperato, mi s'era messo a guardare più che mai altrove, altrove per conto suo. (360–61)

> I may say that, from that day on, I have made a habit of laughing at all my misfortunes and torments. At that moment I saw myself as an actor in a tragedy more comical than any that could be

imagined: my mother had run out with that madwoman; my wife was in the other room busy . . . we'll skip that! Marianna Pescatore there on the ground, and I myself, not knowing where to turn for my daily bread, quite literally, my bread for the next day. My beard was all floury, my face scratched and wet, whether with blood or tears from too much laughter I didn't know yet. I went to the mirror to examine myself. They were tears, but I was also thoroughly scratched. Ah that eye of mine, how it pleased me at that moment! Out of sheer desperation, it had begun to look off in the wrong direction more than ever, gazing off on its own account. (38)

These comments indicate the centrality of the entire experience to Mattia's development. From then on, in the terms of the text, he habitually reacts to even the worst misfortunes and torments with a response that is exactly the opposite of what one would normally expect: he laughs. This idiosyncratic reaction does not mean, to be sure, that Mattia simply turns tragedy into comedy. Instead, his characteristic manner of perception is to see the two inseparably mixed, each relative to the other and each dependent on the other for its meaning. The crucible in which the comic and tragic are blended, as is so often the case in Pirandello, is made up of both violence and humor, blood and the tears of excessive laughter ("il troppo ridere"). The passage's form of presentation in regard to these reflections is also characteristic of Pirandello: "Mi *vidi*, in quell'istante" ("At that moment I *saw myself*"). Reflexive verbs of perception, and especially of sight, recur regularly in the narration and dialogue of Pirandello's most self-involved and skeptical characters (*skeptesthai:* to look, consider). As in the narrator's introductory comments to the scene, moreover, the metaphorization of the experience of everyday life is not only self-reflexive but also literary, and in this passage specifically theatrical: "Questa scena merita di essere rappresentata. . . . Mi vidi, in quell'istante, attore d'una tragedia che più buffa non si sarebbe potuta immaginare" ("This scene deserves to be performed in full. . . . At that moment I saw myself as an actor in a tragedy more comical than any that could be imagined"). Finally as is also typical of Pirandellian experience and perception, Mattia is both inside and outside the events of his own discourse, again at once the self-reflectively "mature" *subject* and the naive *object* of first-person representation.

The importance of the blending of comedy and tragedy, participation and observation, and distance and involvement is evident from the passage itself. But why should we place so much emphasis on maturity? The chapter is entitled "Maturazione." The English translator renders this neither as "Maturity" nor even "Maturation" but, correctly, as "Ripening," undoubtedly taking his cue from the chapter's later description (arising from the narrator's perusal of a less than definitive library book on trees by Giovan Vittorio Soderini) of the way in which worldly wise fruit vendors turn a quick profit by buying unripened fruit and then giving it the semblance of maturity through bruising. As the narrator comments, "Ora così venne a maturazione l'anima mia, ancora acerba" (367; "And this is how my spirit, still green, ripened to its maturity," 44). Simply stated, the condition toward which Mattia's spirit is ripening through the events of the chapter is the one described by Pirandello in his roughly contemporary essay *L'umorismo* (1908) as that of the umorista.[6] Indeed, the first edition of the essay was dedicated, fittingly enough, to the character's memory, "Alla buon'anima di Mattia Pascal bibliotecario."[7]

In "Maturazione" Mattia's development as an umorista is still not complete, nor does he in fact laugh at every misfortune and torment. By the end of the chapter, however, as he suffers not only the continuing deterioration of his marriage but also the deaths of his two infant children and that of his mother, he is well on his way toward the disconcertingly self-reflexive and incessantly shifting perspective of umorismo. The primary facets of the development of this perspective are present *in nuce* in the series of comments quoted previously. These include, according to the essay, first, the perception of the comic, that something is contrary to the normal expectations of everyday life, or "l'*avvertimento* del contrario"; second, the internalization of the reaction, or "il *sentimento* del contrario," in the characteristic passage from perception to sentiment; third, the ever-present activity of reflection—including self-reflection—from which the "sentimento del contrario" arises and which it then further stimulates; and, fourth, the constant tendency to decompose ("scomporre") the form of experience into its constituent elements so that they may be examined both separately and in relation to one another and, if possible (though for the full-fledged umorista such a feat never really is possible), reassembled in workable and more livable fashion as a new fusion of what the essay terms life and form, "vita" and "forma."

In the context of this perspective, it is easy to see why the "scene" that at first threatens to be merely a repetition and extension of the unpleasant squabbles involving Mattia, his wife, Romilda, and the widow

Pescatore turns out to be not just painful, as expected (though it certainly is that, too), but also laughable. Mattia's perception of the scene's peculiar mixture of the tragic and the ridiculous bears the hallmark of Pirandellian umorismo. With the knowledge gained from retrospective review, Mattia as the *narrator*, a past master in the ways of umorismo, recounts the importance of his reaction as a *character* in terms of his own psychological and moral development ("da allora ho fatto il gusto a ridere di tutte le mie sciagure e d'ogni mio tormento"; "from that day on, I have made a habit of laughing at all my misfortunes and torments"). In Mattia's commentary, he breaks up, or "decomposes," the experience and recasts it in the imagery of the theater (precisely: "tragedia . . . buffa"), thus picking up the thread of the introductory metaphor of theatrical success. He then recounts the act of consulting his reflection in the mirror in order to check the liquid on his face (which, as it happens, is covered not with blood but with tears of laughter, although, in the typically painful experience of the incipient umorista, Mattia's tears are running down well-scratched cheeks). This gaze in the mirror, combining elements of narcissism with fundamental self-doubt, again confirms the understanding of Mattia's reactions within the framework of umorismo. The umorista's characteristic act of specular self-reflection and the imagery accompanying it turn up again and again throughout Pirandello's major works, and they recur with special emphasis at the beginning of *Uno, nessuno e centomila*. In the scene at hand, as is indicative of Pirandello's attention to the psychological workings of umorismo's disconcerting self-absorption, Mattia's gaze focuses initially on his face but then is drawn from the general effects of his tears to the particular detail of his distinctive eye, on which, at least for the moment, his regard becomes fixed: "Ah quel mio occhio, in quel momento, quanto mi piacque! Per disperato, mi s'era messo a guardare più che mai altrove, altrove per conto suo" ("Ah that eye of mine, how it pleased me at that moment! Out of sheer desperation, it had begun to look off in the wrong direction more than ever, gazing off on its own account").

The object of Mattia's pleasure is the wandering eye that in his youth had been so stubborn even special glasses had proven unequal to the task of straightening it permanently (333; 12). This eye serves two symbolic functions in the narrative, both of them implicit in the description of Mattia's reactions before the mirror. First, Mattia's eye emphasizes the importance of individual perspective in coming to terms with questions of truth and falsity. Repeatedly in the course of *Il fu Mattia Pascal* and in

Pirandello's major works between 1904 and the late 1920s, the perception of a problem turns out to be an integral part of the problem itself. That is to say, things exist *only* as their existence is perceived; or to put this still another way, there is no such thing as absolute existence apart from perception.

The other symbolic function of Mattia's eye indicates why this typically Pirandellian position is not merely an instance of post-Kantian relativism or of Sartrean existentialism *avant la lettre*. True, individual perception is of primary importance in Pirandello's schemes, and meaning is always relative to it. But seeing merely that Pirandello's major characters are condemned to exist *as* individuals is insufficient for evaluating Pirandello's thought. Beyond this, it is necessary to see that they and their views—like Mattia's eye—are not only individual but also aberrant. Even though the point of view of the umorista provides an incisive critique of human perception and experience in Pirandello's representation of daily life, this perspective is not a universally held one, nor can it be. In its inevitable alienation from others and even from the subject's own original reactions, the self-reflexive perspective arising from "il sentimento del contrario" colors the everyday view of the umorista in a way that consistently differs from the perspectives of other members of society. At the same time, social norms (as well as the minor codes of social comportment, such as the prescribed propriety of covered legs for mature women) continue to exist, despite the fact that the umorista is constantly at work decomposing the edifice of social organization and belief, thereby exposing the arbitrariness and contingency of society's constructions. The reason that society continues to construct such formal edifices of belief and practice is simply that it must do so in order to function, just as the umorista must continue to decompose them. What this *mutual* relationship means, therefore, is that even though the fully developed perspective of umorismo is by definition aberrant, it nonetheless depends on existent social constructions—albeit in an oppositional fashion—for the workings of its perceptions. It may be antisocial but never, strictly speaking, *a*social.

In suggesting the significance of individual perspective, and especially of a point of view that habitually goes against the grain of the established order of social life, Mattia's wandering eye poses problems that recur in the novel as major factors in the text's treatment of characters and events. But in spite of, or perhaps because of, its symbolic importance, its "role" is far from unambiguous. Indeed, one of the central problems that its description suggests—one of the most revealing for assessment of Pirandello's conception of umorismo—is never resolved. In brief, the problem is this: does the perspective of the umorista come from birth or from worldly experience? That is, can anyone, given the right set of circumstances, develop this perspective, or is there some rare, inborn propensity to this manner of perception (due perhaps to intelligence and flexibility, as the umorista might want to claim, or perhaps to foolishness and contrariness, as other characters in Pirandello's works occasionally say)?

That Mattia's eye seems naturally disposed to wander ("un occhio, il quale, non so perché, tendeva a guardare per conto suo, altrove," 333; "one eye, which, I don't know why, tended to gaze off on its own account, in the wrong direction," 12) would seem to imply that the answer to this problem lies on the natural side of a nature/experience (heredity/environment) dichotomy. On the other hand, the concept of ripening through "bruising" seems to indicate that the solution lies on the side of experience. When considered more closely, however, the underlying dichotomy, like other Pirandellian oppositions, is not nearly so clear-cut as this. The ripening of the individual character, like that of the fruit vendors' produce, is in fact a naturally predetermined part of life, with or without bruising. The bruising may well be necessary for the full development of the perspective of the umorista, but a certain *predisposition* to this perspective is in all probability just as necessary (as is suggested here by Mattia's *youthful* eye). Doubtless, this combination is rare. Either the predisposition or the experience, in the absence of the other, is probably insufficient to create the perspective.[8] It is in part for this reason that the unpredictable play of chance and fortune retains such great power in Pirandello's thought, as evidenced not only in the novel's extensive episode at Monte Carlo but also in the circumstances of Mattia's first "death." (There is, furthermore, a historical aspect to this problem, as Mattia's deprecation of Copernicus in the "Premessa seconda" humorously suggests; but even though it may well be true that modern man is especially given to the relativism and the anxious self-reflection of umorismo's perspective, the state of modernity itself is clearly not enough to turn all humankind into umoristi, at least not as modernity is portrayed in Pirandello's works. In one sense just the opposite is true, since the instability of modern life seems to create a special need for the inflexible absolutism of naive yet zealously maintained belief, such as that of Henry IV's hypostatized Irish priest.)

The problem of the origins of the perspective of umorismo thus remains an open one in *Il fu Mattia Pascal*, as it does elsewhere in Pirandello's works. Moreover, this is not the only major difficulty posed but left tantalizingly unresolved in the novel. The conclusion itself is framed as a dual opposition regarding Mattia's life and death that at first seems simple but, on closer examination, reveals itself to be as complex as the questions concerning Mattia's eye. Furthermore, since the eye plays a major part in the intricate metaphorization of doubling that eventually leads to the novel's notably inconclusive ending, it is worthwhile to review the eye's symbolic functions in the sections of the narrative that follow these seemingly inauspicious beginnings.[9]

After Mattia learns of his "death" from the newspapers, he changes his identity and begins to travel. His only regret, at least initially, is that even in his role as the happy and carefree Adriano Meis, replete with new hairstyle and clothing, he retains the distinctive characteristic of Mattia Pascal, that refractory eye. Indeed, during one of his habitual conversations with himself in the mirror, he complains of "quest'occhio *di lui*, di quell'imbecille" (416; "that eye, *his*, that imbecile's," 90). At first, however, he does nothing. He is alone and free, liberated originally by chance, but now taking willful advantage of his freedom in expectation of the happiness that, he thinks, is sure to come with it. But once in Rome, Mattia/Adriano's continuing annoyance with his eye is augmented both by the genuine desire to present an attractive appearance to Adriana, the youthful object of his desire, and by his pressing fear of discovery ("Mi trovai, senza saperlo, davanti allo specchio, come se qualcuno mi ci avesse condotto per mano. Mi guardai. Ah quell'occhio maledetto! Forse per esso colui [lo Spagnolo] mi avrebbe riconosciuto," 480; "Without realizing it, I found myself in front of the mirror, as if someone had led me there by the hand. I looked at myself. Ah, that damned eye! Perhaps on account of it he [the Spaniard] might have recognized me," 151). As a result of this mixture of hope and fear, Mattia/Adriano decides to undergo the surgery suggested by Signorina Caporale (457; 129), the operation that seems to have been approved not only by Adriana but even by the mirror itself ("lo specchio ha parlato," 460; "the mirror has spoken," 132).

Technically, the operation is a success, but both its practical and its symbolic ramifications are, to say the least, unforeseen. Once Adriano comes to admit, as he has in fact feared for some time, that his "freedom" is really tyranny, that life without a social past is tantamount to life as a shadow without a body and so without a present or future in any society, and that happiness, in his condition as Adriano Meis, is therefore impossible, he has little difficulty (by means of a faked suicide and a cryptic note) in returning to his old identity as Mattia Pascal. There is a catch, however. He can restore his facial appearance through the expedient of having a barber attend to "quell'imbecille" (now Adriano rather than Mattia), thus undoing the original disguise. But he cannot change his new eye so easily: "Ecco, qualche cosa d'Adriano Meis mi sarebbe tuttavia rimasta in faccia" (552; "So something of Adriano Meis would still remain in my face," 218). This comment echoes Mattia's earlier lament at the beginning of his new life as Adriano Meis, "'Ah, quest'occhio,' pensai, '. . . rimarrà sempre suo nella mia nuova faccia!'" (406; "'Ah, this eye,' I thought, '. . . will still remain his in my new face!'" 81). At first glance, the later passage seems the mirror image of the former, as though the second doubled the first. But this is not the case. Like Mattia's second "death," the later description of the eye, in terms of the symbolic organization of the narrative, emphasizes not sameness but difference. In his role as Adriano, Mattia could and did change the original eye to suit his new identity, but the "late" Mattia Pascal does not consider changing his eye back to its old state, even if it were possible to do so. This merely points up the fact that the apparent doubling in *Il fu Mattia Pascal* is never perfect; and Mattia's changing reactions to the eye again serve as a confirmation of this fundamental lack of balance, or, in other terms, of this progressive difference rather than sameness. This difference is also apparent in Mattia's view, as an umorista, of the self as an object. When Mattia first notices and comments on his eye in the mirror (in "Maturazione") he seems to take his image as that of an other, as the specularly distanced double of himself; but at the same time he sees the eye as an integral part of himself, because it is his, and uniquely so: "Ah quel *mio* occhio, in quel momento, quanto mi piacque!" ("Ah that eye *of mine*, how it pleased me at that moment!"). After Mattia's irrevocable "fall" into the perspective of umorismo at the news of his "death," however, his eye becomes the definitive mark not of the self but of the other, of the person Mattia used to be and from whom he is now alienated. This mark remains with Mattia wherever he goes, so that the self is never again unified once the knowledge of the contingency and arbitrariness of its own construction has fully taken hold. Henceforth, with the fall into the conscious self-reflectiveness of umorismo, the self is a priori always doubled, even though, again, always imperfectly. The subsequent image of the eye in the mirror, therefore, serves to reconfirm not only the doubling but also the spiral of this inevitable, now internal imbalance and alienation.

This same type of disequilibrium is noticeable in the symbolic functions of naming in the story and in the story's temporal organization as a narrative. To take just one example of the importance of naming, the choice of the character's original surname buttresses the narrative's play of perspective in several ways. There is perhaps a secondary reference to the turn-of-the-century theosophist Théophile Pascal, two of whose books are mentioned as part of Paleari's collection (*Les Sept Principes de l'homme* and *ABC de la Théosophie*, 435; 109). But the primary allusion is undoubtedly to the celebrated philosopher. In part, Pascal's thought figures in the novel because of his well-known formulation of man's immeasurable smallness amidst the spatial and temporal infinity of the universe (which Mattia, while discussing the disastrous effects of the discoveries of Copernicus on man's perception of himself in the "Premessa seconda," recasts in historical terms as "la nuova concezione dell'infinita nostra piccolezza," 324; "the new idea of our infinite smallness," 3). This type of self-reflective "perspectivism," however, was not the only aspect of Pascal's thought that attracted Pirandello's interest. In the essay *L'umorismo*, Pirandello attributes to Pascal a concept that was a recurrent preoccupation, though in different contexts, for both writers: "Non c'è uomo, osservò il Pascal, che differisca più da un altro che da sé stesso nella successione del tempo" ("Pascal observed that there is no man who differs from another man more than he differs, with the passing of time, from himself").[10] This notion of temporal succession and difference becomes a point of recurrent, even obsessive discussion in *Uno, nessuno e centomila*, but its effects are also present in *Il fu Mattia Pascal*. It explains to an extent why even though perfect doubling, or sameness, is in reality impossible for Pirandello, attempts at disregarding difference in favor of sameness are nevertheless inevitable. According to the Pirandellian reformulation of these concepts through the events of the narrative, with temporal succession comes difference, so without difference there would be no succession, no time, and therefore no worldly existence. But without sameness, the worldly result would be equally shattering to the concept of the individual, since there would be no identity.

This strangely embattled combination of similarity and difference, or, more precisely, of inevitable difference masquerading as sameness, is, in Pirandello's works, the key to understanding the temporal organization underlying not only the individual persona but also that of the functions of naming and, finally, of narrative fiction itself. The story of Mattia Pascal thus becomes the story, over time, of Mattia, Adriano, and Mattia again, with significant changes in regard to the "character" at every step of the way. Just as the novel exists both as a unified, completed whole, narrated by a knowledgeable first-person narrator, *and* as the formal progression of its narration, so Mattia seems one character, participant and narrator, but one who is in fact different at every stage of the plot and, indeed, at every moment of his own discourse. After his fall into umorismo, moreover, he knows this difference, though imperfectly, even as he attempts to minimize its consequences. Traditionally in first-person narrative, such problems would be resolved by the novel's conclusion, enfolding narrator and character, actor and teller, but as we shall see, such a reading of the end of *Il fu Mattia* Pascal is too facile.

As an actor/creator within his own story, moreover, Mattia attempts to construct a complete character once and for all, Adriano Meis ("*questa costruzione fantastica* d'una vita non realmente vissuta," 413, my italics; "*this imaginative construction* of a life not really lived," 88, my italics); yet Adriano is just that—a construction—and as such, is doomed to progressive decomposition under the reflexive workings of umorismo's perspective. Again the underlying problem is a familiar one: perception over time. As the poetic fantasy of the moment, the making of "Adriano" gives undeniable pleasure to its creator: "Mi procurò una gioja strana e nuova" (413; "It brought me a strange, new joy," 88). But no matter how pleasurable its creation might be, the construction as such cannot last in the world, because every time Mattia is required to reaffirm and explain his "existence" as Adriano Meis, he must outwardly insist on the truth of *identity* even while he sees, within himself and despite his own "fantasy," the undeniable *difference* and thus the construction's falsity. The original idea and the world in which it must succeed or fail on its own remain antagonistic although linked entities. As in Henry IV's rebukes of his servile and unimaginative counselors, who so readily submit to the conventions of language, identity, and authority, the knowledgeable decomposition of the conventions of language in *Il fu Mattia Pascal* eventually extends to the decomposition of *all* metaphorical constructions, which is to say, both of the self as identity and of narrative fiction as truth. Pirandello's position in these works, however, is not simply to reaffirm the other side, to imply that constructions are false and thus valueless and that identity is merely a sham and therefore to be avoided at all costs. Instead, his critique of these notions falls somewhere between such poles. He sees that they *are* false but, at the same time, that human perception and human society itself (as affirmed, too, at the conclusion of *Liolà*) must depend on such falsehoods if individual and social life is to continue.

The inconclusive complexity of this position is one of the reasons why it is important to pay careful attention to the details of the character/narrator's seemingly offhanded affirmations at the novel's opening and again at its closing in regard to the limits of what he knows, what he is called, and who, in truth, he is:[11]

> Una delle poche cose, anzi forse la sola ch'io sapessi di certo era questa: che mi chiamavo Mattia Pascal. E me ne approfittavo. Ogni qual volta qualcuno de' miei amici o conoscenti dimostrava d'aver perduto il senno fino al punto di venire da me per qualche consiglio o suggerimento, mi stringevo nelle spalle, socchiudevo gli occhi e gli rispondevo:
> "Io mi chiamo Mattia Pascal."
> "Grazie, caro. Questo lo so."
> "E ti par poco?"
>
> * * *
>
> Nel cimitero di Miragno, su la fossa di quel povero ignoto che s'uccise alla *Stìa*, c'è ancora la lapide dettata da Lodoletta. . . .
> Io vi ho portato la corona di fiori promessa e ogni tanto mi reco a vedermi morto e sepolto là. Qualche curioso mi segue da lontano; poi, al ritorno, s'accompagna con me, sorride, e—considerando la mia condizione—mi domanda:
> "Ma voi, insomma, si può sapere chi siete?"
> Mi stringo nelle spalle, socchiudo gli occhi e gli rispondo:
> "Eh, caro mio . . . Io sono il fu Mattia Pascal." (319, 578)

> One of the few things—perhaps the only one—that I know for certain is that my name is Mattia Pascal. I used to take advantage of this. Every now and then when a friend or acquaintance had taken leave of his senses to the point of coming to me for some suggestion or advice, I would shrug my shoulders, close my eyes slightly, and answer:
> "My name is Mattia Pascal."
> "Thanks a lot. I know that much."
> "Well, does it seem so little to you?"
>
> * * *
>
> In the cemetery at Miragno, over the grave of the poor stranger who killed himself in the millrace, there is still the stone with the words dictated by Lodoletta [Skylark]. . . .
> I took the wreath of flowers as promised, and every now and

then I go out there to see myself dead and buried. Occasionally a curious passer-by follows me at a distance, then, on the way back, accompanies me, smiles, and—considering my condition—asks me:

"Well, might one ask [know] who you are, after all?"

I shrug my shoulders, close my eyes slightly, and answer:

"Ah, my friend . . . I am the late Mattia Pascal." (vii, 244)

The character changes, his knowledge and situation change, and so does his name. But is the change, overall, an effective and valid one? The answer, as readers of Pirandello will recognize, is both yes and no. In a way, the addition of "late" to Mattia Pascal's name does seem to designate a new entity. There is, moreover, another significant shift between the two frame passages, a change that occurs despite the passages' similarities in descriptive lexicon, in rhetorical organization, and in the thematic concerns of knowledge and identity. This shift appears to be from the guarded admission of attribute to the open affirmation of essence, that is, from "my name is" to "I am." Once again, however, the narrator has it both ways. He seems to affirm positive identity, but the *entity* identified is one that, in terms of human society, must by definition remain a *nonentity*. So, is Mattia Pascal dead and buried, or does Mattia Pascal exist in the world? There is no single answer to this question, which remains, nonetheless, an unavoidable one. The joke is on the text's curious interlocutor, or on the reader, who would try through questioning or interpretation to pin the text down to one position alone. For Pirandello, truth, like human identity itself, is always doubled already, even though imperfectly so, as the concluding reflexive verbs of motion and perception reaffirm once more: "Ogni tanto *mi* reco a veder*mi* morto e sepolto là" ("Every now and then I go [literally, take *myself*] out there to see *myself* dead and buried"). In the latter passage this doubleness is also suggested, albeit in a secondary manner, by the use of the technically plural "voi" form.

But if by the novel's conclusion there are two names and at least two selves that they name (even though imperfectly), one already underground and one still walking in the sun, who then *is* (the late) Mattia Pascal and what is the nature of his roles and the import of his experiences, "strange and different" (320; viii) as they may be? One role that Mattia fulfills for certain (and significantly so, as Pirandello himself suggests in his commemorative dedication to *L'umorismo*) is that of "bibliotecario," or librarian. Initially, Mattia takes this job out of financial necessity, but his adoption of the role is more thoroughgoing than it may at first appear. Even though he jests at the expense of the story's original librarian, the old and infirm Signor Romitelli, who reads with obvious difficulty, keeping his head close to the page and using only one eye while reciting the lines aloud in incremental repetition (364; 41–42), Mattia himself, upon seeing the news of his "suicide," reads the report in precisely the same halting, repetitious, one-eyed manner, as though debilitated and suddenly aged (394–95; 69–70). But, as we have seen, Mattia's initial period in the library does not last for long. Once he learns of his "death" and becomes a "free" man, his days as a lowly librarian appear to be over. From then on, or so it seems to him, his role is simply to profit from the good fortune that chance has provided him and to enjoy his new life, or, as the text has it, "to live, live, live" (104; "vivere, vivere, vivere," 431).

Mattia's new role, which inaugurates the second section of the narrative, turns out to be far more difficult and more painful than he had imagined. This is true in part because of the reasons already suggested and in part because of the basic human capacity—heightened still further for the umorista—of feeling oneself live ("sentirsi vivere"), the self-reflexive faculty described by Paleari in chapter 13 as mankind's "poor privilege" (155; "tristo privilegio," 484). The "bella illusione" that results from this specifically human privilege—also noted by Paleari and discussed openly by Pirandello himself in L'umorismo and elsewhere—is that human beings mistake "come una realtà fuori di noi questo nostro interno sentimento della vita, mutabile e vario, secondo i tempi, i casi e la fortuna" ("for external reality our inner feeling of life, which varies and changes according to the times, chance, and fortune"). As a traveler, Mattia himself had noticed a similar mix of internal sentiment and supposedly external reality in his own perception of objects as images (420–21; 95). The narrator comments on this perceptive and interpretative faculty, which structures the perceived objects in relation to internal sentiments and images while developing their relations, and which therefore contributes to making "objective" reality pleasant or unpleasant to the individual. This faculty is designated by the narrator as fantasy. The interrelations of seemingly objective perception and subjective interpretation, which during Mattia's travels are formulated in the theoretical terminology of abstract analysis, are demonstrated actively at work in the subsequent portion of the text when Mattia, as Adriano, breaks his silence of more than a year's solitary traveling to tell Adriana and Signorina Caporale of his "adventures." The following series of discussions is colored first by his surprise at his internal wealth of impressions from his experience that come alive as he speaks and then by his reactions to the external evidence of his audience's delight:

> Quest'intima meraviglia coloriva straordinariamente la mia narrazione; dal piacere poi che le due donne, ascoltando, dimostravano di provarne, mi nasceva a mano a mano il rimpianto d'un bene che non aveva allora realmente goduto; e anche di questo rimpianto s'insaporava ora la mia narrazione. (455)

> This intimate surprise colored my narration in an extraordinary manner; and as the two women, listening, showed their pleasure, there was born slowly within me a longing for a happiness that I had never really enjoyed, and this longing also gave flavor to my narration. (127)

The introductory comments to this passage are based on an elaborate metaphor intended to describe the gradual liberation of Mattia's narrative and his growing powers as a narrator ("A poco a poco, superati gli scogli delle prime domande imbarazzanti, scansandone alcuni coi remi della menzogna, che mi servivan da leva e da puntello, . . . la barchetta della mia finzione poté alla fine filare al largo e issar la vela della fantasia"; "Little by little, having passed the reefs of the first embarrassing questions, dodging some with the oars of falsehood, which served me as my lever and my support, . . . the fragile bark of my fiction could at last take to the open sea and hoist the sails of fantasy"). This introduction is, of course, openly and playfully "literary," echoing the traditional tropes of autobiographical lyric commonplace since the Renaissance. Moreover, the theory of narrative representation expressed here—which is that narration is at once the process and the result of the description of prior external event and character as well as of internal affective reactions to various external stimuli—picks up and extends the general discussion of types of narrative and their worth and utility in the modern world begun by the narrator in the "Premessa seconda." This sort of self-reflexive theorizing and practice, demonstrated in a series of passages that point not only to the character's psychological development but also to his narrative procedures (in a subtly embedded switch on the previous distinctions between the function of the narrator and that of the character) is one of the modernist discoveries of Pirandello's prose, which, as Robert Dombroski and others have noted, tends to take itself and its own creation as primary topics in both literary and psychological terms.[12] Mattia is no longer only an "actor," as he had been in "Maturazione," but is now a creator as well. Rather than simplifying or resolving the difficulties of interpretation posed by the narrative, however, the novel's increasingly self-conscious examination of its own subject matter and techniques, and of the changing roles of its main character, merely reaffirms the complexity and inconclusiveness of the story itself.

In the narrative's last section, as a final gesture toward resolving such problems, the text provides a concluding discussion between Mattia (in his reincarnation as now unofficial *bibliotecario*) and his librarian colleague, Don Eligio Pellegrinotto. Their exchange appears at least to elucidate the "moral" of the story if not to abolish all doubt concerning it. In its rhetorical organization, the commentary recalls the dialogues between Renzo and Lucia at the end of *I promessi sposi*, although Pirandello's text includes snares that are even more insidious than those set by Manzoni:

> Abbiamo discusso a lungo insieme su i casi miei, e spesso io gli
> ho dichiarato di non saper vedere che frutto se ne possa cavare.
>   "Intanto, questo," egli mi dice: "che fuori della legge e fuori di
> quelle particolarità, liete o tristi che sieno, per cui noi siamo
> noi, caro signor Pascal, non è possibile vivere." (577–78)

> We have discussed the events of my life at length, and I have told
> him often that I don't see what lesson can possible be drawn from
> them.
>   "In the first place," he says, "that outside of the law, and outside of those particular characteristics of our lives that, happy or
> sad as they may be, make us ourselves, my dear Signor Pascal, it
> is not possible to live." (243)

As a concluding statement, these words—presented in the sudden immediacy of the present tense—carry the weight and authority of Don Eligio, Mattia's trusted friend and mentor, at whose prodding the narration was begun and in whose hands the finished manuscript is ultimately to be entrusted (321; 1; and, as the scholarly footnote by Don Eligio on page 489 [Eng. trans., p. 160] perhaps indicates, to whom it has in fact already been entrusted). If indeed this *were* the moral of the story, in and of itself, it would certainly help to answer many of the narrative's most vexing questions. It would explain why all Mattia's energy and will during his existence as Adriano and therefore outside of the history, social relationships, and responsibilities of normal everyday life are inadequate to make him either happy or free.[13] It would affirm, moreover, Mattia's earlier complaints that outside the law, and the formal edifice of social order that it ensures, he is, as far as the law itself is concerned, nothing but a shadow, a sham—in short; "nessuno" (518; "no one," 187). At the same time, again reminiscent of the lessons of the philosopher Pascal, it would establish once and for all that any attempt to live as pure "life," or "vita," caught up in a sort of timeless and therefore absolutely spontaneous Bergsonian *élan vital*, as at the gaming tables in Monte Carlo, without any regard for the necessity of constancy or *durée* in determining knowledge and truth, is doomed to failure from the very start (perhaps, conversely, just as any attempt to live only as a "construction," only as a fixed form without the corresponding movement of interior life, is equally doomed).

But Don Eligio's statement, alas, makes up only part of the concluding exchange. He is no more Mattia's perfect double than the earlier librarian, Romitelli, had been. Indeed, as soon as Don Eligio finishes, Mattia adds his contradiction in his characteristically witty and self-reflexive (and here perhaps even playfully Dantesque) fashion: "Ma io gli faccio osservare che non sono affatto rientrato né nella legge, né nelle mie particolarità. Mia moglie è moglie di Pomino, e io non saprei proprio dire *ch'io mi sia*" (578; "But then I point out to him that I have not returned at all either within the limits of the law or to the particular details of my former life. My wife is the wife of Pomino, and I really can't tell *who I may be* [literally: *to me*]," 243–44).

So, back to the beginning. Law may be necessary for society, but that does not mean in any sense that the law is reasonable or that living within its formal conditions suits Mattia at all (as Mattia objects in an exemplary instance to Berto's brother-in-law, the precociously erudite and supercilious "avvocatino": "Scusi! Questa è legge turca!" 559; "Excuse me! This law is suited for Turks!" 225). Even though Mattia is in one sense back in society, living with his Aunt Scolastica and passing his time writing in the library, in another sense, as an ambulatory corpse, he continues to exist outside society's order. In point of fact, when the entire story is considered from the perspective of these final paragraphs, it becomes clear that Mattia has *never* been able to live comfortably within society's rule as a stable, responsible adult. This was the case at the heyday of his sexual activity, during the early days of his marriage and his constant battles in his *piccolo borghese* ambience with the widow Pescatore (with whom Pomino, Mattia's other imperfect double, has managed to get along), during his travels as a solitary wanderer, and during his stay in Rome; and it is now true for

Mattia again, back in Miragno, as a dead man returned to life but not to all the ways and "particulars" of his former life. He is at last fully "mature," but as a character he is far from stable or unified. This continuing lack of stability is one reason why it is important to note that Pirandello's dedication to *L'umorismo* is a commemorative one, to a soul dead and gone: "Alla *buon anima* di Mattia Pascal bibliotecario." There is no single, unified Mattia Pascal at the end of the novel, but more than that, when Mattia is seen in the disturbing light of umorismo's ambiguously inconclusive "final" perspective, perhaps there never has been one in any lasting social sense. So, when all is said and done and the story has come to its close, who is this character who, in the typically "tragicomic" knowledge and perspective of umorismo, is at once completely constrained by circumstances and utterly free, inside and outside of his own "life," even inside and outside of the voice of his own discourse? Well, to make a long story short—and to take the narrative, for the moment, on its own terms—he is indeed, both figuratively and literally, (the late) Mattia Pascal.

The relationship between *Il fu Mattia Pascal* and *Uno, nessuno e centomila* is a strikingly close one.[14] At times during the first sections of *Uno, nessuno e centomila*, it almost seems as though Pirandello's intent was to pick up and extend the concerns of the earlier novel by beginning the story of Vitangelo Moscarda somewhere near the midpoint of Mattia Pascal's development as an umorista. The later novel was first published in installments in *Fiera letteraria* in 1925–26; but Pirandello had alluded to the project in his correspondence as early as 1912, so it is probable that he had nurtured the story throughout this entire period. Indeed, at its appearance, *Uno, nessuno e centomila* was without question the most comprehensive and systematic presentation of his philosophical and literary ideas to date. Because of the interest in the problems of social environment evident at the narrative's conclusion, moreover, the novel also provided a foretaste of the concerns of the subsequent, more socially oriented plays of the late twenties and the thirties.

In terms of narrative self-consciousness, the most obvious difference between *Il fu Mattia Pascal* and *Uno, nessuno e centomila* is one in degree that, in the course of the story, becomes—or, more accurately, appears to become—a difference in kind. Whereas the earlier novel takes form as a representation of the discovery of psychological and artistic self-reflexivity, *Uno, nessuno e centomila* is a programmatic exposition not only of the process but also of the consequences of such discoveries. Generally speaking, therefore, it would seem that *Il fu Mattia Pascal* looks back to the traditional novel of the nineteenth century, in which the issue of self-reflexivity, while important, is approached only indirectly, and that *Uno, nessuno e centomila* is similar to contemporary and subsequent modernist texts, in which self-consciousness, in a direct manner, assumes the primary focus of the narrative.[15] Cast in these terms, the discourse of the earlier narrative sounds in essence both representational and transparent, whereas that of the later one appears nonrepresentational and opaque. But under scrutiny these generalizations begin to break down. Indeed, as we shall see in relation to the later text's concluding passages, the primary problem in interpretation and assessment of *Uno, nessuno e centomila*, as so often is the case in Pirandello's major works, is that it simply will not remain in any single rhetorical *or* hermeneutic category.

The novel begins, in a scene reminiscent of various sequences in *Il fu Mattia Pascal*, with the major character regarding himself in a mirror.[16] The importance of self-reflection, rather than being tucked away amid the ongoing order of narrative events, thus receives major emphasis by being directly broached in the opening paragraphs. It quickly becomes apparent, furthermore, that the functions of self-reflection serve as the mainspring not only of these early passages but also of the entire story.[17] The doubling and multiplication openly thematized in this first specular gaze lead, through the remainder of the story's introductory sections, to a series of hypotheses and tentative conclusions. What Vitangelo discovers in these pages is indicated in summary fashion in the novel's title. The emphasis on the subjective-objective problems of perception is, if anything, even stronger here than it had been in *Il fu Mattia Pascal*. Vitangelo Moscarda—or Gengè, as his wife, Dida, affectionately refers to him—had been "one" individual as long as he enjoyed the illusion that the person he perceived himself to be was the same as that perceived by everyone else. But with the discovery that others (e.g., his wife, his neighbors, the townspeople) regard him differently from the way he regards himself, he feels that, as a living, breathing body, in and of himself, he is "no one." This condition extends that of Mattia Pascal, who found himself to be "nessuno" before the law in specific circumstances (518; 187), by making Vitangelo's state of "nobodiness" seem necessary and permanent rather than merely contingent and temporary. Vitangelo finds that apart from others' perceptions of him—which in fact determine his identity and thus his existence—he is nobody, so much so that "un filo d'aria poteva farlo [quel corpo] starnutire, oggi, e domani portarselo via" (759; "a draft of air could make it [that body] sneeze today and tomorrow could carry it away," 42). But at the same time, as long as his identity depends on the perceptions of other individuals, he feels himself to be a different being for each of them, or "centomila" ("a hundred thousand"): thus *uno, nessuno* and *centomila*.

In order to understand this situation better and, if possible, to rectify it, Moscarda embarks on the project at the heart of the story. Vitangelo's scheme is more thoroughly planned and more willfully pursued than Mattia's had been, but it is important to see that both of them result from a mixture of choice *and* chance (Vitangelo's glance in the mirror and his wife's comments, Mattia's original "death"). Vitangelo resolves, first, to attempt to see himself as others do, and second, should the first task prove impossible, to decompose all of those characteristics, those various masks, which others mistake for his essence and by which they think to "know" and identify him.[18] In pursuit of this goal of self-decomposition, he gradually commits a sort of social suicide by divesting himself of his wife, of the bank that he has inherited from his father, and of all the other belongings and attributes that have contributed to making up his reputation in society. Eventually, it seems that he finds an ally and confidante in the figure of Anna Rosa, one of his wife's friends. But even though she helps for a time to allay the pain of Vitangelo's solitude (which, of course, has resulted from the very goal he has set for himself), the end of their brief "relationship" is just as unhappy, though in a dramatically different way, as that between Moscarda and his actual wife. Indeed, the entire project—when carried out *within* society—is, in practical terms, an utter failure. Nonetheless, this is not the end but in a sense the beginning of Moscarda's story, since this very failure gives rise to the narrative's concluding situation and, along with it, the character's final perspective, from which the entire story, once again in first person, is then narrated. In terms of the overall narrative, however, even this culminating perspective is not nearly so comprehensible or so clear-cut as the narrator eventually attempts to make it sound.

As mentioned previously, the novel opens with Moscarda regarding himself in the mirror. His wife asks what he is doing, and he replies that he is checking to see if there is anything wrong with his nose, since he has felt some pain in one of his nostrils. This initial exchange sets the stage for a disconcerting discovery—that, at least to his wife, his nose appears to droop down to the right. Vitangelo's discovery of the self as other, as a being at once different from what it had perceived itself to be and *con-*

scious of this difference, is, as in *Il fu Mattia Pascal,* one of the crucial discoveries of the umorista.[19] But there is more than this to Vitangelo's discovery. Following upon his opening realization that he is not only the subject but also the potential object of his own and others' perceptions comes the knowledge that at each new moment he becomes a different being, both for himself and for others, with the inevitable progression of circumstances and the passage of time. The demystified narrator playfully attempts to make the reader share in the implications of these discoveries, moreover, even while Vitangelo as a character is undergoing the arduous process of initiation into the knowledge of his own alienation from himself and from others: "Oh Dio, voi impallidite. Riconoscete forse anche voi ora, che un minuto fa *voi eravate un altro?*" (770; "Good heavens, you're pale! So now perhaps you too are beginning to realize that, a moment ago, *you were a different person?*" 62).

Moscarda's initial loss of composure gives rise to his first endeavors, in which he attempts to regain his sense of stability by seeing himself as others see him, or, in Pirandello's characteristic complement to Paleari's previous formulation ("sentirsi vivere"), by seeing himself live ("vedersi vivere"). But Vitangelo finds that this is impossible for the reasons that, at least in Pirandello's dialectics, "seeing" is akin to knowledge and knowledge remains on the side of stasis, or "forma," whereas "living" is akin to motion (i.e., flux, change), or in the earlier Pirandellian formulation "vita," and that even though the two sides of the dialectic can and do mix, they cannot be resolved. In a recapitulation and extension of Paleari's laments to Mattia Pascal, Moscarda is condemned to feeling (i.e., sensing) himself live without ever seeing (i.e., knowing) himself live. Moscarda can, of course, look in the mirror and see himself, but in the very instant in which he becomes conscious of doing so—and this consciousness is necessary for Pirandellian self-knowledge—his image becomes that of an other, with the result that he can only see the other live, not the self. Moscarda's first self-conscious gaze in the mirror, like Mattia's though even more clearly, thus represents his fall into the seemingly endless subtleties of Pirandellian dialectics. In the course of the subsequent series of humorous encounters with the other in the mirror, Moscarda comes to understand the difficulty of the task that he has begun.

Vitangelo's opening sense of instability in regard to his personal identity is complemented, in book 3, by his discovery of the instability of his professional identity. Once again, Dida plays an important part in this discovery, though perhaps an innocent one, since she confirms precisely what he has begun to fear: that in his *piccolo borghese* role of banker, which he inherited from his father and has always considered his profession, and from which, quite understandably, he has taken his identity in society, he is regarded by others not as "banchiere" but as "usurajo" and by Dida herself as a cuddly but feckless idler, "uno stupido" (794–95; 100–101). Intervening in the story between these two discoveries—one concerning Moscarda's identity in a personal sense, the other in a social sense—is an extended consideration of an institution that is both personal and social, language itself.

The questioning of the nature and validity of language includes consideration of the functions of "titles" (such as banker, usurer, and later criminal) and the workings of naming (e.g., Vitangelo/Gengè, Moscarda/Mosca, the unfortunately named "Signor Porcu"), both of which were put in question in an implicit fashion during the course of *Il fu Mattia Pascal*. But once more the investigation in *Uno, nessuno e centomila* goes much further, including open consideration of the fundamental units of language, words themselves. The problem, here as elsewhere in Pirandello's work of this period, arises from the disjunction between the personal aspects of individual *intention* and the social matrices of linguistic *communication*. In order to make this point, the narrator indulges in a hypothetical "conversation":

> Dopo una buona oretta di conversazione, ci siamo intesi perfettamente.
>   Domani mi venite con le mani in faccia, gridando:
>   "Ma come? Che avete inteso? Non mi avevate detto così e così?"
>   Così e così, perfettamente. Ma il guajo è che voi, caro, non saprete mai, né io vi potrò mai comunicare come si traduca in me quello che voi mi dite. Non avete parlato turco, no. Abbiamo usato, io e voi la stessa lingua, le stesse parole. Ma che colpa abbiamo, io e voi, se le parole, per sé, sono vuote? Vuote, caro mio. E voi le riempite del senso vostro, nel dirmele; e io nell'accoglierle, le riempio del senso mio. Abbiamo creduto d'intenderci; non ci siamo intesi affatto. (769)

After something like a good hour of conversation, we understand each other perfectly.

> The next day you come to me with your hands to your face yelling:
> "But what's this? What did you understand? Didn't you tell me thus and so?"
> Thus and so, yes, exactly. The trouble is that you, my friend, will never know, nor shall I ever be able to communicate to you, the way in which what you say to me is translated inside me. You were not speaking Turkish, certainly not. We both used the same language, the same words. But is it our fault, yours and mine, if words, in and of themselves, are empty? Empty, my friend. You fill them with your meaning as you speak them to me, while I, taking them in, inevitably fill them with my own. We thought that we understood each other; we did not understand each other at all. (59–60)

The view of words as empty containers, the senses of which are filled in by each individual speaker or hearer (with the logical result that their meaning in social communication will never correspond perfectly with individual intention and understanding, or if so only by chance), is in fact an extension of the view of individuals expressed by Vitangelo in the midst of his early discoveries. Indeed, it is in the course of his willful self-decomposition of himself as an individual that he comes upon the problem of the individual in society and, so, upon that of language as interpersonal expression of individual intent. Vitangelo concludes that if he is to locate some stable *point de repère* amidst this disconcerting morass of relativism, he must investigate his background and his roots, which have contributed to his own image in social as well as in personal terms. But his investigation into his personal background and his familial history, which he terms the "condizioni" of his life, provides no solace. Over some of these "conditions"—his birth, station in life, and "profession"—he has had no control, and even the ones that he can control remain inevitably open to (mis)interpretation by others. Even after his investigations, his *image* continues to be just as empty as any word, to be filled with sense by everyone who perceives him. If anything, as long as he remains within the social system, which, like language, is an established system beyond the control of any individual constituent, such conditions lead only to the social and personal confusions of the type "banchiere" = "usurajo." The "roots" of his past, like those of language, are, in *Uno, nessuno e centomila*, true etymologies; but merely examining the linguistic and human *etymon*, within its given system of historical relationships, is insufficient to change the overriding *logos* in either a personal or a social sense.

In part, Vitangelo's personal and social difficulties in these early and middle sections of the novel can be understood to result from the continuing inadequation of the Pirandellian opposition, *vita* and *forma*. It is apparent from the start that Vitangelo's project entails an investigation of his life in terms of the various forms it assumes for himself and for others. As he says early in the narrative, however, "Purtroppo non avevo mai saputo dare una qualche forma alla mia vita" (780; "Unfortunately, I had never been able to give any sort of form to my life," 78). At first, Vitangelo approaches this particular self-knowledge with humor and a measure of lucidity. But his most lucid moments, perhaps not surprisingly given the context of his project, are those in which he sees his madness reflected most clearly—when he sees the inevitable multiplicity of his being and his inability to control or even to gauge its endless avatars—or, as Vitangelo himself describes it, "la coscienza della pazzia, fresca e chiara, signori, fresca e chiara come una mattinata d'aprile, e lucida e precisa come uno specchio" (813; "the consciousness of madness, as clear and fresh, my friends, as clear and fresh as an April morning, and as lucid and precise as a mirror," 130). As the story proceeds, moreover, Vitangelo's humor at the complexity of this situation, along with the comic effects of the early narration, gives over to despair. Vitangelo's initially good-natured curiosity, the desire to see himself as others see him, is succeeded in the story's later sections by his repugnance at seeing himself being watched by anyone, which is to say, seeing his vital spirit being given a *form* by anyone ("Io non posso più vedermi guardato," 842; "I cannot stand being looked at anymore," 173). Finally, this repugnance results in his horror at feeling his being enclosed in the "prison" of any form whatever (868; 215). In the end, for Pirandello as for Lacan and even Narcissus, the perfect reflection means not only the fascination of the loss of identity, of losing the self within the other, but also the horror of totally fixed identity, and so of the trap of ultimate stasis, or death.

The problems of the imbalance of "life" and "form" in *Uno, nessuno e centomila* are significant, moreover, for the constant (re)creation of the individual and social subject as well as for the creation of artistic forms. This importance is clearest in the narrator's extended discussion of the scandalous behavior of the local sculptor's assistant, Marco di Dio. The specifically artistic self-reflexivity of this portion of the narrative extends far beyond that of *Il fu Mattia Pascal*'s treatment of either the unexpectedly problematic "Portrait of Minerva" or the notations of the differences between the stoically classical and self-reflexively modern temperaments of the *Oresteia* and of *Hamlet*. In *Uno, nessuno e centomila*, the discussion of art and life (and particularly of the unfortunate confusion between aesthetic form and the rules of social behavior) is crucial both for the thematics of artistic representation and for the development of the story's action. Indeed, the discussion is essential to an understanding of the novel, since it involves a critique not only of perception and understanding in human society but also of that other category so central to Pirandellian analysis, the individual and communal will.

Marco di Dio mistakes art's timeless, aesthetic representation of life for life itself—immediate and real—and in so doing alarms the young boy (the model in the unwitting sculptor's rendition of the classical grouping "Satiro e fanciullo") and offends the moral sense of everyone in the upright community of Richieri (809; 123–24). By confusing the realms of art and life, Marco di Dio finds himself caught in a crime against society. This is the townspeople's judgment of his act, since they consider his violation of the moral code from an external perspective. The narrator, however, in presenting Marco's deed and its motivation from within, comes to a conclusion that is at least more complex than that of society, if not in fact contrary to it. Seen from within, the momentary passion that permits the previously dormant unconscious beast to dominate Marco di Dio is not only an attribute of bestiality but also one of humanity. That is, all mankind is made up of an infinite play of often unconscious desires, some of them laudable and some not. The unity of the individual, which is necessarily posited by society's code of moral comportment, is a convenient fiction that covers over the real multiplicity lying at the very core of the Pirandellian subject.

This multiplicity is distinctly emphasized by the narrator, who adduces the examples of the Christian saints and of Julius Caesar to prove the point that far from being the *opposite* of humanity, bestial drives are an *integral* part of human beings (this is reminiscent of the polemics of contemporary psychoanalysis, with which Pirandello had a close though uneasy relationship). When the saints, for example, experienced temptations that were far from saintly, as even the most expurgated versions of their lives insist that they did, their temptations were attributed to demons. Their saintliness was demonstrated by their resistance to such temptations, but Pirandello's point is that far from representing external threats, these stories of Christian heroism portray what are actually internal desires. In terms of Marco's behavior, the expression of his desire is considered antisocial, but if that is the case, then what are we to make of the aberrant behavior of such an exemplary figure as the great Caesar? If he is to be regarded as truly himself only when he acted as an auhoritative, self-controlled sovereign beyond reproach—and not, for example, when he became intimately involved with Nicomedes, king of Bithynia—then our view of Caesar is a false one. No matter how pleasing it may be to our sense of moral comportment, the conception of "Caesar" as "uno"—as the name by which we designate an exemplary leader and *only* that—substitutes the lie of moral identity for the truth of inevitable multiplicity. As the narrator puts it:

> Il guajo è questo, sempre, signori: che dovevano tutti quanti esser chiamati con quel nome solo di Giulio Cesare, e che in un solo corpo di sesso maschile dovevano coabitare tanti e anche una femmina; la quale, volendo esser femmina e non trovandone il modo in quel corpo maschile, dove e come poté, innaturalmente lo fu, e impudicissima e anche più volte recidiva. (810)

> The difficulty, as always, is this, my friends: that each and every one of them had to be called by the single name of Julius Caesar, and that in a single body of masculine sex so many had to live together, including a woman, who, wanting to be a woman and not finding the way to do so in that masculine body, did the best she could, and even though unnaturally, she succeeded, shamelessly and repeatedly. (125–26)

Even though the lecherous satyr within Marco di Dio escaped only once, amidst the sultriness of the summer's afternoon, with his imagination excited and confused by his master's art, his condemnation in the eyes of society is not temporary but lasting. He is branded forever as a result of that momentary act, despite the fact that he subsequently takes a wife, with whom he makes preparations for their imminent departure for England (always, however, delayed) and even takes up the study of English, walking around town reciting, together with her, "'Is Jane a happy child?' 'Yes, Jane is a happy child.'" In fact, Vitangelo's father was the only one who treated the two of them with any respect whatever, listening to their troubles and lending them money (for which treatment, in light of the inexplicable difference between his behavior toward them and the town's communal condemnation, they first distrusted and later hated him, with a ferocity eventually turned on Vitangelo himself as his father's heir). Because of this close if strange relationship, Vitangelo decides to experiment further with the couple's reactions, giving them their house free of charge along with the sum of ten thousand *lire* so that Marco can install and equip an inventor's laboratory for himself.

In the plot of the novel, Marco di Dio thus assumes a central part in Vitangelo's project of social suicide, since as a result of this "donazione" everyone in town thinks that Vitangelo has lost his head as a usurer, as a banker, *and* as a citizen. In terms of the thematics of the narrative's treatment of Marco's behavior, moreover, there is another aspect that at first seems secondary but that returns, later on in the story, with obvious importance. This aspect is not restricted to knowledge, desire, or action alone, but, rather, includes all of them together, which is to say, it is a matter of will. In the text's description of Marco di Dio's bestial act, the individual is no longer presented as an empty void regarded from without but rather as a boiling caldron of desires seen from within. As is also true in the text's consideration of the constantly shifting "identity" of the individual perceived from necessarily multiple external perspectives, the concept to be emphasized from this internal perspective is once again the Pirandellian dialectic of stability/instability, but now in an expanded context.

From the beginning of the novel, with Vitangelo's fall into the knowledge of the multiplicity and contingency of his very being, he has desired somehow to reestablish his prelapsarian sense of himself as one, as "uno." His "donazione" to Marco di Dio, with its resultant contradiction of the title of usurer, was intended as a step in this direction. Vitangelo's subsequent attempt at dissolving the entire bank carries him further along this line, but he is temporarily blocked by Quantorzo's demonstration at the end of book 5 that the bank is not, strictly speaking, Vitangelo's alone but instead belongs to and depends on other individuals and groups. In response to Quantorzo's objections, Vitangelo erupts in a violent manifestation of his internal desires: "So un corno io di queste cose! So che voglio, voglio capisci? voglio ritirare i miei denari, e basta così!" (856; "I don't know anything about these things! I just know that I want to, I want to, understand? I want to withdraw my money, and that's all there is to it!" 196). The thrice-repeated volley ("scarica") of "I want" reduces Quantorzo to a posture of supplication, but this is not enough for Vitangelo. His intention is not to threaten or scare others with what they take to be his madness, but to destroy his "identity" as (for Quantorzo) a usurer and as (for Dida) "Gengè." However, since they continue to implore him in the very same terms as before, he again explodes in fury and walks out of the room: "Finiscila [Dida], col tuo Gengè che non sono io, non sono io, non sono io! Basta con codesta marionetta! Voglio quello che voglio; e come voglio sarà fatto!" (858; "Cut that out, [Dida], with your Gengè. That's not me, that's not me, that's not me! Enough of that silly marionette! I want what I want; and what I want will be done!" 198).

As a result of this second thrice-repeated (and ironically puppetlike) outburst, Vitangelo begins to regain the sense of himself as "one," as a unified subject, master of his will and capable of using it to affect others in a meaningful way. This affirmation of individual will, moreover, goes along with the sentiment of internal stability amidst the now irrevocably unstable world. At the beginning of the narrative's subsequent section, he says:

> Diventavo "uno."
> Io.
> Io che ora mi *volevo* così.
> Io che ora mi *sentivo* così.
> Finalmente!
> Non più usurajo (basta con quella banca!): e non più Gengè (basta con quella marionetta!). (859, my italics)

> I was becoming "one."
> I.
> I who now *willed* myself thus.
> I who now *felt* [sensed] myself thus.
> At last!
> No longer a usurer (enough of that bank!): and no longer Gengè (enough of that marionette!). (202, my italics)

The multiplicity and contingency of Vitangelo's being are thus countered by his violent reassertion of his unity and freedom in a moment of willful action. In this scene, "life" takes over and asserts its force and the transcendent singleness of purpose of its drive ("Vita/angelo"). But like the earthly presence of angels, the assertion itself is necessarily fleeting. Moscarda has the internal sentiment of the unity of his being—similar to the sentiment that he terms in book 7 the "God within" and similar too, in part ironically, to the momentary internal sentiment of Marco di

Dio—but for Vitangelo, this unity cannot last. As he becomes "one" and knows this unity, life hardens into unified form and, so, becomes subject once more to all the winds of time and all the vagaries of perception—both the perceptions of Vitangelo himself and those of others. As this process unfolds, it becomes apparent that Vitangelo is no more truly free than Mattia Pascal had been. The later novel's two differing views of the subject—as empty counter and as driving force—simply do not jibe in the world of men, at least as that world is constituted up to the novel's concluding paragraphs.

In the course of the story, moreover, Vitangelo's willful assertion of unified intent in action demonstrates still another worldly failing: it simply does not work. In the end, Quantorzo, Firbo, and the bank's other officers and associates win out, in part because of Vitangelo's debacle with Anna Rosa (and the court's consequent judgment against him) and in part because the "conditions" upon which society depends cannot be effectively overthrown by the violent act of any individual, no matter how forceful or serious such an act may be. As had been clear, too, by the end of *Il fu Mattia Pascal*, once the umorista has learned that the individual subject, as "uno," is a metaphor and only that, he can no longer accept society's modus vivendi of taking metaphorical falsehood as truth. In *Uno, nessuno e centomila*, moreover, the metaphor of the individual subject is seen to be no different in this regard from those of language or of the broader "constructions" of social and religious institutions. The only real options for Vitangelo would thus appear to be the destruction of society and/or of the individual-social relationship, but established society, as Vitangelo's failures with the bank demonstrate, will not accept either of these solutions. Nor is there any workable way, within society, to bring together Vitangelo's conception of the "empty" form of the individual with his growing awareness of the active force of vital life. As long as he remains within the social order as it is constituted at present, both Vitangelo's project and his underlying hopes are blocked at every turn.

Given this state of affairs, the novel's concluding "resolution" is at least comprehensible if not entirely convincing. Following Vitangelo's mix-ups, setbacks, and, at best, half-successes with Anna Rosa, the judiciary, and even the Church, he ends up withdrawing from the life of the town and retreating to a hospice in the countryside. He has seen, at last, that any solution to his dilemmas must come from outside the actual social system, since it is that system itself which both creates and depends on such dilemmas. His life at the hospice represents an attempt to reconcile the opposing claims of *vita* and *forma* in favor of *vita* by externalizing internal subjective consciousness into the disunified flux of objective "reality." He describes this new life in the book's final paragraphs:

> L'ospizio sorge in campagna, in un luogo amenissimo. Io esco ogni mattina, all'alba, perché ora voglio serbare lo spirito così, fresco d'alba. . . . E l'aria è nuova. E tutto, attimo per attimo, è com'è, che s'avviva per apparire. Volto subito gli occhi per non vedere più nulla fermarsi nella sua apparenza e morire. Così soltanto io posso vivere, ormai. Rinascere attimo per attimo. Impedire che il pensiero si metta in me di nuovo a lavorare, e dentro mi rifaccia il vuoto delle vane costruzioni.
> La città è lontana. Me ne giunge, a volte, nella calma del vespro, il suono delle campane. Ma ora quelle campane le odo non più dentro di me, ma fuori, per sé sonare, che forse ne fremono di gioia nella loro cavità ronzante, in un bel cielo azzurro pieno di sole caldo tra lo stridìo delle rondini o nel vento nuvoloso, pesanti e così alte sui campanili aerei. Pensare alla morte, pregare. C'è pure chi ha ancora questo bisogno, e se ne fanno voce le campane. Io non l'ho più questo bisogno, perché muojo ogni attimo, io, e rinasco nuovo e senza ricordi: vivo e intero, non più in me, ma in ogni cosa fuori. (901–2)

The hospice stands in the open country, in a very pleasant place. I come out every morning at daybreak, for the reason that I wish thus to preserve my soul, with all the freshness of dawn. . . . And the air is fresh. And everything, from second to second, is as it is, revived to take on appearance. I turn my eyes quickly in order not to see again anything come to a halt in its appearance and die. Only in this way can I go on living from now on. Being reborn second by second. Seeing to it that thought does not once more start working in me and refashion in me the void that goes with empty constructions.
 The city is far away. There comes to me occasionally, upon the vesper calm, the sound of its bells. I, however, no longer hear those bells within me, but without, ringing for themselves and perhaps trembling with joy in their resounding cavities, in a beautiful blue sky filled with a warm sun, amidst the twittering of sparrows or the cloudy winds so high and deep, in their aerial

bell towers. To think of death, to pray. Certainly there are people who still have this need, and it is to their needs that the bells give voice. I no longer have any such need, for the reason that I am dying every instant, and being born anew, without memories: alive and whole, no longer within myself, but now in everything without. (267–68)

The narrator's life in the country takes place in a continually shifting present, in which he identifies himself with the seemingly objective existence of external nature. This way of life depends on a pair of related assumptions and procedures: the narrator assumes that it is possible to deny internal, subjective stasis in favor of external, objective flux, and he abandons the continuity of connected time and belief (memories, prayer, death) for the spontaneity of life lived in constant rebirth, moment by moment, free from the fixed forms of intellectual constructs and social "conditions." Recast in the concepts of current linguistics and psychoanalysis, this is a distinction between the stable, condensed unity of metaphor and the disjunctive displacement of metonymy, and, at least in appearance, at the expense of metaphor in favor of metonymy.

Pirandello himself includes considerations both of social life and of language in the third of the final chapter's five paragraphs, which directly precedes the two cited above. Before that, however, in the chapter's opening, he is at pains to point out the contrast between Vitangelo's perspective and the hilarity of the onlookers and participants in court at the sight of his institutional uniform, made up of beret, clogs, and turquoise smock—which is, in short, their reaction to the external appearance of this new Vitangelo Moscarda. In these same paragraphs, the narrator discusses the ultimate fruits of his project, all of which differ sharply from the townspeople's continuing beliefs and practices. As a result of his most recent experiences he has now given up on all unified understanding, images, or external reflections of the self ("Non mi sono più guardato in uno specchio, e non mi passa neppure per il capo di voler sapere che cosa sia avvenuto della mia faccia e di tutto il mio aspetto," 900; "I have not looked in a mirror since then, and it doesn't even enter my head to want to know what has become of my face and the rest of my appearance," 266). Moreover, he has seemingly forsaken any further attempt to fix individual essences by means of communally understood names, and he deprecates others for their need to continue in the folly of such illusions.

At first glance this entire ending chapter, entitled, appropriately enough, "Non conclude," seems the fitting if extreme consequence of Vitangelo's actions and of his meditations on the two basic units with which the narrative has been engaged all along, words and individuals. As we have seen, the examination of these two units has led to a critique of the broader systems of relations in which they function, which is to say, language and society. Underlying the entire project—as should be clear from the novel's opening, with Vitangelo/Gengè standing before the mirror of his life and discovering the multiplicity of his being by means of his wife's offhand remark—is a Pirandellian critique of the workings of human perception and the logic of belief. Up until the final three paragraphs of the narrative, it seems as though this critique merely extends, though in more systematic and direct fashion, the discoveries and conclusions of *Il fu Mattia Pascal*, while giving special weight to Mattia's half of the ending opposition between his understanding of the purport of his "story" and Don Eligio's. The middle paragraph of *Uno, nessuno e centomila*'s concluding chapter, however, takes the step that the earlier narrative could not or would not take. In the often discussed central passage, the narrator announces his break with established society, which means, for him, his break with the regulated metaphors for life that necessarily depend on the deceptions of form. Once again, though more succinctly than before, he frames his announcement in terms of the functions of naming and the status of the individual subject:

> Nessun nome. Nessun ricordo oggi del nome di jeri; del nome d'oggi, domani. Se il nome è la cosa; se un nome è in noi il concetto d'ogni cosa posta fuori di noi; e senza nome non si ha il concetto, e la cosa resta in noi come cieca, non distinta e non definita; ebbene, questo che portai tra gli uomini ciascuno lo incida, epigrafe funeraria, sulla fronte di quella immagine con cui gli apparvi, e la lasci in pace e non ne parli più. Non è altro che questo, epigrafe funeraria, un nome. Conviene ai morti. A chi ha concluso. Io sono vivo e non concludo. La vita non conclude. E non sa di nomi, la vita. Quest'albero, respiro trèmulo di foglie nuove. Sono quest'albero. Albero, nuvola; domani libro o vento: il libro che leggo, il vento che bevo. Tutto fuori, vagabondo. (901)

> No name. No memory today of yesterday's name; of today's name tomorrow. If the name is the thing, if a name in us is the con-

cept of everything that is situated outside of us, and without a name there is no concept, and the thing remains blindly indistinct and undefined within us, very well, then, let everyone take that name which I once bore and engrave it as an epitaph on the brow of that image of me that they beheld; let them leave it there in peace and not speak of it again. For a name is no more than that, an epitaph. Something befitting the dead. One who has reached a conclusion. I am alive, and I reach no conclusion. Life knows no conclusion. Nor does it know anything of names. This tree, the tremulous breathing of new leaves. I am this tree. Tree, cloud; tomorrow, book or breeze: the book that I read, the breeze that I drink in. Living wholly without, a vagabond. (267)

In this crucial passage, names are rejected as externally fixed constructs, static, unchanging, and therefore illusory in their relation to what they supposedly name, which, in this context, is taken to be ever-shifting, vital, internal life. In other words, by establishing identity, names impose "objective" form on "subjective" life at the expense of life itself. Constructions, intellectual concepts, conclusions, even memory, as an imposition of fixed form on the vital fluidity of thought, are all to be eschewed in the narrator's new mode of being. The associations among form, stasis (along with abstractly conceptual or connected time), linguistic constructs, social organization, and death, all of which had been implicit in earlier sections of the novel, are here made crystal clear. At the same time, the opposing elements of Pirandellian thought—vitality, flux (along with purely linear or constantly changing time), linguistic spontaneity, freedom, and life—are valued as the primary characteristics of the narrator's new existence. Far from being the beginning of rational self-reflection, this new life represents, or perhaps it should be said, embodies, its end, in what now amounts to a continual flight from the sort of dualistic *self-consciousness* with which the narrative began.

In one sense, this position does seem to provide a solution to Vitangelo's problems, by permitting him to exercise his will in taking the step that Mattia Pascal had taken only by chance. It should be asked, however, whether this new and more radical movement outside society is really as convincing as Vitangelo wants it to sound. This is an important question, since it has implications both for the status of the individual subject in this "new" existence and for that of his own discourse, which, after all, is, at this point in the narrative, the novel itself. We might begin an approach to this question by noting that at the end of the conclusion's central paragraph, in the course of describing the externalization of his vital energy into the natural world around him, the narrator mentions one object that is *not* natural: "Sono quest'albero. Albero, nuvola; domani libro o vento: il libro che leggo, il vento che bevo" ("I am this tree. Tree, cloud; tomorrow book or breeze: the book that I read, the breeze that I drink in").

Because of the inclusion of this patently nonnatural artifact, it is clear that the narrator's existence does not represent merely a Leopardian immersion in the "infinity" of nature (as Vitangelo's "dolcissima angoscia," or "sweetish anguish," at his perception of the countryside's "così smemorata lontananza" near the beginning of chapter 2 of this concluding book had seemed initially to suggest). Rather, the narrator's new mode of perception and experience includes absorption into all external phenomena, natural or factitious, and extends even to the experience of literary products. At the same time, this strangely self-reflexive literary notation serves to remind us, as readers and participants, that reading is not the only literary activity with which we are dealing here. The narrator is in the act of narrating his own story. In these concluding paragraphs he shifts into the present tense, indicating his current point of view. That he could *read* a book, as an external object into which he could pour his subjective being in this new sort of "vagabondage," is probably beyond dispute. But—since the narrator himself implies the question, we might as well ask it—how could he ever *write* one, and especially such a unified aesthetic product as a novel? Now it is true that *Uno, nessuno e centomila* demonstrates, particularly in the opening chapters, ample measures of humor, anxiety, and facetious commentary, all of which—when combined with the novel's essayistic presentation, its occasional lack of interest in plot, and the direct addresses and asides to the reader (far more disruptive in their effects than the "editor's" footnote by Don Eligio in *Il fu Mattia Pascal*)—serve repeatedly to break up the novelistic order of presentation and thus contribute to the sort of dizzy spontaneity of the story's narration. But the other side can be argued at least as easily. The methodical division of the novel into eight "books," each with internally if not always logically subdivided and ordered chapters, along with the pretense in broad terms of a more or less unified plot (i.e., social suicide), replete with subplots and an openly self-identifying first-person narrator, all contribute to the creation of an artifact that seems too unified and, in the traditional sense of narrative fiction, too meaningful—in short, simply too artful—to be produced by the narrator as he presents himself at the novel's conclusion (which is, it should be stressed again, the condition in which the narrator, in retrospective first-person narration, tells his story). Therefore, the odd effect of the implicitly self-reflective comment on books amidst the novel's polemically anti-reflective conclusion is to make us ask the question that first-person narration seems to answer on its face but that, in this example, no understanding of destiny and will, desire and intent, emotion and logic, is sufficient to resolve: Who (the devil) speaks?

The question—in this context even more so than at the end of *Il fu Mattia Pascal*—is, of course, asked in vain. At the conclusion of *Il fu Mattia Pascal*, the narrator is not, it is true, sure of the purport of his "story." But the recitation of a tale to the end of discovering its meaning is one of the many traditional ploys in the organization and production of narrative fiction. Mattia's ambivalence about the meaning of his experience does in fact run much deeper than the use of such a ploy generally indicates, but it is obvious that, once again, *Uno, nessuno e centomila* goes further still. This was Pirandello's last novel. It is not extreme to say that, with it, he attempted to abandon definitively both the old Romantic notion of the individual subject *as* individual and the traditional nineteenth-century assumptions of the organic development of character and plot in first-person fiction. Pirandello does this in part by adopting within the narrative the linear progression of a dramatic soliloquy—in which it may appear that the role of the fiction's narrator/creator, at least in the guise of logical organizer, is no longer crucial—as opposed to a traditionally "novelistic" and logically unified frame. This is an advance on the discoveries and techniques of the early narratives and even on the "notebook" format of *Serafino Gubbio*. Whereas the narrator of *Il fu Mattia Pascal* had remained within the system of his text both as unwitting object and as demystified (though not all-knowing) speaking subject, the narrator of *Uno, nessuno e centomila* at the end of his story deserts the logic of his narrative system altogether, thus leaving the reader, who has participated over the course of the entire process, with a question that, it seems, cannot even be approached in a logical or systematic fashion, much less answered. What the earlier story had put in doubt—the traditional beliefs about the nature of human perception and understanding and the means of re-presenting that worldly experience in the novel—the later one, in its concluding paragraphs, seems to abolish.

But perhaps this critique of the novel's inconsistencies—which reflect *Uno, nessuno e centomila*'s fundamental and irresolvable disjunction between the subject and the object of its own narration—is, in one sense, excessive. Is it not possible, it should be asked, to imagine *a state of mind in which the speaker would consider the self as totally and unalterably other*, in the process taking the internal memory of the subject as the external story of the object (without regard to the normal rules of cause and effect and the consequent emotional responses) and would then narrate this memory, this life, with apparent spontaneity, as the "life" of an other? The answer to this question—which is psychosis—may not provide a resolution to the novel's basic ambiguity, but it does lead us, if by a somewhat indirect path, back from the narrative's concluding *vertige* to our own beginning, to the Lacanian epigraph as well as to the shock to traditional Italian culture and literature both caused by and evinced in Pirandello's work.

This is, of course, another way of saying that even though Pirandello's earlier work sets about "decomposing" the metaphors on which the notions of the self and of society depend, such decomposition alone is no longer enough in Pirandello's later work. Attempts to protect the notion of the unified subject by isolating the individual *from society without making any other adjustments*—such as Vitangelo's Narcissian endeavors to be "alone" in book 1—are doomed to failure from the outset. Early in his career, Pirandello had already seen the alienation pervasive in contemporary society, but by the time of his last novel, he also saw that simple isolation, in the form of the subject alone with his reflection in the mirror, leads not to freedom but to death. Nevertheless, in the terms of the novel, moving back into society gives rise to the paranoia and now internalized alienation that goes along with such a move, that is, with the shift from the self-consciously doubled but isolated "specular" ego back into a fully social context (as is so apparent, too, at the conclusion of *Enrico IV*). If it is ultimately self-defeating, therefore, to change the naive social subject—Vitangelo as Gengè—into a knowledgeable but isolated individual—"Moscarda . . . Moscarda . . . Moscarda" before the mirror in book 3—so is it equally pointless to carry out, however methodically, the social "suicide" of the individual as long as that individual remains *within* society. Thus, by the 1920s, Pirandello had seen (like the Futurists, but with markedly different conclusions) that the next step in his overall project was unavoidable: to conceive of changing not only the individual or the relation between the individual and society but also society itself. The outcome of this realization is clearest in the concluding section of *Uno, nessuno e centomila*, in the description of life at the hospice, but Pirandello had been proceeding toward it since at least as early as the composition of *Il fu Mattia Pascal*. This conclusion eventually leads to the overtly socially oriented plays of the late twenties and thirties, all of which are concerned with portraying the nature of human life and art and the relation between individuals in some sort of a society—sometimes a patently mythic one, sometimes a merely "fantastical" one—that would be different from the contemporary life of the Italian twenties and thirties, different, that is, from the repression and anxieties of political and social life under either supposedly liberal industrial capitalism or Fascism.[20]

This is not to say that any of these "solutions" are successful in terms of art or life. The later ones tend to leave contemporary society further and further behind, though they do not demonstrate any clear, concrete way of attaining their goal of another type of world. In *Uno, nessuno e centomila*, however, the problem is somewhat different from that in the later plays. Although the novel's ending way of life seems radically strange, even psychotic, it is, in a sense, not radical enough. Rather than finally relinquishing the categories of his previous view of individual and social life in the contemporary world, Pirandello simply splits the dialectics of *vita/forma* in half, forsaking the latter and its ramifications (stasis, internal reflection, unity, duration, the constructs of contemporary society itself, and the like) and espousing the former in the purest sense possible. In part, this procedure leads to the fundamental ambiguity underlying the relation of the novel's "speaker" to the creation of his own discourse; but it also means, despite the conclusion's appearance of novelty, that the dialectics underlying Pirandello's narrative really have not changed. No matter how far Pirandello's modernist vitalism has progressed in his narrative, at this stage it still has not made the radical break with his earlier dualistic thought and work that will be evident in such later, increasingly "mythic" dramas as *La nuova colonia* (1928), *Lazzaro* (1929), *La favola del figlio cambiato* (1933), and his last play, *I giganti della montagna* (performed posthumously in 1937). Nevertheless, by staying within these limits, the relentlessly self-conscious critique of human perception and understanding carried out in *Uno, nessuno e centomila* ties it, along with Pirandello's other major novels (despite the recurring D'Annunzian echoes), to the techniques and interests of the self-involved psychological realism of the 1920s and 1930s, and perhaps most directly to Italo Svevo's great psychological novel, *La coscienza di Zeno*.[21]

FIVE

The Genre of Literary Confession and the Mode of Psychological Realism

The Self-consciousness of *Zeno*

> "So you got well, hah."
> "I got busy. . . . Maybe that's the same thing."
> William Faulkner, *The Hamlet*, bk. 1, ch. 3

Italo Svevo's novels are all intimately concerned with the detailed portrayal of their central character's attitudes, desires, and reactions. Because of Svevo's preoccupation with such topics as mental health (as opposed to mental aberration), individual motivation, and human self-perception over time, his narratives demonstrate many of the same preoccupations as do the works of Pirandello and, to a somewhat lesser degree, the contemporaneous novels of Massimo Bontempelli. Svevo's novels are of particular interest because of the ways in which they combine the basic effects of literary self-consciousness with those of psychological self-consciousness. This is especially true of *La coscienza di Zeno* (1923; *The Confessions of Zeno*), written in the period of the diffusion of Freudian psychoanalysis just after World War I. But it is also true, at least to an extent, of the two fin de siècle novels that preceded Svevo's masterpiece in the mode of psychological realism, *Una vita* (1892; *A Life*) and *Senilità* (1898; *As a Man Grows Older*).[1]

Una vita opens with a letter from Alfonso, the main character, to his beloved mother, in which Alfonso describes his unhappiness with his employment (as a clerk in the correspondence office of a bank) and expresses his desire to return home, to be free once again to read the volumes of his poets "all'ombra delle quercie" (134; "in the shade of the oaks"). The saccharine, childish, yet obviously sincere tone of this opening letter contrasts sharply with the cold, impersonal, and evasive communication that both concludes the narrative and confirms Alfonso's death by suicide. But neither Svevo's use of the contrastive framing device of the implicitly paired letters nor Alfonso's literary predilections constitute the most obviously self-reflective aspect of the narrative as literature, which is instead the collaborative project undertaken by Alfonso and the youthful object of his desires, Annetta (who is also the daughter of the bank's founder). Their joint project is nothing other than the writing of a novel. The uncertain progress of this literary enterprise, in its inception, complications, and eventual abandonment, parallels the progress of the relationship between the two characters even as it provides the material reason for their regular meetings. Although the narrative of *Una vita* is often flat and listless, the literary collaboration at its center serves to focus the psychological development of the proudly obstinate yet helpless main character in a doubly revealing "literary" light.

This combination of psychological and literary reflection recurs in *Senilità*, though in the later novel these two factors are more successfully integrated, since they function together in terms of both character development and thematics. The central character is again a writer. As the narrator explains at the outset, Emilio Brentani (similar in part to Alfonso and to Svevo/Schmitz himself) has maintained two careers, one as a relatively insignificant clerk in an insurance office and the other as a novelist, having published a locally well-received first novel before settling into a state of literary inertia. Emilio's three most important continuing relationships in the story are those with his sister, Amalia; with his "amante," Angiolina; and with his sculptor friend, Balli, who also has had special relationships both as an artist and as a man with Amalia and with Angiolina. While the almost incestuously close relation between Emilio and Amalia is psychologically determinant in Emilio's life, and while his friendship with Balli provides a spur to his desires in terms of competition as well as *amicizia*, it is the relation with Angiolina that inspires, and at times hinders, his creative imagination as a writer.

His first novel, the writing of which had propelled him out of his inactivity following the death of his father, portrayed the relation between an ingenuous young man, modelled on Emilio himself, and a young woman drawn according to the literary mode of the times as "un misto di donna e di tigre" (525; "a mixture of woman and tigress"). Near the middle of *Senilità,* Emilio begins a new novel, though now he has a *real* model for his narrative: the woman from whom, he believes, he has separated himself in life only to re-create her in art:

> Riprese ora la penna e scrisse in una sola sera il primo capitolo di un romanzo. Trovava un nuovo indirizzo d'arte al quale volle conformarsi, e scrisse la verità. Raccontò il suo incontro con Angiolina, descrisse i propri sentimenti, —subito però quelli degli ultimi giorni—violenti e irosi, l'aspetto di Angiolina ch'egli vide al primo incontro guastato dall'animo basso e perverso, e infine il magnifico paesaggio che aveva contornato agli esordii il loro idillio. Stanco e annoiato, abbandonò il lavoro, contento di aver steso in una sola sera tutto un capitolo. (525–26)

> Now he took up his pen again, and in a single evening he wrote the first chapter of a novel. He was discovering a new direction to his art that he wanted to follow, and he wrote the truth. He related his encounter with Angiolina and described his own feelings—immediately, those of the most recent days—violent and angry, how the aspect of Angiolina that he had seen in their first encounter was ruined by her ignoble and perverse spirit, and finally the magnificent scenery that had surrounded their romance at its beginning. Tired and annoyed, he stopped working, happy to have hammered out an entire chapter in a single evening.

Emilio's partial disillusionment concerning Angiolina—which is just one more in a series of false starts and reversals concerning his evaluations of her character—provides the "truth" that is to be the new ground for his art. The next day, however, when he returns to carry his work forward, he is astounded to find not only that the male character is dissimilar to him, the supposedly "true" model, but that the woman is also very different from what he had intended ("'Incredibile!' mormorò. L'uomo non somigliava affatto a lui, la donna poi conservava qualche cosa della donnatigre del primo romanzo, ma non ne aveva la vita, il sangue"; "'Incredible!' he murmured. The man did not resemble him at all, while the woman retained something of the woman-tigress of the first novel, but without any of the life, the vitality").

Emilio's discovery of his failure to recapture the "truth" of life in his art leads to his further doubts: "Pensò che quella verità che aveva voluto raccontare era meno credibile dei sogni che anni prima aveva saputi gabellare per veri" ("He felt that the truth that he had wanted to narrate was less believable than the dreams that years before he had been able to pass off as true"). The result of Emilio's reflections regarding this crisis of representational language is his resumption of his literary silence. Even though Emilio tells himself that he will take up his work later on, perhaps even the next day, he does not do so. According to the narrator, Emilio simply does not feel strong enough to study his own failings and overcome them in literary expression.

Along with Emilio's inability to write, to express his desires and hopes through literary creation, comes his desire to see Angiolina again, just as their earlier separation had given rise to the composing of that ill-fated first chapter. This seesaw between relations experienced in life and relations re-created in art recurs at the end of the novel in a remarkable fashion. Indeed, even though Emilio's powers of observation are stressed on various occasions throughout the later sections of the narrative (particularly in chapter 11), only at the story's conclusion—after the seemingly sudden illness and tortured demise of Amalia and the definitive break between Emilio and Angiolina—are Emilio's perceptions again depicted specifically as those of an imaginative *literary* artist.[2]

Just prior to this conclusion, Emilio, now following the model of his new-found friend, Elena Chierici, attempts once more to renew his daily life and his relation to art. But he does so without success or pleasure, at least while he is still in thrall to his memory of Angiolina in its current form (592–93). When Angiolina scandalizes the city by running off with her latest lover, a married cashier employed at a local bank, Emilio's first reaction is pained surprise. Over time, however, her absence provides the condition in which Emilio can come to terms both with Amalia's death and with Angiolina's narcissistic refusal of him. He does this by retaining in his memory the physical beauty of Angiolina while endowing her with the moral qualities of his sister. The result of what the narrator terms this "strange metamorphosis" is a sort of psychological hagiography, in which Angiolina, contrary to every indication regarding her character in the novel itself, becomes the symbolic exemplar of the chaste ideal *and* the lover, a wondrously comforting *and* alluring *mater dolorosa:*

> Anni dopo egli s'incantò ad ammirare quel periodo della sua vita, il più importante, il più luminoso. . . . Nella sua mente di letterato ozioso, Angiolina subì una metamorfosi strana. Conservò inalterata la sua bellezza, ma acquistò anche tutte le qua-

lità d'Amalia che morì in lei una seconda volta. . . . Egli la vide dinanzi a sé come su un altare, la personificazione del pensiero e del dolore e l'amò sempre, se amore è ammirazione e desiderio. . . .

Quella figura divenne persino un simbolo. Ella guardava sempre dalla stessa parte, l'orizzante, l'avvenire. . . . Ella aspettava! L'immagine concretava il sogno ch'egli una volta aveva fatto accanto ad Angiolina e che la figlia del popolo non aveva compreso.

Quel simbolo alto, magnifico, si rianimava talvolta per ridivenire donna amante, sempre però donna triste e pensierosa. Sì! Angiolina pensa e piange! Pensa come se le fosse stato spiegato il segreto dell'universo e della propria esistenza; piange come se nel vasto mondo non avesse più trovato neppure un *Deo gratias* qualunque. (594–95)

Years afterwards he became enchanted with his admiration of that period of his life, its most important and its most luminous one. . . . In his mind, that of an idle man of letters, Angiolina underwent a strange metamorphosis. She conserved her beauty unaltered, but she also acquired all of the qualities of Amalia, who died in her another death. . . . He saw her before him as though placed on an altar, as the personification of thought and sorrow, and he loved her always, if love is admiration and desire. . . .

The figure itself became a symbol. She always looked in the same direction, towards the horizon, the future. . . . She awaited! The image embodied the dream that he had once had while he was next to Angiolina and that the child of the masses had not understood.

That great, magnificent symbol at times came to life again as a lover, but still remained sad and thoughtful. Yes! Angiolina reflects and weeps! She reflects as though the secret of the universe and of her own existence had been explained to her; she weeps as though in the entire world she could no longer find even the simplest *Deo gratias.*

It should not come as any surprise that Svevo's text does not stand behind this concluding vision, or that Svevo himself, as the cleverly versatile novelistic ironist, does not affirm the validity of Emilio's Romantically self-deluding psychological perspective, in which the character turns the failures of his past into the illusion of his present and the world's future through his idealized reflections.[3] The stubborn narcissism of Emilio's final vision—by means of which his own inertia, melancholy, and guilt are protectively enshrined on this D'Annunzian altar of his imagination—is implicitly criticized not only by its obvious lack of correspondence with the prior descriptions and events of the novel overall but also by details within the passage itself ("egli *s'incantò* . . . letterato *ozioso* . . . metamorfosi *strana* . . . *se* amore è ammirazione e desiderio . . . che la figlia del popolo *non aveva compreso*"; "he *became enchanted with* . . . *idle* man of letters . . . *strange* metamorphosis . . . *if* love is admiration and desire . . . that the child of the masses *had not understood*"). As is suggested here, in the self-enchantment of his old age, as an idle, bourgeois author, Emilio glories in the supposed nobility of his past by re-creating a Romantic image of love that includes admiration and desire but leaves out activity itself. In the process, he interprets his ex-lover and her class as a reflection of his own system of psychological traits and values, while the third-person narrator transposes the denials of the past into the overblown affirmations of the present ("Sì!") by switching into the present tense. It is fairly clear, at least in this passage, that Emilio is the one who has not "understood."

The distance from which the novelist regards this sort of hagiography on the part of his character finds further confirmation near the end of *La coscienza di Zeno*, in the later novel's treatment of similar reactions experienced by Ada after Guido's death and by Zeno in regard to his own childhood. But before we can approach the question of perception (and misperception) over time in Svevo's last and most complex novel, it is necessary to consider both the story's organization and its character in some detail. From the opening pages of *La coscienza di Zeno*, it is apparent that this novel is, if anything, even more concerned with psychological self-consciousness than either *Una vita* or *Senilità*. But that notwithstanding, it may also appear initially to be a less pertinent example of *literary* self-consciousness than the earlier two. Among other things, Zeno is a businessman and only that, rather than a part-time or a full-time fiction writer, and his reflections are therefore not usually concerned with artistic creation in any direct way. But even though it would be excessive to claim (as does Linda Hutcheon) that "*La coscienza di Zeno* is as much a discourse on literature and language" as examples of Italian "metafiction" of the

1960s and 1970s, it is nonetheless true that literary self-involvement is central to Svevo's last novel for the reason that it operates at the very deepest levels of the narrative's organization.[4]

The impetus for Zeno to write his autobiography, beginning with a historical analysis of his penchant for cigarettes, comes from his psychoanalyst, Doctor S., whose remarks open the novel. In the doctor's preface, in which he explains his reasons for publishing Zeno's manuscript (as a "vendetta" for Zeno's withdrawing from analysis), the psychoanalyst refers to the manuscript first as a "novella," or story, then as an "autobiografia," or autobiography, and finally as "queste memorie," or "these memoirs"; and he concludes by suggesting the potential utility of further psychoanalytic commentary on the manuscript's accumulation of "tante verità e bugie" ("so many truths and lies"). Towards the end of Zeno's own narration, however, the character has another word for his narrative: "confessioni," or confessions. This special type of autobiography, based on the established literary genre of the edited confession as well as on the contemporary discipline of psychoanalysis, gives Svevo a traditionally literary way to focus the novel's psychological realism.[5] In other words, the primary genre of the confession and the secondary play of editor and author provide Svevo with a pair of traditional narrative formats, each of which he recasts in a literary version of modern-day, psychoanalytic discourse. Zeno, in both literary and psychological terms, thus becomes an "osservatore" not so much of the world as of the self. Indeed, Zeno is in this regard both Svevo's best character/novelist, and the "author" of one of the most psychologically self-conscious narratives possible.

I should hasten to add, however, that even though psychological and literary self-consciousness are frequently interwoven in the late-nineteenth- and twentieth-century novel, in which the psychological development of the individual in the world of bourgeois society is often the common narrative denominator, these two sorts of self-consciousness are not necessarily the same thing. In *La coscienza di Zeno* as, for example, in Pirandello's *Il fu Mattia Pascal* (which also includes the background play of editor and first-person "author") the weight of the balance between psychological and literary self-consciousness falls on the side of psychology, which thus comes first in importance, and it does so much more obviously than in, to take another example from Pirandello, *Uno, nessuno e centomila*. Having said this much, however, we are further obliged to determine exactly what the psychological, or (to adopt the novel's term) the psychoanalytic, status of Zeno's "confession" really is.

As the critics who have recently considered the novel from the viewpoint of psychoanalysis have all perceived, the novel invites a certain analytical, if not to say skeptical, attitude towards Zeno's consistently first-person but far from unambiguous discourse. It does this in part by prefacing the narrative with the remarks by Doctor S., who, as we have noted, laments his inability to offer his further "commento" to his ex-patient on the mass of truths and lies accumulated in the following pages. The critique of the relation between representation and truth goes much further here than it had in Svevo's earlier novels. Zeno himself also puts in doubt the entire procedure of writing down his confessions by questioning the validity of standard Italian when written by someone whose native speech and thought patterns are Triestine, not Tuscan Italian. This plainly self-serving questioning extends, moreover, well past semantics or even grammar to include the selection, or the deletion, of the episodes to be narrated:[6]

> Il dottor presta una fede troppo grande anche a quelle mie benedette confessioni che non vuole restituirmi perché le riveda. Dio mio! Egli non studiò che la medicina e perciò ignora che cosa significhi scrivere in italiano per noi che parliamo e non sappiamo scrivere il dialetto. Una confessione in iscritto è sempre menzognera. Con ogni nostra parola toscana noi mentiamo. Se egli sapesse come raccontiamo con predilezione tutte le cose per le quali abbiamo pronta la frase e come evitiamo quelle che ci obbligherebbero di ricorrere al vocabolario! È proprio così che scegliamo dalla nostra vita gli episodi da notarsi. Si capisce come la nostra vita avrebbe tutt'altro aspetto se fosse detta nel nostro dialetto. (928; cf. 936–37)

> The doctor also attaches too much faith to those blessed confessions of mine, which he refuses to give back to me to look at again. My God! He has studied nothing but medicine and so has no idea what writing in Italian means for those of us who speak in dialect but do not know how to write it. A written confession is always untruthful. With every Tuscan word that we utter we lie. If only he knew how we tend to talk about things for which we have the words all ready and how we avoid those that would oblige us to look things up in the dictionary! That is precisely how we choose, from among all of the episodes in our life, the

ones to be related. Naturally our life would take on quite a different aspect if it were told in our own dialect. (368; cf. 377)

This passage is important in a general sense not only for its expression of linguistic self-consciousness (which follows on a series of considerations of the power of words extending throughout the narrative) but also for its expression of narrative self-consciousness, in its open consideration of the role that linguistic limitations play both in the selection of narrative events and in the veracity of narrative itself. But in terms of the immediate context of these remarks, their self-reflexive examination of the truth or falsity of narrative discourse reflects specifically on psychological revelations of the story's previous paragraphs, in which Zeno provides a brief literary and analytic account of what he considers psychoanalysis to be, declaring not only that he is "finished" with it ("L'ho finita con la psicanalisi," 927; 366) but also that he never needed it in the first place:

> La mia cura doveva essere finita perché la mia malattia era stata scoperta. Non era altra che quella diagnosticata a suo tempo dal defunto Sofocle sul povero Edipo: avevo amata mia madre e avrei voluto ammazzare mio padre.
> Né io m'arrabbiai! Incantato stetti a sentire. Era una malattia che mi elevava alla più alta nobiltà. . . . E non m'arrabbio neppure adesso che sono qui solo con la penna in mano. Ne rido di cuore. La miglior prova ch'io non ho avuta quella malattia risulta dal fatto che non ne sono guarito. . . . Io chiudo gli occhi e vedo subito puro, infantile, ingenuo, il mio amore per mia madre, il mio rispetto ed il grande mio affetto per mio padre. (928)

> By rights, I ought to have been cured, since my disease had been discovered. It turned out to be the very same one diagnosed long ago by Sophocles for Oedipus: I had been in love with my mother and wanted to kill my father.
> I didn't even get angry! I listened enchanted. It was a disease that elevated me to the highest nobility. . . . And I still do not feel angry, even now that I am here alone with pen in hand. Instead I can laugh about it wholeheartedly. The surest proof that I did not have that disease is the fact that I have not been cured of it. . . . When I close my eyes, I see immediately before me—pure, childish, and innocent—my love for my mother, my respect and my great affection for my father. (367–68)

In these paragraphs, Zeno's ironic denigration of psychoanalysis, which he considers nothing but a "sciocca illusione, un trucco buono" ("a silly illusion, a harmless trick") designed for hysterical old ladies, culminates in his affirmation of the purity and innocence of his childhood, in his enduring love for his mother and his respect for his father. Zeno's initial "enchantment" with Doctor S.'s brand of psychoanalysis—in a procedure contrary to Emilio's concluding "enchantment" with his own past in *Senilità*—eventually gives way to the character's perspective of ironic detachment. This process points up one of the major differences between the two novels, since Emilio ends in a state of blind belief whereas Zeno *claims* knowledgeable withdrawal. But such an understanding of Svevo's novelistic oeuvre is, of course, far too limited, since, despite Zeno's position as the first-person narrator of his own story, his discourse, however self-assured, is far from unquestionable.

One of the perspectives from which Zeno's narration can and should be questioned is that of Freudian thought itself. The concluding affirmation of the passage cited above, for example, brings to mind the psychoanalytic aspects of two scenes related earlier in Zeno's narrative. One of these concerns his earlier behavior as an illicit smoker, and the other describes the death of his father. Zeno tells of his experiences as a smoker because of the doctor's suggestion that he begin his autobiography by relating his earliest memories of what he regards as his illness, the habit of smoking.[7]

As Zeno relates, he began smoking cigarettes that were given to him by a young friend whose father sent more money than he needed for himself. When Zeno felt that there was a difference in the number of cigarettes given to Zeno's brother and the number he received, he began making up the difference by stealing from their own father. Despite the concluding affirmation of the lengthy passage cited earlier in regard to the purity and innocence of Zeno's childhood, he initially describes his thievery and his father's ingenious reactions to it precisely in terms of a *loss* of "innocence" (603; 6). When Zeno continues stealing—taking his father's half-smoked Virginia cigars—he comes very close to being caught. Zeno remembers the scene of his escape as one that should have included his brother but from which his brother is instead excluded. Zeno's father appears as an intruder, too, since the isolated pair in the scene is made up of Zeno, who is supposed to be sleeping but is actually awake, and his mother.

Zeno is lying clad in his bathrobe (having just been undressed by his mother) on a couch in the children's room, where his mother sits beside him, occupied with her sewing. When Zeno's father enters, Zeno's mother protects her son by feigning ignorance in regard to the missing half-smoked cigar, while she furtively demonstrates her complicity to Zeno by her smile, which remains at length on her face and which subsequently remained so alive in Zeno's memory that it makes a startling reappearance: "Quel sorriso mi rimase tanto impresso che lo ricordai subito ritrovandolo un giorno sulle labbra di mia moglie" (604; "That smile made such an impression on me that I remembered it immediately when I saw it again one day on the lips of my wife," 7). It is not difficult to see, from the general perspective of Freudian thought, that Zeno's initial reference to his loss of innocence, followed by the "dolcezza" ("sweetness") of his experience lying at the side of his mother's "caro corpo" ("dear body") in a scenario from which his brother is excluded and in which his father is rejected in favor of Zeno (whom the father is also constrained to treat with respect) is all part of a standard Oedipal situation.[8] This does not mean that Zeno wants literally either to eliminate his father or to sleep with his mother, but that, symbolically, he does in fact achieve aspects of both of these goals through his mother's momentary complicity and his own eventual marriage. In the meantime it is fairly clear that his smoking—with its phallic symbolism, its underlying phenomenon of desire spurred by prohibition, and its suggestion of the patient's fixation on what might be termed, following Melanie Klein, a "part object" stemming from an oral and therefore pregenital stage of psychic development—constitutes not the disease itself but rather its sign. Although the dreams and various other psychic material reported by Zeno throughout the narrative alter and complicate this basic picture, none of them changes it completely.

It is not my intent here, however, to determine more exactly the nature of that malady, be it hysterical or obsessive.[9] Such a determination would be both tricky and cumbersome due in part to the incongruity and the patently equivocal status of Zeno's own discourse. In the beginning, Zeno's project is to provide material that the psychiatrist might be able to use. With that goal in mind, and to make the doctor's job easier, Zeno has read a tract dealing with psychoanalysis ("Non è difficile d'intenderlo, ma molto noioso," 600; "It is not difficult to understand, but very boring," 3). Zeno's initial enthusiasm for the doctor's suggestion, however, only adds to the problem of interpretation from the very start. Precisely to what extent Zeno's desire to please the doctor colors his narrative, or to what extent his eventual rejection of psychoanalysis *in toto* influences the dated narratives of the concluding chapter, is impossible to ascertain with certainty. Therefore, rather than attempting a detailed (psycho)analysis of the multilayered motivations of Zeno's true-false discourse, in which he at times tries to assist the doctor and at other times admittedly deludes him with lies (941; 382), I intend only to retrace a few of the more obvious paths of interpretation offered by Svevo's text itself.

These paths lead, in terms of the novel's development, to the climactic scene of the next section, which carries the openly Freudian title of "La morte di mio padre," or "The Death of my Father." This scene—in which the hand of Zeno's dying father strikes the son's cheek as though in reproach—spurs Zeno's feelings of guilt, as is confirmed by his overzealous denials and by his further account of the casual conversation between the medical assistant and the family domestic. It is unclear whether Zeno feels that he is being reproached by his father for a specific reason (his attempts to restrain the dying patient) or for a more general one as well (his lack of belief in absolutes, such as Christianity, and his habitual ironic derision, both of which his father had bemoaned earlier in the chapter). What is clear, however, is the extension of the Freudian thematics of this chapter to Zeno's often tense relations with the other important masculine figures of authority in the novel; these include Zeno's father-in-law, Giovanni Malfenti (who complains during an often discussed dinner scene in chapter 6 that Zeno seems to want to see him dead), Zeno's brother-in-law, Guido (before his shift to brotherhood and finally his demotion to childhood as his business and personal failures mount in chapter 7), and, as is only logical in terms of Freudian theory, Doctor S. himself. In the concluding paragraph of this chapter, moreover, Zeno relates his return to the "religion" of his childhood and his habit of imagining his father still alive, which for Zeno means that his father is able to hear Zeno's excuses and to accept them. This conclusion thus recalls Doctor S.'s introductory comments on truth and falsity in Zeno's discourse at the same time that it leads to the next chapter, concerning Zeno's choice of a wife, in which truth, falsity, illness, and self-perception all come together in a curious scene at a bar, whence Zeno eventually exits with a pronounced limp.[10]

Zeno enters the bar late at night, having been unable to fall asleep, his mind filled with Signora Malfenti's imagined reproaches for his attempt at "playing footsie" ("giocar di pedina") with Ada. Although he does not expect to see anyone he knows, he is recognized by an old friend, Tullio, who is afflicted so seriously with rheumatism that he is forced to use a crutch to walk. Zeno pretends to be sympathetic to his friend's affliction and then goes on to tell of his own troubles, exaggerating his difficulties to such an extent that he very nearly moves himself to tears. After Tullio (who also smokes excessively) describes his affliction in precise physiological and even mechanical terms, Zeno leaves the bar limping, and he continues to limp for some time.

The quick progression within this scene from Zeno's *feigning* interest ("fingere," 681; 92) to his active though easy *simulation* of both interest and sympathy (*simulare*) points up an important aspect of Zeno's active *creation* of his character as a self-made patient, or—as he and others say later in a depiction that recalls Molière—a "malato immaginario." The fictional text's self-reflexive treatment of the powers of "simulation" continue, moreover, all the way to the concluding sections of the story, in which Zeno's ability in this field is by turns affirmed and denied, as is Guido's. Indeed, Guido's ultimate success/failure in the arena of creative self-presentation is recapitulated in his final worldly act, since what seems his last *staged* suicide turns out, for reasons beyond his control, to have an all too real denouement. But in spite of the importance of this line of thematics for the novel as a whole, the crucial aspect of the scene with Tullio is the way in which simulation blends with the underlying issue, that of disease.

The paragraph preceding Zeno's entry into the bar describes his vague conviction of being ill but, as usual, without any specific declaration regarding the origin of his illness ("Da molti anni io mi consideravo malato," 680, cf. 607; "For many years I had considered myself ill," 92, cf. 11). However, he does point out the beginning of his really painful *physical* sickness ("la malattia 'dolente'"), which turns out to be none other than his meeting with his actually afflicted friend in the bar. As we have noted, this scene is connected by contiguity to Zeno's fancied games of footsie with Ada (in which all that the hapless Zeno has ever managed to reach with his foot is the wooden table leg). The image of the lifeless wooden leg is picked up in that of the crutch, which eventually leads to the half-humorous description of the human leg as a "macchina mostruosa" ("monstrous machine"), requiring fifty-four muscle movements ("ordigni") for every step. Moreover, the image of walking, which begins with the playfully sexual "pedina" and leads to Zeno's limping, unifies the scene and articulates it in terms of the narrative progression by tying it not only to its introduction but also, in turn, to the introductory passage at the beginning of the next chapter ("La moglie e l'amante"; "Wife and Lover"), in which Zeno, having finally settled for Augusta, describes the progress of his multiple courtship and its surprisingly happy result by using a term that in any other context would seem odd indeed. Who would have predicted such an outcome, Zeno wonders, "quando avevo *zoppicato* da Ada ad Alberta per arrivare ad Augusta?" (725, my italics; "when I had *limped* from Ada to Alberta to arrive at Augusta?" 140, my italics).

Zeno's expression of surprise that his marriage seems to be turning out so well thus incorporates reference to the "limping" that began, as we have seen, during his courtship of Ada. Since this imagery now extends from one of the Malfenti sisters to three of them, the question suggested by the text appears at least fairly clear: who is it that limps from one woman to the next only to end up with the one destined for him (i.e., the one whose smile is linked to that of the suitor's mother)? The answer to this question is not as straightforward as it may seem, since Zeno is not Oedipus and has not married his own mother, however close Augusta may be in various respects. In other words, even if Freud was right—and on this issue, in terms of the novel, he seems not to have been far from it—coming to terms with Zeno's internalization of the incest taboo (so tenuously drawn between Alfonso and his mother in *Una vita*, or between Emilio and Amalia in *Senilità*) may further our understanding of, yet does not in any sense solve or resolve, Zeno's problems.

But what, after all, *are* his problems? The central one, which, again, involves both sickness and the peculiarly human capacity to think abstractly, to perceive the self as another over time, returns us to consideration of Zeno's original limp and the scene at the bar. Since the primary topic of discussion there involved the ability to move rapidly and successfully through space in an analyzable yet continuous fashion, it is not hard to see that the other primal limper for Svevo's text, along with Oedipus, is at least by cultural tradition another Greek, Zeno of Elia. "Zeno's paradox" and Zeno's problem (in regard to his chain-smoking as well as in broader terms) have been definitively treated by John Freccero.[11] Zeno's paradox has to do with the apparent impossibility of perceiving, at one and the same time, both flux and stasis, existence and essence, the flow of temporal continuity and the discrete moments of discontinuous time. For Svevo, of course, the emphasis of the paradox falls not on physical motion but on human self-perception in time, which is to say, on the confrontation, evocative of Pirandello's major novels and plays, between stable personal identity and undeniable worldly change. For Svevo's Zeno, man's inherent difficulty is due to the fact that his rational powers impede his natural freedom of existence by stopping or fixing the self in time through the faculty of analysis. *Psycho/analysis*, as the form par excellence of psychological *self*-consciousness, thus comes to represent, for the "occhialuto uomo" (955; "bespectacled man," 398) such as Zeno himself (238; 188), not health but the worst form of disease. Zeno sees the problem, that "La vita attuale è inquinata alle radici" ("Life today is poisoned to the roots"), and that the more rational man gets, that is, the more mechanically sophisticated and self-reflexive, the worse off he is. But at the same time, Zeno also believes that he sees a solution.

Zeno's solution runs along two paths, one individual and tentative, the other communal and absolute. For the human race, constantly more subject to the mechanically abstract, external "ordigni," or machines, of its own making (as opposed to the natural, internal "ordigni" of the leg's fifty-four muscle movements), Zeno's only proposal for a return to health is through total destruction: cleansing through explosion and annihilation, in what the text's remarkable finale terms "una catastrofe inaudita prodotta da . . . un esplosivo incomparabile . . . [in] un'esplosione enorme che nessuno udrà" ("an unheard-of catastrophe produced by . . . an incomparable explosive . . . [resulting in] an enormous explosion that no one will hear"). For Zeno as an individual, the solution is less dramatic: neither self-destruction nor self-analysis through review of his past but immersion in commercial activity. In and through "buying" (*comperare*), Zeno finds the strength and the nonreflective, temporally unbounded action that signal his "cure"—both his cure from his malady and his cure from psychoanalysis itself. He thus substitutes a seemingly pure, nonreflective, and continuous present for the analytic "disease" of discontinuous time (such as neatly divided past/present/future). In other words, Zeno definitively abandons the doctor's initial admonition to write about his past and to see himself "whole" ("intero") because seeing himself at all entails reflection and reflection entails doubling, the result of which is the denial of wholeness rather than its affirmation.

In this way, Zeno appears to free himself from the trap of self-conscious reflection, but without succumbing to the sort of temporal delusion evident in the hagiography of the now frozen and therefore illusory past (as Emilio does at the end of *Senilità* and as Ada does after Guido's death). Zeno also seems to have freed himself from his sick obsession with time, which had included everything from temporal change and duration to the disorders of the calendar and even the weather as "il tempo" (940, cf. 919; 381, cf. 357). At the end of the narrative, Zeno claims to be concerned only with living in the present and with the force of his new life, active and liberated from the disease of self-reflection and therefore happy, whole, and free: in short, healthy.

There are several specifically literary aspects to Zeno's developing perspective that are worthy of note. Some of these, though not all, have already been mentioned in other contexts: first, the importance of creative simulation in the competitive relationship—at times one of brother and brother, at times one of parent and child—between Guido and Zeno (an ability that extends specifically to the creation of fables, not unlike those of Svevo/Schmitz's own literary and journalistic enterprises); second, the power of language ("parole") to create as well as reflect worldly meaning; third, the orthographic intertwining of the Malfenti sisters' names, all of which begin with A, and among whom Zeno (A to Z) limps from one to the next in a new version of his namesake's paradox; fourth, the story's various secondary similarities in naming, several of which are clearly emphasized by the text (Carla/Carmen, 838; cf. "Gerco"/"Greco"); and finally and most importantly, Zeno's discovery of the efficacy and the trickiness of simulated images when used as the route to understanding things in general and his own psychic apparatus in particular. In the middle sections of the narrative, Zeno is convinced of the usefulness of images or figurative analogies ("Per intendere bene le cose, occorre lavorare di immagini," 864; "To understand the situation it is necessary to resort to images," 294). But later on, Zeno asserts the potential deceptions of such a procedure, especially as regards psychoanalysis:[12]

> Il dottore mi confessò che, in tutta la sua lunga pratica, giammai gli era avvenuto di assistere ad un'emozione tanto forte come la mia all'imbattermi nelle immagini ch'egli credeva di aver saputo procurarmi. . . . Ed io non simulai quell'emozione. . . . E così che a forza di correr dietro a quelle immagini, io le raggiunsi. Ora so di averle inventate. Ma inventare è una creazione, non già una menzogna. Le mie erano delle invenzioni come quelle della febbre. . . . Avevano la solidità, il colore, la petulanza delle cose vive. A forza di desiderio, io proiettai le immagini, che non c'erano che nel mio cervello. . . . [Ma] appena svanite, le ricordavo ma senz'alcun eccitazione o commozione. Le ricordavo come si ricorda il fatto raccontato da chi non vi assistette. Se fossero state vere riproduzioni avrei continuato a riderne e

a piangerne come quando le avevo avute. In verità, noi non avevamo più che dei segni grafici, degli scheletri d'immagini. (928–29)

The doctor confessed to me that during the whole of his long practice, he had never met with an emotion as strong as mine when I came up with the images that he believed to have suggested to me himself. . . . And I did not simulate that emotion. . . . And by dint of pursuing those images, I finally overtook them. I know now that I invented them. But invention is a creative act, not merely a lie. My inventions were like the fantasies of fever. . . . They had the solidity, the color, the presence of living things. By the strength of my desire I projected these images, which had existed only inside my brain. . . . [But] as soon as they had vanished, I remembered them without any excitement or agitation. I remembered them as one remembers an event told by someone who was not present at it. If they had been real reproductions, I would have continued to laugh or cry in the same way as when I had them. In point of fact we were left with nothing more than graphic signs, mere skeletons of images. (368–69)

Zeno's belief in the utility of images and his potent emotional reaction to his supposed youthful memories drummed up for the doctor prove utterly inadequate to change the fleeting force of false images into the lasting power of true experience. In this instance, Zeno's emotional reaction is genuine, but its object is specious, ephemeral, and ultimately depersonalized. Zeno's creative though dubious act of invention results in signs that, since they are not tied to real past experience, end up as images devoid of continuing import beyond the notes registered by the (perhaps) duped doctor. Unlike Ada or Emilio, in the end Zeno cannot convince himself of the truth of these false images, no matter how arduously and artfully produced and projected they may be. At the same time that the images create an actual if complex experience in the *narrated* present by reference to an illusive past, they are also commented on by Zeno in the *narrating* present ("*Ora* so"; "I know *now*"). Zeno's discussion of them therefore reinforces the deeply embedded play of deluded past and knowledgeable present, "then" and "now," that, while it does not result in the total demystification of the speaking subject (Zeno's assertions to the contrary notwithstanding), does run throughout Zeno's discourse up to the concluding sections of the novel.[13] Near the conclusion, however, as we have noted, Zeno renounces "definitively" both the division of his life into discrete compartments and the attempt to recapture his past—whether by images or not—in favor of his total immersion in the present, as though a man, even while standing still himself, actually could be absorbed into the continuous motion of a river's current (940; 381). In a passage near the beginning of the narrative's penultimate entry, dated 26 June 1915, Zeno restates in no uncertain terms both his renunciation of all desires to relive his past and his belief that he has finally escaped his preoccupation with health and disease by living actively and nonreflectively, day by day (944; 386).

Zeno's cure, effected through his resolution to live actively in the present and to abandon reflective analyses of his past, indeed to avoid self-conscious reflection altogether, resembles the underlying beliefs and values of fiction writers (and occasionally of their characters) as diverse as Verga, Pirandello, and William Faulkner.[14] But, as in the novels of these writers, the affirmations of Svevo's main character in regard to the character's own health and well-being do not stand unchallenged. As we have seen, part of the literary and psychological effect of Svevo's narrative is to put in question *all* of Zeno's "confessional" discourse—whether it be ironic or sincere, insightful or misguided, evasive or direct—from his initial statement of his problem to its ultimate "solution." But on the other hand, even though it is true that in *La coscienza di Zeno* such questioning begins much earlier than the questioning of the perceptions and motivations of the main characters in *Una vita* and *Senilità*, it is equally true that not only the relation between text and narrator but also that between character and author—despite all of Zeno's neurotic rationalizations, self-justifications, and narcissistic projections—is in important respects more closely intertwined in *La coscienza di Zeno* than in the earlier novels, perhaps, in the end, inseparably so.

This is so partly because, even though Zeno demonstrates the constant tendency to create alibis that is a distinguishing feature of so many of Svevo's major characters, Zeno's alibis, in human terms, are at once more universal and more complexly engaging than those of the other figures in Svevo's repertoire.[15] It is undeniable that Zeno's conviction of health is in large part merely a result of autopersuasion, that he attempts to discard his life-long "conviction" of being ill (with which he claims to have been born, 607; 11) simply by convincing himself that he is now cured of his maladies; and it is also the case that this new conviction runs far deeper and is far more complicated than Ada's belief in her willful delusion regarding Guido's sainthood, which can exist only in an illusory world created by "parole non vere" (923; "false words," 362)—which is to say, in an illusion that is always the result of such words. At the same time, however, Zeno succumbs only halfway to his own illusions, persisting in the realization that what is sick is not so much any one individual as mankind itself.

Indeed, in the same concluding passage in which Zeno announces his "persuasion" of his definitive cure through the activity of buying (dated 24 March 1916, almost a full year after the previous entry), he also persists in describing life as being like a disease, from which no one recovers: "A differenza delle altre malattie la vita è sempre mortale. Non sopporta cure" (954; "Unlike other diseases, life is always mortal. It admits of no cure," 397). Rather than getting better, "la vita attuale," or "life today," is only getting worse. With every new "advance" toward abstraction and rational development, "man" (i.e., all mankind) becomes sicker and sicker.

In part these concluding notations repeat elements of what Zeno has already said on several occasions. As a result of his excessive meditations on Ada's affliction with Basedow's disease, for example, he concludes that life is full of poisons ready to afflict whomsoever comes to rest in a single point or attitude even for a moment:

> Ma io ammalai con lei di una malattia lieve, ma lunga. Per troppo tempo pensai a Basedow. Già credo che in qualunque punto dell'universo ci si stabilisca si finisce coll'inquinarsi. Bisogna moversi. La vita ha dei veleni, ma poi anche degli altri veleni che servono di contravveleni. Solo correndo si può sottrarsi ai primi e giovarsi degli altri. (858)

> But I became ill along with her from a disease that was mild, yet long-lasting. For too much time I thought about Basedow. In fact I believe that at whatever point of the universe one settles down one ends up becoming poisoned. It is essential to keep moving. Life has its poisons, but it has other poisons, too, that serve as counter-poisons. Only by constantly moving about can one avoid the former and profit from the latter. (287)

As in Zeno's earlier identifications with Tullio, Guido, and others, his morbidly internalized preoccupation with Ada—again in romantic terms, as the subsequent paragraphs make clear—and with her disease is another aspect of his psychological weaknesses. The general solution that he proposes here, of constant motion (i.e., external activity as opposed to stasis, reflection, and so forth), fits into his overall view of mankind's malady while providing very little solace, since, as he notes shortly afterward, the motion of constant activity is no more possible than is one of its particular variants, constant kissing (868; 298). There really is no perfect mean, moreover, since even those who seem healthy are just on their way to being sick, merely stopped at a momentary resting point somewhere between the diseased poles of frenetic desire and total lethargy. Regardless of the idealized example of Augusta (whom Zeno, nevertheless, regularly betrays, regardless of his affirmations to the doctor), all mankind is subject to these poisons of life, and the most any individual can hope for is the temporary relief produced by the "counter-poison" (not "antidote") of nonpensive, yet also serenely nonfrenetic motion. For Zeno, "in tutta l'umanità, la salute assoluta manca" (858; "in all of humanity, there is no such thing as perfect health," 287). Such is life in terms of the individual as well as in terms of the race: no one is thoroughly free from disease, and no one escapes alive.

Because of the overriding nature of Zeno's realization of both the human condition and its current development, the expansion of his perspective to encompass broader social considerations in his final prediction of communal apocalypse—as the only way to real health via the elimination of all parasites, indeed of literally everything worldly—seems logical enough. But it is important to see once more that even though Zeno claims that he is cured, his new strength and health exist only within the framework of disease that surrounds all mankind, Zeno included. Zeno's characteristic mixture of truth and falsity in his assertion of his newfound health is doubtless one means of reacting to the crisis, or sickness, of bourgeois life that ran throughout middle Europe, including Trieste, a crisis that is reflected in the works of writers as diverse as Franz Kafka, Robert Musil, and Thomas Mann and that found its most catastrophic expression in World War I.[16] That mankind was sick, and that consciousness of his malady was a necessary though not a sufficient condition of his cure, was understood by Svevo as well as by his character. Svevo's own reaction to this consciousness was not, however, to attempt a cure by buying but, rather, by writing, by immersion in the creation of art, which Zeno at one point defines as the distinctive combination of "vita e dolore" (744; "life and suffering," 162). In other words, Svevo attempts to counter the temporal inconsistency and randomness of real life by effective and *lasting* simulation. In a famous diary entry, Svevo remarks, "Insomma fuori della penna non c'è salvezza" ("In short, outside of writing, there is no salvation"), a belief stated clearly and extended to include all humanity in the famous first paragraph of "Le confessioni del vegliardo" ("The Confessions of an Old Man") of 1928.[17] Through the faculty of the creative imagination and the elaborate frame of the confessional autobiography, edited by Doctor S. (N.B.: Svevo/Schmitz), Svevo thus actively turns his consciousness of his own situation into the *self*-consciousness of his character, while infusing Zeno's discourse, through the simulating, writerly activity of the *author's* cure, with the true "lie" of Zeno's disease and his asserted recovery, both of which now have a psychological and physiological beginning but, outside of the total, apocalyptic destruction of human society, have no worldly end. Within Zeno's and Svevo's understanding of the world, all men are thus irremediably "occhialuti" (bespectacled) in their capacity for abstraction and rational reflection, including not only Zeno but also Svevo himself.

In view of the totality of this situation, the only hope is to know that condition. In this case, however, knowledge does not mean escape but, up to the very point of apocalypse, its opposite: "L'uomo diventa sempre più furbo e più *debole*" (955, my italics; "Man becomes continually more cunning and continually *weaker*," 398, my italics). Having abandoned, as Zeno laments, the law of natural selection through the introduction of mechanical supports, modern man has come to depend on those supports in a sense that is absolute rather than haphazard or limited. But though Svevo's interest and belief in the world were far more concrete than Pirandello's, the impulse to escape it remains, as well as a possible worldly route: activity. The result of this activity, on the part first of Zeno's author and then of Svevo's character, with the good doctor following somewhere in between, is initially an approach toward understanding of the self and later a retreat from it, both of which combine in one of the most psychologically realistic and self-conscious confessional discourses imaginable in the novel up to the time of *La coscienza di Zeno*. Only after the cataclysm predicted for the modern bourgeois world at the novel's end could Svevian man have truly exclaimed *non*-self-consciously, "Io sono guarito!" (953; "I am cured!" 396). But by that time, of course—as Svevo, now in contradistinction to his character, saw all too well—there would be no one to hear this joyous affirmation, much less to give it voice.

SIX

Silone and Neorealism

After the inwardly focused psychological novels of Pirandello and Svevo—and after the years of Fascist censorship between the two wars and the mix of lyricism, psychology, and highly elliptical worldly representation in writers like Federigo Tozzi and Corrado Alvaro—the next major phenomenon in Italian narrative was neorealism. In regard to literary self-reflection, the procedure generally followed in neorealist fiction (somewhat similar in this respect to Verga's verismo) is to place the issues of representation squarely *within* the world portrayed by the text. Such potentially self-reflexive topics as the relation between discourse and meaning, the worldly status of fantasy, and the production of symbolic truth itself are thus described and discussed unobtrusively in the narrative as parts of everyday life.

Signs and History in Silone's *Vino e pane*: The Dilemma of Social Change

Although Ignazio Silone's *Vino e pane* (*Bread and Wine*) is not, strictly speaking, a neorealist novel, the narrative is illustrative here because of the clarity of such representational procedures. The first version of the novel, written in the mid-1930s during Silone's Swiss exile, actually precedes postwar neorealism by almost a decade, and it is often considered to be of lesser stature than the neorealist fiction of writers like Alberto Moravia, Elio Vittorini, and Cesare Pavese.[1] Nonetheless, *Vino e pane* is of particular interest in this context for its exemplary demonstration of representational technique within a realist aesthetic, in that the novel openly treats the topic of the relation between symbolic signs and worldly referents even while adhering in a fairly consistent way to the straightforward description of local life in prewar Italy.

Silone's *Vino e pane* depicts the difficulties of active resistance to the Fascist state. For most of the novel, these difficulties are portrayed through the actions of the characters, especially those of the priest, "Don Paolo." In reality, "Don Paolo" is the identity assumed by the novel's clandestine revolutionary activist, Pietro Spina.[2] Since the "real" day-to-day role of the activist repeatedly jars with the "fictive" (but equally day-to-day) role of the priest, the validity of Pietro/Paolo's acts is constantly put in question by means of the narrative events.[3] Ultimately, the various implications of this questioning come together to form a pair of interrelated, broader questions: Can we change society simply by changing our identities, by agreeing to discard or significantly modify our old roles and values and to assume new ones? And even if we can, how can we control the results of such a change so that they will be beneficial rather than harmful?

The action of the novel both grows out of and embodies these questions, which stem from Silone's two great themes, politics and religion (or, for Silone, social action and individual morality). But in the events of the novel, the questions themselves are never resolved. Several of the reasons for this lack of resolution are made clear, however, on the discursive level of the narrative during a series of conversations in one of the novel's central chapters, chapter 13, between Don Paolo and his peasant interlocutors at the inn in the rural Abruzzi where the disguised activist is in hiding.[4]

Since these discussions are about the qualities and rules of symbolic meaning, they provide a special opportunity for the novel to examine its own status and techniques as fiction. Silone does in fact take advantage of this opportunity, but, remaining within the systems of representation normally available to realist narrative, he does so only indirectly, by presenting this potentially self-conscious commentary through the voices of the novel's characters in everyday conversation. Moreover, because of the heated nature of the chapter's disputes, the self-reflexive implications of the abstract principles involved in the discussions and the further application of these principles to the problems of the overall narrative seem, at this point in the text, muted, to say the least. Comprehension of these principles, however, and of the conflicts among them, is in fact central to an understanding not only of chapter 13 but also of the entire story as both a political and a social novel.

The first of these discussions concerns a game of cards underway at the inn in Pietrasecca. Don Paolo is called upon to settle a dispute that has arisen among the players. When the argument begins, Don Paolo is upstairs at his writing table, "curvo su alcuni fogli che recavano questa intestazione: *Sull'inaccessibilità dei cafoni alla politica*" (140; "bent over some notes with the title 'On the Peasants' Lack of Political Capacity'" [*literally:* On the Peasants' Inaccessibility to Politics], 129). With the noise of the games and the conversations downstairs, he finds it difficult to concentrate on his work. Meanwhile, one of the men below suggests that Don Paolo be asked to settle the argument. Hearing his name mentioned, Don Paolo descends the stairs to appear before the crowd of players and onlookers; but before the peasants tell him what they want of him, he must participate in their ceremonial welcome: "Cessarono d'incanto le discussioni e tutti offrirono da bere al prete. Egli ringraziò, cercò di scusarsi, ma infine dovette accettare di fare il giro della stanza e di avvicinare le labbra a ogni bicchiere, secondo il costume" (141; "All the talking stopped at once and everyone offered the priest something to drink. He thanked them and tried to excuse himself, but he finally had to go around and touch his lips to each glass, according to the custom," 130).

As set forth at the opening of chapter 13, the problems encountered in the game are due to the circumstance that the back of the most important card in *settemmezzo*, the king of diamonds ("il re di denari"), has become so worn in every deck that the card can be recognized by anyone. To solve the problem, a player suggests that, by agreement of all the players, the king be exchanged for another card, the three of hearts ("il tre di coppe") and that the value of the king be transferred to the three. Another player opposes the suggestion, and the dispute begins: "'È impossibile' aveva subito detto un altro giocatore, un certo Michele. 'Anche se fossimo tutti d'accordo, sarebbe impossibile'" (140; "'That's impossible!' somebody else said, a certain Michele. 'Even if we all could agree, it would still be impossible,'" 129).

At issue here is the value—natural or merely conventional, inherent or merely agreed upon—of the various cards. The questions of the properties and the production of symbolic meaning become even clearer as the discussion proceeds.[5] Another player, Mascolo, sides with Michele: "Il re di denari è sempre il re di denari. Potrà essere sporco, segnato, forato, ma rimane quello che è" (140; "The king of diamonds is always the king of diamonds. It could be dirty or marked or it could have a hole in it. But it's still what it is," 130). In other words, the essence of the king and the role that goes with it always remain fixed, regardless of the varying attributes of the card that symbolizes the king in the game. The reason for this timeless unity of sign and referent, despite any illusion of worldly change or difference, is supplied by Mascolo's opening words: "Ma è naturale" ("But it's natural").

The opposing side is again taken up by Daniele, the player who had made the original suggestion concerning the exchange of the king and the three. As before, he argues that the agreement of the players is adequate to change the value of the cards: "Basta mettersi d'accordo" (141; "All we have to do is agree on it," 130). Now, however, he puts special emphasis on the practical rather than simply the logical aspects of his proposal: "Il giuoco andrà meglio se nessuno riconoscerà in anticipo chi ha in mano il re di denari" ("The game will go better if no one can see who has the king of diamonds in his hand"). As the conversation proceeds, Mascolo counters the argument from practicality and reasserts the correctness of his own position by subordinating practicality to epistemology: "Tu dici che il giuoco andrebbe meglio? . . . Forse, ma sarebbe un giuoco falso" ("You say the game would go better? . . . That may be, but it would be a false game").[6]

This last complication is probably enough to render the situation complex beyond any single, clear-cut solution. But before Mascolo mentions this complicating factor, Michele asserts a further difficulty *within* the arguments of those who favor construing meaning as arising from agreed-upon convention rather than from nature and/or essence: "'Il nostro accordo non basta,' ripeteva Michele. 'C'è la legge'" ("'But our agreement is not enough,' said Michele. 'There's the law'"). For Michele, then, even if it were possible to change the value of the cards, and even if the agreement of the players were a necessary condition for any change to occur, such an agreement in and of itself would still be insufficient for the change actually to take place. According to this line of reasoning, there are definite hierarchies in the production of symbolic meaning, and these hierarchies transcend the limits of the will of any single group of players. The logic of legality takes precedence over the intentions of the particular players involved in any specific context.

It is at this point—in the midst of the welter of disputes and confusions concerning nature and convention, essence and attribute, truth and falsity, logic and practicality, custom and law—that Don Paolo is called upon to intervene. At first the priest tries to avoid the role of arbiter that the peasants want to assign to him. Since the disagreement involves interpretation of a class of symbols outside his supposed field of expertise ("sacred images"), Don Paolo attempts to excuse himself. But the expectant audience will accept no refusal, and one of the more vocal peasants, Sciatàp (who had first mentioned the priest as a possible judge), closes off Don Paolo's every line of escape.

Seeing no alternative, Don Paolo jumps in with both feet. What follows, with notable directness, is a brief for the arbitrariness and the conventionality of the sign. With the king of diamonds in his hand, Don Paolo begins by asking Michele, "Credi tu che questa carta abbia un valore per sé stesso, oppure che l'abbia ricevuto?" ("Do you think this has value for itself, or do you think someone gave it a value?"). Michele persists in arguing for its necessary and essential rather than contingent or accidental value: "Essa vale più delle altre, *di per sé, essendo* il re di denari" (my italics; "It's worth more than the others *because it is* the king of diamonds," my italics). But Don Paolo overcomes every objection with ease. He shows that the card's value is variable rather than fixed, since its role differs according to the game in question (*tressette, briscola, scopa*). Moreover, the card's value is not only assigned arbitrarily, but it is also assigned by conventional agreement. As for the problem of whose agreement, the solution is simple: by agreement of the players themselves. The crucial question of *which* set or sets of players is glossed over through Silone's use of "choral" indirect discourse in a key passage; but the remaining issues at stake, as well as the seemingly inevitable conclusions, are handled by Don Paolo with an impressive degree of clarity:

"Questo carta ha un valore fisso o variabile?" disse ancora il prete. . . .
"Varia sempre di valore" disse Michele. "Varia secondo i giuochi."
"Chi ha inventato i giuochi?" disse il prete.
Nessuno rispose.
"Non credete che il giuoco sia stato inventato dai giocatori?" suggerì il prete.
Vari acconsentirono subito. Di tutta evidenza i giuochi sono stati inventati dai giocatori.
Il prete concluse:

"Se questa carta ha un valore variabile, secondo l'accordo e la fantasia dei giocatori, a me pare che voi potete farne quello che vi pare."

"Ben detto, bravo, benissimo" gridarono in molti. (141–42, my italics)

"Is its value fixed or variable?" said the priest. . . .
"It varies according to the games," said Michele.
"Who thought up the games?" asked the priest.
No one answered.
"Don't you think the players thought up the games?" suggested the priest.
Several agreed right away. There was every reason to believe that the players had thought up the games.
The priest concluded, "If this card varies according to the players' agreement and fantasy, it seems to me you can do with it what you want."
"Bravo! bravissimo!" many of them yelled. (130–131, my italics)

Don Paolo is encouraged and flattered ("lusingato") by his success. He continues with an example from the experiences (well known among the peasants) of the loquacious Sciatàp as an immigrant in America: "'C'era una volta qui a Pietrasecca' disse 'un uomo che si chiamava Carlo Campanella, e c'è a Nuova York un uomo che si chiama Mr. Charles Little-Bell, Ice and Coal. È una sola persona o sono due?'" ("'Once upon a time there was a man here in Pietrasecca,' he said, 'a man called Carlo Campanella, and in New York there's a man called Mr. Charles Little-Bell, Ice and Coal. Is this one person or two?'"). Others begin to respond, but Sciatàp insists, "Sono io che devo rispondere" ("I'm the one to answer that"). His answer is to be expected: "È il medesimo che ha cambiato nome" ("It's the same one. He changed his name"). The progression from playing cards to personal names extends the terms of the previous discussion without any apparent change in the logic involved, and Don Paolo's argument remains the same as before: "Se un uomo può cambiare nome, perché non può cambiarlo una carta da giuoco?" ("If a man can change his name, why can't a playing card change its name?"). The priest's decision is clear. The connection between sign and referent is determined by convention rather than by nature; there is no inherent reason why the king of diamonds, rather than any other card, should have the role it has. Once this issue is decided, the rest of the problems seem to fall into line: at least in this instance custom and law are effectively the same, since both of them grow out of and depend on the agreement of the users of the language under consideration, be that the language of playing cards or of proper nouns; the interests of logic and practicality go hand in hand in the determination of symbolic meaning; and validity is determined by mutual accord of the members of the group concerned, not by a fixed value over which the group has no final control.

If this were all that Don Paolo intended to demonstrate with his examples and explanations, his presentation would be significant primarily for its analysis of the issues outlined up to now in relation to the epistemology and utility of symbolic meaning in aleatory contracts and personal appellations. As is typical of Silone's development of his material in the novel, however, the discussion of these sorts of "language games" is merely a preamble to Don Paolo's major argument, which concerns not so much the signs of cards and individual names as those of political roles. This crucial part of Don Paolo's explanation follows immediately upon the previously cited exchange. In the succeeding discussion, the issues appear to be no different, and once again the side of essence/nature is upheld by Michele:

> "Se un uomo può cambiare nome, perché non può cambiarlo una carta da giuoco?" disse il prete.
> "Un re è sempre un re" disse Michele.
> "Un re è un re finché regna" disse don Paolo. (142)

> "If a man can change his name, why can't a playing card change its name?" asked the priest.
> "A king's always a king," said Michele.
> "A king is a king as long as he rules," said Don Paolo. (131)

During Don Paolo's elaboration of his response, however, it becomes apparent that something is profoundly different in this part of the discussion. This difference is the addition of the now insuppressible element of temporality (which had perhaps been at work even before the beginnings of the dispute, with the gradual wearing away of the cards themselves). The temporal aspect of the production of symbolic meaning can no longer be glossed over, as it had been earlier through the pretense that all of the players of *settemmezzo* were a unified, homogeneous group, rather than *various* groups of originators, inheritors, and/or modifiers of the customs in question. Moreover, as is again typical of *Vino e pane*, the element of temporality leads specifically to consideration of the category that proves so vexing to Pietro/Paolo throughout the narrative: history itself.

In the subsequent treatments of the nature of political roles, the action of history functions in a way that it had not seemed to as long as the discussion concerned the arbitrary signs of games of chance and proper names rather than the icon ("sacred images") and what Peirce terms the index, both of which constitute classes of signs in which either history or nature is of undeniable importance. This is not to say that real kings are in fact icons or indices or anything of the sort, but only that the symbolic properties of their worldly roles are more complicated than those of the seemingly arbitrary signs discussed previously. Don Paolo begins this part of the discussion by stating, "Un re è un re finché regna." The priest's intent, however, is not to dwell on this statement but to arrive at the conclusion of the syllogism, to which he proceeds immediately: "Un re che non regna più, è un ex re, non è più un re" ("A king who no longer rules is an ex-king, he isn't a king any more"). Of course, Don Paolo's point is that the relations between political figures and political roles, like the values of cards and proper nouns, are not timelessly "given" but are determined by the conventional agreement of the members of the body politic. In theory and perhaps in practice, such figures can, therefore, be changed by mutual accord of those same members. In order to demonstrate this point further, and to emphasize the potential for popular revolt against "kings" and other rulers, Don Paolo finally adduces the examples of historical events (only slightly veiled) in Russia and Spain.

At this stage in the chapter, with the boisterous approval of the now satisfied audience, Don Paolo's decision in regard to the process of signification in the game and his extension of that decision to include political roles and other forms of meaning seem entirely successful. Nonetheless, there are three major institutions, each of great importance in the novel, that foster and support views of the properties of symbolic meaning in regard to social and political roles that are utterly opposed to Don Paolo's. The opposition of two of these institutions, the Catholic church and the Fascist state, is immediately apparent; that of the third is perhaps less obvious, but its effects are, if anything, more pervasive and more decisive in both the plotting and the thematic development of the novel.

The view of the Church on the significance of worldly rank and role is formulated succinctly at the end of chapter 10 by Cristina Colamartini, the daughter of Pietrasecca's first family, who has made the decision to take the veil and serve Christ. She and Don Paolo are discussing the problems of reconciling "i doveri del proprio rango e quelli della propria anima" (119; "one's duties to one's rank and those to one's soul," 109). According to Cristina, "ognuno che resti nel mondo, vi occupa un rango che gli impone degli obblighi" ("everyone who stays in the world has a rank which imposes duties on him"). As usual, Don Paolo assumes the position of the spiritually motivated activist (and in the subsequent dialogue, Cristina, unaware of the priest's true identity, actually compares Don Paolo to Pietro Spina). Don Paolo says, "Ma quando i doveri del rango . . . diventano inconciliabili con quelli dell'anima, allora non c'è che da rispedire i primi senz'altro al diavolo" ("But when the duties of rank . . . become irreconcilable with those of the soul, there's no alternative but to abandon the former" [*literally:* to send the former to the devil"]).

In response, Cristina asserts her interpretation of Church doctrine regarding the inequality of social roles and the possibility of worldly change: "L'insegnamento ufficiale della Chiesa mi sembra però differente. . . .Le ineguaglianze sociali sono state anch'esse create da Dio e dobbiamo umilmente rispettarle" ("But it seems to me that the official teaching of the Church is different. . . . Social inequalities were created by God and we must humbly respect them"). The implications of Cristina's position are easy to see. For the Church, the relation between social roles and the figures who occupy them is neither arbitrary nor conventional. Both the roles themselves and the selection of those who must fill them are ordained by God. Theoretically, this system could be changed, but only through the will of God, not through that of man—if true, a disturbing situation indeed for the activist committed to change by social revolution.

In chapter 13, the views of the Fascist state are represented by the village schoolteacher, Signorina Patrignani (whose surname is probably meant to combine a play on *patria,* or "fatherland," with one on *patrigno,* or "stepfather"). Shortly after Don Paolo's remarks at the inn concerning the card game, the schoolteacher complains to him that the subsequent discussions of his "story" about the king of diamonds and the three of hearts have disrupted her classes and, worse, that the students have been repeating the priest's words without having understood them. She describes the ignorance of the villagers ("questa gente") to Don Paolo, and explains that they almost always understand just the opposite of whatever is intended by "una persona istruita come noi" ("educated people like ourselves"). As she remonstrates with the priest, however, the narrator suggests the blindness of the schoolteacher's own acceptance of the inherent value of the party's "emblem," which she wears over her heart, and depicts the comical fashion in which the symbol bounces up and down like a boat at sea with her every sigh (143; 132).

Whether or not the uneducated villagers and their children have misunderstood the implications of Don Paolo's explanations, it is apparent that the schoolteacher, who is convinced that she *has* understood him, has not actually followed any of his arguments. As may be seen from her reading of *Le notizie di Roma* (*The News from Rome*) to the group gathered at the inn, and from her responses to Magascià, Sciatàp, Grascia, and the others who question her, Signorina Patrignani espouses the standard doctrine of the state: the relation between the state's discourse and truth is absolute and unchanging as well as unquestionable; the figure in power, "il capo," occupies his place by right and by destiny and does not depend for his authority on the conventional agreement of anyone, much less on that of the peasants; his relation to his role and the power that goes with it is fixed, not variable; the people owe him allegiance, not vice versa. If what the state says does not make literal sense (as in the *Notizie*'s official description of the success of what is termed the "rural revolution"), then its assertions must be understood in a "senso spirituale" (145; "spiritual sense," 133). Signorina Patrignani's tricolor emblem suggests the effectiveness of the Fascist party's strategy (typical of social and political groups) to appropriate standard signs, such as in this instance the national flag, in its quest to consolidate and extend its power in society. Moreover, even though, during Signorina Patrignani's reading, the peasants jest at the *Notizie*'s continual confusion of literal and figurative language, the object of their scorn remains fragmented and personalized. In other words, they deride not the state but the state's individual representative (and they object to her pronouncements as much from their contempt for an overbearing woman—"quella disgraziata" [147; 135]—as from their distrust of the state's version of the "news").

In regard to the political power of the state, then, Pietrasecca is neither the logical nor the feasible seat of revolutionary change. One of the reasons for this can be clarified through identification of the third institution that the novel depicts as opposing Don Paolo's position. That institution (surprisingly enough, given Don Paolo's hopes) is the peasantry itself. The peasants' opposition is not so obvious as that of the Church and state, but it is nonetheless widespread. The narrator's notation of the "acclamazioni degli *ubbriachi*" (the peasants' "*drunken* cheers") hints that Don Paolo's victory at the inn may actually be due more to the emotions of his audience than to the logic or even the practicality of his solution. He plays the role of arbiter among the peasants with skill, and his audience responds with appropriate enthusiasm; but whether that enthusiasm is inspired by the substance and the actual applications of his argument or merely by his performance is, for the time being, unclear.

There is also a difficulty of even greater significance in Don Paolo's position, one that becomes obvious by the conclusion of chapter 13. It is indicated, though subtly, in the very first moments of Don Paolo's participation in the dispute among the peasants—or more precisely, even before his participation. At Don Paolo's entrance amid the players, as described in the passage cited earlier, the peasants quickly fall silent and offer the priest something to drink. Don Paolo's reaction as an individual is particularly noteworthy in relation to the issues under discussion in the following scene: "Egli ringraziò, *cercò di scusarsi*, ma infine *dovette* accettare di fare il giro della stanza e di avvicinare le labbra o ogni bicchiere, *secondo il costume*" ("He thanked them and *tried to excuse himself*, but he finally *had* to go around and touch his lips to each glass, *according to the custom*"). Perhaps because of Don Paolo's aversion to the ceremony of the greeting, or perhaps because of his continual discomfort in the role of priest, he initially attempts to avoid participating. Eventually, however, he has no choice but to accept the role in which he has been cast, as priest and judge, as well as the customary actions that go with it. Don Paolo's personal distaste for this particular custom and for the stratification of roles which it affirms is, in this case, hardly adequate to breach the convention within the peasantry's sphere.

As for the possibility of the peasants' complying with Don Paolo's subtly expressed wishes and changing the custom involved by mutual accord, the narrative makes it thoroughly clear that the "cafoni" of Pietraecca would not even consider making such a change. The peasants' almost universal acceptance of their role and their deep-rooted fear of any real change are, in fact, the subjects of discussion in the following sections of the chapter. As is obvious during the later conversations, even the peasants' constant "complaining" (148; 136) functions as a safety valve for their feelings of malaise and thereby ensures that the customary position of the oppressed will *not* change. They are actively opposed, moreover, to any change in the standard, accepted social roles of men and women. According to Grascia, "Quando è la donna che insegna all'uomo . . . i figli nascono gobbi. . . . Non c'è nulla di più disgraziato . . . di una gallina che voglia fare il verso del gallo" (146; "When women teach men, the children are born hunchbacks. . . . There's nothing worse than a hen that wants to change places with a rooster," 134–35). The one instance in which the peasants actually voice objection to Don Paolo as a group occurs when the priest wants to pay for a second bottle of wine in a row, since it is the *custom* for *everyone* to offer drink in his turn, the peasants included. Their words indicate their belief in accepted custom, and, at the same time, the irony of their misunderstandings of, and /or disagreements with, all that Don Paolo has hoped to demonstrate: "'Spetta a noi' dissero. 'Conosciamo le regole della creanza'" (148–49; "'It's our turn,' they said. 'We know the rules of courtesy,'" 137). The peasants joke about social customs and about the Church's "rules" ("precetti"), but they also follow both, so to speak, religiously. Nor can Don Paolo himself finally escape the rules of established social convention. As though to emphasize once more the priest's inevitable complicity, the text includes another notation uniting the customary distinctions of social hierarchy with those of religious rite: "'Bevete prima voi' [Daniele] disse al prete. 'Servirà di *benedizione*'" (149, my italics; "'You drink first,' [Daniele] said to the priest. 'That'll be the *blessing,*'" 137, my italics).

Changing the established social and political system through mutual accord of all the members is, plainly, a far more difficult and complex proposition than Don Paolo had originally hoped. This difficulty and complexity are crucial for the novel. Even though the relation between certain signs and their referents may be construed, following Don Paolo's demonstration, as arbitrary and conventional rather than as natural and fixed, this decision does not mean that a system of signs in social and political life is subject to change willy-nilly. Indeed, the deck has been stacked against Don Paolo from the very beginning, as the rest of the chapter makes clear. The natural/conventional opposition, like that between rule-governed and free behavior, is simply inadequate. What earlier had seemed a choice between neatly opposing positions in regard to the symbolic qualities of social signs and roles now appears as a series of distinctions at differing levels of signification and understanding, all involving different contexts and different kinds of symbolic meaning. Moreover, once the meaning of any sign has been instituted and reaffirmed through the patterns of usage and the interrelations between signs in a given system, the weight of history gives the sign a status that makes its relation to its referent appear much closer to the realm of necessity than to that of arbitrary convention. The difficulties in changing the rules implicit in this system of roles may be seen at work not only in the beliefs and habits of the aristocracy, the clergy, and the bourgeoisie, but also in those of the peasants.[7] At the same time, any individual "speaker" will have an ingrained, personal relation to the symbols representing his own experience, as Sciatàp's verbally referential nickname ("Shut up!") and his insistence in response to Don Paolo's question ("Sono *io* che devo rispondere") both demonstrate. Whoever would work against the established order of the sign through social revolution, therefore, must be committed to work against the historical forces of communal use and of individual acceptance as well. Merely exchanging the names or even the roles of the game's objects will never be enough: for a meaningful revolution to occur, the game itself must change.

There are several further notations toward the end of chapter 13 that are important to consider in the light of the peasantry's resignation to its role. The first of these comes at the conclusion of Sciatàp's description of the peasants' inbred diffidence, their constant complaints, and their fundamental inability to change their way of thinking:

> "Si nasce e si cresce nello stesso pensiero" disse Sciatàp. "I più lontani ricordi della nostra mente che cosa sono? I nostri vecchi che si lamentavano. I nostri figli che cosa ricordano della loro infanzia? Noi che ci lamentavamo. Si credeva che non potesse venire il peggio, ma il peggio è venuto. Anche i ciechi, anche i sordomuti lo sanno. Non ho mai incontrato una persona che la pensasse diversamente." (149)

> "We're born and raised with the same thought," said Sciatàp. "Our earliest memories? They were of the old people complaining. What will our children remember of their childhood? Our complaining. We thought it could never be worse, but it got worse. Even the blind and the deaf-mutes know it. I've never met anyone who thought differently." (137)

Sciatàp's reference to "deaf-mutes" ("anche i sordomuti lo sanno") is a common phrase from popular speech and adds to the realistic effects of the dialogue; but it also serves to recall an incident in the previous chapter that occurred between Don Paolo and the village's "sordomuto." Despite the filth of the deaf-mute's hut, located in the most remote corner of the village, as Don Paolo enters he has no inkling of the young man's condition. The priest tries to strike up a conversation, and undeterred by the other's lack of verbal response, Don Paolo ends up delivering what seems the prologue to a lecture on the unity of the peasants and workers in the Russian revolution of 1917. He does not get to the lecture itself, since Matalena, the inquisitive and overly possessive innkeeper, finds Don Paolo ("her priest") and tells him, in her astonishment, the nature of the deaf-mute's affliction. When Don Paolo returns to the inn, one of the peasants remarks that at first he had considered Don Paolo's ability to converse with the deaf-mute "un miracolo" (139; "a miracle" 127) but that later he realized it was only "uno sbaglio" ("a mistake"). Don Paolo denies that his attempt was either of these, but the peasants ignore his assertion and comment that the deaf-mute is, indeed, very intelligent; and they conclude that his affliction may be a chastisement from God for his exceptional intellectual capacities.

At this point, Don Paolo asks a question that links the thematic development of this earlier chapter to the conversations of chapter 13: "'Da che mondo è mondo' egli disse 'i cafoni si lamentano, ma restano rassegnati. Continuerà sempre così?'" (139; "'The peasants have been complaining ever since the world began,' he said. 'But they're resigned. Will it always be like that?'" 127). On occasion in the novel's beginning and middle chapters, and with especially dramatic effects in the later chapters, the answer to this question seems, perhaps, to be no. But in chapters 12 and 13, as well as in the novel generally, the answer seems in fact to be yes. Even the other important reference to deaf-mutes in the novel, moreover, the "falso sordomuto" of the opening chapter, serves primarily to suggest the layered complexity of the relations between truth and falsity in worldly roles (such as that of the activist-priest Peter/Paul) and leads only to the tentative and ambiguous implications of Don Benedetto's warning about the future of the state and those presently in power, not to any definite understanding or real action in regard to the difficulties of the peasants' situation (17; 18–19).

The peasants' demonstration of their lack of ability to think in terms of any condition differing from the one they have "always" known accounts for Don Paolo's despair at the conclusion of chapter 13. Their incapacity to conceive of everyday life in anything other than the available designations of the customary social and political roles and values results in their dependency on the language of superstition (such as the cows' horns the peasants "can't do without" in their struggle with the evil eye [155; 143]) and on that of political myth. These limitations keep the peasants in a state of adamant provincialism and make them subject to what Silone terms elsewhere the "worst tyranny," one of "words" (as exemplified in chapter 13 in the schoolteacher's use of the threat of "the Communists" in order to "save" her from having to think during her exchange with the peasants at the inn [145; 134]).[8] Furthermore, even when Magascià and Daniele affirm that everyone knows that the peasants think ill of the state's imposed taxes, of prices, of the draft, and of other laws, there is no indication whatever that they regard these as anything but necessary evils, which is to say, as further examples of things to be lamented—and accepted.

The chapter's conversations lead to another notation of importance, one that occurs in the description of Don Paolo on his return to his worktable and to the papers he had been reading at the chapter's opening, those entitled "Sull'inaccessibilità dei cafoni alla politica." This topic was a favorite of nineteenth- and early-twentieth-century dialectical materialism. The usual leftist position, from Marx on, was simply the affirmation of the idea expressed in the title. Still, Pietro/Paolo had hoped otherwise, as is so evident in the scene of the card game. At the conclusion of the chapter, however, his doubts, at least for the moment, far outweigh his hopes. He sits thinking "con la testa tra le mani" ("with his head in his hands") and then begins to write what turns out to be chapter 13's concluding (and, for Don Paolo, far from optimistic) lines: "Forse essi hanno ragione" ("Perhaps they are right").

Even if change were portrayed as definitely possible or easy in the narrative, a further problem would still exist: how to insure that such change would yield positive rather than meaningless or negative results. This is the problem that Don Paolo had posed to himself, again recorded in his notebook, at the end of chapter 9:

> È possibile partecipare alla vita politica, mettersi al servizio di un partito e rimanere sincero? La verità non è diventata, per me, una verità di partito? La giustizia, una giustizia di partito? L'interesse dell'organizzazione non ha finito col soverchiare, anche in me, tutti i valori morali, disprezzati come pregiudizi piccolo-borghesi, e non è diventato esso il valore supremo? *Sarei dunque sfuggito all'opportunismo di una Chiesa in decadenza per cadere nel machiavellismo di una setta?* (103, my italics)

Is it possible to take part in politics, to serve one party, and to remain sincere? Hasn't truth become for me the party's truth? and justice party justice? Has not the organization ended up by extinguishing in me all moral values, which are held in contempt as petit bourgeois prejudices, and has not the organization itself become the supreme value? *Have I then not traded the opportunism of a decadent Church to fall into the Machiavellianism of a sect?* (96, my italics)

Similar concerns are expressed later in the novel by Pietro's fellow activist, Uliva, during a conversation with Pietro Spina in Rome. Uliva, bitter and tortured by doubts, predicts that the present bureaucracy will merely be replaced by another, with equally insidious effects: "All'attuale inquisizione nera succederà un'inquisizione rossa. All'attuale censura, una censura rossa" (192; "The present black inquisition will be followed by a red inquisition. There'll be a red censorship instead of the present one," 177).[9] Don Paolo's doubts and Uliva's prediction of doom should also be compared with a comment made near the novel's beginning by Doctor Nunzio Sacca, Pietro Spina's childhood companion, who states his objection in direct relation to Pietro's change from belief in God to belief in the proletariat while retaining "il fanatismo. . . . [e] lo stesso assolutismo di una volta" (41; "the fanaticism. . . . [and] the same absolutism as before," 41).

To these problems, the reasonable control of change for good and the avoidance of fanaticism and corruption, as well as to that of the possibility of valid change, the novel provides no solution. The problems of praxis ("'Anche le rivoluzioni sono dei fatti' disse don Paolo," 174; "'Revolutions are facts, too,' said Don Paolo," 160) are no easier to solve than those of theory. The way to achieve the goals of social justice and freedom, which are suggested by Don Paolo at the conclusion of chapter 13 but derided as only a "sogno," or a "dream," by Grascia, Magascià, and Sciatàp, remains, at best, uncertain. As Sciatàp says, it is a fable that every now and then is repeated to no avail whatsoever: "I lupi e gli agnelli pascoleranno assieme nello stesso prato. I pesci grossi non mangeranno più i pesci piccoli. Una bella favola" (150; "The wolves and the sheep will graze together in the same pasture. The big fish won't eat the little fish any more. A fine fable," 137). By the end of the chapter, it is clear that only in the language of dreams can the fable of true social justice even be considered. As a dream, the notion seems beautiful, but as a meaningful social actuality, impossible.

Despite the skeptical and offhanded tone of Sciatàp's remarks at the chapter's ending, his discussion of this fable includes, beyond his knowledge, a detail of special significance in the overall organization of the novel. Sciatàp's description of the wolves and the lambs "in the same pasture" recalls Cristina's extraordinary experience with the wolf in the sheepfold as a baby and her seemingly charmed preservation from harm (115–16; 106). The reference also foreshadows the reappearance of the wolves later on with the snowfall (287–88; 265) and the specifically Christian ritual of Cristina's preparation for death as she falls to her knees, closes her eyes, and crosses herself in the midst of the howling wolves at the novel's conclusion. But this concluding ritual—like the rite of the "bread and wine" in the peasants' ceremony of mourning for the sacrificed Luigi Murica (291–93; 269–71), and like Pietro Spina's self-revelation, his promise to return, and his escape—offers no definite solution to the logical and practical problems raised in the text. Pietro/Paolo's goal is clear enough: his hope to combine the spiritual ideals of faith with the practical ends of socialist revolution, in what earlier is described as a sort of fancied union of Jesus Christ and socialism outside both the party and the Church (195; 180).[10] But the attempts to change social and political roles and values, and to avoid the corruptive potential of authority itself, appear as inconclusive and ambiguous at the end of the novel as they had at its beginning.[11]

It is important to see that this lack of resolution in the narrative is not merely a final mystification. This conclusion does contribute a sense of challenge and vitality to the end of the novel; but more to the point, it permits Silone's text to retain the rigor and also the complexity of its argument, which are apparent in the discursive sections of chapter 13 and which by the end may be seen in operation in the narrative's plotting as well as in its dialogue and description. There are no solutions at the conclusion of the narrative because, as demonstrated by the discursive array of assertion, counter-assertion, and growing complexity through the entirety of chapter 13 with its semantic parables ("C'era una volta . . ."; "Once upon a time . . ."), no clear-cut answers are available to the deeply ingrained problems of meaning that the novel raises.

To say that *Vino e pane* is a historical-political novel with strong autobiographical elements and that it was written in the mid-1930s, before any solutions to these problems in Italy were foreseeable, is to ignore the novel's continuing lack of resolution in the 1955 revision. The questions of resistance and change, as well as of social and political representation, grow as the novel proceeds. By the conclusion, given the complexity of the book's subject matter, any definitive answers would appear either forced or overly facile. At the same time, the narrative's open display of the issues of symbolic representation, and therefore of the properties and means of its own production as "fantasy," marks it as a particular kind of modern novel, self-conscious of its very status as representational fiction even as it masks that consciousness by filtering its self-knowledge through the discourse and actions of its characters. This is a perfectly legitimate approach for realist fiction, since language and symbolic meaning are not only the constituent elements of fictional narrative but also regular parts of the everyday world. In terms of the themes and events of chapter 13, and indeed of the entire narrative, the difficulties and uncertainties of the roles of "spina" (thorn) and "spada" (sword) in resistance to Italian Fascism have, in Silone's text, no end. But by the conclusion of the novel, the underlying problem, at least, is clear: How can a "thorn" *really become* a "sword"?

Postilla on Neorealism

Although the narrative of the Italian neorealists had important forerunners, the major period of the movement, in both literature and film, was during the years immediately following World War II. This is true in part because the fall of Fascism and the eventual liberation, with the subsequent opening up of Italian public life, gave rise to an outpouring of discourse about personal (yet shared) experiences, in what Italo Calvino has termed the communal, almost anonymous "smania di raccontare," or "rage to narrate."[12] It is perhaps worth noting in passing that the *locus classicus* of the sort of odd, at times near-comical obfuscation adopted of necessity by Italians *before* this opening up of discourse is a passage in Vittorini's *Conversazione in Sicilia* (1938–39, 1941), in which the local travelers on the train out of Messina can refer to the two Fascist officials outside only by the "senhal" of their metaphorical "puzza" (stench).

Since the primary subject matter of neorealist narrative is the country's recent experiences, the usual social and political topic of these works is the struggle against Fascism and the wartime suffering of the Italian populace, especially the working class and the peasantry. Although the group of authors most often considered to be part of the neorealist movement includes significantly disparate members (among others, Vittorini, Pavese, Moravia, Bilenchi, Viganò, Brancati, Fenoglio, Pratolini, and the young Calvino), their works of the period do share, at least in general terms, a common aesthetic. That aesthetic, like Silone's in *Vino e pane*, is a representational one. The commitment to worldly representation, when combined with the drive to tell about experience rather than to tell about telling, means that the weight given the effects of self-consciousness in neorealist narrative is slight.[13] It is true that certain novels of this group of writers and of this period do include significant self-reflexive aspects (perhaps most notably Vittorini's *Uomini e no* [1945], in which the status of the narrative itself is constantly put in question because of the uncertainty of the narrating identity). But extended treatment of these works in the context of literary self-consciousness, beyond consideration of the instructive example of Silone's novel written in exile and eventual discussion of Calvino's first novel in terms of his overall development as a writer, would be a misrepresentation both of neoralist narratives themselves and of the conditions of their creation.

Exceptions to this combination of representational aesthetic and historical milieu, such as Pavese's richly poetic and obsessively self-involved first-person narrative, *La luna e i falò* (1950), most often indicate that the force of neorealism within the narrative in question is already on the wane.[14] Indeed, over the course of the economic and cultural revival during the following decade, narrative aesthetics again assumed very different guises, with literary self-consciousness once more becoming an important issue. One of these guises was the revivification of the historical novel, recast as a meditation not only on human history but also on the novel's own status as a contemporary re-presentation of that history, as exemplified most incisively by Giuseppe Tomasi di Lampedusa's *Il Gattopardo*.

SEVEN

Lampedusa's Il Gattopardo

Figure and Temporality in a Historical Novel

Through the progression of the fictional narrative, Lampedusa's *Il Gattopardo* (1958; *The Leopard*) develops simultaneously a model of historical change and a critique of that model.[1] Not content with this sleight of hand, Lampedusa presents both the model and its critique by means of the seemingly antithetical modes of allegory and irony, or more precisely, through the interaction of the two. This heterogeneous mixture defines *Il Gattopardo* as a modern narrative that is at once perceptive and mystified, one in which the potentially disruptive functions of self-knowledge are contained only through the complementary and no less vigorous operations of *méconnaissance*.[2]

This active narrative development, proceeding by means of an increasingly obvious play of suppression and disclosure, is the most self-consciously presented aspect of the novel. This is not surprising, since the issues at stake—the workings of language, the meaning of representation, the nature of historical truth and historical change, and the very status of the historical novel—are the most reflexively pertinent ones that the narrative poses. These issues are particularly clear in the later sections, but their seeds are present from the very beginning of the story. Before dealing with the novel's examination of the techniques and concerns of representational fiction, however, it will be useful to sketch a few of the book's more significant characters in their relations both to each other and to the history of nineteenth-century Italian politics and society. Such a review is helpful not only because the depiction of the characters is central to the novel's gradual display of self-consciousness, but also because the story's cast of characters, like its overall organization and its thematic development, is especially rich and varied.

The characters can be arranged schematically in relation to the central figure of the Sicilian *principe*, Don Fabrizio. The exemplary figure of the old guard is Sua Maestà, Ferdinando II (whose post–1848 military tactics earned him the epithet "King Bomba"), with an occasional supportive voice supplied by Don Fabrizio's brother-in-law, "quel Màlvica." Between them, with the later and much more open addition of the "scimmiette" ("little monkeys") of the ball scene, the latter two figures represent a peculiarly Bourbon combination of tradition and gaucherie, emblems of a class still powerful yet in obvious decline. Opposite them and still in the first rank stand the figures of Italy's political, economic, and cultural future, Don Calogero Sedàra and Chevalley. Though Chevalley belongs to the lesser nobility, his *piemontese* birth and French name, as well as his spirited optimism, attest to the distance between him and Don Fabrizio. Sedàra represents a class on the rise, replete with the self-assertiveness and narrow perspective traditionally attributed to the profiteers of economic flux. Indeed, Chevalley, in his conference with Don Fabrizio, offers his own opinion of his companions in Italy's future as "gente senza scrupolo e senza prospettive" (209; "people with no scruples and no vision," 211), thus recalling a prior condemnation, voiced in surprisingly similar terms, of "la gente nova e i subiti guadagni," or "new people and quick profits" (*Inferno*, 16.73). In concert with Sedàra's sudden economic advance and social ascent (the second due to the coming marriage of Angelica to Tancredi) the "merits" of Don Calogero are depicted somewhat more generously in the latter portions of the book (157ff.; 159ff.), though his markers are still by no means all positive, as the sight of exposed drawers at the conclusion of the ball scene amply demonstrates.

Beneath this first rank there stands a second, positioned as a mirror image of the primary characters. These secondary characters have a certain importance in the narrative, and for brief periods they may even threaten to eclipse the primary ones, as does Don Tumeo in the hunting scene in chapter 3 or Don Pirrone in his return home in chapter 5. But even when they attain prominence, they still remain symbolically dependent, functioning only in implicit relation to their more significant counterparts. There is also a general difference in class, with the second rank serving as a bridge between the elevated stratum of Don Fabrizio and its distant opposite, the pit of "Peppe Mmerda." But even though these distinctions of class are important in historical terms, they are not absolutely determinant in defining interrelations among the fiction's characters, since the characters themselves represent clusters of abstract qualities—

economic, political, cultural, and intellectual—rather than monistic social entities.

In this regard, Don Pirrone may be seen as the secondary counterpart of Don Fabrizio, a type of surrogate ecclesiastical *principe,* who enters S. Cono just as triumphantly as Don Fabrizio had earlier returned to Donnafugata and who dispenses moral and political advice with the same mixed success as His Excellency. Like Don Fabrizio before him, Padre Pirrone manages, at his personal loss, to effect a solution to the familial difficulties heightened by the vagaries of "amore" during "l'estate di San Martino," or Indian summer (176, 232; 178, 233). Moreover, the Jesuit himself betrays his deep and somewhat elitist sense of kinship with the prince in his lamentation of the all too rare solaces of life, "mathematics [and] theology" (230; 232). Finally, flanked on either side of Don Pirrone are Ciccio Tumeo, the hunting companion at Donnafugata, and Ciccio Ferrara, the bookkeeper of the house outside Palermo.

In psychological terms all these characters, as well as the many others supporting them, may be considered secondary in their essential lack of self-knowledge: Don Pirrone in his openly biased and occasionally facile simplifications, Tumeo in his unknowing "snobbismo," and Ferrara in his dissimulating "anima illusa e rapace di un liberale" (40; "deluded and rapacious soul of a liberal," 44). As we have seen, too, in regard to the characters of the first rank, the narrative's most condemnatory remarks are reserved for the figure representing the rising capitalist class, Ciccio Ferrara, who unlike his counterparts, Russo and Sedàra, does not even act on his own initiative. That the valued term thus becomes self-knowledge indicates the importance of this function for the minor characters, for Don Fabrizio as the dominant character, and, no less significantly, for the entire text.

Moving back and forth across these three realms there is a central mediating figure, but this figure is not the prince. Indeed, Don Fabrizio could serve as mediator in terms of knowledge and, at times, in terms of attitude, but he does not act—or more accurately, he refrains from action in the world of men. At the same time that his faculty of vision allows him to see the world for what it is, it forever separates him from that world. He pays for this particular turn of mind in the unbridgeable gap between himself and the villagers he wishes to counsel, who cannot distinguish between Don Fabrizio's explanations and his expected ironic comments (124; 127), as well as in the distance between himself and his social peers, who avoid him not so much out of respect, as he believes, as out of fear

(256; 256). Indeed, in symbolic terms he even pays physically for his acute vision with "quella congiuntivite cui era soggetto" (126; "the conjunctivitis to which he was subject," 129). Consonant with this narrative primacy of thought over deed, the events of the historical period—of the military, economic, and social turbulence of the Risorgimento—fall not within the narrative proper but in the interstices between segments. Rather than venturing outside his carefully delimited sphere on his own, Don Fabrizio receives and interprets reports from emissaries of the world of time and change, some of which serve to make up the dialogical frame of narration (as, for example, the reports furnished by the king, Russo, Ciccio Tumeo, Chevalley, and Pallavicino). In this way, the narrative concentrates not on the historical world but on the play of consciousness within its central character, a figure twice removed from what he terms "i fatti" and fully at ease only in the presence of those few who seem to demonstrate "un animo simile al suo" (288; "a mind kindred to his own," 288), or better, when left to himself and the pure animal instinct of Bendicò or the predictable abstraction of the stars. The novel is filled with the residua of history, with overt "realistic" references to event and personage; but as far as the narration is concerned, the events of recorded history exist purely as exteriority, having vanished to leave only the traces reflected in the energy of the characters' reactions and in the narrative's abstract model of change.

The figure who does most to develop this model—the narrative's mediating character—is Don Fabrizio's alter ego, his nephew Tancredi. It is Tancredi who first offers the seemingly circular formulation that has such an effect on Don Fabrizio and that every other major "Garibaldian" character, from Russo to Chevalley, echoes in some way: "Se vogliamo che tutto rimanga come è, bisogna che tutto cambi" (36; "If we want everything to stay as it is, everything will have to change," 40). But, of course, this optimistic formulation, representing an apparently total resolution of change and stability, of flux and stasis, is not the sole position on this topic taken within the narrative. Paolo, Tumeo, Maria Stella, Concetta, and others all openly refuse, at one point or another, to recognize either the necessity or the fact of change, though their positions are undercut by emotional reactions to perceptions of personal failings, just as even the purest optimism of the *garibaldini* is clearly buoyed by desire for adventure and/or profit. At the same time, Don Fabrizio's original response to the indications of change must be considered in relation to his strong sense of class and tradition, to his feeling of consanguinity with those of the "medesima risma," or "same stock" (260; 260). It is true that by the period of chapter 1 Don Fabrizio's vision has clearly set him off from "suo cognato Màlvica . . . portavoce della folla degli amici" (18; "his brother-in-law Màlvica, the spokesman for their many friends," 22) as well as from the Bourbon royalty. But until Tancredi's expressions of optimism and his putative revolutionary actions, Don Fabrizio has literally no way to turn. Though in many respects he regards himself as a man of "modern tastes" (254; 254), his position and interests seem to link him irrevocably to the forces of the past and to what Don Pirrone terms, perhaps too generously, the robust "collective memory" of his class (224; 226). In a way, then, Tancredi would seem to furnish an almost miraculous bridge back to the world, the mediation by which Don Fabrizio may at once retain the essence of his past and win the energetic Garibaldian future.

The incident of the "pesche forestiere" ("foreign peaches") at the end of chapter 2 provides a more specific frame of reference for these abstract relationships. When Tancredi encounters his uncle before the fountain of Amphitrite and pretends to reprove him for his lascivious interests, Don Fabrizio fears that Tancredi wishes to broach the subject of his daughter, Concetta, with its curious miasma of love and death. But of Concetta Tancredi says nothing. Instead they examine the "pesche forestiere," and Tancredi voices his approbation of his uncle in this alternate role of "*agricola pius.*" The next scene is that of the ceremonial dinner, during which the mere presence of Angelica is sufficient to arouse the natural interest of all the males, the prince included, "vecchio cavallo da battaglia com'era" (91; "old war horse that he was," 95). At dinner Tancredi tells the story of the *garibaldini's* entry into the convent and ventures the double entendre that proves so fascinating to Angelica and so disturbing to Concetta. At the evening's conclusion, Don Fabrizio retreats to take a moment of solace alone with the stars and Bendicò, after which he can sleep; "Basta, dormiamoci su" (98; "Enough, let's sleep on it," 102).

On the next day comes the visit to the convent, no longer that of the tumultuous *garibaldini* and the future but rather that of Beata Corbèra, the Santo Spirito, and the past. In accordance with the letter of fedual privilege, and perhaps to make amends with Concetta (goddaughter of the deceased King Ferdinand), Tancredi requests permission to enter as one of the prince's retinue. At this point there is some confusion, as well as an especially caustic rebuke by Concetta, and the matter is dropped. The visit proceeds, and Tancredi disappears. The reader's discovery in chapter 8 that in terms of the narrative only one of these convents is "real" takes

Figure and Temporality in a Historical Novel 201

on crucial importance for subsequent interpretation, but for the moment it need not concern us.

The chapter concludes with Don Fabrizio's vision of Tancredi delivering the ripened peaches to an unexpected destination. As in the scene by the fountain, Tancredi is again dressed in dark blue, "il colore della mia seduzione" ("my color of seduction"), and once more Don Fabrizio notes his step is "leggero come un gatto" ("light as a cat's") (86, 103; 90, 106). What the prince had fancied in imagination his nephew accomplishes in deed, transporting the remarkable fruit where Don Fabrizio could not, or would not, go. As his uncle watches unseen behind the window, Tancredi moves along with the domestic at his back, deftly avoiding the narrative's playfully constructed emblems of both the old guard ("monello spadaccino"; "sword-waving urchin") and the new ("pisciata di mulo"; "urinating mule") and at last gaining the suddenly respectable and no less figurative "porta di casa Sedàra" ("door to the Sedàra house").

Several further comments should be made in regard to the implications that this incident holds for the central characters. First, as a mediating figure, Tancredi manages to maintain his position of energetic optimism through almost the entire text. He switches from disreputable *garibaldino* to soldier of the king, a new and somewhat different "Maestà" but royalty nonetheless, titular head of "l'esercito *vero*" (173; "the *real* army," 175). With Angelica he takes the voyage to "Cythera," beyond the worldly limits of time and space and into the land of "perennial desire." On their return to the "world of the living" (187; 189), Tancredi appears certain not only of the joys of the future but also of the seigneurial privileges of the past, and once again he turns his uncle's fancies of "lussuria atavica" (112; "atavistic lust," 116) into virtual realization, as though nothing had changed and all his privileges remained in force "dopo una vana rivolta" (176; "after a vain revolt," 178).

Once more it should be noted that this is an extreme position. It is an important aspect of the narrative's model, but neither is it that model's sole affirmation nor is it Don Fabrizio's position. Indeed, the prince indicates repeatedly that the very fact of worldly change implies neither cyclical stability nor improvement but debasement: "E dopo sarà diverso, ma peggiore" (213; "And after it will be different, but worse," 214). The prince and his land may be caught up momentarily in the "flusso della storia universale" (211; "flow of universal history," 211), but in response to Chevalley's heartfelt exhortations to collaborate, Don Fabrizio offers only the traditional enigmas of the island, the timeless solace of sleep and that of pure abstraction, "perché noi siamo dèi" (210; "because we are gods," 212).

For Don Fabrizio, then, his young nephew cannot finally represent the way back to the world. The bridge Tancredi constructs provides the material fortune and the feminine "bellezza" necessary to accompany his self-knowledge, personal energy, and traditional familial background. But Tancredi also has a further requisite attribute, youth and its concomitant optimism, that in mundane terms both gives him the future and forever denies it to his uncle. Don Fabrizio, caught straddled across two worlds, remains to the last in the dilemma of "un uomo di scienza . . . uno scettico" (142; "a man of science . . . a skeptic," 144). As Paul de Man has written of ironic skepticism in an essay on allegory and irony: "Irony divides the flow of temporal experience into a past that is pure mystification and a future that remains harassed forever by a relapse within the inauthentic. It can know this inauthenticity but it can never overcome it. It can only restate and repeat it on an increasingly conscious level, but it remains endlessly caught in the impossibility of making this knowledge applicable to the empircal world."[3]

At this point, therefore, it is necessary to distinguish Don Fabrizio from his figurative alter ego. This process of distinction is carried out within the text itself, as a counterpoint to the more regularly stated and more forthright assertions of similarity, beginning with the same fountain scene we have already discussed: "Per la prima volta gli sembrò che un senso di rancore lo pungesse alla vista del ragazzo" (86; "For the first time he felt a sense of rancor prick him at the sight of Tancredi," 90). This splitting of the subject in regard to the functions of maturity and love serves to define both the figure of the prince and that of Tancredi. It is not surprising, then, that the resolution of the prince's interior rancor is to be found neither in the barred world of his past nor in Chevalley's future of quasi-Aristotelian potentiality, nor yet in Tancredi's illusory mediation of youthful enthusiasm. The ironist's knowledge that originally separates the prince from the world continues to bar his reentry into it, offering resolution only in the transcendent imagery of pure and timeless perfection, in the stars and in death.

In this way Venus and her promised "appuntamento" become the central image not only of Don Fabrizio's later years, but as he comes to discover, of his entire existence. In fact, she was always there, "sempre fedele, aspettava sempre don Fabrizio alle sue uscite mattutine, a Donnafugata prima della caccia, adesso dopo il ballo" (273; "always faithful, always waiting for Don Fabrizio on his early morning outings, at Donnafugata before a hunt, now after the ball," 272–73). These are also the terms of his final journey: "Giunta faccia a faccia con lui sollevò il velo, e così, pudica, ma pronta ad esser posseduta, gli apparve più bella di come mai l'avesse intravista negli spazi stellari" (291; "When she was face to face with him she raised her veil, and there, modest, but ready to be possessed, she looked lovelier to him than she ever had when glimpsed in stellar space," 292). In a fashion similar to what Tancredi's optimistic formulation of worldly change had seemed to accomplish before, this image from a transcendent realm does resolve the apparent antinomies of flux and stasis, change and stability. For Don Fabrizio, however, this is not the beginning of time, but its end.

As each image of the "real" world of "carcasses and blood" is resolved in another of death and so of time, Don Fabrizio moves away from the world rather than into it. This progression is already under way by the narrative's opening scenes, with the interlocking yet constrasting images of the hideous corpse of the dead soldier in the garden and Bendicò's carefree excavations among the fancied "tumuli di smilzi giganti" (15; "graves of tall, thin giants," 20). The trip to the prince's favorite estate, moreover, to the garden world of "Donnafugata," is part of this same process. Don Fabrizio can know this unbridgeable distance between himself and the world of men and events, but he cannot eliminate it. Any attempt to do so leads finally to the nausea of inauthenticity fully as sensible as that felt amidst the "stomachevole" ambience of the Bourbon palace or amidst the "scimmiette" of the ball scene. By the end, he knows this too. The dance with Angelica, stage-managed by Tancredi, provides at the high point of the narrative a moment of near union with a purified yet earthly divinity, with what Ciccio Tumeo fancies as the odor of paradise itself (264; 264). But the moment ends with the final and inevitable sense of separation: "Soli vogliono stare gli innamorati, o magari con estranei; con anziani e, peggio che peggio, con parenti, mai" (265–66; "Lovers want to be alone, or at least with strangers; with older people and, worst of all, with relatives, never," 265). Now more than ever, the stars, "le sole persone per bene" ("the only really decent people"), have come to represent Don Fabrizio's only possible emergency exit (263; 262).

There is, of course, another self-distinguishing ironist at work within the text, operating both through and beyond the youthful astuteness of Tancredi and the aging skepticism of Don Fabrizio. Despite some criticism to the contrary, the narrator distinguishes himself from the characters as well as from the fictional events of the narration both in terms of voice and knowledge.[4] This essential narrative differentiation permits the narrator not only to present his characters through the seemingly immediate *style indirect libre* but also to regard them from an established distance, speaking in his own voice detached from both character and event. Very often the implicit judgments underlying this detachment appear identical to those of Don Fabrizio. But this is not always so, and the narrative attitudes toward all the central characters tend to become more openly critical as the novel progresses, and especially during the ball scene. In part, the effect of separation is achieved through verbal self-identification, often implying shared knowledge either of the cultural elements of the background ("come si usa da *noi*," 107, my italics; "as is done among *us* [i.e., in Sicily]," 112, my italics), or of the perspective of the reader implied by the text ("il padre del *nostro* Gesuita," 217, my italics; "the father of *our* Jesuit," 219, my italics; or again, "rincresce dirlo," 92, 93; "sorry to say," 95, 96). This type of verbal detachment fades as suddenly as it appears, thus exemplifying the essentially spontaneous nature of the ironic intrusion (what de Man terms irony's "synchronic structure").[5] Yet in terms of the overall narrative, the ironic knowledge that shapes the fundamental relationship between the narrator and his own narration is not synchronic but continuous, as we shall see.

Through the play of apparent immersion in the world and knowledgeable separation from it (including such distancing effects for the reader as the mention of events outside of the historical novel's temporal frame), the narrator defines the inevitable duplicity of his relationship to his text, a relationship that is seemingly parallel to that established between Don Fabrizio and his own ironist's perception of "the world." But these relationships are neither synonymous nor truly coincident, even in their fundamental duplicity. This is true because through the additional separation of the author and reader from the world of the narrative at hand, the self-identified figure of the narrator is forever barred from even the illusion of coincidence with the fictional character to whom he appears so similar in both attitude and knowledge.

Despite the discussion thus far, it would be inaccurate to claim that Lampedusa's novel relies exclusively on irony for its mode of presentation. Indeed, in many ways the apparently antithetical mode of allegory dominates. The allegorical elements of the narrative appear from the very first pages, beginning with the frescoed images of the gods and including the figure of "il Gattopardo" itself. These mythological and zoomorphic representations occur within the consciousness of the principal characters as well as apart from them in the occasional discursive sections during which the narrator speaks solely in his own voice. In organizational terms, the constant mythological associations—Classical, Christian, Semitic, and Eastern—also serve as underlying parallels for certain portions of the text. In this way, Tancredi's appropriation of the reputedly magical "frutti . . . giallognoli," or yellowish fruit, recalls Hercules' theft in the garden of the Hesperides, just as the lovers' withdrawal into the fabulous world of "desiderio perenne" recalls the ideal yet restricted consummation of Eros and Psyche.[6]

There is also a wealth of allegorical reference to more properly "literary" sources (including, among others, Aesop's political fables, the *canti* of the Late Romantic poet and patriot Aleardo Aleardi, the *Quixote*, and the Ariostesque "fuga di Angelica"), along with allusion to Dante's special perspectives on the historical degeneration embodied in the old man of Crete (79; 83), the "aiola" of the transitory world (138; 141), and the transcendent stars of eternity.[7] Finally, the literary/legendary name of Tancredi and the mythological one of Fabrizio (*fabbro*, "smith-Vulcan") tend to emphasize the active ability of the younger character as well as the essential ambiguity of the older. In this ambiguity, and through his own interior discourse, Don Fabrizio is ironically tied to and distinguished from that other figure so difficult of definition, initially referred to as "un cornuto," or cuckold (57; 61) and only afterwards the apparent victor: "Lui stesso [don Fabrizio] aveva detto che i Salina sarebbero sempre rimasti i Salina. Aveva avuto torto. L'ultimo era lui. Quel Garibaldi, quel barbuto Vulcano aveva dopo tutto vinto" (286; "He [Don Fabrizio] had said himself that the Salinas would always remain the Salinas. He had been wrong. He was the last. That Garibaldi, that bearded Vulcan, had won after all," 286).

This mixture of active allegorical intertextuality and "realistic" presentation accounts for the ease with which seemingly mimetic details take on symbolic values of love and power within the narrative, as we have seen, for example, at the conclusion of Tancredi's "theft."[8] Indeed, "history" itself, in its factitiousness as an abstract model of change exterior to yet in some ways incorporated in the text, provides a link between the allegorical and mimetic functions, so that the passage of the reigns of the gods serves to parallel both the rhythmic changes of nature and the transfer of sovereignty between the two historical "re" (46, 107; 50, 111). In this dependence upon anterior models, the mode of allegory tends to provide a source of depth and temporal duration in apparent opposition to the spontaneity of irony. Yet despite their seeming antinomy, the two modes in fact exist simultaneously within the text, in a relation that is not one of opposition but rather of interaction.

An examination of the hunting scene at the beginning of chapter 3 should clarify this narrative process. The chapter begins with a seemingly objective description of seasonal change, a subject broached several times in the course of the story:

> La pioggia era venuta, la pioggia era andata via; ed il sole era *risalito* sul trono *come* un re assoluto che, allontanato per una settimana dalle barricate dei sudditi, *ritorna a regnare* iracondo ma raffrenato da carte costituzionali. Il calore ristorava senza ardere, la luce era autoritaria ma lasciava sopravvivere i colori, e dalla terra rispuntavano trifogli e mentucce cautelose, sui volti diffidenti speranze (107, my italics)

> The rains had come, the rains had gone, and the sun was *back* on its throne *like* an absolute monarch kept off it for a week by his subjects' barricades, *and now reigning once again,* choleric but under constitutional restraint. The heat refreshed without burning, the light domineered but let colors live, there sprouted cautiously from the soil clover and mint, and on the faces appeared diffident hopes. (111, my italics)

Whether the background reference within the passage is to the previously mentioned "colpo di Stato di Giove contro Saturno" (46; "Jove's *coup d'état* against Saturn," 50) or to the unsuccessful revolt of the Giants (which would correspond more precisely to the text's stated return of one and the same king) is not, for the moment, of pressing importance. Rather, the most significant aspect of the passage is the ease with which the natural, mythological, political, and historical associations are carried through. The fact of change is noted, but it is quickly mitigated by the return of monarchical stability. At the same time, political power is more closely restrained than before ("raffrenato") in the historical form of a constitutional monarchy. The kingdom is unified and peaceful, with hope tempered only by caution, and there is room once more for "colori" and "trifogli" (thus picking up the image of Tancredi's now official "tricolore" of chapter 1).

This unobtrusive allegorization, however, is not the only manner of presentation within the chapter's introductory paragraphs. A few lines later, the now openly self-identifying narrator illustrates the results of the scarcity of game in the Sicilian landscape: "Così come don Ciccio si reputava fortunato se a sera poteva sbattere sul tavolo un coniglio selvatico, il quale del resto veniva *ipso facto* promosso al grado di lepre, come si usa da noi" (107; "Just as Don Ciccio considered himself lucky to be able in the evening to slap onto the table a wild rabbit, which at any rate would be promoted, as is done among us, *ipso facto* to the rank of hare," 111–12). The metaphorical relation "coniglio"-"lepre" depends not on mythological or political reference but on the narrator's knowledge of Sicilian customs. Furthermore, this is a coded body of custom in which the narrator himself shares ("da noi"). At the basis of the metaphor is a misrecognition, perhaps originally spontaneous, motivated either by hope or by the self-deception of despair, but now conventionalized into formal, agreed-upon practice (see, for example, the unremarked reference to "lepri," or hares, in the formal dinner scene of chapter 2 [93; 97]). Unlike the presentation of the previous paragraph, here the metaphorical relationship at the core of language is purposefully dissected ("*ipso facto*") by the knowledgeable narrator, who later, at least on this particular point, refuses further self-mystification ("Era un coniglio selvatico," 120; "It was a wild rabbit," 123). This theory of metaphor as a trope depending upon identity through transference recalls, among others, both Vico and Rousseau. The theory is developed throughout Lampedusa's text, and in this pasage takes the form error → lie → convention. Such a clear statement of ironic self-knowledge on the part of the fictional narrator should logically abolish the confusion between figurative and literal discourse, thus rendering further allegorical-realistic presentations of the type of the previous paragraph impossible. Nonetheless, the narration does not cease, nor does the narrator desist in his balancing of the two modes of discourse that are now openly coexistent within his text.

The continuation of the fictional presentation in the face of this stated narrative self-knowledge serves to indicate, on the part of the narrator, an instance of active *méconnaissance*. As such, it furnishes a parallel to the psychological reactions of Don Fabrizio. The prince enters Donnafugata knowing, as Tancredi has stated, that at least in some respects change was inevitable, both in historical and in personal terms. This incontrovertible process provides enough of a threat to Don Fabrizio's most highly valued mental state, his "pur dubbia calma" ("precarious calm"), that he permits himself to be deceived and initially contributes to his own deception, thus assuring both change and debasement: "Ed il Principe, che aveva trovato Donnafugata immutata, venne invece trovato molto mutato lui, che mai prima avrebbe adoperato un modo di dire tanto cordiale; e da quel momento, invisibile, cominciò il declino del suo prestigio" (74; "And the Prince, who had found Donnafugata unchanged, was found very much changed himself, for never before would he have adopted so cordial an expression; and from that moment, invisibly, began the decline of his prestige," 78). This same process recurs when Don Fabrizio receives the news of Concetta's youthful affections. The prince strives actively to reduce his personal anxiety, which arises in part from sudden awareness of his own inevitable aging. This is the same type of perceived threat which has at times led him as far as willful self-deception in his reaction to Concetta and her difficult ways. The result of this particular disturbance, crucial to later developments in the story, is that Don Fabrizio first solves the problem in abstraction, in his own mind, and then goes to sleep ("e si appisolò," 85; 89).[9] This is an instance of the intentional withdrawal into the calm of "un sonno che rassomigliava al nulla" (31; "a sleep that seemed like the end of all things," 38), which punctuates Don Fabrizio's reactions through the first three chapters and which, according to the prince himself, defines the condition of the entire island (204; 206).

In fact, this modus vivendi of eliminating noticeable difference between the past and the future is what permits Don Fabrizio to sleep, since it effectively reduces the anxiety arising from a disturbing perception. This is also the organizational core of the méconnaissance that permits the confusion of Tancredi's original formulation of historical change as well as the blurring of distinction, in chapter 3's opening paragraph, between absolute and constitutional monarchy (a confusion heightened by the initially ambiguous "come"). The effects of debasement remain suppressed from consciousness, to become fully recognized only later, if at all. As a misrecognition of a partially perceived fact, this process works to reduce the anxiety of the original perception. It does this by replacing the tension of difference with a transient state of fictional identity, thus leading to a peace felt as pleasure. This psychological combination of action and passivity, with its obvious Freudian overtones, is eventually thematized in the text through Don Pirrone's depiction of the universal human condition: "Tutti noi, egualmente soggetti alla doppia servitù dell'amore e della morte" (227; "All of us, equally subject to the double slavery of love and of death," 229).[10] In purely formal terms the organization of the prince's psychological méconnaissance is again that of metaphor itself, momentarily abolishing necessary difference through a false assertion of an identity that in its turn threatens to become prolonged as stable convention. This process is equally essential to Don Fabrizio's mental functioning and to the completed form of the narrative as a fictional metaphor for historical "reality." Similar to the narrative's "coniglio"-"lepre" model of transference, both Don Fabrizio's characteristic méconnaissance and its linguistic counterpart in the text arise from a passion (anxiety, fear, love, hope) that appears absolutely anterior but in fact results from a perception the effects of which are not just prior but also continuing. As long as the active antecedents of méconnaissance remain hidden from view, it continues to function, either by permitting an individual's existence in the world or by allowing the continuation of the fictional text despite a certain degree of self-knowledge. However, as the pressure of awareness increases, or as the mometary disjunction of irony tends toward prolongation, the model itself threatens to self-destruct, vanishing in the cataclysm of self-knowledge. And this, as we shall see, is very nearly what happens within the narrative of Il Gattopardo.

For the time being, of course, the narrative does not cease its fictional progression, nor does Don Fabrizio cease to utilize the forms of fiction and even those of "malafede," or bad faith (p. 52; 56). Indeed, the prince insists repeatedly on the social necessity of "buone creanze" (good manners), both before and after the opening of chapter 3. The same character capable of concise disclosure of the figure of others' naive "amore" (84 et passim; 88 et passim), as well as of detecting the conventional deception at the heart of the metaphor of political representation ("512 = 512"), is equally subject to both the pleasures of abstract constructions and the very power of naming ("l'autentico Gattopardo").

A crucial scene in this regard is the killing of the "coniglio selvatico," or wild rabbit, alluded to previously:

> Don Fabrizio si vide fissato da grandi ochi neri che, invasi rapidamente da un velo glauco, lo guardavano senza rimprovero, ma che erano carichi di un dolore attonito rivolto contro tutto l'ordinamento delle cose; le orecchie vellutate erano già fredde, le zampette vigorose si contraevano in ritmo, simbolo sopravvissuto di una inutile fuga: l'animale moriva torturato da una ansiosa speranza di salvezza, immaginando di potere ancora cavarsela quando di già era ghermito, proprio come tanti uomini. (120)

> Don Fabrizio found himself stared at by big black eyes quickly overlaid by a glaucous veil; they were looking at him with no reproof, but full of tortured amazement at the whole order of things; the velvety ears were already cold, the vigorous paws contracting in rhythm, the seemingly still-living symbol of a useless flight; the animal died tortured by anxious hopes of salvation, imagining it could still escape when it was already caught, just like so many human beings. (123)

It may initially appear that the principal textual reference ("proprio come tanti uomini"; "just like so many human beings") is directed toward the self-deluded and now fallen members of the prerebellion aristocracy ("Quel Màlvica! Era stato sempre un coniglio," 56; "That Màlvica! He'd always been a rabbit," 60). However, intervening between Màlvica's futile departure and the useless "fuga" of the hunters' prey, there occurs another flight, that of "il Gattopardo" himself: "Il diletto dei giorni di caccia era altrove, suddiviso in molti episodi minuti. . . . nel fuggire, insomma" (107–8; "The joy of these days out shooting lay elsewhere, subdivided in many tiny episodes. . . . in fleeing, in fact," 112). In the previously cited passage, moreover, the very "symbol" of useless flight is the rhythmic contraction of the now grotesquely vigorous *zampette*.

As we have seen before, Don Fabrizio's progressive movements, first to Donnafugata and then into the "immemoriale silenzio della Sicilia pastorale" (108; "immemorial silence of pastoral Sicily," 113), seem to lead him away from the world and from time itself. This flight occurs in the midst of, and at least partially in response to, the phenomenon that Don Fabrizio himself terms "la stupefacente accelerazione della storia," or "the stupefying acceleration of affairs" (115; 119). In certain ways this escape appears successful, utilizing the mediation of abstract images to annihilate the last traces of temporality. But in the terms of the narrative this very "fuga" from time and place occurs in time and in space. In more concrete terms, even the artistry of Don Fabrizio's imagination does not succeed in permanently erasing "Donnafugata con il suo palazzo e i suoi nuovi ricchi" ("Donnafugata with its palace and its new rich"). Like the animals he chooses to hunt as a pastime, he is himself "incappato" ("caught") in the social circumstances of his time and of his class (112; 116). As distinct from them, however, as well as from "quel Màlvica," Don Fabrizio both feels and recognizes the nature of his situation. In the succeeding portions of the narrative, this distinctive combination of self-knowledge and willful self-mystification eventually separates him from even the most compatible of his fellows. But irrespective of whether he is alone or with others, the motivated méconnaissance in which he momentarily indulges—the perception of the Sicilian landscape as further removed in time than Donnafugata, or even than "una utopia vagheggiata da un Platone rustico" (109; "a utopia dreamed up by a rustic Plato," 113)—is foredoomed both by its nature as a fiction and by its occurrence within the inescapable progression of time.[11] Just as the previous metaphorical expression of hope, "Grazie a Dio, mi sembra che tutto sia come al solito" (70; "Thank God, everything seems as usual," 74), represented not only a wish but also an underlying anxiety based on Don Fabrizio's perception of change, so his half-recognized and half-relished flight during the hunting scene represents the tension of the two aspects of time common both to narrative fiction and to cognitive life, of isolated moment and continuing progression. At this point we should recall the basic image of the opening section of chapter 3, with its as yet indecisive mixture of departure/return, victor/vanquished, hunter/hunted, and living/dead, now fully recognizable as a metaphor not only for flight and its perception but also for time itself.

Before moving from the third chapter, we should return to the allegorical confusion of the opening reference. As noted previously, the continuing use of mythological allusion, begun by the narrator and attributed as well to almost all the Sicilian characters, lends an aura of allegorical duration to the text not only as a literary artifice but also as the representation of the habitual perceptions of the Sicilian populace. But even the attribution of a certain flexibility in popular perspective is not sufficient to account for the narrator's apparently willful and repeated confusion of Saturn and Jove, and especially not for the blurring of political distinction between absolute and constitutional monarchy. Indeed, both of these distinctions have already been made within the text itself ("Del resto, neppure Giove era legittimo re dell'Olimpo," 46; "Anyway, even Jove wasn't the legitimate King of Olympus," 50). Nor is this the only such instance of apparent contradiction within the narrative. Even taking Tancredi as the active Hercules of the theft in the spring-fed garden and Don Fabrizio as the god's elderly exemplar rising in the fashion of an "Ercole ... fumante" (79; "Hercules ... steaming," 83) to the heavens, this still does not resolve Tancredi's repeated distinction between his uncle's roles as libidinous rogue and as "agricola pius" (87, cf. 35; 90, cf. 35).

One manner of resolving this confusion is simply to regard both characters as dual avatars of the various principal deities, with "il sole" as the island's only true ruler. In many ways this position of intentional ambivalence is the one adopted by the text. Thus, Don Fabrizio serves in one sense as the figure of Saturn, the Romans' *agricola pius* prudently cultivating his garden world, and in another the elderly *roué* of Jovian repute, the hero both of the Parisian "sgualdrinella" Sarah and of Mariannina during his Palermitan descents. Tancredi, already linked to his uncle through the physical resemblance of his distinctive blue eyes, through his intellectual attitude, and in part through birth, becomes Don Fabrizio's full representative both in the arena of political power and in the arena of sexuality ("un tantino ignobile. E [don Fabrizio] stesso era come Tancredi," 98; "slightly ignoble. And he himself was like Tancredi," 102). Indeed, it is precisely the half-mortal Hercules (in the alternate opening reference) that Jove requires in order to repulse the Giants' revolt and to effect a safe return to his throne. On Tancredi's part, this complex relationship of synonymy, in which he simply reflects what he already both represents and desires, is thematized by his lingering Narcissian glance at his own "correttezza elegante" just prior to the family's "triumphal" entry into Donnafugata: "Quando aveva tirato fuori l'acqua dal pozzo a molti usi, si era guardato un momento nello specchio del secchio, e si era trovato a posto" (63; "When he had drawn the water from the well of many uses, he had glanced at himself for a second in the mirror of the bucket, and he had found himself in good order," 67). And again this narcissistic attention to correctness and stability seems entirely appropriate, considering the neatly circular nature of his original historical formulation (a formula of the type that has been under vigorous attack in Italy during recent decades as "antistoricismo").

Nonetheless, this is the very model of historical change that is never permitted to stand alone in the text without its complementary and continuous critique.[12] Balancing the motivated ambiguity underlying the chapter's first paragraph ("re assoluto" ↔ "re costituzionale") is the series of previously denoted shifts of mythological dynasty, each entailing its particular and significant social change. In similar fashion, Don Fabrizio's semi-willful illusion of the annihilation of time within the Arcadian countryside is soon balanced by the text's "fable" of the irrepressibly industrious ants, heralding the age of the little man already under way beneath "il sole costituzionale": "Ma se una fucilata aveva ucciso il coniglio, se i cannoni rigati di Cialdini scoraggiavano già i soldati borbonici, se il calore meridiano addormentava gli uomini, niente invece poteva fermare le formiche"

(121; "But even if a shot had killed the rabbit, if the bored guns of [General] Cialdini were already dismaying the Bourbon troops, if the midday heat was already putting men to sleep, still nothing could stop the ants," 125). The original mythological misapprehension may thus be seen as an instance of the same confusion of the two aspects of time that has permitted the occasional self-mystification of Don Fabrizio but that has not finally succeeded in returning him to the world either in his own "character" or in that of his nephew. In terms of allegorical reference, the alternating separation and confusion of the two gods, Saturn and Jove, exactly parallels the attempted splitting of the "subject" of Don Fabrizio in defense of the precarious balance: knowledge/mystification.[13] To cite de Man on the development of the subject-object relation: "The dialectical relationship between subject and object . . . is now located entirely in the temporal relationships that exist within a system of allegorical signs. It becomes a conflict between a conception of the self seen in its authentically temporal predicament and a defensive strategy that tries to hide from this self-knowledge."[14]

The process of allegorical confusion, like that of historical, social, and psychological méconnaissance, permits Don Fabrizio to maintain a sense of personal control even against the onrushing "fatti." The desire for stability, achieved under the auspices of abstraction, may lead as far as the convincing "illusion" that even "gli astri obbedissero ai suoi calcoli (come, di fatto, sembravano fare)" (15; "the stars obeyed his calculations [as, in fact, they seemed to be doing]," 19). But by presenting the opposite view, effected through character, narrator, and contrasting segments of textual organization, the narrative manages to develop both model and critique as two essential elements of the same process, each providing implicit review of the other. In some ways the island, as well as the nation in which it officially shares, has remained the same; yet in other respects—socially, politically, culturally—all is perceptibly different. Furthermore, the total narrative becomes progressively clearer in regard to these matters, even to the point of ultimately revealing the illusion of all the gods (258; 258), whereas Don Fabrizio remains to the end willing to face real change only if he can maintain some inner sense of control and stability. Thus, he succeeds astutely in explaining the underlying nature of Sicily (in conversation with the well-meaning outsider Chevalley), while claiming for himself the lack of "la facoltà di ingannare se stesso" (207; "the faculty of self-deception," 209), and only a moment later admits, "Ed io stesso, del resto, se queste cose le avesse dette lei, me ne sarei avuto a male" (212;

"And anyway, I myself, if *you* had said these things, would have been offended," 213).

Up to this point, our analysis of Lampedusa's novel has remained focused on elements either actually noted by the text or clearly implied by the narrative progression. But in regard to the misapprehension of the reigns of the deities, there is an aspect that at first the narrative appears to suggest only vaguely. As a Roman deity, Saturn is more often associated with the Greek Cronus, the Titan overthrown by his son, Zeus (Jove, Jupiter), and to whom Don Fabrizio appears to be compared more than once (as in the description of his "innocente nudità titanica," 79; "innocent titanic nudity," 83). Oddly enough, it is during his most Saturnian scenes (in the early shaving scene, for example, and in the garden at Donnafugata) that Don Fabrizio tends to regard Tancredi not as an avatar of himself but rather as "un altro," fully capable of inspiring indignation and even rancor. These two difficult moments hinge on elements of temporal passage and on sexual activity; and, as such, they suggest something more than the mere confusion of the dualistic aspects of stability and change that the model of Cronus and Zeus would indicate. With the addition of the element of romance, along with the unpleasant "subject of Concetta," Tancredi threatens to become fully an other, not only in terms of political power but also of sexuality. Don Fabrizio may harbor a vaguely Oedipal jealousy of the Tancredi-Angelica relationship (112, 162, et passim; 116, 164, et passim), yet he is necessarily barred from open apprehension of these particular feelings in regard to his daughter. Don Pirrone, in broaching the subject of Concetta's emotions with Don Fabrizio (79–84; 83–88), unwittingly suggests the most terrifying threat of all, forcing Don Fabrizio into the untenable position of the second deity that stands behind the Roman Saturn, not Cronus but the Titans' father and previous ruler—born of the earth yet god of the heavenly "stelle"—the figure of Uranus (cf. 120; 124). This is the very fate, of symbolic dethronement *and* mutilation, against which Don Fabrizio reacts so vehemently because so unknowingly. He can gain Tancredi as a son only by permitting him to become an other, thus either accepting him openly as a threat or giving up the essential, "youthful" part of himself that Tancredi represents. Indeed, it is only as the conversation between Tancredi and Don Fabrizio in the garden turns safely to different topics, to the "pesche forestiere" and the people of Donnafugata, that the prince finally regains his former feelings for his nephew. This full méconnaissance, indicated only by the prince's otherwise inexplicably severe reactions and by the apparent confusion within the text, provides a substantial measure of the underlying energy of the following scenes in both organizational and thematic terms. In his own words Don Fabrizio depicts his people as a race apart: "noi siamo dèi." But he does not say, or seem consciously to know, which gods he really means.

By the time of the opening scenes of chapter 3, then, the various possibilities of temporal succession have all been clearly stated: that nothing will change, that all will change yet remain the same, that all will be different. The figure below represents these positions schematically in an arrangement that is similar to our opening discussion of character.[15] Once

Saturn		Sun	Jove	
Absence of Motion		Motion without Change	Full Motion	
Uranus	Cronus→	(Tancredi)	Difference (*Piemontesi*)	Debasement (*Garibaldini*)

again this deployment indicates an apparent attempt on the part of the narrative to create a "natural" mediation between two polar opposites. The first position represents not so much true temporality as the annihilation of time, achieved only by means of Don Fabrizio's willful dream in the Sicilian countryside and by the island's metaphorical "sonno." The second is represented by the circular passage of the seasons and Tancredi's original political assessments. The third is depicted most typically in the text's repeatedly negative evaluations of the social and political elements of the new regime. Don Fabrizio adopts each of these positions at one time or another, progressing through a spiraling series of alternations in regard to both the historical and the more "personal" elements of the narrative.

Here again, it is important to note that in terms of the narrative what seems the central mediation is in fact neither "natural" nor successful, since the members of the original opposition are not truly opposing entities but two aspects of the same underlying function. Don Fabrizio's escape into timeless abstraction is not any more effective against the necessary degeneration of his physical corpus than is the island's "morfina" against the rising forces of the new regime. Rather than denigrating or valorizing Don Fabrizio's situation, the narrative's multilayering of reference has the overall effect of exposing him in the fundamental irresolvability of his predicament in personal, social, and historical terms. Through the generative energy of its essential misapprehension, his willful flight from time ends not in Arcadian escape but in the ultimate "silenzio" of death and, in symbolic terms, of violent death at that. Once more, however, considered in relation to its symbolic underpinnings, the subject of Lampedusa's novel is more accurately the entire process of dying than death itself. As in the opening myth, the necessity of temporal progression begins not with Zeus but with Cronus, behind whom lies the original mutilation forever barring the way back to "eternity." Don Fabrizio is fully at ease only with the earth ("fratello dei suoi rozzi villani," 88; "brother to his rough peasants," 91) or with the timeless and controlled abstraction of the stars. As is again crucial to the overall narrative critique of temporal illusion, the one mediating position he cannot indefinitely maintain is the "solar" méconnaissance of motion without change.

In its basic elements, then, Don Fabrizio's is a critique of both perception and judgment. Crucial to its resolution is the ironist's distinguishing apprehension that knowledge, as a dominant term, contains within itself not-knowing, the ultimate inability to "know all." Rather than annihilating exterior existence this knowledge then takes the world itself, in both immediate experience and abstract model, as the "text" upon which its critique is effected, progressing by turns through readings and misreadings. In a parallel process, the narrative initiates and carries forth a critical examination of its own, one that encompasses and *transcends* Don Fabrizio's. We have already seen an element of this in the narrator's concise treatment of the metaphor "coniglio"-"lepre." There are many similar instances of this sort of patent linguistic investigation, beginning with the "parole bellissime," or "beautiful words," of the straw man Màlvica (18; 22) and including the sardonic "Verbo"-*"frac"* ("Word"-"tails") analogy of the dinner scene (89; 93). As the narrative develops, however, this procedure takes a new and seemingly precarious turn, pointing the text's analysis increasingly toward the very validity of language. The narrator notes, for example, that Don Fabrizio's mystified "subjects" cannot distinguish between his use of irony and of simple referential statement, a challenge that at times even the narrator declines: "Non era mai possibile conoscere quando il Principe ironizzasse o quando si sbagliasse" (148; "It was never possible to tell when the Prince was being ironic and when he was simply mistaken," 150). For Don Pirrone's sister, Sarina, the world around her threatens to become "una edizione . . . illeggibile" (234; 236), just as earlier the narrative found discrimination between the "real" avatars of the *Quixote* to be so difficult (142; 144). Finally, even the Jesuit father manages to hide the nature of truth not in silence but in discourse, through utilization of the casuistic distinction between "favola" and "menzogna" (241; "fable" and "lie," 242).

As these instances of linguistic inquiry mount up within the text, their effects spread beyond individual characters and even beyond confinement to the narrative's sections of dialogue and description. What begins as a subtle critique ends, in the novel's last pages, as a directly posed problem of major consequence for the understanding of the entire text. A central moment in this process occurs during the prince's review of his life, in the course of which the narrative first denotes the valued "conversazioni" with Giovanni "prima che questi scomparisse" ("before he disappeared") and then parenthetically appends the comment "alcuni *monologhi*, per esser veritieri, durante i quali aveva creduto scoprire nel ragazzo un animo simile al suo" (288, my italics; "a few *monologues,* if the truth were told, during which he had thought to find in the boy a mind kindred to his own," 288, my italics). The apparent innocence of the clarification only serves to underline the importance of the potential negation, which is an especially disturbing one. Up to this time, the background figure of Giovanni has been regularly presented as the prince's natural likeness, as the absent "type" whose role Tancredi fills in exchange. This seemingly casual notation, contaminating the previously unquestioned indications of the rapport between the two, causes a moment of narrative *vertige* that is difficult to resolve. Through it, the essential reliability of the prince's perspective is put in doubt. It is true that this notation joins its predecessors as a further reminder of the limitations of language. Yet at the same time, it initiates a process of forced critical review, by means of which the reader is directed not only forward, through apparent prefiguration, but also back against the narrative development, in a search for information that now appears solely as absence.

The partial negation within the explicit contrast between "conversazioni" and "monologhi" is the penultimate instance of doubt leading to the text's most disturbing expression of self-knowledge, the carefully presented "metatextual" moment of Concetta's concluding discovery. When Tassoni unwittingly furnishes the revelation of Tancredi's "frottola guerresca," or "tale of war" (312; 312), the narrative places in relief both Concetta's relation to her past and the basic enigma of original motivation in regard to each of the central characters. The very scene that Concetta had originally considered as an emblem of a lost battle may in fact have been an indication of Tancredi's underlying affection. According to Tassoni's report, Tancredi's true feelings were that "'era tanto cara . . . che se non mi fossi trattenuto la avrei abbracciata lí, davanti a venti persone ed al mio terribile zione'" (312–13; "'she was so sweet . . . that if I hadn't restrained myself I would have embraced her then and there, in front of twenty people and that imposing uncle of mine,'" 312).

This alternate reading of Concetta's delusion ("ormai quasi storica") can be supported in part by a cursory review of the text. From this later perspective both the garden scene and the scene at the "real" convent appear intentionally ambiguous. As for the dinner scene itself, it should be recalled that it is placed within a chapter dominated by the active perceptions of Don Fabrizio, whose bias in regard to a Tancredi-Concetta alliance is colored in ways beyond his immediate apprehension, as we have seen. Furthermore, Don Fabrizio's reactions remain a source of inexplicable vexation to him even after the union of his nephew and Angelica has been assured (265; 264). Moreover, the prince's original reaction was not in favor of Angelica but of anyone else *except* Concetta, even though the narrative was perhaps preparing the way through the quiet verbal echo between Sutèra and Sedàra (84; 88). Finally, the narrative does not fail to note the true nature of Tancredi's status as a desirable match (252; 252), thus supplying conclusive affirmation of his ability to attain success in the world regardless of the financial underpinnings of the marriage "contract."

This is not to say that Concetta now appears to have withdrawn from the contest too soon or that the Tancredi-Angelica pairing was not inevitable. The concluding scene does not affirm either side; rather, it shades both of them, or any other seemingly "definitive" reading, with irresolvable doubt. If the reader chooses between the various possible interpretations, as the desire for understanding may well tempt one to do, this choice—in terms of plot as well as character and theme—only adds another motivated "palata di terra . . . sul tumolo della verità" ("shovelful of earth on the grave of truth"), since, on this critical point, the narrative remains purposefully inconclusive:

> Ma era poi la verità questa? In nessun luogo quanto in Sicilia la verità ha vita breve: il fatto è avvenuto da cinque minuti e di già il suo nocciolo genuino è scomparso, camuffato, abbellito, sfigurato, oppresso, annientato dalla fantasia e dagl'interessi: . . .
> tutte le passioni . . . si precipitano sul fatto e lo fanno a brani; in

breve è scomparso. E l'infelice Concetta voleva trovare la verità di sentimenti non espressi ma soltanto intravisti mezzo secolo fa! La verità non c'era più. La sua precarietà era stata sostituita dall'irrefutabilità della pena. (315)

But was this the truth? Nowhere has truth so short a life as in Sicily; a fact has scarcely happened five minutes before its genuine kernel has vanished, has been camouflaged, embellished, disfigured, squashed, annihilated by imagination and self-interest: . . . all the passions . . . fling themselves onto the fact and tear it to pieces; in short is has vanished altogether. And poor Concetta was hoping to find the truth of feelings that had never been expressed but only glimpsed half a century before! The truth no longer existed. The precariousness of fact had been replaced by the irrefutability of pain. (314)

What is the reader to make of such a disconcerting passage? This culminating instance of textual self-knowledge demonstrates what Kenneth Burke has termed the ironic "perspective of perspectives," a function recently rediscovered by Jean Ricardou, Lucien Dällenbach, and others as the mise en abyme.[16] At this point in the text the irony previously present as both trope and epistemological perspective becomes itself fully thematized as a mode of narrative presentation. In its retroactive effect upon the entire narrative, this statement knowledgeably discloses and confronts its own essential fictionality, as well as that of all perception, representation, and judgment motivated by underlying human passions, either psychological or material ("annientato dalla fantasia e dagl'interessi"; "annihilated by imagination and self-interest"). Through this disclosure, the narrative supplies a systematic duration to the apparent spontaneity of its ironic elements, thus becoming a metatextual allegory of its own temporal presentation. As a critique of human perception in time, *Il Gattopardo* thus becomes the story of its own factitiousness, the rise from "il fatto . . . scomparso," or "the vanished fact," to historical novel. In this way, the narrative demonstrates the unity of its basic temporal and modal organization. To quote again from de Man: "Yet the two modes, for all their profound distinctions in mood and structure, are the two faces of the same fundamental experience of time."[17]

In terms of the theory of narrative developed within the text, Lampedusa's thus becomes an historical novel with a critical difference, one that arises from the stated conflict between the referential and figural functions of language and provides, not a choice between the two, but instead a knowledgeable statement of the inability of historical fiction to judge. Both the dynamics of the narrative development and the clear statement of this inability push the literary skepticism of Lampedusa's text well beyond Manzoni's self-conscious indications of critical doubt as to the referential validity of fiction in general and of the historical novel in particular. At the same time, they tie *Il Gattopardo* to another, far more insistent fictional critique of the nature and aims of historical novels in postwar Italy, Morante's *La Storia* of 1974. Just as the island's skeptical inhabitants respond to even the simplest questions with the intentional "enigma" of ironic withdrawal (42; 46), so the progression of Lampedusa's narrative seems at first to indicate and then to deny solution.

Once more, however, it is imperative to note that the narration does not terminate with this moment of reflexive knowledge. Just as the text's "demystified" dominant character longs for the timeless yet specious unity of created myth to provide the salve of both explanation and transcendence, so the narrative continues in the active fusion of its two presentational modes. Concetta demonstrates the continuing effectiveness of figural representation in her sudden revulsion at the sight of "il povero Bendicò"; and in similar fashion the image of the concluding "fall" becomes a metaphor for the entire house, as Jeffrey Meyers has shown.[18] Ironically, as the narrative's caveat so plainly exemplifies, it is this very knowledge of its limitations that inspires the narration to continue. In both "worldly" and fictional terms, then, every approach to truth may be seen to lead not into silence but back into the self-mystifying passions of speech, in an unending process of self-allegorization.

As a book about time, and about human self-perception in time, Lampedusa's novel undoubtedly derives part of its fascination from the sense of "fallimento" inherent in its review of "il Risorgimento." Its critique appears to draw further energy, moreover, from the corresponding atmosphere of disillusionment following the short-lived triumphs of the modern Italian Resistance. This combination of historical reference and contemporary concern gives *Il Gattopardo*'s self-conscious critique its special piquancy, since it calls into question not only the nature of fictional representation but also that of worldly "truth" itself, both historical *and* contemporary. Despite the book's unprecedented popular success in the 1950s, or perhaps because of it, the novel has not yet received abundant serious critical attention, discounting the original misapprehensions and accusations of "antistoricismo."[19] Again perhaps ironically, given the political and social malaise of postwar Italian life—in which everything seemed to move, yet very little, if anything, seemed really to change—Lampedusa's book entered its historical moment as the self-consciously diagnostic representation of a perspective whose only cardinal sin is "quello di 'fare,'" that of doing anything at all. At once self-conscious analysis and potential "sfida," it thus continues to embody what remains the unresolved predicament of the postwar period, self-knowledge without final self-destruction.

EIGHT

System, Time, Writing, and Reading in Gadda's La cognizione del dolore

The Impossibility of Saying "I"

The relationship between language and other systems of thought and praxis, scientific as well as philosophical ones, occupied Carlo Emilio Gadda's concerns from his early studies on. These studies included the work he did for his *laurea* in electrical engineering (as well as for his subsequent professional experience first in Italy and then in Argentina) and his readings on the topic of his unfinished thesis for a second *laurea*, which was to have treated the philosophy of Leibniz. Gadda's interest in systems of order (of predictability and/or closure) and disorder (of uncertainty and/or randomness) was already apparent in the book of philosophical-scientific essays entitled *Meditazione milanese* (*Milanese Meditation*), composed in 1928.[1] As Gadda's fiction repeatedly demonstrates, however, when these seemingly logical questions are applied to the actions of human beings, they are inevitably complicated by the all too human aspects of desire, knowledge, and will. Because of such complicating factors, the otherwise logical problems of system and method in Gadda's narratives quickly take on the distinctively Gaddian flavor of aggression, of melancholy, and, just behind these, as though in melancholy's mirror, of terror.

The elements of literary self-consciousness so rife in Gadda's novels serve repeatedly to highlight these affective and logical difficulties, which Gadda perceives as integral parts of the worlds that his works create and describe. In *La meccanica* (*Mechanics*), written primarily between 1928 and 1929 but not published until 1970, the most notable aspects of literary self-consciousness are those that will recur in still more marked fashion in his mature fiction, such as the fascination with the incorporation of dialect into literary language, the fairly open intertextual allusions to the Latin and Italian literary tradition (as embodied most notably here by the figures of Caesar, Manzoni, and D'Annunzio), and the intrusively self-identifying authorial commentary and footnotes, all of which serve to emphasize the author's powers *and* his evasiveness, including his ability to make his appearance in his own works however he pleases, in a manner that makes one think of Hitchcock or Truffaut, or, even more relevantly, of Joyce.

The self-conscious aspects of *Quer pasticciaccio brutto de via Merulana* (*That Awful Mess on Via Merulana*), published at first in installments in 1946–47 and then in book form in 1957, go considerably further than those of *La meccanica*. In Gadda's *Pasticciaccio*, the author's obsession with the lexical and grammatical eccentricities of multiple dialects (predominantly those of Naples, Rome, and the province of Molise) works continually to focus attention on the novel's own heterodox language and on its status as a linguistic artifact. As both earlier and later in Gadda's narrative production, a checkerboard of specifically literary allusions and pastiches recur in the *Pasticciaccio;* but they take a back seat to the most insistently self-proclaiming literary element of the narrative, its form as a mock *giallo*, or detective story, in which each new turn in the labyrinthian puzzle openly calls for a new attempt at interpretation both from the narrative's central character (the investigating police officer, Don Ciccio Ingravallo) and from the reader. Indeed, as the narrator comments in chapter 7, the entire book often appears to take on the form of an ongoing *referto*, or police report, although its account, like Gadda's other works, is destined to remain inconclusive and in certain respects open-ended.

Even though both *La meccanica* and *Quer pasticciaccio* are self-reflexive in important ways, by far the most significant of Gadda's three novels in terms of literary self-consciousness was the last to be completed, *La cognizione del dolore* (*Acquainted with Grief*).[2] This is the case partly because in *La cognizione* the question of self-reflexivity is posed in regard to a character who is not only the protagonist but also, within Gadda's story, a writer himself, indeed, the writer of a novel. Like Gadda's other novels, *La cognizione del dolore* has a complicated publishing history. The bulk of the novel first appeared between 1938 and 1941 in the Florentine literary review *Letteratura* (the same review that published the installments of the *Pasticciaccio* in the 1940s). This and subsequent material were then put together and published by Einaudi in 1963. As distinct from Gadda's other novels, however, *La cognizione*'s first publication between two covers was not the final version to appear. In 1969, the novel was brought out by Braziller in an English translation that included two concluding chapters which had been written much earlier but which had never been published. By Gadda's agreement, this material was also added to Einaudi's definitive edition of 1970. Since these two concluding chapters affect both the plot and the themes of the novel in a fundamental way, the 1970 version is in many respects a new novel rather than merely a reissue of an earlier one or a new edition with an unimportant addendum. On account of this new and very different form—and despite the significance of the novel's thematics for the social and political period in which it was first written—I have chosen to consider *La cognizione del dolore* as a novel completed in 1970, one that, from the historical perspective of its *reception*, falls after rather than before the neorealism of the postwar years and Lampedusa's revivification of the historical novel in the late 1950s. Among other results, this choice places Gadda's *Cognizione* closer to the "Gruppo 63," which acknowledged Gadda as one of their few Italian models, and thus ties Gadda's novelistic production more closely to the interests and practices of the Italian experimental novel of the 1960s.

The version of 1970 does not change *La cognizione*'s setting or the opening parts of its format. The novel is still a linguistically complex pseudo-*giallo* laden with autobiographical details and set in a fictitious South American country that obviously bears greater similarity to Gadda's Lombardian Brianza than to any existing region or country of Latin America. In the versions prior to 1970, the novel's meandering story line, consisting principally of the oddly ambivalent relationship between mother and son and of the vaguely threatening relation between the night watchmen's organizations overseen by the state (reminiscent at least in its social and official attributes, of Italian Fascism) and the Pirobutirro family as homeowners, has no particular ending. In the early editions, rather than reaching any sort of conclusion the novel simply wanders off, as though the form of its own discourse were indeed as haphazard and "loquacious" as is, in the narrator's words, life itself (7; 5).

In the 1970 version the novel is still open-ended, but it is no longer totally inconclusive. With the addition of the mother's terrifyingly violent murder, revealed in what is now the last chapter, the possibilities for interpretation of the plot (i.e., who killed her and why) are at least set forth, if not decided. As in *La meccanica* and, mutatis mutandis, in *Quer pasticciaccio brutto de via Merulana*, the novelistic technique of delayed exposition does eventually lead to a revelation of sorts, however uncertain and tenuous the project of interpretation may remain. This second of the two chapters included in 1970 has received a great deal of critical commentary—no doubt because of the crucial information it adds to the novel's plot as well as the violence that this information reveals. This has not been so, however, for the first of the two added chapters. This lack of critical attention is especially pertinent in the present context because of our focus on *literary* self-consciousness: in the first of these two appended chapters the son, Gonzalo, is said to be at work on a novel. To see just why *this* revelation is essential to the novel's thematic complexity, however, it is necessary first to retrace the major yet far from unambiguous path that language and writing have followed throughout the narrative as a whole.

The first striking passage in this regard occurs in chapter 3, more or less midway through the first of the novel's two main parts.[3] Gonzalo is in the process of telling Doctor Higueróa that his reclusive mother has a repugnance not only for doctors but for any medical attention whatever when, out of the blue, Gonzalo erupts in what the doctor finds an incomprehensible condemnation of the first-person pronoun:

> "Bel modo di curarsi! . . . . a dire: io non ho nulla. Io non ho mai avuto bisogno di nessuno! . . . . io, più i dottori stanno alla larga, e meglio mi sento . . . . Io mi riguardo da me, che son sicura di non sbagliare . . . . Io, io, io!"
>
> E di nuovo si lasciava prendere da un'idea, e levò la voce, rabbiosamente: "Ah! il mondo delle idee! che bel mondo! . . . . ah! l'io, io . . . . tra i mandorli in fiore . . . . poi tra le pere, e le Battistine, e il José! . . . . l'io, io! . . . . Il più lurido di tutti i pronomi! . . . ." (123)

> "A fine way to take care of yourself! . . . . to say: 'there's nothing wrong with me. I've never needed anyone! . . . . The farther away the doctors stay from me, the better I feel . . . . I can take care of myself, that way I'm sure not to make mistakes'. . . . I, I, I!"
>
> And again he allowed himself to be seized by an idea, and he raised his voice, angrily: "Ah! the world of ideas! What a fine world! . . . . Ah! the I, I . . . . among the almond blossoms . . . . then among the pears, and the Battistinas, and José! . . . . The I, I . . . . The foulest of all pronouns!" (86).

When the doctor gives voice to his amazement at his patient's outburst ("Quando uno pensa un qualchecosa deve pur dire: io penso";

"When a person thinks something or other, he still has to say: 'I think'") Gonzalo responds first by mixing Descartes together with Hamlet, in a typically Gaddian pastiche, and then by extending his condemnation to include all personal pronouns:

> ". . . . I think; già: but I'm ill of thinking . . . ." mormorò il figlio. ". . . . I pronomi! Sono i pidocchi del pensiero. Quando il pensiero ha i pidocchi, si gratta, come tutti quelli che hanno i pidocchi . . . . e nelle unghie, allora . . . . ci ritrova i pronomi: i pronomi di persona . . . . "

> ". . . . 'I think,' true: 'but I'm ill of thinking'. . . ." the son murmured. ". . . . Pronouns! They're the lice of thought. When a thought has lice it scratches, like everyone who has lice . . . . and in the fingernails, then . . . . you find pronouns, the personal pronouns."

Gonzalo's rage derives in part from what he perceives as his mother's claims of self-sufficiency, her asserted lack of need for anyone else, including him. Of course, the son's own narcissism is offended by his mother's exclusion of him, since, from Gonzalo's point of view, everyone should need him—even though, if that were the case, if someone actually did require his active attention, he would doubtless refuse such an advance because of the other side of his self-absorption: narcissistic withdrawal. More than anything, Gonzalo wants the right of first refusal, which on his part will predictably lead to his rejection of every offer; and this psychological ambivalence and confusion on the part of the focus character accounts for a good deal of the confusion and uncertainty in the narrative itself.

Despite this apparent hegemony of the "io," with which all relations seem to begin and end, its status is precisely what Gonzalo insists on calling into question. As is regularly the case, Gonzalo casts his recrimination in seemingly abstruse terms, in this instance in the terminology of linguistics—which is one of the reasons why the doctor finds his comments so difficult to comprehend. But any reader of Gadda will be quick to apprehend that the import of the son's bitter remark moves well beyond language itself to the other systems of logic and social relations on which language depends and for which, in Gadda's narratives, it often serves as a model. According to Gonzalo, the impersonality of thought gives way to the individual identity of the thinker in the form of the pronouns which name that identity, but the system of relations between individuals, thoughts, and pronouns is itself far from stable. The "io" is the shiftiest and the most offensive of all pronouns because, while supposedly representing the fixity of subjective identity, it in fact only accomplishes such identification through systematic isolation of the subject, that is, through exclusionary violence and through the unwarranted assertion of unified sameness at the expense of difference. This distortion is possible only because the "io" appears to remain the same even though it names different people and different versions of the same person over time. Gonzalo claims, moreover, that this representational lie extends to all the personal pronouns, and in the following paragraphs he concentrates on the "io/tu," or "I/thou," relationship (124–25; 87–89).

This extension of Gonzalo's otherwise Pirandellian considerations of the status of pronouns well past questions of epistemology to social relations, when coupled with the speaker's anguish, suggests that something more important than the abstract logic of various systems is at stake here. Indeed, what Gonzalo is really objecting to becomes apparent as his ramblings—seemingly disjointed and diffusive but, for all that, aiming toward a specific end—culminate in the chapter's concluding lines. After proceeding with his condemnation of the "io" that breaks up the continuity of being and the impersonal unity of ideas, Gonzalo finally gets around to the "io" that he dislikes most: that of the controlling authority of society, here the state, which would oversee his possessions and control him through taxes and levies. Both the doctor and the peon (who for the moment does not understand that Gonzalo's wrath is directed also at him) remain silent as Gonzalo explicitly criticizes the "io" of all the "altri," or others, of society. At the same time, Gadda, through his character's excesses, *implicitly* puts in doubt the health of Gonzalo's own bourgeois "io," with its fetishistic attachment to its possessions:

> "Io, io, io! . . . . Ma lo caccerò di casa! Col pacco de' suoi diritti legato alla coda . . . . fuori, fuori!". . . .
>
> "Il muro è gobbo, lo vedo . . . . ma il suo segno, il suo significato rimane, e agli onesti gli deve valere. . . . Dacchè attesta il possesso: il sacrosanto privato privatissimo mio, mio! . . . .che è possesso delle mie unghie, dieci unghie, delle mie giuste e vere dieci unghie!" . . . .
>
> ". . . . Dentro, io, nella mia casa, con mia madre: e tutti i José e le Battistine e le Pe . . . . le Beppe, tutti . . . . Via, via! fuori

> . . . . fuori tutti! Questa è, e deve essere, la mia casa . . . . nel mio silenzio . . . . la mia povera casa . . . ." (127)
>
> "I, I, I! . . . . But I'll drive him out of the house! With his packet of rights tied to his tail . . . . out, out! . . ."
>
> "The wall is humpbacked, I see it . . . . but its sign, its meaning, remains, and for everyone honest it should retain its value . . . . For it attests to possession: the sacrosanct private, most private mine, mine! . . . . which is the possession of my fingernails, ten nails, of my right and true ten nails!" . . . .
>
> ". . . . Inside, I, in my house, with my mother: and all the Josés and the Battistinas and the Pep . . . . the Beppas, all . . . . Away, away! out . . . . out with all of them! This is, and must be, my house . . . in my silence . . . . my poor house." (90–91)

As "io" progresses to "mio," "I" to "mine," the train of Gonzalo's thought becomes somewhat clearer. By first putting in doubt the status of the individual subject in regard to his mother, Gonzalo merely begins the loop that will end not with questioning but instead with his affirmation of his own individual unity amidst the endless hordes of "others." That this affirmation occurs only as a reaction to the threat of others' encroachment on his possessions and his house (here in the obvious Freudian association of the house with the mother), merely reaffirms the precariousness of Gonzalo's forced perception of personal stability and integrity. This integrity is especially precarious, moreover, when it is seen not so much in personal as in social terms, in the relation between the world of Gonzalo's property and the world outside.

This odd mixture of openness and closure, impersonality and individualization, identity and differentiation, had already been present, however subtly, in Gonzalo's initial condemnation of the "io," the "foulest" of all pronouns, and in his description of pronouns as the "lice" of thought caught in one's fingernails. But the social as well as logical and psychological aspects of Gonzalo's reasoning (if it may be termed that) are apparent only in the image's reprise, when he speaks in anguish of the "possesso delle *mie* unghie, dieci unghie, delle *mie* giuste e vere dieci unghie" ("possession of *my* fingernails, ten nails, of my right and true ten nails!"). As we noted earlier in terms of the two attitudes of Narcissus, one the megalomaniacal feeling that the world only mirrors the self, the other that the self only exists in withdrawal from the world and in total self-absorption,

Gonzalo again espouses a system of personal and social relations that is at once, and in seemingly contradictory ways, open and closed, never ending and perfectly complete.

In this scene, these thematics of openness, closure, and melancholy are connected with the act of writing through a *secondary* reference, one made in passing to the early years of Gonzalo's lifelong occupation and writing, when his father's extravagance in building the familial villa with its ostentatious belfry meant that there were not sufficient funds to heat the house, with the result that Gonzalo's fingers, covered with chilblains, were too cold to hold the pen for his studies (all of which Gonzalo recollects under the rubric of "castighi," or punishment, 125; 88). At this point in the novel, therefore, the self-reflexive aspects of the text remain principally focused, first, on language as a system rather than on writing or narrative as such and, second, on the relations between language and the unity, or disunity, of the individual subject.

This cluster of linguistic and psychological interests, along with the often discussed "unfinished" nature of Gadda's works (especially in evidence prior to the 1970 editions of *La cognizione*), explains the admiration that many of the members of the trenchantly avant-garde Gruppo 63 had for Gadda as a novelist. The fascination with language and with the rapport between language, meaning, and society is apparent both in the theoretical essays and in the experimental novels of such Gruppo 63 writers as Edoardo Sanguineti, Nanni Balestrini, Angelo Guglielmi, and Giorgio Manganelli. Though their highly self-conscious fictions did not immediately demonstrate any convincingly successful line in regard to these topics in literary practice (partly, to be sure, because of the extraordinary literary and political diversity of the group's members), their widely publicized meetings and discussions following their first gathering in Palermo in 1963 did place these topics at the forefront of Italian critical discussion. Before reviewing where these issues lead within Gadda's narrative, however, we should return briefly to the psychological aspects of the relation between mother and son, which is central to the novel's eventual denouement, and to those of Gonzalo's other familial relations.

Gonzalo's rage, which is one of the major symptoms of the inexplicable disease that the doctor hopes to treat, is abundantly apparent in his relationship with his mother. She often seems to be the object of his outbursts, whether she deserves such treatment or not. Indeed, the scene just discussed opens with a mild rebuke from the doctor on this very point. Gonzalo was upset by the taxes levied on the estate, the responsibility for which he and his mother inherited at his father's death, and he had ended up yelling at her, even though he claims he did not mean to do so: "Ma intanto ha gridato . . . e ha gridato con lei!" (122; "But still you shouted . . . and you shouted at her!" 85). There are, of course, two other family figures, both absent, who are also objects of Gonzalo's wrath and/or his remorse: his father and his brother. The parallels with the situations of Coriolanus (mentioned in the text), Oedipus, and Christ are important here;[4] but, given the added ingredient of the absent brother, the most pressing and most instructive similarity in Gadda's novel is the autobiographical one between Gonzalo and Gadda himself.[5]

Gonzalo's anger at his spendthrift father can be viewed in practical and in symbolic terms. As a child, Gonzalo felt he suffered deprivation because of his father's excessive expenditures on the villa, and he continues to suffer because of the state's imposition of taxes on the property, taxes that the son claims he is ill-prepared to pay. In symbolic terms, matters are somewhat less straightforward. As the figure of the arbitrariness of authority, the father ends up being collapsed with the state in a way that, had the father lived, would have seemed odd at best in real life, since the father, too, would have been subject to the state's powers. The father's absence facilitates this symbolic conflation of the forces of authority, but it also makes Gonzalo's relation to his nemesis all that much more difficult, since, in practical terms, Gonzalo finds himself doing battle against a figure whom he literally cannot defeat. Nonetheless, a victory of sorts *is* possible, albeit a tenuous and uncertain one. For the bell tower—which is at once the image of phallic authority and expression *and* the agency of Gonzalo's own expressive undoing (since, because of it, he could not even hold his pen)—Gonzalo has a present remedy: expression through writing. This does not mean that Gonzalo necessarily has the last laugh, since he must constantly renew this expressive activity if his victory, however partial, is not to be overturned by the lasting force of the state and the continuing burden of the taxes on the villa. In both a practical and a symbolic sense, therefore, time itself is what makes Gonzalo's victory possible while also making it *only* that: time, by means of its creation of an absolute past as well as its continuous progression furnishes the condition that makes the game potentially winnable even while making it unending and therefore winnable only *in potentia*.

The relationship between Gonzalo and his brother is even less clear than that between father and son. All that is evident—here as in Gadda's own life—is that the death of the brother has caused a continuing sense of loss in the closest survivors. At the end of the narrative, just before the revelation of the horrible attack on the mother, Gonzalo's bed is found unslept in and his worktable bare except for an open book and a photograph, of his brother, untouched by time, still smiling "dopo tant'anni!" (263; "after so many years!" 231). So even though the connections between Gonzalo's writing, his feelings for his brother and father, the passage of time, and his rage are less clear than the mechanics of his relation with his mother, which is the rapport foregrounded in the latter sections of the narrative, it is nevertheless important to see that these background relations are implicated in Gonzalo's own psychological makeup and in his current day-to-day relations with others.

It is not difficult to see what the major components of that makeup are.[6] Its outward signs are evident in both the form and the content of Gonzalo's discourse: in the obsessive self-reference, jealousy, and paranoia of the narcissist; in the free-floating anxiety that attaches first to one object and then to another without ever permitting a satisfactory, stable object relation (or an extrafamilial relation of *any* sort, since even though Gonzalo claims to have willfully renounced marriage in favor of freedom, it is obvious that his freedom to exercise his will, to love and work on his own in the world, is not so much the point as is the character disorder that impedes him from engaging in any meaningful worldly endeavor outside the home); and, finally, in the rage that incites his often belligerent logorrhea and that, on occasion, manifests itself not only in his words but also in his threatened deeds (such as in his openly hostile treatment of his father's portrait [96–97, 186; 59–60, 153]; in his menacing eruption at his mother even as he seems to realize that he should have identified himself—"sono io"; "it's I"—and asked her pardon [247; 214]; and in his outrageously high-handed treatment of the peon [205–12; 172–79]).

What could possibly be the cause of such bizarre symptoms? This is, of course, the one question that Gadda's text elicits but refuses to answer. We can nonetheless hazard an approach toward the internal reasons for this psychic mechanism (as distinct from its external constellation of symptoms) by reconsidering the problems of the narcissistic character disorder and of grief. In a well-known essay, Freud pointed out that whereas mourning generally has a defined series of stages (from the initial reaction to the loss of the beloved, to working through the ambivalent memories and feelings attached to the lost object, and then to eventual recovery), melancholia, as a prolonged facet of the personality, does not necessarily have either a clearly established external origin or a definite course of development.[7] While mourning involves the loss of the object and subsequent ambivalence, melancholia adds to these a third factor, what Freud terms the regression of libido into the ego, which, in a violent confusion of identity and difference, then takes the other as the self by internalizing the ambivalence toward the lost object—in the keys of both love and hatred—thus perpetuating the struggle around the object *within* the subject. This struggle—now an internal one—is a battle over which the subject has no immediate control, and its one possible resolution is for the internally cathected libidinal energy to become free again, the results of which, however, are continual rounds of mania and/or the *re*-deflection of the libido into (now libidinally reinforced) narcissism. For Freud, this continuing conflict, inherent in the mechanism of melancholia, acts like a painful internal wound, one that cannot be easily healed since it cannot be directly reached.

It is essential to see that Gonzalo's familial attachments to his father and brother, whether understood in the mode of rage or of lament, are so significant in the novel precisely because they are so vaguely defined. Gadda portrays the effects while leaving the causes to be divined by the reader. In the end, the symbolic presentation of these familial relations confirms Gonzalo's personality and his difficulties as a narcissist in a way that is perhaps less obvious than is done through his relation with his mother but that, for all its indirection, is no less powerful. Indeed, as post-Freudian studies of narcissistic character disorders have shown, the next step in the deepening of such disorders often leads to antisocial personality structures, which add, to the phenomenon of extreme narcissism, severe superego pathology.[8] So even though in practical terms Gonzalo is not the likeliest perpetrator of the awful crime revealed at the novel's conclusion, the violent expression of his seemingly inexplicable rage could, by *symbolic* extension of Gonzalo's menacing comments and of what the reader already knows about him, turn him into one of the possible suspects for that role.[9]

As is evident over the course of the narrative, and as we have seen earlier from another perspective, the vagueness and uncertainty of Gonzalo's familial development is most precisely focused in the primary textual relationship, that between Gonzalo and his mother. Again, the ambiguity of attachment and withdrawal is an aspect of each character's reaction to the other. In the later parts of the novel, the dialectic of openness and closure *within* each character's personality and *between* them is set against the backdrop of the father's house, with its emptiness and its Freudian game of exclusion (involving the mother's primal *horror vacui* [180; 146]; the "marriage bed" [265; 234]; and even allusion to the Dioscuri, of which only one now survives [181; 148]). But the imagery and the thematics of the later parts of the novel remain murky. All that can be stated with certainty is that the "male oscuro" ("obscure illness") of the earlier sections of the novel is ever-present here, too, with its thematics of order and disorder, identity and difference, reason and uncertainty, system and randomness, and its constant miasma of seemingly necessary yet also inexplicable grief.

These thematics come together in a particularly pointed way in the scene in which Gonzalo is revealed to be at work on a novel, as though writing and representation were of special cogency in understanding what *La cognizione del dolore* is all about. The discussion of Gonzalo's activity as a novelist is preceded in the first of the two added chapters by a series of allusions to, and/or jokes on, Plato, Manzoni, and Carducci, as well as by various references to Gonzalo's studies. At the same time, it picks up the thread of literary discussion and reference that runs throughout the novel (including, from the very first pages, autobiographical self-reference: "uno scrittore arzigogolato e barocco, come Jean Paul, o Carlo Gozzi, o Carlo Dossi, o un qualche altro Carlo anche peggio di questi due, già così grami loro soli," 52; "a labyrinthine and baroque writer, like Jean Paul, or Carlo Gozzi, or Carlo Dossi, or some other Carlo even worse than these two, already so sorry in themselves," 13). It is clear from the first part of the novel—in which the Pirobutirro family is described as "tutta gente di penna" (101; "all people of the pen," 63), and in which, shortly afterwards, the doctor cautions Gonzalo against his habitual reading and, worse, against writing his "memoirs," and prescribes instead what the doctor considers healthful fresh-air activity—that Gonzalo is not only studious but also an author of sorts, one of the narrative's "letteratàzzi" (157; "litterateurs," 122). But only in the added material of the concluding sections does the narrator expand on Gonzalo's writerly occupation:

> Gli piaceva talora di fantasticare: e si lasciava fare come una carezza, da chi? da chi? se non dalla vana luce d'un pensiero, labile come raggio d'autunno.

> Immaginava che qualche sodalizio gli avrebbe regalato un piccolo orologio, da polso, visto che nessuna donna ci aveva pensato, mai: nessuna donna? la mamma, la povera mamma. Fantasticava che la patria maradagalese lo incuorasse a perfezionare quel suo scarabocchio di romanzo:
>
>> e te molesta incita
>> di poner fine al *Giorno*
>> per cui, cercato, a lo stranier ti addita.
>
> Ma sapeva benissimo che se ne fregavano tutti, nel modo più completo, e che il romanzo, legato a dei personaggi veri e a un ambiente vero, era stupido quanto i personaggi e l'ambiente. Stai fino! C'era altro da fare e a cui pensare, nel Maradagàl e in tutto il Sudamerica a quei lumi di luna. E soprattutto era certo, o quasi, di doversi considerare un deficiente.
>
> Un romanzo! Con dei personaggi femmine! Con quel po' po' di pratica che Cristo gli aveva fatto fare, tanto non intorpidisse, della psiche umana! Della psiche! E anche della sua stessa. (238–39)

He enjoyed daydreaming at times: and he allowed himself to receive a kind of caress, from whom? from whom? if not from the vain light of a thought, ephemeral as the ray of autumn's sun.

He imagined that some society would present him with a little watch, a wristwatch, since no woman had ever thought of it, ever: no woman? Mama, poor Mama. He daydreamed that the Maradagalese fatherland would encourage him to perfect his scrawl of a novel:

> and, vexatious [the fatherland] urges you
> to complete *The Day*
> for which, sought after, you are pointed out to the foreigner.

But he knew very well that none of them gave a damn at all, and that the novel, bound to real characters and a real environment, was as stupid as those characters and that environment were. Fat chance! There were other things to do and to think of, in Maradagàl and in all of South America in times like these. And above all he was sure, or almost, that he was to be considered a fool.

A novel! With female characters! With all that experience
that Christ had made him have, so he wouldn't become dull, experience of the human psyche! The psyche! And also of his own.
(206–7)

In terms of the thematics of openness and closure that we have considered so far, the most noteworthy aspect of this passage is Gonzalo's concern for the limitations inherent in novelistic representation. Before Gonzalo's thoughts lead him to such considerations, however, he first notes the
pleasure of indulging himself in fantasy and in the "vain light" of thought,
an image that foreshadows the vain and sorrowful decadence of the poem
appended at the novel's conclusion, entitled "Autunno," or "Autumn."
Gonzalo then imagines the honorary gift to be conferred upon him, one
that fulfills the obligation of recognition as no woman had ever done, with
the possible exception of his mother. The novel on which Gonzalo is
working, the narrative that would be the true object of the award, is then
alluded to by means of a verse from Parini's (uncompleted) satirical poem,
Il giorno; and this last step finally takes Gonzalo's meandering thoughts up
to his consideration of representational limits.

What, in Gonzalo's opinion as expressed here, is the problem with
novelistic representation? In brief, since novels are tied to real characters
and a real environment—which is to say to the literary depiction of characters in relation to others and to their physical surroundings—the literary product is bound to be as limited, or as "stupid," as those characters
and that environment. In aesthetic terms, the problem that Gonzalo outlines has to do with the nature and value of meaning in representational
fiction. According to these reflections, the meaning of any narrative can
only be as significant as the subject matter that it seeks to re-create. Gonzalo's despair at what he takes to be the uselessness of fiction in the real
world spurs him not only to castigate the endeavors of fiction-writing in a
country and in a period in which there were many more important things
to do, but also to deprecate himself as a writer, which is to say, in this
context, as a fool ("un deficiente"). This passage seems fairly straightforward, especially by comparison to the halting, self-contradictory nature
of so much of Gonzalo's reflections; but the instructive addition of the
qualification "o quasi" ("or almost") again underscores the characteristic
uncertainty of Gonzalo's thoughts. This sentence leads, moreover, to the
character's expression of his deep-rooted ambivalence about his literary

project, which was to include not only female characters but also his experience of the human psyche in general and of his own mind in particular.

As is so often the case in Gadda's novel, what seems here to begin in celebration leads to denigration and ends—though, as we shall see, the term "end" is appropriate only by half—in ambivalence and confusion. Fantasy and the pleasures of thought seem at first to be good, that is, as long as they are unrestricted, abstract, as ephemeral as daydreams. Once imagination is channeled into expression through the rigors of writing, and, worse, submitted to the limitations of specifically novelistic discourse, its value is diminished not only for Gonzalo but also, in his opinion, for his entire potential audience. As creative randomness hardens into fixed system—much like the abstract thought that is described as becoming infested with the "lice" of pronouns in Gonzalo's earlier diatribe—fantasy's worldly import and its intellectual significance necessarily become limited. This position is consistent, more or less, with Gadda's comments throughout the *Meditazione milanese* and with several of his most marked narrative interests and procedures in *La cognizione*: first, in the repeated play on the oddities and the veracity of literary representation in his own works and particularly in the *locus classicus* of Carducci's "Canzone di Legnano"; second, in the text's various jokes on language as system and limitation (242, n. 1, et passim; 210, n. 54, et passim); and third, in Gadda's constant questioning of the integrity of the individual subject in terms of both understanding and will.[10]

Despite such indications, however, Gadda's text is not a brief for randomness as opposed to determinism, freedom as opposed to restriction, openness as opposed to closure, or for either side of any similar opposition. This is the case because, in Gadda's work, the two sides of such oppositions can never be satisfactorily split. Both parts remain mixed together, and both remain in force. Just as surely as attempts at systematic rigidity lead to exclusion and diminution of value, randomness and uncertainty lead to anguish and, beyond that, when reincorporated into rigidity, to terror. It is neither fixity nor uncertainty by itself that gives rise to the "male oscuro" with which Gonzalo's will and his whole being are afflicted but rather the perception of chaos *in relation to* order. As Gonzalo seems to believe near the conclusion of the earlier version of the novel, a few pages before his excursus on novel-writing, "nulla accade senza ragione" (214; "nothing happens without a reason," 181). But this does not mean that the reason can be divined or understood amid the *real* mixture of order and disorder that constitutes the world. The perception that this mixture is finally incomprehensible results, for the narcissistic subject of *La cognizione del dolore*, in the vertigo that is constantly renewed by his perception of the world itself. Oddly enough, though again understandably so within the framework of narcissism, this vertiginous reaction seems at once the result of the perception of chaos and the cause of chaos. In short, the "invisible" illness is itself the moving force of the grief that is so painful because, as we have seen, it is now untouchable, both prior and omnipresent. In this respect, it is akin to Gonzalo's perception of the awful notes hovering in their system of "clauses" over the human-fashioned world of man and that of nature—and over the profound, unknowable abstraction of time and space as he looks across his property just after his ambivalent reflections on his novel of the human psyche—"come la cognizione del dolore" (240; "like the knowledge of grief," 208).[11]

Is there a version of material life that would provide an escape from this impasse? How could one create a universe in which everything was open yet at the same time closed, random yet ordered, free yet at the same time logical, understandable, reasonable *and* comfortable? This is the *cul de sac* of narcissism: the longing for a world in which one perceives the disordered existence of others, of "gli altri" to which Gonzalo constantly alludes, only in relation to the stability of the self, as the Platonic image of specular reflection in the pupils of others near the end of Part Two suggests.[12] But neither the impasse nor the longing to escape it has any worldly egress, and this for a basic reason, apparent in one of the elements of Gonzalo's reflections that we have not yet considered, his obsession with time. Gonzalo's ruminations on the temporal advancement of human generations and on the passage of time occupy a central position in his excursus on novels cited above; and his typically ambivalent invocations/imprecations of time ("Gli anni!"; "The years!") resound like a leitmotif throughout the narrative, especially in its middle and later sections. But the point at which time, and the movement of human life through time's open yet closed system, is of most urgent significance occurs in the second of the two appended chapters, during the description of the mother's hideously battered body.

The discovery and depiction of the body is the high point of the chapter, indeed the climactic moment toward which the novel's plot now seems, in retrospect, to have been slowly building all along. The discovery scene resembles that of the murder in *Quer pasticciaccio brutto* in certain effects of description and attitude (though in *Quer pasticciaccio* the murder comes near the beginning rather than at the conclusion); and it recalls, in its temporal notations, both the horror that death, as the end of one aspect of time, evokes in Don Ciccio and the overall aura of sorrow that is regularly associated with the detective's perception of time throughout the novel. In the narration of La cognizione's concluding chapter, moreover, the temporal progression of the narrative *itself* is underscored by the striking alteration in narrative pacing, rhythm, and focus. The combination of these effects serves to reemphasize the specifically narrative (rather than merely linguistic) self-consciousness that has been part of the story since Gonzalo's excursus on fictional representation.

When the concluding chapter opens, Gonzalo and his mother are absent from the scene, and the focus has suddenly shifted to the pair of cousins who work as night guards for a neighboring property owner. After a brief introduction to the guards, the narrative relates the guards' approach toward the Pirobutirro villa and then, following the general alarm, the approach of the larger group within the house toward the mother's bedroom, all of which is described in lucid, streamlined prose. Gone are Gonzalo's meanderings, his labyrinthian psychological conflicts, his oddly deflected statement of his concern for his studies and his books, and his mother's assertions and protestations. In these pages, the narrative proceeds as though it were in fact a *giallo,* one that was at last getting to the point. It is true that what the guards eventually find does not solve any of the narrative's dilemmas, but in the shock of the revelation, it does provide the narrative's apex, the various aspects of which are repeated almost immediately in the description of the communal reaction at what is gradually disclosed by the doctor's semiritual cleansing of the body:

> Per detergere, ci vollero pazienza e tempo, al dottore, mentre i presenti inorridivano . . . . L'emorragia aveva imbrattato il capo, il viso, le labbra, il coagulo si era aggrumato e stagnato ne' capelli, nell'orecchio destro, sulla faccia, sotto il naso: anche dal naso era venuto molto sangue: il lembo del lenzuolo, il cuscino, ne erano atrocemente arrossati.
>
> Si comprese da tutti, al riscontrare delle tracce di sangue sullo spigolo del tavolino da notte, verso il letto, che il capo così ferito doveva avervi battuto violentemente; forse qualcuno doveva averla afferrata a due mani, pel collo, e averle sbattuto il capo

contro lo spigolo del tavolino da notte, per terrorizzarla, o deliberato ad ucciderla. Terribile fu e permaneva a tutti l'aspetto di quel volto ingiuriato, ch'essi conoscevano così nobile e buono pur nel disfacimento della vecchiezza.

Ora tumefatto, ferito. Inturpito da una cagione malvagia operante nella assurdità della notte; e complice la fiducia o la bontà stessa della signora. Questa catena di cause riconduceva il sistema dolce e alto della vita all'orrore dei sistemi subordinati, natura, sangue, materia: solitudine di visceri e di volti senza pensiero. Abbandono. . . .

Nella stanchezza senza soccorso in cui il povero volto si dovette raccogliere tumefatto, come in un estremo ricupero della sua dignità, parve a tutti di leggere la parola terribile della morte e la sovrana coscienza della impossibilità di dire: Io. (268–69)

To cleanse required patience and time, of the doctor, while the onlookers were horrified. . . . The hemorrhaging had bloodied the head, the face, the lips; the coagulation had clotted and stagnated in the hair, in the right ear, on the face, below the nose; also from the nose had come a great deal of blood: the edge of the sheet, the pillow, were atrociously red with it.

It was understood by all, at seeing the traces of blood on the edge of the night table, toward the bed, that the wounded head must have struck against it violently; perhaps someone had gripped her with both hands, by the neck, and slammed her head against the edge of the table, to terrify her, or with intent to kill her. For all, the sight of that outraged face was terrible and so remained, when they had known it noble and good even in the decay of old age.

Now swollen, wounded. Debased by a wicked cause operating in the absurdity of the night; with the Señora's trust and her very goodness as accomplices. This chain of causes led the sweet and lofty system of life back to the horror of the subordinate systems, nature, blood, matter: solitude of viscera and of faces without thought. Abandonment. . . .

In the unaided weariness where the poor countenance had to collect itself, swollen, as if in an extreme recovery of its dignity, it seemed to all that they could read the terrible word of death and the supreme awareness of the impossibility of saying: I. (236–37)

The "chain of causes" that contaminate the "lofty system of life" with the baser, literally "thoughtless" systems of "nature, blood, matter" results in the same end—though with a specially violent and horrible twist—that all systems involving individual humans necessarily reach sooner or later, depending on the eccentricities of desire and will and the worldly motions of chance: "decay" and death. For the individual, death is an end. For all others, however, it is only an end point, since life goes on. The continuation of life in terms of the audience is given by Gadda's text, moreover, in the layered elements of a metaphor that is both linguistic and literary: the viewers "read" the "terrible word of death" and, at the same time, the end of the other's expressive subjectivity, the impossibility of *her* saying "I."

The seemingly unnatural horror of the scene, which even ritual is inadequate to cancel completely, is thus transmitted to the bedside audience in the natural *and* human terms of the ending of individual subjectivity amidst the communal perception of death. The abstract, apparently logical system of pronouns leads, as in the anguish underlying Gonzalo's earlier deprecations, to complex, *un*systematic questions of subjectivity and perception. That these perceptions in fact stimulate the re-creative imagination and the interpretive faculties of the onlookers (expressed in the strangely impersonal but not depersonalized, because communal, form "Si comprese da tutti"; "It was understood by all") only underscores the complexities of all perception and all descriptive systems. Such systems, of course, include the novel's own organization as a *giallo* with a striking conclusion but with no definite indication of the crime's perpetrator, a necessary element in the normal interpretative closure of the genre. In the end, just as Gadda's novel is finished without closure, so the system of the doctor's art is capable of working against the horror of the absurdity of incomprehensible and therefore terrifying violence only in part, since nothing in this world is absolute; all is contingent, uncertain, incomplete, including, as the narrator suggests in the very next sentence (the first in the final paragraph), art itself: "L'ausilio dell'*arte medica,* lenimento, pezzuole, *dissimulò in parte* l'orrore" (my italics; "The help of *medical art,* soothing, bandages, *dissimulated in part* the horror," my italics).

When systems come in contact with human beings, no system is perfect—not time, not language, not writing, not even art. Reasons and relations among causes and effects necessarily exist, but no one can know them all. They remain, as Don Ciccio knows, inevitably multiple, contingent. If, as Heidegger saw, the perception of time's finality, of death, turns human beings back on themselves and so back into the infinite contingencies of their existence in and through time, that progression is still not the *cause* of grief but only its *motion*. Man perceives the motion, whereas the cause, like the "cause" of Freudian melancholia, remains hidden, or at best partially glimpsed, perceived in its effects rather than in its presence.

This motion is also, of course, that of Gonzalo's halting, anguished ruminations and more generally of Gadda's narrative itself, though it is important at this point to begin to distinguish the author from his character. It is true that the character disorder of narcissism is one that wants to stay forever open *and* closed, in the fashion of Narcissus poised above the pool without being either distracted by others or immersed in death. It may seem, moreover, that writing, art, can provide a way to maintain this situation by immortalizing it. But again, such a solution can succeed only by half. Gadda's disinclination to finish his works was notorious, and all of the elaborate extratextual apparatus of *La cognizione del dolore* (from the spurious introductory claim by the editor, through the numerous "authorial" footnotes, to the concluding poem) only reaffirms the author's distaste for a unified, closed artifact. But despite Gonzalo's anguish and Gadda's own concerns, writing is never as unending, as expressively "loquacious," as life itself. Its system, finally, is bound within the covers of the printed book. True, the reader, with every reading, reactivates that system and brings it to life once again; and in this sense, evocative of William Faulkner's equally humanist understanding of the "motion" of art, writing does escape the dead end of narcissism's eventual conclusion.[13] But this is so only for the character and for the book itself, not for its author. The author must live in the world and meet his end there too, as the narrator of *La cognizione* knows so well: art can dissimulate the world's horrors, but only in part.

The self-conscious effects and the insistent "metacommentary" of Gadda's novels can and do suggest that their author knows this impasse, but they cannot lead him out of it.[14] In the end, balanced between the chaos of utter randomness and the rigidity of utter certainty, Gadda's novels conclude by offering yet another vision of the relation between these two aspects of life and of the "obscure" or "invisible" illness that the perception of this relationship engenders. At the end the author, if not his book, must cede to the *force majeure* of system and time over which he has only partial control, consigning his own discourse to the world, in which it is thus cut off from the sovereign life of authorial subjectivity. As this subjectivity becomes an object for others, it suffers the inevitable fate at the conclusion of all worldly systems, open and/or closed, knowledgeable and/or mystified, rational and/or irrational: death. However, by acquiescing to the finished system of the printed book, Gadda gives up his sovereignty as subject while regaining it as object, through the literary sorcery that permits the writer to disappear as presence only to return as the expressive revenant of his own discourse, in the ghostly capacity to speak *despite* the inability to say or to write "I." As the activity of writing hardens into its product, into the established order of the written and published word, the author dies the literary version of the "little death" that grants him, although now in another guise, renewed life. In the end, the startling array of self-reflective literary devices (including the pastiches for which Gadda is justly renowned) that contribute to distinguishing the author from his character also aid him in establishing his own privileged—however contingent—position as creator.

The literary self-consciousness of Gadda's novel is even more radically fragmented than that of Pirandello's Uno, nessuno e centomila, since now both the individual subject and the novel itself are internally divided, contingent, and split, in their form and their substance, from the very start. Gadda's radical conception of the individual in society and of the work of art was no doubt the reason for the appeal that his works held for the experimentalist Italian writers of the 1960s and 1970s; but before moving on to other recent authors, there is one further passage in this concluding chapter that might help to clarify our considerations so far and to extend them to include, in a more open fashion, some of Gadda's social concerns.

We have seen how time, death, and art come together in the novel's final scene within the activity of reading. Although this is the most obvious conjunction of such elements within this particular frame, it is not the only one. This conjunction also occurs more subtly in an earlier scene, one already alluded to from a different perspective, when the intruders enter the son's room and see the photograph of his deceased brother on his writing table, the brother standing by his plane with a machine gun in his hand and a smile still on his face "dopo tant'anni!" ("after so many years!"). One of the group lingers to look carefully at the photograph and then reads a few lines of the open book on the otherwise cleared table. The lines—"Ma le leggi della perfetta città devono . . . ." ("But the laws of the perfect city must . . . .")—concern a primary topic in idealist civil philosophy from Plato to the Enlightenment and beyond. (In fact Plato's *Laws* has been mentioned earlier in the novel, along with the *Timaeus*, the *Parmenides*, and the *Symposium*, as part of Gonzalo's regular reading material.) After this brief delay, the reader rejoins the others, and a few paragraphs later, the narrative ends with the discovery of the mother's body.

The inevitable failure of the kind of ideal society outlined in utopian thought, with its enlightened leaders and populace and, in Plato's version, its system of guardians—indeed the failure of any social system that neglects to come to terms with the inescapable disorder of human life and with the evil causes "operating in the absurdity of the night"—seems fairly clear in Gadda's novel, particularly in light of the narrative's concluding scene. Oddly enough, in Gadda's thought the rigid narcissistic posturing of social superiority is what leads the way to the reciprocal violence and the communal horror of warfare (suggested in the photograph by the machine gun and the plane), which signals not the order of social community but the breakdown of that order on an international scale, an insight that Gadda had begun to set forth in his critique of Fascism in *Eros e Priapo*. The outrage of the concomitant destruction of life is one of the results of a rigidity that cannot tolerate flexibility or of an order that does not knowledgeably provide for the possibility of disorder (though not for disorder's dominance in the opposite yet paired extreme of social anarchy). This outrage, this loss of life's "dignity," is in fact one of the synonyms for death, to which it stands in a relation of reciprocity rather than of cause and effect. As the narrator of *La cognizione* comments in the novel's opening chapter in regard to the attempts at proving an absolute theorem by means of experiments with a live cat (which prove the theorem but also result in the animal's melancholy and finally in its death): "Ogni oltraggio è morte" (77; "Every outrage is death," 39).

Art, like the photographic representation of Gonzalo's aviator brother (evocative of Gadda's own deceased aviator brother) or like Gadda's own self-consciously literary creations, can mitigate the horror of death, can deny its fact with a seemingly invincible—because frozen, timeless—smile. But it can do so only to a certain extent, since it entails the relinquishing of authorial sovereignty and since it depends on the viewer, the reader, the audience, for its magic to work. At the same time, the audience's understanding, its ability to participate, imagine, and interpret, is something over which the creating subject does not have final control. Indeed, the transient viewer/reader of the photograph and of the book within Gadda's text does not understand the photograph of the brother or the import of the book's passage in any sense that is similar to the external, empirical reader's understanding of Gadda's novel. As an artist, Gadda can use his self-reflexive knowledge of this situation to shield himself from the unpredictable contingencies inherent in the reception of his works, but he cannot escape them altogether. All he can do (like Svevo in this regard) is to place his wager on the purgative and so finally healthful activity of writing itself, in the hope that the metaphorical death of the artist will eventually mean the continued life of his works in and through others, in and through his works' existence in the world.

Something of the sort is suggested, too, by the imagery at the very end of La cognizione del dolore, as, outside the room where the doctor is completing his task, wringing the water and alcohol from the bloodstained bandages, the cock suddenly crows ("perentorio e ignorante, come ogni volta"; "peremptory and unaware, as always") and, in a pastiche of the epic simile typical of Gadda for its play on cause and effect, rouses the dawn from the distant mountains: "La invitava ad accedere e ad elencare i gelsi, nella solitudine della campagna apparita" ("[The cock] invited it to proceed and to number the mulberry trees, in the solitude of the countryside, disclosed"). Despite the awful, incomprehensible night of death, life continues, not only in and through those who have witnessed and perhaps understood something of the meaning of the mother's death but with in the daily dawning of nature itself. At the same time, the interpretative faculty of the empirical reader is aroused—even if also frustrated and/or confused—by this inconclusive conclusion, which seems to trail off rather than really end, and through which Gadda's book now continues to live in its audience. In a doubly analogous fashion, the Signora, too, gains new life, both inside and outside the book, as the dark blood of her murder is transformed through the conventions of literary symbolism into the life force of nature, in the color of the mulberry trees numbered in their order by the proceeding dawn. Life's force *and* its stability are thus restored, though for the moment only, in art and in reality. The senseless, yet not meaningless, death at the heart of Ovid's story of Pyramus and Thisbe, which underlies the literary symbol, as well as the abortive nighttime meeting of the would-be lovers kept by society from consummation of their bliss, is once again replayed in the eerie confusion of its parts and in the oddly deflected revisions and metamorphoses of narcissistic desire, in which both man and nature now appear to play their parts. The conclusion of Puck's romantic comedy (the illusive nocturnal hobgoblin mentioned as perhaps inhabiting the grounds directly after the now absent Gonzalo's meditations on the novel), with its full-blown Shakespearean pastiche of Ovid's tale, takes on the darker cast of its nighttime meaning in combination with what is here the real though "invisible" evil of death. But again, the interpretative vitality of this last descriptive gambit can succeed only if the reader's faculties also participate, thereby turning the "death" of the character and that of her author into the renewed life of literary experience, and the renewed challenge of literary interpretation.

NINE

History and the Trial of Poetry

Everyday Life in Morante's *La Storia*

It may come as a surprise to find a discussion of Elsa Morante's *La Storia* (1974; *History*) situated between treatments of Gadda and Calvino.[1] *La Storia* is not at all self-conscious in the way or to the extent that the works of Gadda and the later works of Calvino are, or as are myriad other contemporary Italian novels. Nevertheless, given my intent to trace the historical development of a *mode* of presentation rather than that of a *genre*, inclusion of Morante's masterwork in a study such as this is especially instructive. Among the many varieties of literary self-consciousness occurring in secondary ways during the postwar decades, a particular sort of self-reflexive interest is demonstrated by Morante's narrative, not only in its active critique of the essence and the uses of poetry (or, broadly considered, creative fantasy) but also in its consideration of the very possibility or impossibility of poetry's continued existence. These concerns, when considered in the context of the novel's amalgam of Christian and Marxist ethical polemics, mark *La Storia* as a literary product of an important though concisely delimited era in Italian cultural life, roughly that following the social and political quake of 1968 and preceding the peculiar series of aftershocks during the years 1976–80. Although the narrative is in many respects less constantly self-conscious than either Morante's subsequent novel, *Aracoeli* (1982), or her two previous novels, *Menzogna e sortilegio* (1948; *House of Liars*) and *L'isola di Arturo* (1957; *Arthur's Island*), the self-conscious effects of *La Storia* are both consistently focused and carefully aimed. What the accumulated meaning of these effects points up is, first, the social trial of poetry in the modern world, and, second, the tremendous stake that all mankind has in that trial's outcome.

This ordeal, though not its conclusion, is what Morante's narrative *in toto* eventually comes to represent. However, since *La Storia* is a historical novel, with a consequent commitment to worldly representation, Morante's portrayal of the ordeals that poetry must endure is presented first of all as a part of ordinary, day-to-day existence, solidly rooted in the life and times of the narrative's main historical period, the years during and immediately following World War II. As a result of this representational aesthetic, therefore, Morante's approach to her material in *La Storia* is occasionally reminiscent of the indirectly self-conscious procedures of such earlier realist authors as Verga, Silone, and the postwar neorealists.

At the same time, though again in indirect ways, the novel's *own* poetic aspects are also presented as participating in this everyday process. In part because of the narrative's realistically framed poetic self-reflexivity, *La Storia*'s poetic and representational procedures combine to form an aesthetically unified yet extremely disturbing picture of the novel's principal subject matter, the lives of a simple, half-Jewish schoolteacher, Ida Ramundo, her children, and their familial acquaintances in war-torn Rome. The complexity of Morante's narrative derives from the multiplicity of this representational and poetic focus, since, on one level, the novel portrays the family's everyday experiences, while on another it depicts the difficulties of the worldly functioning of creative fantasy, and on a third it inserts its own discourse into that same set of difficulties, in a mixture of overtly historical and covertly contemporary social representation and diagnosis.

The variety of these narrative concerns—for the representation of historical events through the experiences of a restricted group of characters and for the functions of the creative imagination within those experiences—is signaled even before the story's beginning, on the book's title page, which reads in full: *La Storia. Romanzo,* or *History: A Novel.* The side of this apparent dialectic that is most often treated by the novel's critics, with several notable exceptions, is that of "History."[2] History itself, in Morante's conception, subdivides into History with a capital *H* (the official History of economic power and international politics) and history with a small *h* (the daily lives of the little people that make up the vast, unsung preponderance of the world's population). Within the novel, the machinations of History are discussed and, most often, denigrated by the openly self-identifying narrator in the broadly evaluative Historical sections inserted into *La Storia*'s primary discourse, which is constituted by the highly detailed representation of the daily lives of Ida and her offspring. The combination of these two differing sorts of narratives, the family saga and the reports of supposedly great Historical events, when further complicated by such framing devices as snatches of verse, a cryptic diary entry (cited as anonymous but in fact taken from Gramsci's prison letters), and even a set of endnotes, gives the novel the form and the effects of literary accretion. This formal accretion, reminiscent of a baroque artifact, encompasses both the traditional effects of the historical novel and the reportage procedures of the inserted Historical essays (which sometimes dovetail with the family's story, and sometimes do not, in a process that in a formal sense is reminiscent of the "Camera Eye" and "Newsreel" techniques of Dos Passos). Thus, *La Storia*'s overall effect, in terms of form as well as meaning, is a historical narrative aimed in various ways both at history and at History, one that, regardless of the misapprehensions of its initial critical reception, is typical of neither seventeenth- nor eighteenth- nor nineteenth-century narrative but is, rather, thoroughly eclectic and in that respect characteristically contemporary.

The straightest pathway into the other side of the story's titular dialectic, which is to say, into the fantasy world of the novel as *poesia*, is through the figure of *La Storia*'s most strikingly original and most engaging character, the child at once too strange and too beautiful for this world, Useppe. Among the many ways in which Morante shades her portrait of Useppe as a natural poet, one of the most telling is the text's depiction of Useppe learning to talk. Useppe is the fruit of the rape of his mother by a lonely German soldier, which is described in graphic detail in the narrative's opening section. Irrespective of his origin, the child is almost miraculously innocent, as is affirmed repeatedly by the narrator and as is suggested obliquely by the text's trenchantly anti-Freudian reference to one of the folktale forms of the immaculate conception, in which children are born from the eyes of their mother rather than from the womb (405; 345). The childlike qualities of joy and wonderment that permeate the portrayal of Useppe are evocative of some of Morante's early poetry and also of her first ventures in fiction writing, the children's stories that were collected and published in the 1940s and 1950s; nonetheless, the overall depiction of Useppe's life is cast in a mold that is anything but cheerful, since the child is destined to die from grand mal, which he has probably inherited from Ida.

While Useppe is acquiring the rudiments of language, however, that destiny remains well in the background. The process itself is worth considering in its various stages both for what it reveals about Useppe's poetic character and for its implicitly self-reflexive attention to the ways in which language and imagination come together in the everyday world. The description of Useppe's first words, at about the age of one year, is introduced by a reference to the jubilation with which he regularly experiences his universe: "Non s'era mai vista una creatura più allegra di lui" (120; "A merrier baby than he had never been seen," 103). Although Useppe is restricted to the family's small apartment, his good-natured and imaginative view of life transforms his miserable environment into a world that is as fascinating as it is infinite:

> Tutto ciò che vedeva intorno lo interessava e lo animava gioiosamente. . . . E se, come accade, la luce solare, arrivando indiretta al soffitto, vi portava, riflesso in ombre, il movimento mattiniero della strada, lui ci si appassionava senza stancarsene: come assistesse a uno spettacolo straordinario di giocolieri cinesi che si dava apposta per lui. Si sarebbe detto, invero, alle sue risa, al continuo illuminarsi della sua faccetta, che lui non vedeva le cose ristrette dentro i loro aspetti usuali; ma quali immagini multiple di altre cose varianti all'infinito. Altrimenti non si spiegava come mai la scena miserabile, monotona, che la casa gli offriva ogni giorno, potesse rendergli un divertimento così cangiante, e inesauribile. (120)

> Everything he glimpsed around him roused his interest and stirred him to joy. . . . And if, as happens, the sunlight reached the ceiling indirectly and cast the shadows of the street's morning bustle, he would stare at it fascinated, never tiring of it, as if he were watching an extraordinary display of Chinese acrobats given especially for him. To tell the truth, one would have said from his laughter, and from the constant brightening of his little face, that he didn't see things restricted to their usual aspects, but as multiple images of other things, varying to infinity. Otherwise, there was no explaining why the miserable, monotonous scene that the house offered every day could afford him such splendid, inexhaustible amusement. (103–4)

In this novelistic version of the Platonic cave, Useppe's imagination and wonderment are enough to change the shadows coming from the world outside into infinite sources of delight. Proceeding in the same vein, the narrator goes on to describe how Useppe learns such words as *star*, *swallow*, and *sun* and the ways in which he uses them. This early stage of Useppe's cognitive and linguistic development, in which the child believes he identifies the essence of things by naming their most salient material attribute (such as color, light, or motion), once again involves Useppe's powers of imaginative extension and transformation:

> Una delle prime parole che imparò fu *ttelle* (stelle). Però chiamava ttelle anche le lampadine di casa, i derelitti fiori che Ida portava da scuola, i mazzi di cipolle appesi, perfino le maniglie delle porte, e in séguito anche le rondini. Poi quando imparò la parola *dóndini* (rondini) chiamava dóndini pure i suoi calzerottini stesi a asciugare su uno spago. E a riconoscere una nuova ttella (che magari era una mosca sulla parete) o una nuova dóndine, partiva ogni volta in una gloria di risatine, piene di contentezza e di accoglienza, come se incontrasse una persona della famiglia.
>   Le forme stesse che provocavano, generalmente, avversione o ripugnanza, in lui suscitavano solo attenzione e una trasparente meraviglia, al pari delle altre. Nelle sterminate esplorazioni che faceva, camminando a quattro zampe, intorno agli Urali, e alle Amazonie, e agli Arcipelaghi Australiani, che erano per lui i mobili di casa, a volte non si sapeva più dove fosse. E lo si trovava sotto l'acquaio in cucina, che assisteva estasiato a una ronda di scarafaggi, come fossero cavallucci in una prateria. Arrivò perfino a riconoscere una *ttella* in uno sputo.

> One of the first words he learned was *ttars* (stars). However, he also called the lightbulbs in the house ttars, and the forsaken flowers Ida brought from school, the hanging clusters of onions, even the doorknobs, and later on also swallows. Then when he learned the word *wallows* (swallows), he also called his socks hanging out on a line to dry wallows. And each time he would recognize a new ttar (which was perhaps a fly on the wall) or a new wallow, he would burst into a glory of laughter, filled with contentment and welcome, as if he had come upon a member of the family.
>   The same things that, usually, arouse aversion or repugnance,

in him inspired only attention and a transparent wonder, just like everything else. In his endless journeys of exploration crawling on all fours around the Urals and the Amazon and the Australian archipelagoes, which the furniture of the house was to him, sometimes he was lost. And he would be found under the sink in the kitchen, ecstatically observing a patrol of cockroaches as if they were wild ponies on the prairie. He even recognized a ttar in a gob of spit.

The transformation that things undergo in Useppe's linguistic imagination serves to heighten similarities by ignoring basic differences and by interchanging essences and attributes. In cognitive as well as imaginative terms, this procedure is also, generally speaking, that of the creation of metaphor. In this respect, Useppe repeats the beginnings of the history of the race, since like Vico's first men he perceives the world and expresses those perceptions first in poetry rather than in prose. At the same time, his poems are not "fictional" or feigned, since they represent real, direct perception of his world: Vico's *vera narratio* and Useppe's truthful fables are two aspects of the same manner of discovering and naming daily—yet also wondrous—surroundings.

The text goes on to list other words that Useppe learns while confined in the apartment and that he uses in similar fashion: *tole* for *sole* (sun) and also for the light, the sky, and the windows; *ubo* for *buio* (dark) and for the night and the furniture under which he passes in the darkness; *opi* for *voci* (voices) and for noises in general; *ioia* for *pioggia* (rain) and for water; and *no* for the world outside, forbidden to him by his mother's interdiction. Eventually, of course, Useppe does journey outside, and these early ventures into what he considers a "vero giardino lucente," or a "real shining garden," are doubly wondrous because his guide is his older brother Nino ("Ino"), whose presence is the most cherished aspect of Useppe's realm.

As is obvious from these and a great many other examples, the effect of Useppe's delight in, and his imaginative response to, the world around him is to make that world marvelous, at least in his eyes. For Useppe, the things of the world and the words that name them possess a power of their own. Even normally "repugnant" aspects of life undergo this fabulous transformation. To a certain degree, Useppe's jubilation is infectious, and he provides Nino with a good deal of pleasure as he tries such words as *farfalla* (butterfly), *bandiera* (flag) and finally his own name, uttering "Useppe" for "Giuseppe" and thus supplying the name with which Nino immediately baptizes him. But it is also important to see that the extent to which Useppe's joy can be transferred or even communicated to others is limited.

These limitations are due in part to Useppe's uniqueness. Although Useppe's acquisition of language and his vivaciousness are similar to the cognitive development and the exuberance of many other children, the child's faculties of imagination and wonderment portrayed in the novel are clearly distinct from those of others, as though Useppe were indeed the lost angel of light caught alone in the snare of History's darkness. Useppe differs to an even greater degree, moreover, from adults. He is undeniably close to nature, to the birds, dogs, cats, and other animals whose language he understands; but in human society he remains a foreigner, an emissary from the kingdom of poetic fancy and creative goodwill destined for only a brief sojourn in humanity's corrupted world. As the novel's epigraph from Luke 10:21 suggests, the revelation embodied by Useppe remains unseen or misunderstood under History's rule. The differences between Useppe and other people (including Nino) show up in many minor ways, but in no respect is the difference between Useppe and others more apparent than in the dual role of jester and poet into which he grows as the novel progresses.

Following the end of the war (and Useppe's stint as court jester to the clan of the *Mille*), Useppe and his dog Bella share a notably close relationship with Davide Segre, the young Jewish anarchist and drug addict who had made his appearance at the *Mille*'s quarters several years before and who turns up again on the street by chance. Along with Useppe's imaginative linguistic creations and his love for stories, his penchant for making up his own fictions has already been mentioned in the narrative. As Ida hesitantly tells the doctor who is trying to ascertain the cause of Useppe's seizures, "Credo che si racconti da solo delle storie . . . o forse poesie . . . favole . . . Però non vuole farle conoscere a nessuno" (398; "I believe . . . he tells himself stories . . . or poems perhaps . . . or fairy tales . . . But he doesn't want anyone else to know them," 339). In the narrative's concluding section, in response to a question from Davide ("A che pensi?"; "What do you think about?") and at Bella's encouragement, Useppe finally reveals his avocation: "'Io faccio le poesie!' gli comunicò arrossendo di segretezza e di confidenza" (522; "'I make up poems!' he told him, blushing with secrecy and trust," 492).

When Davide asks if Useppe writes his poems, he responds that he does not want to have anything to do with the *written* word (which is to say, within Morante's polemic, the Historical word of established power and oppression); instead, he thinks up his poems and says them aloud. When asked to whom, he answers that he tells them to Bella, who acknowledges the privilege of complicity by wagging her tail. In response to Davide's request for a sample, Useppe thinks of a series of verses and sings them out on the spot, each line representing an entire, spontaneously created poem with the appropriate stops indicated by breaths taken in between:

"Le stelle come gli alberi e fruscolano come gli alberi.
"Il sole per terra come una manata di catenelle e anelli.
"Il sole tutto come tante piume cento piume mila piume.
"Il sole su per l'aria come tante scale di palazzi.
"La luna come una scala e su in cima s'affaccia Bella che s'annisconne.
"Dormite canarini arinchiusi come due rose.
"Le 'ttelle come tante rondini che si salutano. E negli alberi.
"Il fiume come i belli capelli. E i belli capelli.
"I pesci come canarini. E volano via.
"E le foie come ali. E volano via.
"E il cavallo come una bandiera.
"E vola via." (523)

"The stars like trees and they rustle like the trees.
"The sun on the ground like a handful of little chains and rings.
"The sun just like lots of feathers a hundred feathers a thousand feathers.
"The sun up in the air like lots of stairways.
"The moon like a stairway and at the top Bella looks out and hides.
"Sleep, canaries, folded up like two roses.
"The ttars like swallows saying hello to each other. And in the trees.
"The river like pretty hair. And the pretty hair.
"The fish like canaries. And they fly away.
"And the leaves like wings. And they fly away.

>   "And the horse like a flag.
>   "And it flies away." (443)

Although Useppe's poem is clearly not meant as an artistically polished masterpiece, neither does the narrator intend it merely as a frivolous antic or as a lighthearted narrative ploy, like such earlier examples of Useppe's cuteness as his "thinking" by holding his head between his hands or his answering the telephone in childish imitation of adults. Indeed, the details of the verse tie in with earlier sections of the narrative in particularly telling ways. His active metaphorization of the elements of everyday life by establishing a link between disparate phenomena recalls his earlier acquisition of language both in a general sense and in such words as "rondini," "cavallo," "vola via," and "ttelle" (for "stelle"). The touches of *romanesco* give evidence of his daily life in Rome ("s'annisconne," "arinchiusi," "foie"), while the images of birds and especially those "folded up like two roses" hark back to his experiences amid the clan of the *Mille*. His choice of poetic objects betrays his recollection of the lullabies Ida inherited from her parents as well as his closeness to nature, and his treatment of them demonstrates not only his intimate affections ("Dormite canarini"; "Sleep, canaries") but also his lack of possessiveness, his open, unfearful, and in that sense non-Freudian (because nonconflictual) affective relationships with the contents of the world around him. In one sense, even loss here does not seem tragic, since these elements—unlike Nino—seem subject to endless replenishment like the joyous balloons of his world: "E volano via" ("And they fly away"). But there are also implicitly darker elements in this passage, since a good deal of the animal imagery as well as the images of "flying away" repeat Useppe's earlier comments to Nino (who *does* fly away, however metaphorically, leaving Useppe behind), and since the poem's imagery of enclosure and hiding also reflect Useppe's own enclosure and his progressive solitude, particularly in these final portions of the narrative. At this point in the story, these meanings remain secondary, but it is nonetheless important to see that they are at work, however subtly, even here.

Later on, just prior to Useppe and Bella's encounter with the fancied river pirates, Useppe's spontaneously created and now more highly articulated poetry again seems to demonstrate his good-natured interest in the spectacle of his ever-changing natural surroundings as well as his capacity for both wonderment and humor (632; 534). But again, despite the fact that Useppe's poetry arises from joy, a joy that once more touches Bella too (who pricks up her ears and gives a humorous bark at the sound of the word "cat" in the poem), its reproduction here is darkened by the shadows of doom. Almost immediately after the poem's conclusion, the narrator adds the remark: "Questa, poi, che io sappia, è stata l'ultima poesia di Useppe" ("This, as far as I know, was Useppe's last poem").

Though the narrator's comment is quite specific, its bleakness in regard to Useppe's future as a poet and as a representative of the functions of poetry in the world is generalized in the text. Useppe is the poet of joy and innocence; as such, he represents a key element in Morante's view of the world, the center of all that is spontaneously positive and productive in humanity and in nature. But as long as History reigns (or what Marx, in a different context, termed the stages of prehistory), as long as the brutal logic of international monopoly capitalism and political repression holds sway, there is no lasting place for Useppe's little spot of utopia.[3] His death, in both symbolic and real terms, merely reconfirms the impossibility of his mission in the world as that world is presently constituted. Useppe thus comes to represent not only the figure of the poet, doomed to perish unheeded and misunderstood in the fallen world of History's scandal, but also poetry itself, that life-giving and life-sustaining force of innocent joy, of "immaculate" creation, necessarily stifled by the present tyranny of everyday life.

That Useppe represents poetry-as-innocence is fairly clear in the text, but even so he is not the novel's only poet. The other poet in *La Storia*, the representative of poetry-as-anguish, is the miserable, self-torturing Davide Segre. As opposed to Useppe's poetic celebration of innocence, Davide's poetry manifests his hope only as it occurs in strict relation to his despair. His commentary on Useppe's poetry—that Useppe's extensive use of "come" ("like") points to the absent agency of the creator of material similarities and so to a metaphysical God—finds its poetic analogue in Davide's utopian verse. The relation between Davide's poetry and his own life is not, however, as simple or direct as in Useppe's case. Whether the subject of Davide's verse is politics (as in the poem entitled "Ai compagni"; "To the Comrades"), love ("Primavera"; "Spring"), or religious experience ("Ombre luminose"; "Luminous Shadows"), the point is not the *connection* between the world and his poetic expression of hope but rather the stark *contrast* between his actual experience and his utopian sentiments. In other words, Davide's poetry differs from Useppe's in that Useppe's poems repeat primarily the child's unblemished personality and his joyful relation to the world, whereas Davide's verse stands as a metaphorical representation of his hopes for change in a world that is *undeniably* corrupted and corrupting. Davide's poems thus express his social desires in the context of his thoroughly gloomy alienation. His poetry is probably never sufficient in itself to bridge the gap between his experience and his hopes, or even to make him forget the troubles of the world. Indeed, while he is busy creating poems to appease Useppe's insatiable poetic appetite, Davide is also injecting himself with the "medicine" that will eventually lead to his death by overdose. As time goes on, moreover, and as Davide's alienation becomes more acutely felt, the power of poetry as an antidote to the cold facts of life, or even as a respite from them, grows weaker and weaker.

The extent of Davide's misery is notably apparent in the course of his inebriated harangue delivered to the barroom audience of card players, during which his passionate hope in the possibilities of mankind's social future is overshadowed only by his current state of anguish (564–98; 478–506). The possibilities that Davide sees and attempts to argue for find their expression as a mixture of anarchist utopian thought and evangelical Christianity. This is an explicit formulation of many of the implicit biases running through the entirety of Morante's text, the sort of biases that she had evinced earlier in several of her expository writings and perhaps most forthrightly in her polemical collection of poetry published by Einaudi in 1968, *Il mondo salvato dai ragazzini* (*The World Saved by Children*). Indeed, the section of the 1968 collection that is entitled "Addio," or "Goodbye," is addressed to Morante's young American companion, Bill Morrow, who had died of a drug overdose and whose experiences may also have served as a model for Davide's character in *La Storia* and for the circumstances of his death (including his "childish, almost tender" last breath [621; 525]).

That Davide's harangue is affected both by the wine (to which, as a drug addict, he is unused) and by his intensely bitter emotional state is easy to see; but at the same time, the subject matter of his discourse is of particular significance at this late stage of the narrative. In the course of Davide's drunken ramblings (amidst a setting similar to that of Renzo's inebriated discourse at the Inn of the Luna Piena), one of the most interesting aspects of his remarks is his accusation of History itself: "La Storia, si capisce, è tutta un'oscenità fino dal principio, però anni osceni come questi non ce n'erano mai stati" (584; "History, of course, is all an obscenity from the beginning, but years as obscene as these have never existed before," 495). This outburst follows a description of Davide in which the narrator notes that the speaker seems suddenly and unaccountably aged, so thoroughly so that even his latent sexual ardor, which normally burns with the "grazia tragica" ("tragic grace") of a stigmata, seems all at once to have dried up and withered away. Davide, using terminology that echoes the book's narrator, goes on in Nietzschean fashion to denounce the scandal of History, once again History with a capital H, the scandal that is not only obscene but also worsening.

It is fairly clear in this section, therefore, that Davide's speech both furthers the narrator's entire polemic against "History" and fits into that same polemic as part and parcel of the narrator's argument. Just as Useppe is the naturally innocent, prelapsarian poet who, as Davide affirms a while later, stimulates belief in human *potential* because he is simply "troppo carino per questa mondo" (599, cf. 397; "too sweet for this world," 507, cf. 338), Davide is the poet of the last age, at once the Vichian "youthful" old man who actually carries the age of the world inside of him *and* the prophetic voice of Christian sacrifice, suffering, and apocalypse. Davide thus joins the numerous other young men of the narrative—vital, spirited, yet living on borrowed time—as one more object of human sacrifice. His anarchist/Christian harangue contributes to the narrator's overall condemnation of History's scandal, therefore, even as it plays a part in the narrative's description of the history in which Useppe and the other characters also figure as participants and victims. Paired together, Davide and Useppe are the two sides of the narrative's conception of poetry, one the poetic voice of innocence and joy and the other the communal public seer of corruption and suffering. Although in this sense they are the embodiment and the expression of two different aspects of history, they are both caught in History's vise and so in the end, despite their differences, are similarly fated.

Because of the negative slant of the narrator's argument as a whole, Useppe's joyfulness and innocence should not be blown out of proportion. His fate under the sentence of History is suggested repeatedly throughout the novel, most often by the shadow in his eyes that all his expressions of joy are insufficient to hide from Nino and the others. Useppe's end, moreover, symbolically confirms the "genealogical imperative" of his lineage, harking back both to the early death of the story's first Giuseppe, Ida's anarchist Calabrese father, and to that of Ida's husband, Alfio, who actually died of cancer but whose death is attributed by Ida to the less sacral and therefore more utterable, because less frightening, "malattia del secolo" (43; "disease of our time," 37).

Not surprisingly, all of the narrative's most pointed elements of literary intertextuality reflect this same view of the motions of History. These include the Manzonian scene of the bread (here flour) riot (334–36; 285–87); the Dantesque description of Davide's suffering in the infernal world of industrial hell (411–22; 349–59); the Dostoevskian allusion in the selection of Davide Segre's *nom de guerre* (Piotr); the direct reference to Manzoni's *Colonna infame* (569; 482); and the verses by César Vallejo and Miguel Hernández that frame the narrative. This view also underlies another aspect of the novel's self-reflexivity (here specifically narrative self-reflexivity), Useppe's fascination with "stories" and his desire that his mother's "favoletta," or roughly "nursery rhyme," be constantly repeated in the fervent yet vain hope that its ending will turn out to be happy rather than sad (290; 247). The implications of this last passage are in one sense more disturbing than the narrator's casually self-reflexive commentaries on writing scattered through the narrative (such as that on Nino's boisterous sloganeering [135; 116]; on Davide's attempt to turn his own body into a bloodstained text [416; 353]; on the "authorial" style of Davide's missives from Mantova [422; 359]; or on the morbidly impersonal chronicle of the newspaper report announcing Useppe's death and Ida's funeral watch [647; 547]), since in terms of this particular example of Useppe's experience in the world of History, even fairy tales end in sorrow.

No treatment of literary self-consciousness in *La Storia* would be complete without consideration of the narrator herself, the complex and often disconcertingly intrusive figure who does the most to emphasize the distinction between history and History. The narrator's feminine gender, linking her directly with Morante, is confirmed by the form of the adjectives that refer to the speaker here and there throughout the text. The perturbing aspect of the narrator's presentation (and self-presentation) is not, however, primarily a matter of gender but one of attitude—which is to say, of knowledge, perspective, and tone. In this regard, the relationship that the narrator establishes between herself and her audience—between her own discourse and its readers—is a topic of special moment.

Almost everyone who has discussed the book in print since its appearance has had something to say about the active role that the narrator assumes in not only presenting but also commenting on and even criticizing her text. Her intrusions—at times so heavily ironic as to be snide rather than merely witty or even cutting—have more often than not given rise to a good deal of critical displeasure. The major questions are whether or not this reaction is created intentionally, and if so, what the narrator's goals might be in taking this tack. In certain instances her ironic commentary is directed toward the supposedly great leaders of History's brigade ("Benito," "Adolfo," et al.), whereas in others it is aimed at events and characters of lesser Historical import (the various bureaucrats portrayed throughout the text, the doctors who attempt to diagnose Useppe's illness). In still other situations her intrusive comments are not so much ironic as coy; these include her early avowal of ignorance in regard to the local geography and customs of Calabria (28, cf. 53; 24, cf. 45), and her desire to call Useppe by that name since that was the way she had always known him (131; 113). The latter effects cast the problem of the narrator's perspective in a new light, since they have to do not only with the narrator's knowledge and her point of view, but also with the broader conventions of realist discourse, which is to say with the relation between the narrator and the supposedly *real* world described by her *fiction*.

Morante published *La Storia* in 1974 after a lengthy career that included, as I have mentioned, poetry and many other types of narrative, from children's stories to a psychologically focused family saga (*Menzogna e sortilegio*) to realist fiction with a strong component of fantasy (*L'isola di Arturo*). In the course of this earlier work, she had experimented with a wide variety of narrative voices, tones, and perspectives. It is clear, then, that notwithstanding several of the negative technical assessments of her work in the course of the extraordinarily lively debate that followed the novel's publication,[4] Morante was well aware of both the detailed effects and the general impact that her choice of presentational technique in *La Storia* would have. By adopting this manner of presentation in the "historical" parts of the narrative as well as in the interspersed "Historical" sections, she breaks the conventions of the historical novel in a way that is far more thoroughgoing, and ultimately far more disruptive, than merely dividing the text into two completely discrete types of discourse.

Through these techniques of presentation, Morante's narrator becomes omniscient in a peculiarly distinctive sense, since she is all-knowing to such a degree that she can include the limitations of her knowledge as part of the affirmations within her own discourse. Paradoxically, therefore, by stressing her limitations the narrator does not weaken but actually strengthens her own authority, in part because the acknowledgment of weakness only reconfirms the narrator's overall position of strength (which, again, in the genre of the historical novel is a conventional as well as a logical position) and in part because the narrator's open admission of her limits only accentuates the far greater limitations of the reader, whose position vis-à-vis the narrator remains one of dependency. That some of the book's actual readers have disliked and at times even heartily resented this sort of self-conscious effect on the part of the narrator—this insistent breaking up of the traditional conventions of representational transparency and narratorial anonymity within the historical novel—has also been apparent since the novel's earliest critical reception. Oddly enough, this negative reaction is precisely the one that puts us on the track to approaching our second question: *what* was Morante's intent in choosing to present her material as she did?

Although *La Storia* is cast in the mold of a historical novel, any attempt to read it merely as an example of seemingly transparent, representational fiction will be frustrated, as we have seen, both by the purposefully slanted Historical introductions and by the spontaneously self-conscious and often pointedly challenging interruptions of the narrator. It is not hard to see that this is realism in the line of Brecht rather than that of Auerbach or even of Lukács. It is true that, in terms of the aesthetics of literary models and effects, this sort of realism—in which the reader is repeatedly reminded both of his or her position as reader and of the responsibility for interpretation entailed by any representation of "History" or "history"—does disrupt the conventions of traditional realist discourse. But this result takes on even greater importance in *La Storia* when the book's first audience of readers is considered from a historical perspective, and more narrowly, from that of Italian political history.

Nineteen seventy-four was by no means an insignificant year in Italian culture, but by any measure it was part of an inestimably momentous period for Italian politics. Under Enrico Berlinguer, the recently elected secretary of the Communist party, it appeared to many, including writers, academics, journalists, and others associated with the Italian Left, that new solutions to Italy's age-old social and political problems might actually be on the horizon. Questions like the status of the family, the social role of women, the possible reorganization of the Italian economy (following the end of the postwar "economic miracle" and the 1973–74 crisis), and the reform of countless other institutions, from the universities to the labor unions to the press, were being regularly addressed throughout the country. In this highly politicized and often heady environment, it is not surprising that Morante's patently political novel created the stir that it did. I have discussed elsewhere the publishing aspects of *La Storia*'s initial success (in terms of marketing and publicity "hype") and the literary elements of its critical reception (in terms of the breakup and decline of the previous avant-garde of the Gruppo 63 and other neo-experimentalists).[5] In this context, it may suffice to remark that at *La Storia*'s appearance in 1974, the Italian Left, riding on the surge of optimism of the early 1970s that preceded the massive setback and subsequent confusion at the polls in 1976, was less than comfortable with a book as pessimistic, depressing, and insistently prodding as Morante's novel.

Although the pertinence and the force of the novel's statement and the historical climate of its reception may easily be lost on subsequent generations (and different nationalities) of readers, the circumstances of the book's initial appearance should not be taken lightly. By confronting head-on such topics as sociopolitical oppression and victimization, potentially non-Freudian, spontaneous love, and the relation between utopian anarchism, Marxism, and millennial Christianity (from Davide Segre's theory of infinitely multiple Christs, all recognized by their use of the same word, to Useppe's angelic goodness), Morante's novel staked out positions in several of the most embattled regions of the social, political, and cultural debates in the early and mid 1970s. That the book was a work of fiction, and therefore one that required from its readers reflection and interpretation before its place in those debates could be assessed, only made the public's reaction to it that much more complicated. This was true in emotional as well as intellectual terms, all the more so because of the strange mixture of representational responsibility, ironic withdrawal, and pathos that both infuses and derives from the narrator's voice.[6]

Nowhere is this distinctive mixture more apparent than at the novel's conclusion, in the scene of Ida's reaction to Useppe's death (646–49; 546–48). The scene begins with Useppe's lifeless body on the floor of the apartment's entryway where he fell. His feet are bare, since his sandals had fallen off, and his arms are spread out in the attitude of Christian sacrifice. When Ida returns to the apartment, her reaction to what has happened is to imagine that all the terrors in the history of the world have come together to produce this end:

> Ora nella mente stolida e malcresciuta di quella donnetta, mentre correva a precipizio per il suo piccolo alloggio, ruotarono anche le scene della storia umana (la Storia) che essa percepì come le spire multiple di un assassinio interminabile. E oggi l'ultimo assassinato era il suo bastarduccio Useppe. Tutta la Storia e le nazioni della terra s'erano concordate a questo fine: la strage del bambinello Useppe Ramundo.

Now in the stolid and undeveloped mind of that little woman, as she ran wildly around her small home, the scenes of human history (History) also revolved, which she perceived as the multiple coils of an interminable series of murders. And today the last to be murdered was her little bastard son, Useppe. All History and the nations of the earth had agreed on this end: the slaughter of the little child Useppe Ramundo.

As had occurred earlier in the course of Davide's drunken discourse, the narrator again concurs in Ida's bitter accusation against human history and refines that condemnation by casting history in her own terminology as History. At this point it appears, therefore, that regardless of Ida's severe limitations she has at last understood her plight in the very terms in which the narrator conceives of the world's situation. The next step in the development of this scene, moreover, seems to extend the nature of Ida's understanding. The smile that she has been futilely waiting to see on Useppe's face begins to appear instead, by a "miracle," on her own face. Ida's reaction in this concluding *pietà* links her even more closely to Useppe's experience, since, as the narrator notes, her smile is similar to the expression of marvelous innocence and quietude that earlier had accompanied her own seizures (cf. 29, 69; 25, 59). But the suggestion that Ida has now understood Useppe's fate as well as her own circumstances both in an intellectual sense and in an emotional, even miraculously spiritual one is immediately undercut by the narrator herself, who in an uncannily disconcerting conclusion once again tinged with pathos *and* irony, explains that Ida's response was neither the smile of rational understanding nor that of revelation but instead that of madness. With this, Ida's life, as the narrator goes on to note, effectively ends, and her story is finished.

This conclusion, or something very much like it, was most likely inevitable from the start, given the narrative's view of History. Like many earlier twentieth-century writers, though in a more deeply political manner, Morante sees that all History is nothing but a story of sickness, oppression, and death: in the end, no one escapes alive. Morante's History thus evinces its force in the world of history just as pervasively and as powerfully as Vico's or Manzoni's Providence, but its effects are always negative. Her view of the progression of everyday human life is thus as pessimistic as Verga's but far more stridently so. Unlike Verga, however, or even Lampedusa, Morante sees not only the problems of the historical world of matter and sense but also a solution to those problems, at least *in potentia*.

That solution, quite simply, is the end of History itself. Unfortunately, *La Storia*, as a historical novel, can *suggest* such a solution but cannot *represent* it, since the desired end is not yet part of the everyday world.

Two of the major ways in which the narrative makes this suggestion are ones that we have mentioned before: first, through the figure of Useppe (linked at the end with Davide), and, second, through the agency charged with the task of representation, the narrative voice. Whereas Useppe is the walking embodiment of poetry and of innocent love as well as the novel's principal indication of human potential in a non-Oedipal, evangelical future, the increasing pessimism of the narrative voice regularly serves as a reminder to the reader that, as long as History holds sway, the utopian potential of mankind can never be realized. This constant reminder furnishes the answer to the question of Morante's intent in utilizing such a discomforting narrative voice, though at the same time it must be remembered that not everything in *La Storia* is completely bleak, that occasionally one is permitted to see at least a ray of hope, if not in the novel's plot at least in the final, proleptic entry from Gramsci's correspondence (taken from a notably affectionate letter sent from the prison at Turi di Bari to his sister-in-law, Tania, dated 3 June 1929): "Tutti i semi sono falliti eccettuato uno, che non so cosa sia, ma che probabilmente è un fiore e non un'erbaccia" ("All the seeds have failed except one. I don't know what it is, but it is probably a flower and not a weed"). But such suggestions of hope, especially toward the novel's end, are few and far between.

Morante's book thus takes its place in the highly charged political atmosphere of the Italian mid-1970s not only as a literary depiction of social life but also as a social statement and a political accusation. The political purposes of art had been part of Morante's developing aesthetics for some time, but with the publication of *La Storia* they entered their most intense stage. In a series of remarks to a union-sponsored cultural conference in Rome in 1976, following the censoring of the text of *La Storia* in Franco's Spain, Morante explained the goals of her book in no uncertain terms.[7] Provided with this opportunity, she used it to reaffirm the dual nature of *La Storia* as both an "opera di poesia" ("work of poetry") and as "un atto d'accusa contro tutti i fascismi del mondo" ("an act of accusation against all the fascisms of the world"). Her book thus represents, for her, what Useppe had represented *within* her narrative, a worldly example of the force of poetry, of creative imagination at work in the world, and a key to the understanding and the salvation of human society gone wrong, which is to say, to the understanding of history *and* History. On this topic at the same conference, Morante was at once eloquent and concise: "[*La Storia* è] una domanda urgente e disperata, che si rivolge a *tutti*, per un possibile *risveglio comune*" ("[*History* is] an urgent and desperate request, which is directed at *everyone*, to the end of a possible *communal awakening*").

This affirmation picks up Morante's self-consciously expressed concern for the worldly power of poetry (already present *in nuce* in the lyric poem "Sheherazade" from the collection *Alibi* [1958], used as the epigraph to this book), while it casts that concern in a decidedly political light. To conceive of Morante's aesthetics for a moment in terms of Benjamin's concept of the "aura," the traditional aura of the work of art has returned in the form of the political richness of representational fiction's authentic worldly force. Morante's book thus becomes a self-conscious work of art with a new twist, since the circle of that self-consciousness—of poetry as a factor within the narrative and of the novel itself as a poetic factor in the world of its reception—is completed only as the novel enters the empirical world of its audience. By putting in question the future of human society through depiction of the recent historical past and, in the fashion of a Brechtian epos, by then placing the burden of responsibility for understanding and *change* on the novel's readers, *La Storia* strains at the limits of the form of the historical novel, indeed at the limits of literary representation itself. *La Storia* may thus be seen as an attempt at creating a special sort of *romanzo popolare*, one that, despite the critical misunderstanding that greeted the novel's publication, intends not only to represent the day-to-day world of popular society but also to take its place in that world as a thorn in the side of its audience.

This type of literary self-consciousness, at once disconcertingly self-reflexive and stridently political, was new in Italian postwar fiction. Given this novelty, the difficulties in classifying the narrative—and indeed of reacting to it in any coherent fashion—that were so apparent during the debate following its appearance are perhaps understandable. There had been, it is true, many previous narratives with obvious political content in terms of both subject matter and ideological evaluation—the examples of D'Annunzio and Silone come immediately to mind—but never before had literary self-consciousness itself cut so close to the heart of what it meant to be at one and the same time a work of art *and* a statement of political belief. This development demonstrates, first, that literary self-consciousness is not necessarily a sterile, antisocial game and, second, that it and social commitment in literature are not antithetical, that at least in certain works the two can and do go hand in hand. None of this means, of course, that the intent of Morante as an individual author was sufficient to produce the results for which she hoped, any more than the will of her most "poetic" characters is enough to change their own world. Both at the implicitly self-reflexive end of her novel and at the end of her conference remarks in 1976, Morante noted, with obvious despair, "E la Storia continua" ("And History continues")—as did in her view, therefore, the daily trial of poetry itself.

TEN

Self-conscious Artifacts

Calvino's Fictions

Literary self-consciousness took an extraordinary variety of forms in the course of Italo Calvino's work. His first novel, *Il sentiero dei nidi di ragno* (1947; *The Path to the Nest of Spiders*) is a neorealist depiction of a boy's experiences during World War II amid a uniquely inept band of Ligurian partisans. As such, it is the most straightforwardly representational of Calvino's major works. But despite the fact that in its pages representation of the external world leads and literary self-involvement follows, there are important strains of both linguistic and narrative self-consciousness running through the novel.[1] The stories of *Le Cosmicomiche* (1965; *Cosmicomics*), Calvino's first collection of *fantascienza*, or science fiction, demonstrate the consciousness of their literary status and techniques more directly. Nevertheless, once again the concern for representing something other than the functions of language and the creation of narrative (in this case, the origins and evolution of the earth and its universe) receives paramount emphasis. *Se una notte d'inverno un viaggiatore* (1979; *If on a Winter's Night a Traveler*) is the most programmatically self-conscious of Calvino's fictions. Indeed, the narrative takes its own unfolding as its primary interest, occasionally to the exclusion of all others. At the same time, the novel demonstrates a further characteristic of contemporary literary self-consciousness, not just extreme self-awareness of its nature and workings as a *written* artifact but also as one that is meant to be *read*.

This shift within literary self-consciousness away from attention to writing and toward attention to reading has been a gradual one, both in the development of narrative generally over the past three centuries and more narrowly within the canon of Calvino's works. It is true that interest in the act of reading and in the role of the reader has always been an aspect of novelistic self-awareness (one need only recall the lively games with the reader in *Tristram Shandy* or even Manzoni's commentary on reading and interpretation and his characteristically coy remarks to his hypostatized "lettori"). But it is also true that the function of the reader has been of especially obvious importance over the last few decades, roughly from the Joyce of *Finnegans Wake* to the subsequent strains of "metafiction" in the European, American, and Latin American novel. From this perspective, Calvino's work retraces the lines of current literary discussion and ends with several of the most important questions of contemporary literary concern.[2]

Il sentiero dei nidi di ragno: The World and Its Narration

As I have suggested, Calvino's narratives did not start out with the reader as their principal interest. In the beginning, their focus was on the representation of the world and then on the processes of their own creation rather than on those of their reception. *Il sentiero dei nidi di ragno* demonstrates its consciousness of its literary qualities and procedures in three main ways: first, in the linguistic self-consciousness of its attention to the part that the mastery of language's subtleties play during the initiation of the main character into the partisans' world; second, in the narrative self-consciousness of its borrowings from the folktale tradition in terms of character presentation, settings, themes, plot motifs, and the like; and third, in its treatment of the devices and effects of narration itself during a crucial passage toward the end of the novel when Lupo Rosso ("Red Wolf") tells his "hero's tale" of the final encounter with Pelle ("Skin"), the story's cold-ridden, gun-obsessed turncoat.[3]

The narrative's focus on language and its acquisition is as subtle as it is important. For Pin, the acquisition of new linguistic terms leads eventually to his introduction to and understanding of new cognitive concepts. Since this is a learning process, however, and since Pin constantly overshoots the bounds of his current capacities, the effect of the representation of his struggles is one of irony. Initially, the linguistic aspect of his worldly education is underscored in the text by his bluffing attempt to parade his ignorance as mastery in regard to what seems to Pin to be the arcane vocabulary of the Resistance, such as *Comitato*, *gap*, and the like (64 et passim; 31 et passim). During his detention by the Fascists, the irony of Pin's endeavors to convince the bona fide partisan hero, Lupo Rosso, of his competence thus establishes an evaluative distance between the character and the reader even though the story is narrated in the seeming immediacy of the present tense. This particular irony, associated with the text's demonstration of the worldly importance of language, dissipates as Pin becomes more experienced in the partisans' lingo and in their ways, for the simple reason that as Pin gains experience, he also becomes more sophisticated in his use of language and so at least somewhat less ingenuous. After his escape from detention and his encounter with Cugino ("Cousin"), for example, instead of losing himself in total confusion between figural and literal discourse at the sound of the cook's greeting when he and his guide first approach the camp, Pin simply asks Cugino about the status of his seemingly odd appellation and then, once informed, proceeds enthusiastically to try out the name on his own (90–92; 53–55). A similar effect is created shortly thereafter with the term *troschista*, or Trotskyite (94–95; 57–58), although in this case the final result is to underscore not only Pin's increasing storehouse of linguistic lore but also his continuing political naiveté.

The textual play of ignorance and knowledge in regard to Pin's use of language is not confined to dialogue but also occurs in descriptive passages. Indeed, the narrative's subtle lexical contrasts during the escape scene between what Lupo Rosso actually knows from experience ("conosce") and what Pin only thinks he knows ("sa") from what he has heard about avoiding detection and about the hard facts of death (76–77; 41) again emphasize the lacunae in Pin's worldly development despite his occasionally precocious knowledge of such adult phenomena as violent encounter and sexual intercourse. The narrative's treatment of language is thus a major, though not unique, means of shading its presentation of Pin's development even while the story appears to be narrated from Pin's general perspective. The story's portrayal of linguistic skills, moreover, ties in with the subplot of initiation and thus demonstrates the layered interweaving of mimesis and diegesis in Calvino's fiction even at this early stage of his writing.

The novel's borrowings from the folktale tradition carry even more weight than the text's notations of linguistic effects. The folktale elements usually act as unifying devices buttressing the narrative though not always so. They would not necessarily play a part in narrative self-consciousness, except that they are so pervasive and so obvious in *Il sentiero*, as narrative ploys, that they effectively call attention to themselves as literary devices. The folktale elements have been noted by almost everyone who has commented on the novel, beginning with Cesare Pavese, who suggested their importance in a laudatory review published in the same year as the novel (and then acknowledged by Calvino himself specifically in regard to Pavese's comments in the preface added to the 1964 edition [17; xvii]).⁴ In the course of commending Calvino for not creating characters ("personaggi") in the manner of either the historical or the psychological novel, Pavese points out that Calvino's figures resemble those of a different narrative tradition, which is that of Ariosto (via Stevenson, Kipling, Dickens, and Nievo), or, better, of the chivalric romance, in which not only the character but also his actions and gestures ("il gesto") are portrayed as being all-important even as they are subsumed in the ongoing succession of events. Betraying his own interest in the problem of character formation in modern fiction, Pavese describes Calvino's narrative procedures in terms that recall Propp's insistence on the folktale connection between narrative figure and action in unities conceived of less as characters than as functions: "Un sicuro istinto gli ha fatto ridurre le sue figure, non diremo a macchiette che suona offensivo, ma a maschere, a '*incontri*,' a burattini" ("An unerring instinct made him reduce his figures, I will not say to caricatures, which sounds offensive, but to masks, '*encounters*,' puppets").⁵

Among the novel's folktale elements, many of the more important ones have to do with the characters themselves. The most notable case in point is Pin, who, along with his sister, plays the role of the abandoned child, left on his own in the wide world after the death of his mother and the unexpected departure of his father (who has perhaps established a new family in a city beyond the sea). In the course of Pin's overall search for what at the end is termed an "enchanted land" where everyone is good (167; 120)—a search that is in part ironic, given the strong misanthropy that is part of Pin's character—Pin encounters helpers (Lupo Rosso) and false friends (Pelle, 109; 70) as well as the true friend Cugino. Pin's relationship with Cugino appears to blend with the narrative's plot of initiation, furthermore, since the wondrous image of the hand made of bread with which Cugino initially leads Pin (87; 51) is repeated at the end when *Pin* leads Cugino (192; 142). Certain folktale attributes are also demonstrated by other characters, such as Pin's almost universally known sister (though the specific talents for which she is known are not usually found in children's stories), Lupo Rosso (as the valiant hero), and the quasi-familial band of partisans, which resembles nothing so much as a politicized wartime burlesque of "Snow White" (played here, ironically, by the concupiscent Giglia, or "Lily") and the "Seven Dwarfs."⁶

Several of the story's more prominent themes, topoi, and motifs also stem from the folktale tradition. These include the division of females into two groups, idealized and barred (the deceased mothers of the narrative's conclusion) and utterly evil because too easily attained (Giglia, Pin's "mattress" of a sister, and, in the editions of the novel prior to 1964, the Petacci sisters); the metonymic linking of sexual activity with excretion, a common aspect of children's fantasies; and the recurrent association of sex with violence. This last association is all bound up in "quella storia di sangue e corpi nudi che è la vita degli uomini" (41; "that tale of bloodshed and naked bodies which makes up men's lives," 11), and it encompasses the manifestly phallic P .38, which Pin is competent to fire if not really to aim, Pelle's passion for both women and guns, Dritto and Giglia's unabashedly theatrical wielding of the knives during foreplay (hers very probably belonging to her husband the cook), and the accomplishment of their illicit union just as the guns of battle sound. Still other folktale examples are furnished by the topos of the magic spot of Pin's "kingdom" (185; 136), in which he can weave strange spells and rule as a sovereign, even a god, and in which Cugino is the unthreateningly chaste great friend and the "great magician" (187, 191, 194; 138, 141, 144), and, finally, by the motif of the fabulous concatenation of the possession of the pistol as a symbolic object through the entire story.

In terms of the novel's plot, the tale of initiation is also reminiscent of the folktale tradition. However, like the concatenation of the pistol's possession, this plot—in Calvino's novel as opposed to genuine folktales—is not meaningful in any unified sense. At first glance, the concluding scene amid the dark landscape lit by the fireflies may seem to constitute the folktale's happy ending. But in point of fact, Pin and Cugino, with their discussion of women and of the world in general, are talking more at cross-purposes than anything else. How to live in the world with or without others (that is, both men and women) thus remains a question posed but left unanswered in the text. As with the text's self-conscious notations of linguistic development, the self-consciously elaborated folktale attributes, motifs, and events, as narrative devices, do help to frame this ambiguity; but in and of themselves they cannot resolve it, nor do they serve to indicate any possible resolution other than, perhaps, a suddenly foreshortened version of willful exclusion from the world, of odd-men-out.

The novel's awareness of its workings *as* a narrative is demonstrated, apart from its folktale elements, in several ways. One of these is by general literary allusion; "Pin" perhaps recalls Pinocchio, with the boy's *padrone* Pietromagro as Geppetto, whereas "Kim" may recall Kipling's loyal and equally committed protagonist. A related effect is created by more or less direct literary reference (Zena il Lungo's *Supergiallo,* or *Super-Thriller;* Dritto's memories of *Il conte di Montecristo*). Significantly, a great many of the novel's allusions and references are to works that fall within the general sphere of the romance. This dual backdrop, of both folktale and romance, is of special importance for the text. Considered in this light, the novel's most obvious and by far most significant instance of self-consciousness as narrative and as *narration*—Lupo Rosso's story of his encounter with Pelle—can be understood as the hero's tale it is, the returned knight's account of his victorious battle with the forces of evil before the audience of his peers. Viewed in this way, Lupo Rosso is the chivalric Hero, chosen by his liege lords, Ferriera and Kim, to represent them and their court. Similarly, Pin takes the complementary role of Fool, or the officially abrasive Court Jester, who tells stories to mock his audience and thus serves the group as a prod and a safety valve.

Calvino handles the insertion of Lupo Rosso's narration amid the ongoing events of the narrative with a great deal of care. The introduction of the tale is reminiscent of the suspense techniques common in the *gialli* of which Zena il Lungo is so enamored. The members of the band are discussing the recent treacheries of such defectors and spies as Pin's sister, Miscèl Francese, and others, when one of them mentions Pelle as the worst of all. It is at this point that Lupo Rosso's voice is suddenly heard, as if coming out of nowhere. When the partisans turn toward the sound of his voice, they see that he is covered with the weapons that are now both the spoils of war and the emblems of his (i.e., their) victory over the communal enemy:

> "Pelle," fa Gian l'Autista, "è il più cattivo di tutti."
> "*Era* il più cattivo," dice una voce dietro a loro. Si voltano: è Lupo Rosso che arriva, tutto bardato d'armi e di nastri di mitraglia catturati ai tedeschi. Gli fanno festa: tutti sono contenti quando rivedono Lupo Rosso. (173)

> "Pelle," remarks Gian the Driver, "is the worst of the lot."
> "He *was* the worst," says a voice behind them. They turn around: it's Lupo Rosso arriving, all adorned with weapons and machine-gun belts captured from the Germans. They give him a

warm welcome: they are always pleased to see Red Wolf again. (125)

After this dramatic introduction, the partisans ask what has happened to Pelle, and Lupo Rosso tells the story, first providing the background information (that the *gap* planned and carried out the operation) and then proceeding to the particulars. He tells them that Pelle, in order to keep his armory of collected weapons to himself, usually chose to stay alone in a garret rather than to sleep in the Fascist barracks with the others. One night on his way home, Lupo Rosso continues, Pelle realizes that he is being followed by first one and then a pair and then more and more men in trenchcoats. When Pelle reaches his building and heads up the stairs, at each landing he looks down to see more and more men in trenchcoats standing below him in the dim light, as though they are all the repeated image of that first man, reflected in a "game" of mirrors. Pelle is convinced that reaching his room is tantamount to being home free, with his cache of weapons and grenades for his defense, and he runs up the last flight, opens his door, and bangs it shut behind him. But through the garret's windows he sees another man on the roof, aiming at him. As Pelle raises his hands the door behind him opens, and he sees all the men on all the landings, repeated seemingly ad infinitum. Then one of them fires. Although Red Wolf states that no one knows who the actual executioner was, he concludes this portion of his story by satisfying the curiosity of his listeners in telling them where *he* was and, at least by implication, what role he played in the operation:

> Adesso uno dice: "Lupo Rosso, tu, qual eri, di quelli?"
> Lupo Rosso sorride: si rialza il berretto a visiera sul cranio rasato nella prigione: "Quello sul tetto," dice. (175)

> Now one of them says, "What about you, Red Wolf, which of the men were you?"
> Red Wolf smiles: he raises the visor of the beret on the skull that had been shaved bare in prison:
> "The one on the roof," he says. (127)

The entire story, in its overall organization, its heightening play of suspense and revelation, its descriptive details, and its technique of psychological development in the direct reporting of Pelle's thoughts, is told with consummate narrative skill. The effect on Red Wolf's audience is to be expected: they follow the story breathlessly ("Senza tirare il fiato"). Indeed, this inserted tale is far more unified and dramatically pointed than anything else in the novel. But therein lies the problem. Hand in hand with the question of representational *technique*—at least in realist fiction—goes the question of representational *fidelity*. Red Wolf's story, in its psychological precision (strikingly dissimilar to the rest of the text, as Pavese's comments quoted earlier suggest) and in its dramatic unity, makes a fine story. But because it *is* that—so pointed and so neat—its worldly veracity inevitably comes into question. In terms of its narration, the tale's unity is hardly a drawback, but in terms of the recounting of the events of everyday life it is; which is to say, maybe Red Wolf's tale is a good story, but, at the same time, maybe it is *only* that: *just* a story. Moreover, the novel's narrator, very close to Pin's perspective at this point, alludes to precisely this problem immediately following the notation of the story's effects on its audience: "Alle volte Lupo Rosso esagera un po' le cose che racconta, ma racconta molto bene" ("At times Red Wolf exaggerates a little when he tells his stories, but he tells them very well").

It would in turn be an exaggeration on our part to claim that Lupo Rosso's story is indeed untrue, that it is cut from whole cloth. The circumstances of Pelle's execution in the presence of the other partisans as well as Lupo Rosso's extraordinarily consistent devotion to forwarding the cause of Marxist truth (in which he is similar to Kim but distinct from Pin, who shows little commitment to anything except his own interests) make such a reading extremely unlikely. It must be remembered, nonetheless, that Pelle *is* heartily despised by the band of listeners and that Lupo Rosso's youthful enthusiasm (he is only sixteen) may well lead to his recasting his account in such a way that it becomes the sort of story that he wants to tell and that his audience wants to hear, with all the melodramatic effects and the closed ending that the genre of the hero's tale calls for. The narrator's pointed concluding comment simply underscores this possibility. In this instance, therefore, while the realistic novel's self-conscious commentary on the effects and the validity of narrative points up its *own* overall factitiousness as narrated fiction, it also, and more succinctly, calls into question the relation between the inserted story and its purported referent—in other words, the relation between unified discourse and worldly truth. While Calvino's text does not deny that such a relationship might actually exist, the novel expresses an awareness, embedded within its own narration, of the difficulties that such a relationship entails.

These multiple effects can be approached from still another angle.

One result of the text's indication of doubt is to draw attention not only to the tale but also to its teller. As I have mentioned, Red Wolf's motivations for heightening the dramatic effect of his narration do not stem exclusively from aesthetic considerations but also from his general loyalty to Marxist doctrine (apparent in everything he does and says, extending from his analyses of Pin's capitalist failings to his denunciations of the Fascists and even to his sloganeering) and from his particular dislike for the sort of egotistically unprincipled treachery practiced by Pelle. The apparent unity of the hero's tale, therefore, derives from and further supports Red Wolf's dual denomination as *Lupo*, or in this context, warrior, and *Rosso*, or Marxist. Early in the story, Red Wolf insists on each attribute during his conversations with Pin. When Pin attempts to address him familiarly as "Wolf," Red Wolf responds that without the qualifier "Red" the "Wolf" would be a Fascist animal (66; 33). Through the complexities of the symbolism of naming, Calvino's text manages to incorporate the political and military ideals exemplified by Red Wolf's story even while it includes a narratorial indication of the limitations of those very ideals. The text's presentation of the hero's tale followed by the narrator's final comment thus comprises not only an idealized view of the partisan struggle but also its knowledge of the disorderly practicalities of the real world and its distrust of any idealized unity in terms of either worldly action and political belief or literary representation. The narrator's self-consciously pointed disclaimer in regard to the veracity of Red Wolf's story only reaffirms, therefore, the multiple ambiguities already present in the overall parameters of the novel's techniques of representation as realist fiction and in the functions of naming as both everyday and literary language. In *Il sentiero*, the language of the world as well as the naming and the narration of the world's truth are presented as being at one and the same time unified and disjointed, highly stylized yet compellingly "real." The complexity of this combination, moreover, explains in part why the text's folktale and other narrative elements, even when acting as unifying devices, can frame but cannot resolve the novel's underlying ambiguities, especially at the conclusion.

Despite the importance of the narrative's expression of doubt, however, it must be remembered that the moment itself passes very quickly, as a flickering signal of self-knowledge rapidly left behind in the progress of the story. The narrative's illustrative example of "How to Tell a Story," accompanied by its suggestion of the dangers that may well be inherent in all storytelling, is immediately subsumed within the ongoing concerns of the worldly representation of the partisans' activities and interests. The ephemeral nature of this self-conscious commentary is therefore consistent with the depiction of the novel as primarily representational, knowledgeable about the techniques and the qualities of its own production but not openly obsessed with them. Within the world depicted by the story, moreover, not only narrative but language, too, is seen as ancillary to worldly action rather than as somehow equal or superior to it, as is suggested by the band's communal distrust of Mancino's immaterial "parole e ragionamenti" (132; "words and arguments," 90). *Il sentiero* thus demonstrates its consciousness of its narrative technique and presentation only obliquely, as secondary aspects of the larger story that remains focused on the practical worldly experience giving rise to the author's own discourse, the "experience" defined by Calvino in the 1964 preface as the accumulation of "memory," "wound," and the "change" that these two have worked in the individual over time (23; xxiv). All of these concerns—political belief, social theory, narrative self-reflection, and referential validity—play important roles in shaping the literary text, but all of them, as Calvino affirms in a series of essays dating from the 1950s and early 1960s, do so only in service to the underlying thrust of representational narrative following the liberation and the end of the Fascist censorship, in service, that is, to what Calvino recalls in the 1964 preface as the "rage to narrate" (8; vi).[7] Both in Calvino's fictional practice in *Il sentiero* and in the aesthetic sketched in these essays the just-past, commonly experienced events of the world take the lead while the self-conscious analysis of them, and of the individual writer's literary representation of them, comes quietly but significantly behind.

This play of representation and self-involvement, or, generally speaking, of the seemingly contrary concerns for what Teresa de Lauretis has described as *praxis* and *poiesis*, is an extremely complicated phenomenon in the development of Calvino's work.[8] What may appear in theory as an opposition turns out, in terms of the texts themselves, to be a series of subtly nuanced interactions at various levels of both form and content. Merely to affirm, however, as de Lauretis does, that Calvino's works have always shown an interest in each side of the putative opposition is probably misleading, since such an affirmation vitiates both the force of *Il sentiero*'s representational thrust and the cleverly indirect social, political, and intellectual references in Calvino's other, more obviously allegorical and satirical fictions. But at the same time, it is true that even though the general arc of Calvino's development as a writer has carried his work from representation to abstraction and self-involvement, this progression over the decades has not been simple or direct; and de Lauretis is correct to question the accuracy of any overly tidy historical schema in regard to Calvino's literary production.

What this complexity means, as is the case in so many issues of literary criticism and theory, is that assessment of the tendencies toward external reference and toward self-involvement becomes, in Calvino's works, a question of emphasis rather than one of cut-and-dried formulae. The literary *self-effacement* of *Il sentiero* and of Calvino's contemporary and subsequent realist fictions is considerably less evident in the trilogy of novels published in the 1950s (and collected in 1960 in *I nostri antenati; Our Ancestors*), and still less so in *Le Cosmicomiche* and its sequel of 1967, *T con zero* (*T Zero*). Calvino's more recent novels, those of the 1970s, are by far the most openly self-conscious of his narratives, though again it is worth stressing, as we shall see, that even these texts do not leave the contemporary world of men and action totally behind.

Signs and Science in *Le Cosmicomiche: Fantascienza* as Satire

> *Il rigore della filosofia e della scienza l'ho sempre molto ammirato e amato; ma sempre un po' da lontano.*
>
> *I've always greatly admired and loved the rigor of philosophy and of science; but always from a bit of a distance.*
>
> Italo Calvino, "Intervista," *Autografo*, 1985

The stories of *Le Cosmicomiche* stand at midpoint in Calvino's literary production from the Second War to the present in several important ways.[9] At first glance, the narratives making up the collection seem to depart from the world of everyday life and to take up residence amidst the vast hall of literary fantasy known as science fiction. But on closer examination it becomes apparent that this departure is not total. Rather, the stories fall between the commitment to external reference, or referential transparency, of Calvino's early neorealistic fiction and the cheerful obsession with internal reference, or referential opacity, of his most recent works. Moreover, while the stories of the *Cosmicomiche* take as their primary concerns external topics like the beginnings of the universe and the early development of the world, they do so with regular attention to such internal issues as the workings of language and of narrative. In regard to literary self-consciousness, one of the most useful avenues of investigation into the *Cosmicomiche* is that of the collection's treatment of determinist systems, especially as these systems pertain to the creation of signs and to the predictability of events in a succession that can be construed as narrative order.

Calvino flirts with linguistic and with "scientific" or "historical" determinism throughout the stories. Simply stated, linguistic determinism is the proposition that the available forms of language determine man's ideas about himself and his environment: in other words, one can think only within the limits of the conventional system of linguistic signs, and since the system *is* conventional, it determines the individual's perceptions rather than vice versa.[10] On the other hand, scientific or historical determinism, as presented in the *Cosmicomiche*, is the proposition that man's progressive development and all his perceptions are determined and ordered by a given historical system outside of language (the class system, the logic of cybernetics, the biological evolution of the species).[11]

Calvino's stories can be described as "flirting" with these two determinist systems because the narratives that make up the *Cosmicomiche* never finally espouse any of the various determinisms that they set forth.[12] This procedure of propounding a logical system and simultaneously undermining its certainty, of giving with one hand and taking away with the other, is typical of literary satire. Moreover, Calvino's use of *fantascienza* to serve the ends of satire places him in a well-established tradition that includes Lucian, Ariosto, Bruno, and de Bergerac.[13] One of the most intriguing aspects of Calvino's particular brand of *fantascienza*, however, is the way in which the stories of the *Cosmicomiche* insert themselves in a broader discourse that is not so much traditional or even *sensu stricto* literary. That is to say, investigation of the problem of reference in the collection necessarily moves us beyond consideration of the techniques of satire to the *objects* of satirical treatment. Despite the literary illusion of timelessness that Calvino's science fiction occasionally fosters, these objects turn out to exist not in an atemporal void but in the discourse of society itself, and more specifically, in the social and intellectual debates in Italy during the 1960s.

Although the developing ideological complexity of Calvino's various fictions has often been discussed, his self-consciously astute portrayals of linguistic and historical determinisms in the *Cosmicomiche* have not been analyzed through detailed examination of the stories themselves.[14] His treatments of these types of determinism are clearest in the third and the eighth of the collection's twelve stories, "Un segno nello spazio" ("A Sign in Space") and "Quanto scommettiamo" ("How Much Shall We Bet?"). The third story begins with the collection's palindromically denominated narrator, Qfwfq, telling how and why he made the first sign in his part of the universe, "il primo segno che si faceva nell'universo, o almeno nel circuito della Via Lattea" (42; "the first sign ever made in the universe, or at least in the circuit of the Milky Way," 31). Qfwfq makes this sign in order to get his bearings in the future as he passes it again in the circuit of space ("io una volta passando feci un segno in un punto dello spazio, apposta per poterlo ritrovare duecento milioni d'anni dopo, quando saremmo ripassati di lì al prossimo giro," 41; "once, as I went past, I made a sign at a point in space, just so I could find it again two hundred million years later, when we went by the next time around," 31). From the first, Qfwfq's sign serves several functions:

> Dunque la situazione era questa: il segno serviva a segnare un punto, ma nello stesso tempo segnava che lì c'era un segno, cosa ancora più importante perché di punti ce n'erano tanti mentre di segni c'era solo quello, e nello stesso tempo il segno era il mio segno, il segno di me, perché era l'unico segno che io avessi mai fatto e ero l'unico che avesse mai fatto segni. Era come un nome, il nome di quel punto, e anche il mio nome che io avevo segnato su quel punto. (43)

> So the situation was this: the sign served to mark a point, but at the same time it meant that in that place there was a sign (something far more important because there were plenty of points but there was only one sign), and at the same time the sign was my sign, the sign of me, because it was the only sign I had ever made and I was the only one who had ever made signs. It was like a name, the name of that point, and also my name that I had signed on that spot. (32–33)

At this stage of the narrative, the connection between signs and names, and specifically between Qfwfq's sign and nominative linguistic forms, is apparent in the narrator's description ("Era come . . . il nome di quel punto, e anche il mio nome che io avevo segnato su quel punto"; "It was like . . . the name of that point, and also my name that I had signed on that spot"). Moreover, the problems of referentiality seem multiple yet, all in all, clear. Qfwfq's sign refers to the point ("serviva a segnare un punto"; "it served to mark a point"), and it also refers to the sign's maker ("il segno di me"; "the sign of me"). In another sense, the question of reference includes that of intentionality, since the sign represents not only the maker but also his *desire* to make a sign ("Avevo l'intenzione di fare un segno, questo sì, ossia avevo l'intenzione di considerare segno una qualsiasi cosa che mi venisse fatto di fare, quindi avendo io, in quel punto dello spazio e non in un altro, fatto qualcosa intendendo di fare un segno, risultò che ci avevo fatto un segno davvero," 42; "I had the intention of making a sign, that's true enough, or rather, I had the intention of considering a sign a something that I felt like making, so when, at that point in space and not in another, I made something intending to make a sign, it turned out that I really had made a sign after all," 31). Later on, furthermore, when Qfwfq tries to distinguish his sign from others, the crucial question of intention recurs, even though in a negative sense ("qui non riconosco la mia mano, figuriamoci se a me veniva in mente di farlo così," 49; "I don't recognize my hand in that one, I would never have wanted to make it like that," 38).

The questions of the intentions and the validity of reference become both more obvious and more complex after the principal "event" of the narrative. This occurrence is Qfwfq's discovery that another being, a certain Kgwgk ("il nome fu dedotto in seguito, nella più tarda epoca dei nomi," 46; "the name was deduced afterwards, in the later era of names," 35), has erased Qfwfq's original sign and set one of his own in its place. These two signs now take on their full meaning because of the perceptible difference between them. Along with the perception of differences, and Qfwfq's creation of another sign, come the notions of taste and style ("chiamiamolo stile," 47; "call it style if you like," 36). But Calvino's text does not stop with these patently "structuralist" observations. Instead, Qfwfq goes on to describe how, out of pride and pique, he began to make yet other signs, false signs, to confound the profaner of that first, pure sign: "Così, non potendo fare dei veri segni ma volendo in qualche modo dar fastidio a Kgwgk, mi misi a fare dei segni finti, delle tacche nello spazio, dei buchi, delle macchie, trucchetti che solo un incompetente come Kgwgk poteva scambiare per segni" (48; "So, unable to make true signs but wanting somehow to annoy Kgwgk, I started making false signs, notches in space, holes, stains, little tricks that only an incompetent creature like Kgwgk could mistake for signs," 37).

Now it is true that at first Qfwfq depicts Kgwgk's sign as a bastardized version of his own original, as a sign that signifies only the desire of the also-ran (perhaps as the sequence *k-g-w-g-k* itself can be read as a second-rate imitation of *Qfwfq*). Kgwgk's desire would thus be not that of the creator but only of the johnny-come-lately imitator; and according to Qfwfq this change in relation between the signmaker and his finished product necessarily brings with it a diminution in value: "Era chiaro che quel segno non aveva niente da segnare se non l'intenzione di Kgwgk d'imitare il mio segno, per cui non c'era nemmeno da metterli a confronto" (46; "It was clear that his sign had nothing to mark except Kgwgk's intention to imitate my sign, which was beyond all comparison," 35). Moreover, it is apparent that imitation itself, on the level of the characters (or as Calvino's text has it, the "rivals," [46; 35]) gives rise to competition and to a kind of linguistic violence of successive creations and cancellations of signs. But despite their competition and the early strength of Qfwfq's nostalgia (followed, perhaps not surprisingly, by his later embarrassment at his initial product), this seeming refinement through the process of competitive signmaking does not result in the reestablishment of some sort of purified language, or in a return to a now lost golden age before the perception of forms, when sign and function corresponded perfectly ("prima d'ogni inizio delle forme," 48; "before any beginning of forms," 37). Instead, with the passage of time *all* signs become somehow suspect. As the galactic eras progress and the forms of signs proliferate, first the seemingly stable unity of signifier, signified, and referent, and then even that of sign and function, are gradually unmasked as the illusions that they now appear to be:

> Ma adesso le cose erano diverse, perché il mondo, come vi ho accennato, stava cominciando a dare un'immagine di sé, e in ogni cosa alla funzione cominciava a corrispondere una forma, e le forme d'allora si credeva che avessero un lungo avvenire davanti a sé (*invece non era vero: vedi—per rifarci a un caso relativamente recente—i dinosauri*). (47, my italics)

> Now things were different, however, because the world, as I mentioned, was beginning to produce an image of itself, and in everything a form was beginning to correspond to a function, and the forms of that time, we believed, had a long future ahead of them (*instead, we were wrong: take—to give you a fairly recent example—the dinosaurs*). (35–36, my italics)[15]

As more and more beings participate in the production of signs, the universe begins literally to fill up: "Nell'universo ormai non c'erano più un contenente e un contenuto, ma solo uno spessore generale di segni sovrapposti e agglutinati che occupava tutto il volume dello spazio . . . l'universo era scarabocchiato da tutte le parti. . . . Non c'era più modo di fissare un punto di riferimento" (51; "In the universe now there was no longer a container and a thing contained, but only a general thickness of signs, superimposed and coagulated, that occupied the whole volume of space . . . the universe was scrawled over on all sides. . . . There was no longer any way to establish a point of reference," 39). This crisis of linguistic plenitude and complexity is at once the climax and the conclusion of the story. But the problems apparent here were already implicit in the earlier sections. Indeed, the narrative's development—the form of the story *as* a story—has been the process of making explicit the difficulties inherent from the outset in any system of language.

Early in the narrative, just after the creation of the first sign, Qfwfq acknowledges the problematic interrelations between signs and referents and between the forms of signs and those of thought itself:

> Ci pensavo giorno e notte; anzi, non potevo pensare ad altro; ossia, era quella la prima occasione che avevo di pensare qualcosa; o meglio, pensare qualcosa non era mai stato possibile, primo perché mancavano le cose da pensare, e secondo perché mancavano i segni per pensarle, ma dal momento che c'era quel segno, ne veniva la possibilità che chi pensasse, pensasse un segno, e quindi quello lì, nel senso che il segno era la cosa che si poteva pensare e anche il segno della cosa pensata cioè di se stesso. (43)

> I thought about it day and night; in fact, I couldn't think about anything else; actually, this was the first opportunity I had had to think something; or I should say, to think something had never been possible, first because there were no things to think about, and second because signs to think of them by were lacking, but from the moment there was that sign, it was possible for someone thinking to think of a sign, and therefore of that one, in the sense that the sign was the thing you could think about and also the sign of the thing thought, namely, of itself. (32)

In the early moments, the major problems of reference arise because there is only one sign to refer to all the things of the universe. But by the conclusion of the story the problem concerns not the number of possible correspondences but the fact of correspondence itself. What was originally only a suggestion of linguistic determinism ("chi pensasse, pensasse un segno"; "for someone thinking to think of a sign") seems to end as a full-blown description of the extreme formalist postulate of the determinist conception of language's workings:

> La Galassia continuava a dar volta ma io non riuscivo più a contare i giri, qualsiasi punto poteva essere quello di partenza, qualsiasi segno accavallato agli altri poteva essere il mio, ma lo scoprirlo non sarebbe servito a niente, *tanto era chiaro che indipendentemente dai segni lo spazio non esisteva e forse non era mai esistito.* (51, my italics)

> The Galaxy went on turning but I could no longer count the revolutions, any point could be the point of departure, any sign heaped up with the others could be mine, but discovering it would have served no purpose, *because it was clear that, independent of signs, space didn't exist and perhaps had never existed.* (39, my italics)

At this point it would perhaps seem easiest to affirm that the narrative does in fact describe and espouse the theory of linguistic determinism in its strongest form, that is, that thought and even material existence itself are absolutely dependent on and determined by the forms of language. But for several reasons such a reading of the story is too facile. First, the narrator himself has assured us from the start (with the retrospective knowledge of first-person narration) that his sign was *indeed* the first and that space *had existed* before the sign's creation. Moreover, the narrator has taken many different positions in regard to the relations between words and things in the course of the story, and none has remained unchallenged. This final statement does receive added emphasis because it comes last, but there is no reason to believe that it is in fact definitive. Even here, at the conclusion, Qfwfq is careful to post his disclaimer: *"forse,"* or "perhaps." Third, the only other instance of determinist thought in the narrative (concerning the necessary and stable identity of form and function) has been openly undercut by the narrator himself (in regard to "the dinosaurs"). Fourth, the initial section of the story depicts an instance in which intentions *precede* signs rather than being determined by them. Fifth, the disparagement of the implications of synonymy, manifest in Qfwfq's disgust at Kgwgk's feeble imitation, is presented not as a sophisticated defense of linguistic determinism but merely as a part of the humorous spat between these galactic rivals.[16] Sixth and last, the tone of the piece—ironic, chatty, often jocosely "scientific," on occasion openly paradoxical—works against any single, straightforward acceptance of unified philosophical or scientific postulates. Moreover, as Walter Pedullà has perceived, the effects of comedy and satire break up not only the determinist systems that serve as the *content* of the *Cosmicomiche* but also any appearance of narrative closure or "destiny" in the *formal organization* of the stories themselves.[17]

Rather than constituting a final Peircean affirmation of a unified "visione semiologica" of the universe, Calvino's narrative thus continues to cast critical doubt on the nature of the world's existence.[18] Similar to the other stories that treat linguistic determinism (as in the bizarre example of reverse Cratylism in the chase for Ursula H'x through the letters of space in "La forma dello spazio" ["The Form of Space"]), "Un segno nello spazio" ends with satirical skepticism rather than the naive acceptance of the narrative's concluding suggestion. The joke is on the reader who takes the narrative, or even the narrator, at face value. The text's caveat emptor is displayed in the very first paragraph: "Avevo l'intenzione di fare un segno, questo sì, ossia *avevo l'intenzione di considerare segno una qualsiasi cosa che mi venisse fatto di fare,* quindi avendo io, in quel punto dello spazio e non in un altro, fatto qualcosa *intendendo di fare un segno,* risultò che ci avevo fatto un segno davvero" ("I had the intention of making a sign, that's true enough, or rather, *I had the intention of considering a sign a something that I felt like making,* so when, at that point in space and not in another, I made something *intending to make a sign,* it turned out that I really had made a sign after all").

By the end of "Un segno nello spazio" it is obvious that the neorealistic relationship of event giving rise to discourse posited in Calvino's 1964 preface to *Il sentiero dei nidi di ragno* is no longer the model of linguistic creation in the *Cosmicomiche*. But neither does the opposite hold, that now all events are construed as coming only in and through prior linguistic forms. Rather, the weight of "Un segno nello spazio" falls on the final inability to decide which of these two positions is actually correct. Or more precisely, the story self-reflexively presents the implications of linguistic determinism at the same time that its satirical procedures subtly but persistently question the certainty of this type of determinism.

The narrative procedures used to undermine any system of thought that smacks of determinism are even more evident in the collection's eighth story, "Quanto scommettiamo." The subject of this story is the predictability of the succession of worldly events. As a study of what may be understood as plot, therefore, the story is as intriguing an instance of *narrative* self-consciousness as "Un segno nello spazio" is of *linguistic* self-consciousness. Indeed, as Qfwfq reveals, the entire action of "Quanto scommettiamo," the competitive activity from which both Qfwfq and the Dean take not only their identity but also the proof of their very being, concerns the narrating ("raccontare") of events and the existence of things to be narrated (104–5; 86–87). Like the other stories in the collection, "Quanto scommettiamo" begins with a simple "scientific" postulate that originates outside of Qfwfq's consciousness and that seems ironclad in its logic. But as is equally true elsewhere, the validity of scientific explanation is put in serious doubt, though not totally destroyed, by the irrefutable and infinitely complex facts of experience as demonstrated by the narrative itself (and as at times hinted at by Qfwfq's often ironic tone in his comments about the introductory postulates through the collection). The focus of "Quanto scommettiamo" is on the "logic of cybernetics" and the application of such logic to history.[19] According to the introduction, this logic would explain the *necessary* progression of historical events once the chain of positive and negative "retroazioni" has been set in motion:

> La logica della cibernetica, applicata alla storia dell'universo, è sulla via di dimostrare come le Galassie, il Sistema solare, la Terra, la vita cellulare non potessero non nascere. Secondo la cibernetica, l'universo si forma attraverso una serie di "retroazioni" positive e negative, dapprima per la forza di gravità che concentra masse d'idrogeno nella nube primitiva, poi per la forza nucleare e la forza centrifuga che si equilibrano con la prima. Dal momento in cui il processo si mette in moto, esso non può che seguire la logica di queste "retroazioni" a catena. (103)

> The logic of cybernetics, applied to the universe, is on the way to demonstrating how the galaxies, the solar system, the Earth, cellular life could not help but be born. According to cybernetics', the universe is formed by a series of "feedbacks," positive and negative, at first through the force of gravity that concentrates masses of hydrogen in the primitive cloud, then through nuclear force and centrifugal force which are balanced with the first. From the moment that the process is set in motion, it can only follow the logic of this chain. (85)

The narrative's action is constituted by the events that this logical chain supposedly determines and by Qfwfq's bets with "il Decano (k)yK" regarding the determined outcomes. In Qfwfq's initial surge of enthusiasm for his competition with Dean (k)yK all goes well. He bets on the existence and interaction of the atoms in the postulated hydrogen cloud, and even before the words are said the cloud has begun to form: "Non avevo finito di dirlo, e già attorno a ogni protone aveva preso a vorticare il suo elettrone, ronzando. Un'enorme nube d'idrogeno si stava condensando nello spazio" (104; "I had no sooner finished saying this than around each proton its electron had started whirling and buzzing. An enormous hydrogen cloud was condensing in space," 85).

But as in "Un segno nello spazio," the entire subject quickly becomes more complex. The difficulties inherent in the original suppositions are rendered explicit as the narrative progresses. Some events can indeed be predicted in detailed fashion (the amount of growth in the size of the stars, the distance of the planetary orbits one from another). But others—historical events such as the exact results of battles, the plots of Balzac's fictions, stock market quotations, the results of horse races—cannot be foretold with complete precision. As the conclusion of the story states openly, Qfwfq has misread the possibility of forereading and thus foretelling the orderly succession of the world's events. The result of this impossibility is that Qfwfq begins to lose, and to lose big. He has made his bets on the basis of a totalizing system, and the failings of its calculations, caused by the inevitable element of chance in worldly experience, give the lie to all his predictions. The fundamental lesson is obvious. Some of the phenomena of physical science and the facts of worldly endeavors can be described and even predicted by the logic of "scientific" determinism. But human nature and its development over time cannot be determined so easily. Such simplicity, if it were real, would be "beautiful" in its ideal abstraction and certainty, as Qfwfq says at the conclusion of "Quanto scommettiamo." But it would falsify life by making the world's historical "pasta d'avvenimenti" ("doughy mass of events") readable in a fixed and therefore necessarily misleading way (112; 93). Despite the fact that Qfwfq and Dean (k)yK end up as members of a research institute, in which they can continue their contests, they do not manage to come any closer to devising a reliable system for predicting the events of the world's story.

True, the humorous effects of the presentation—the feverish gamesmanship, the adoption of the terminology of the stock market, the spontaneously ironic tone, the depiction of Dean (k)yK as a stodgy conservative and Qfwfq as a daring "Young Turk," Qfwfq's obvious attempts to appear "scientifically" objective by concealing his jealousy of the Dean's administrative success—all serve to mitigate the heaviness of the narrative's philosophical and historical implications. Nonetheless, the basic hubris of Qfwfq's belief that the "logic of cybernetics" or indeed the logic of any determinist system would be adequate to explain and even predict the "intrinsically illegible" history of human events (112; 93) should be regarded seriously. As in the *backward* evolution of "Lo zio acquatico" ("The Aquatic Uncle"), whose return to the water humorously recalls the probable experience of the world's whales, the progression of life is never so simple as the systems devised to explain it appear at first to indicate. The unpredictable element of chance ("fortuna," 110; "luck," 91) and the fickleness of human emotion and caprice intervene to tarnish even the most "beautiful" schemas in the inevitable process that, in any specific context, "circonda sommerge schiaccia ogni ragionamento" (112; "surrounds submerges crushes all reasoning," 93).

As I suggested earlier, the humor and irony of the *Cosmicomiche* are spontaneous rather than constant, but the underlying satirical treatment of all determinist systems is uniform in its effects. That is, even though Calvino's text adopts satirical procedures only intermittently, the basic polemic against determinist claims of total validity is consistent rather than merely occasional. This consistency, along with its negative thrust, is why I have portrayed Calvino's procedures as satirical rather than as just locally humorous or ironic. In a formal sense, the presentation of the *Cosmicomiche* thus complements Calvino's own description of his openly symbolic (though not satirical) treatment of the developing process of human identity and alienation in the three previous narratives making up *I nostri antenati*.[20] Moreover, the seemingly "aristocratic" withdrawal of Calvino's speakers from the neorealistic representation of the everyday world of matter and sense is only a partial one. Indeed, the most significant objects of satirical treatment in the *Cosmicomiche*, linguistic and historical determinisms, also furnished the subject matter for two of the major debates in the intellectual life of the 1960s in Italy (in both of which Calvino was well versed), the debates over structuralism and social theory.[21] In the best tradition of satirical narrative, even while the stories of the *Cosmicomiche* seem to concern a subject immeasurably distant from everyday life, Calvino's *fantascienza* manages to insert itself into its historical moment as both a commentary on and an implicit critique of any facile acceptance of the determinist postulates so pervasive in contemporary European literary and social discussions. In terms of language and narrative, the stories of the collection are thus at once reflexively self-involved and externally referential, directed both back into themselves and out into the world of their reception.

Se una notte d'inverno un viaggiatore: Or, You Can't Judge a Book by Its Title

Calvino's interest in the functioning and the epistemology of individual signs and of narrative *in toto* continues through *Le città invisibili* (1972; *Invisible Cities*), in which Marco Polo relates to the Great Khan the stories of his real/imaginary "journeys," and *Il castello dei destini incrociati* (1973; *The Castle of Crossed Destinies*), in which the wayfarers tell their tales by means of the *tarocchi*, reproduced *in margine al testo*. In *Se una notte d'inverno* the weight of Calvino's interest expands, however, from notions of authorship, or textual production, and of structure, or textual ontology, to encompass questions of the nature and the workings of reading.[22] As had been true, too, in Calvino's earlier fiction, the text's emphasis on reception parallels contemporaneous critical and theoretical concerns, evident in the writings of such diverse authors as Umberto Eco in Italy, Wolfgang Iser and Hans Robert Jauss in Germany, Roland Barthes in France, and Norman N. Holland, Michael Riffaterre, and Stanley E. Fish in America, to mention only a few of those actively concerned with the role of the reader and the aesthetics of reading.[23] All of these writers, like most critics, are deadly serious in their aims and contentions; and so is Calvino, in a sense. Nonetheless, it would be inaccurate to claim that Calvino's novel merely apes or even adopts contemporary critical enthusiasms in its own discourse. Instead, as was also the case in the stories of *Le Cosmicomiche*, *Se una notte d'inverno* is not just a reflection but also a parody of the issues at stake in current academic and intellectual exchanges in Europe and America, not just the exposition of a theoretical *parti pris* but also, in more practical terms, the scene of a merry chase through the labyrinthian forests of reading.

The novel begins with a direct address to the Reader, who is also, in a quite practical sense, a character: "Stai per cominciare a leggere il nuovo romanzo *Se una notte d'inverno un viaggiatore* di Italo Calvino" (3; "You are about to begin reading the new novel, *If on a Winter's Night a Traveler*, by Italo Calvino," 3). There follows a series of comments, suggestions, rhetorical questions, and exclamations all addressed familiarly to the

Reader and all concerning what might be termed the logistics of settling down to read a book:

> Rilassati. Raccogliti. Allontana da te ogni altro pensiero. . . . La porta è meglio chiuderla; di là c'è sempre la televisione accesa. Dillo subito agli altri: "No, non voglio vedere la televisione!" Alza la voce, se no non ti sentono: "Sto leggendo! Non voglio essere disturbato!" . . . "Sto cominciando a leggere il nuovo romanzo di Italo Calvino!" . . . Prendi la posizione più comoda. . . . Certo, la posizione ideale per leggere non si riesce a trovarla. . . . Bene, cosa aspetti?
>
> Relax. Concentrate. Dispel all other thoughts. . . . It's best to close the door; the TV is always on in the next room. Tell the others right away, "No, I don't want to watch TV!" Raise your voice or they won't hear you: "I'm reading! I don't want to be disturbed!" . . . "I'm beginning to read Italo Calvino's new novel!" . . . Take the most comfortable position. . . . Of course, the ideal position for reading is something that can never be found. . . . All right, what are you waiting for?

This type of direct address recurs regularly in the sections (numbered as chapters) that introduce the various narratives making up the novel. Similar to many of the subsequent stretches of quasi prosopopeia (quasi because the Reader both is and is not present), this initial section includes notions not only of the process of reading but also of material consumption in a consumer society, of the buying and selling of books as commodities in the modern marketplace. The narrative thus takes a step backward and describes—still adopting the familiar second-person singular—first the expectations of the Reader as buyer, then *his* (on which, more later) perusal of the book in the shop window, and finally his purchase of *Se una notte d'inverno un viaggiatore*. The Reader at last arrives home with the new book and, once settled, begins to read.

Rather than simply telling a story, as most of the following interspersed narratives will do, the first titled section of text, "Se una notte d'inverno un viaggiatore," opens by *describing* the beginning of the "novel": "Il romanzo comincia in una stazione ferroviaria, sbuffa una locomotiva" (11; "The novel begins in a railroad station, a locomotive huffs," 10). After a few remarks in the manner of nonlocalized evaluative commentary ("Le stazioni si somigliano tutte," 12; "Stations are all alike,"

11), the next step in Calvino's project is to introduce the character in the railroad station as the fiction's *narrator*, this, too, in the self-conscious manner of direct address:

> Io sono l'uomo che va e viene tra il bar e la cabina telefonica. Ossia: quell'uomo si chiama "io" e non sai altro di lui, così come questa stazione si chiama soltanto "stazione" e al di fuori di essa non esiste altro che il segnale senza risposta d'un telefono che suona in una stanza buia d'una città lontana.
>
> I am the man who comes and goes between the bar and the telephone booth. Or, rather: that man is called "I" and you know nothing else about him, just as this station is called only "station" and beyond it there exists nothing except the unanswered signal of a telephone ringing in a dark room of a distant city.

Next, the Reader is told that the man in the station is caught in a kind of trap as he goes back and forth within the confines of the station: "Sono preso in trappola, in quella trappola atemporale che le stazioni tendono immancabilmente" ("I am caught in a trap, in that atemporal trap that all stations unfailingly set"). Since the mention of a trap could easily go along with the introductory setting of the train station to announce "Se una notte d'inverno" as a *giallo*, the Reader, realizing that this is, or at least could be, a crucial point in the narrative's development, awaits affirmation that such is or is not to be the case. Instead, he gets a warning that regards not only his own potential entrapment by the text's gradual manipulation of details in a suspense plot, but also the author's illusiveness and, finally, both the author's and his own continuing indecision:

> È già da un paio di pagine che stai andando avanti a leggere e sarebbe ora che ti si dicesse chiaramente se questa a cui io sono sceso da un treno in ritardo è una stazione d'una volta o una stazione d'adesso; invece le frasi continuano a muoversi nell'indeterminato, nel grigio, in una specie di terra di nessuno dell'esperienza ridotta al minimo comune denominatore. Sta' attento: è certo un sistema per coinvolgerti a poco a poco, per catturarti nella vicenda senza che te ne renda conto: una trappola. O forse l'autore è ancora indeciso, come d'altronde anche tu lettore non sei ben sicuro di cosa ti farebbe più piacere leggere: se l'arrivo a una vecchia stazione che ti dia il senso d'un ritorno all'indietro,

> d'una rioccupazione dei tempi e dei luoghi perduti, oppure un balenare di luci e di suoni che ti dia il senso d'essere vivo oggi, nel mondo in cui oggi si crede faccia piacere essere vivo. (12–13)
>
> For a couple of pages now you have been reading on, and this would be the time to tell you clearly whether this station where I have gotten off is a station of the past or a station of today; instead the sentences continue to move in vagueness, grayness, in a kind of no man's land of experience reduced to the lowest common denominator. Watch out: this is surely a method of involving you little by little, capturing you in the story before you realize it—a trap. Or perhaps the author still has not made up his mind, just as you, reader, for that matter, are not sure what you would most like to read: whether it would be the arrival at an old station, which would give you a sense of going back, a renewed concern with lost times and places, or else a flashing of lights and sounds, which would give you the sense of being alive today, in the world where people today believe it is a pleasure to be alive. (12)

What is one to make of all this metacommentary? A first conclusion is that *Se una notte d'inverno* is going to be a novel about novels, which, of course, it is. But as one quickly discovers, it is also, literally, a novel *of* novels, old-fashioned as well as new-fashioned ones, of novelistic plots and styles. This ongoing play of narrative organization means that the text's discussion of the aims and techniques of fiction as a genre complements but does not eclipse the text's progressive revelation, as narrative, of the complexities of novelistic discourse and its traditional models (of which the text at·hand is, it must be admitted, a peculiarly parodic and aberrant example, but an example nonetheless). Rather than a static or strictly expository discussion of how to make a novel, therefore, *Se una notte* becomes a story of stories to the second power, a hall of mirrors that seems at once perfectly self-sufficient and, oddly enough, constantly in motion.

This state of affairs is made clear at the beginning of the second chapter, when the mechanism underlying the novel's overall organization comes into play. The Reader discovers—or, better, the narrator describes the Reader discovering—that the book he has purchased shows signs of a strange repetition of sentences and even the recurrence of an entire passage. At first, the Reader takes this to be an example of stylistic refinement ("finezze") on the part of the author, who seems to be underscoring the passage's importance. On further examination, however, the repetition turns out to be merely an error by the compositor: "Accidenti! Da pagina 32 sei ritornato a pagina 17! Quella che credevi una ricercatezza stilistica dell'autore non è altro che un errore della tipografia" (25; "Damn! From page 32 you've gone back to page 17! What you thought was a stylistic subtlety on the part of the author is nothing but a printers' error," 25).

From one perspective, the Reader's initial confusion is a way for Calvino to ridicule a certain type of interpretive procedure that is practiced by some readers and undoubtedly by many critics. But from the perspective of narrative plotting, the defects in the purchased copy serve the more significant end of making the Reader return to the bookstore so that he may secure another copy as a replacement. The bookseller explains that somehow the bindery had mistakenly interspersed the pages of a translation of a novel by the Polish author Tazio Bazakbal (*Fuori dell'abitato di Malbork; Outside the Town of Malbork*) with Calvino's *Se una notte d'inverno*. Since the Reader has actually begun Bazakbal's novel, he insists on being supplied with a good copy of that book, rather than either retaining his present defective copy of *Se una notte d'inverno / Fuori dell'abitato di Malbork* or securing a copy of the Italian novel. But when he arrives home and cuts the paper open, he realizes that this novel is completely different from the one he had been reading before. The Reader, nonetheless, does enjoy the book, in part because of its rich texture of worldly detail, its descriptive illusion of referential plenitude (41; 42). Indeed, the Reader's attention is quickly drawn in by a type of descriptive "suspense" similar to that which the narrator had previously warned against. But even before the first chapter is over, in the middle of a crucial sentence, the Reader is frustrated once again, this time by a pair of blank pages. Because of another error (again explained by the narrator, who appears thoroughly familiar with the mechanics of book production), pairs of blank pages alternate throughout the text with pairs of properly printed ones. Due to his aroused interest, the Reader is again intent on pursuing his reading of the narrative at hand. After making some inquiries, however, he discovers that the novel in question is not Polish at all but Cimmerian, and, what is more, that it has never been translated. A scholar at the local university (who is named, in typically Calvinesque sprightliness, Professor Uzzi-Tuzii) does provide a translation of the opening chapter, but this novel,

Sporgendosi dalla costa scoscesa (*Leaning from the Steep Slope*), by the Cimmerian poet Ukko Ahti, again shows no similarity whatever to either of the previous two.

Not unexpectedly, given the procedures of Calvino's narrative up to this point, other problems quickly develop. It turns out, in chapter 4, that Ahti's text was left unfinished and that only a fragment of it was ever published. Professor Uzzi-Tuzii explains that this very incompleteness is what makes the novel the most thoroughly representative work of Cimmerian prose, since in fact all Cimmerian books are unfinished (69–70; 70–71). The short-lived, ambiguous, and finally unverifiable nature of Cimmerian literature thus parallels that of the now "dead" Cimmerian language, the country's perhaps mythical and certainly obliterated geographical borders (and, since the *Odyssey*, its connotation of obscurity), and even its completely dispersed populace. These attributes also resemble those of the novel at hand, Calvino's own. Sure enough, once again the neatly emblematic and seemingly stable insert-story of the unstable Cimmerian "text within the text" gives over to a lively argument not only about the general nature of referentiality and the pleasures of reading but also about the very status of the Cimmerian text. Amidst a welter of charges and countercharges regarding the publishing of fraudulent material during an anti-Cimmerian propaganda campaign at the close of World War I, an expert in Erulo-Altaic languages and literatures, a certain Professor Galligani, steps forward to assert that *Sporgendosi dalla costa scoscesa* is in point of fact neither Cimmerian nor unfinished. According to Galligani, the original of what Uzzi-Tuzii has been reading is a Cimbrian novel, the title of which was later changed to *Senza temere il vento e la vertigine* (*Without Fear of Wind and Vertigo*) and which was signed with the pseudonym Vorts Viljandi (72–73; 73–74). Following the "Cimbro-Cimmerian debate," the Reader joins a study group to pursue the reading of the Viljandi novel. He immediately makes two discoveries neither of which, by this time, come as any surprise: first, this novel, too, demonstrates absolutely no connection to the previous ones, and, second, it is nonetheless so fascinating that, having once begun, the Reader and his companions cannot stop (75; 76).

By this time, the narrative's standard organization is abundantly clear: introductory section, followed by the beginning chapter of a new novel, leading first to interest but then inevitably to frustration, only to begin the process all over again with the next introductory section. This pattern eventually takes the Reader to a publishing house, where he learns that the translator of the novel(s) making up the texts of the wild-goose chase, Ermes Marana, has hatched a scheme to create books that are nothing more than a flock of forgeries and counterfeits. Among others, Marana has plagiarized the works of Silas Flannery, a hack detective novelist. In the section of the narrative given over to Flannery's diaries, Calvino's novel, as JoAnn Cannon has pointed out, "turns back upon itself" in a particularly suggestive way.[24] Besides bringing most of the important characters of the frame story together, the diaries also (re)reflect the organization and the major themes of *Se una notte d'inverno* and include a choice example of character/creator mise en abyme (197; 197–98). As the diaries make clear, in spite of Flannery's prolific past as a writer, he has developed writer's block and can produce only a few pages of any story before giving up and leaving it unfinished. His torment is due in part to his awareness that fiction and life never seem to meet one-to-one, that what is often conceived of as the fallacy or the problem of referentiality is in fact a continuing crisis without resolution. Nevertheless, despite the clarity that these diaries add through their self-reflective implications, they do not really serve to change much in the narrative. Rather than ending the story or even directing it toward a significantly new course, the diaries simply lead back into the same chain of enticement–suspense–frustration that has been organizing the overall text from the early pages on.

Indeed, one of the most important clarifications contained in the diaries concerns neither referential validity nor narrative organization, but rather the role of the individual female Reader, Ludmilla. Ludmilla has been an important character in the story since her appearance in the bookstore where the Reader first met her in chapter 2. As fate would have it, she, too, had bought a defective copy of *Se una notte d'inverno*. From the time of their initial meeting, she and the Reader have been sharing their experiences of reading, comparing notes and exchanging opinions on the various novels successively in question. In fact, Ludmilla and her sister, Lotaria, are the ones responsible for the Reader's attempts at gathering information at the university and for his subsequent participation in the study group. But even though Ludmilla, as a character who is *par excellence* a "Lettrice," is connected by the *logic* of experience with the Reader (according to the Reader she has read far more novels that he has and remembers them much better), the driving force of their relationship is not based principally either on logic or on reason. Rather, theirs is a relationship of desire.

That the Reader has something more than merely an intellectual interest in Ludmilla is evident from their first meeting, during which the Reader, clearly specified as a masculine "Lettore," is drawn to the female "Lettrice" like a magnet (the metaphor is Calvino's [29; 29]). But in spite of Ludmilla's initial friendliness, their exchange of telephone numbers, and their subsequent discussions and experiences while chasing together down the trail of books (all of which concern some version of male-female involvement), their relationship is not a simple one. Indeed, they are part of a triangle, or rather a series of interlocking triangles, in which the translator/forger Ermes Marana and the writer Silas Flannery both play a part. Marana's motivation for his devilish trickery is his jealousy of the unseen rival, the author (explicitly Silas Flannery, but by extension any "author" who entices readers, including Calvino himself), with whom Marana vies for the attention of the "Lettrice." In the course of Flannery's diaries Ludmilla also figures as a character, indeed as a literary admirer. When she explains why she likes his books, however, Flannery becomes jealous of his own authorial imago, embodied not by his physical being but by the ink, periods, and commas of his prose. He makes a hasty and unsuccessful pass at her (in response to which, as much out of practicality as adroitness, she defends herself with the bulky shield of Webster's International Dictionary [191; 191]). Embarrassed but undeterred by this setback, Flannery plans, at the conclusion of his diary, to send the Reader in search of Marana, "il Falsario," so that he can be alone with the "Lettrice," the true object of his desire.

But Flannery's and Marana's gambits and ruses meet with only limited success. Although they keep the Reader and Ludmilla busy, they do not succeed in keeping them apart. Following their first meeting, the "Lettore" and the "Lettrice" become closer and closer. In chapter 7, only a few pages before the beginning of Flannery's diary, the two of them (at last in bed together) turn the focus of their activities as readers away from the pleasures of reading books to those of reading bodies, which is to say, away from literary texts to the physical "texts" of each other, in all of their sensual, signifying aspects:

> Lettrice, ora sei letta. Il tuo corpo viene sottoposto a una lettura sistematica, attraverso canali d'informazione tattili, visivi, dell'olfatto, e non senza interventi delle papille gustative. Anche l'udito ha la sua parte, attento ai tuoi ansiti e ai tuoi trilli. Non solo il corpo è in te oggetto di lettura: il corpo conta in quanto

parte d'un insieme d'elementi complicati, . . . tutti i segni che stanno sul confine tra te e gli usi e i costumi e la memoria e la preistoria e la moda, tutti i codici, tutti i poveri alfabeti attraverso i quali un essere umano crede in certi momenti di star leggendo un altro essere umano.

E anche tu intanto sei oggetto di lettura, o Lettore: la Lettrice ora passa in rassegna il tuo corpo come scorrendo l'indice dei capitoli, ora lo consulta come presa da curiosità rapide e precise, ora indugia interrogandolo e lasciando che le arrivi una muta risposta, come se ogni sopraluogo parziale non le interessasse che in vista d'una ricognizione spaziale più vasta. (155)

Ludmilla [Lettrice], now you are being read. Your body is being subjected to a systematic reading, through channels of tactile information, visual, olfactory, and not without some intervention of the taste buds. Hearing also has its role, alert to your gasps and your trills. It is not only the body that is, in you, the object of reading: the body matters insofar as it is part of a complex of elaborate elements, . . . all the signs that are on the frontier between you and usage and habits and memory and prehistory and fashion, all the codes, all the poor alphabets by which one human being believes at certain moments that he is reading another human being.

And you, too, O Reader, are meanwhile an object of reading: the female Reader [Lettrice] now is reviewing your body as if skimming the index; at some moments she consults it as if gripped by a sudden and specific curiosity, then she lingers, questioning it and waiting till a silent answer reaches her, as if every partial inspection interested her only in the light of a broader reconnaissance. (155)

The text goes on to note the details of Ludmilla's reading of the Reader, again in a sort of semiotics of perception, in the terms of physical details and general codes and the creation of meaning through differences between and among such codes and details. It then comments on the distinction between the reading of written pages and the reading of lovers' thoughts and bodies (the one is linear, or serial, the other is not, though needless to say, *both* manners of reading are part of Calvino's novel). Finally, it discusses the seemingly contrary notions of repetition toward climax and the unrepeatable singularity of separate events, all of which means that various things are indeed different but that nonetheless there is a kind of "family resemblance" that can unite even the most unsystematically diverse phenomena, as regularly occurs, of course, in narrative fiction. But beyond the text's specific details and its general assertions, the import of this interlude of reading is clear: the "Lettore" and the "Lettrice" are getting constantly more involved with each other notwithstanding the treachery and jealous scheming of Marana, Flannery, et al.

In this respect the conclusion of the novel, however sudden, is not surprising. The Reader, having gone to the library to consult the card catalog in search of the ten interspersed narratives, is advised by another library patron—that is, another reader—that if he really wants to discover the beginning and end of the stories in question (none of which is available), his quest for specific details is unnecessary. According to this reader, there are only two ways of ending any narrative: either the hero and heroine marry one another, or they die. As the new reader says, "Il senso ultimo a cui rimandano tutti i racconti ha due facce: la continuità della vita, l'inevitabilità della morte" (261; "The ultimate meaning to which all stories return has two faces: the continuity of life, the inevitability of death," 259). At this point, apparently realizing his own position as romantic lead, the Reader decides "fulmineamente," or "in a lightning flash," to marry Ludmilla. *Se una notte d'inverno* ends with the Reader and Ludmilla lying in bed reading in "un grande letto *matrimoniale*" (my italics), in what is now the very locus of domestic desire and the erotics of both sexual activity and reading. Ludmilla, tired of reading, puts down her book and turns out her reading light, laying her head against the pillow. She suggests: "Spegni anche tu. Non sei stanco di leggere?" ("Turn off your light, too. Aren't you tired of reading?"). But regardless of whether or not there is a hint here, or whether or not the Reader gets it, he protests that he is not yet ready, and so the book ends with one last instance of both narrative and erotic suspension–frustration–continuation: "E tu: 'Ancora un momento. Sto per finire *Se una notte d'inverno un viaggiatore* di Italo Calvino'" ("And you: 'Just a minute. I'm almost about to finish *If on a Winter's Night a Traveler* by Italo Calvino'").

This cleverly embedded ending, by means of which the more or less unified Lettore-Lettrice frame story and the fragmentary interspersed narratives come neatly together to finish at the same time, provides a momentary illusion of closure. Nonetheless, the narrative's conclusion is neither so neat nor so self-enclosed as it at first appears. It provides no indication whatever as to the resolution of the many subplots or to the Marana-Flannery-etc. schemes (will Ludmilla's marriage be adequate to deter them completely?), nor does it take into account the implications of the shift in authority from the opening "*Stai* per cominciare," in which the narrator seems in charge, to the concluding "'*Sto* per finire,'" in which the Reader, now to a certain extent on his own, seems to have taken over. Even the status of "Se una notte d'inverno un viaggiatore" and the subsequent truncated narratives is left unclear, since it has been pointedly undercut by another reader in the library, who contends that far from being separate narratives, all ten of the interspersed titles, beginning with "Se una notte," actually make up the complete first sentence of a narrative (undoubtedly a mystery) that he himself has read. He knows this to be so, furthermore, because once upon a time all novels began in just that way, as though *Se una notte d'inverno* were indeed the true novel of novels: "Se una notte d'inverno un viaggiatore / fuori dell'abitato di Malbork / sporgendosi dalla costa scoscesa / senza temere il vento e la vertigine / guarda in basso dove l'ombra s'addensa / in una rete di linee che s'allacciano / in una rete di linee che s'intersecano / sul tappeto di foglie illuminate dalla luna / intorno a una fossa vuota / quale storia laggiù attende la fine?" ("If on a winter's night a traveler / outside the town of Malbork / leaning from the steep slope / without fear of wind and vertigo / looks down into the gathering shadow / in a network of lines that enlace / in a network of lines that intersect / on the carpet of leaves illuminated by the moon / around an empty grave / what story down there awaits its end?"). The ending of *Se una notte d'inverno* is indisputably both clever and fitting, though it does not really resolve any of the specific questions that the narrative itself at once poses and incorporates.

We should quickly add, of course, that resolving the plot is the last thing in which *Se una notte d'inverno* is interested. Rather than resolution, the ending serves once again to emphasize the thematics in play (and of play) throughout the text, the many-faceted pleasures of reading and the self-consciousness of the narrative in all its writerly and readerly aspects. It is indeed at precisely this level that the narrative should be questioned. Certainly the pleasures of the text and of textual "intimacy" are manifest in the novel, but rather than being fulfilled, every desire—the desire for information, for mastery, for further revelation—is aroused only to be frustrated. Everything, in short, is always either preliminary or interrupted. What sort of enjoyment is this? Reading itself continues, as though at once opened to and condemned to fragmentary yet endless foreplay. But the reader himself or herself—as distinct from either the "Lettore" or the "Lettrice"—is never really satisfied except with the satisfaction that comes from submission to and participation in constantly shifting preliminaries, that is, with the (*perhaps* joyous) giving into the erotics of continually incomplete satisfaction, of constant *narratio interrupta*.

It is no wonder, then, that one of Calvino's models, mentioned as though by chance in the later sections of *Se una notte d'inverno*, is A Thousand and One Arabian Nights (177; 177). Calvino's novel does make genuine innovations along several lines (particularly in its modernist concern for framing encompassed within its postmodernist predilection both for seriality and for the Chinese boxes of literary frames within frames, as well as in its modernist examination of the notions of literariness, communication, and referentiality within its postmodernist questioning of the very validity of such notions).[25] But the reference to the *Arabian Nights* also reminds the reader—the empirical reader—that concern for and even delight in the process of narration and the pleasures of reading have been part of both the form and the thematics of literature over many centuries and through many different cultures and traditions. At the same time it is true that Calvino's text is conscious of such issues in an especially ingenious and pervasive manner—self-conscious in spades, one might say—and that it forces the *reader* to be conscious of them, too. *Se una notte d'inverno* thus poses again and again, in a particularly demanding and consistent way, not only traditional questions of literary production and meaning but also the currently much debated problems of "innocent" versus sophisticated reading (115; 115) and of "legible" versus illegible texts (182; 183).

It should be clear that *Se una notte d'inverno* goes further than anything I have treated before, in Calvino's works or in others', in terms of questioning the traditional assumptions of character formation, plotting, communication, referentiality, the stability of meaning, and the functions of reading. It takes the sort of giant step—though perhaps even more spacious this time—that Pirandello's *Uno, nessuno e centomila* had taken in the 1920s. This step—not surprisingly, given Calvino's deeply ingrained literary interests—is not so much away from literature's arena as back into it, into fiction's assumptions and models and workings. It is evident that the direction of Calvino's text is away from the straightforward representation of society—in many respects even further away than any of his previous narratives—but it is less clear that contemporary social questions are therefore left completely behind. Indeed, in self-consciously demystifying any stable notion of what it is and what it means to be a reader (a "you") or an author or a narrator (an "I") or even a text, whether as a "lost" object or a "found" one, Calvino implicitly calls into question the category of the individual subject in terms of both worldly meaning and worldly pleasure in literary experience. In this light, his narrative may be viewed as another entrant in the debates extending into the 1980s over the nature and meaning of the subject (unified or disunified, integrated or alienated) in contemporary society and culture. Again, this does not mean that Calvino proposes ultimate solutions outside of literature, or even that he suggests their possibility, but only that in both content and form his text *poses* the problems.[26] No one is to blame, perhaps least of all Calvino, if the novel's only answers to the issues at stake in this dispute are simply further questions self-consciously proffered to the reader. Both the status of the intentionally unnamed Reader in the text (the one who is "read") and the status of the readers of the text (the ones who are, and who identify with, "reading"), whether as members of the literary industry, the academic community, or simply of consumer society at large, have undoubtedly been affected, in many respects more directly than ever before, by the questioning/prodding/beguiling of Calvino's self-consciously written/read fiction.

Calvino's last full narrative, the autobiographically slanted *Palomar* (1983; *Mr. Palomar*), continues this interest in the relationship between self and other, conceived of as either dualistic or multiple, based on either presence or absence, certainty or uncertainty. However, despite repeated discussion of such topics as the activity of reading (including the reading of material, nonlinguistic signs, like the waves of the sea) and the problematics of interpretation (including the investigation of the signs of archeological ruins, which, like the supposed meaning of all stories in the library in *Se una notte d'inverno,* may constitute allegories of life's continuity and death's inevitability), *Palomar* is considerably less self-conscious than *Se una notte d'inverno un viaggiatore.*[27] This is so in part because *Se una notte d'inverno* is not just a highly self-conscious artifact, does not just demonstrate the *effects* of literary self-consciousness, but also *embodies* literary self-consciousness at all of its levels of narrative organization and meaning, which is to say of plotting, style, voice, and thematics. In its self-conscious game of allusion, absence, and progressive emptiness—aiming, perhaps, toward a new type of fullness—*Se una notte d'inverno* thus remains the most complete of Calvino's self-conscious artifacts that we have: indeed, from the perspective of writing and *reading*, the most thoroughgoing example of literary self-consciousness in Italian narrative to date.

ELEVEN

Continuations

Samonà, Manganelli, Eco, and Considerations on Postmodernism

Over the past ten years or so, a great many Italian novels, by writers of widely varying approaches and prominence, have demonstrated important as well as informative aspects of literary self-consciousness. The novelists to be treated here—Carmelo Samonà, Giorgio Manganelli, and Umberto Eco—all evince, in notably different fashions, the general rise in literary self-consciousness after the period of neorealism and particularly the increase of the last twenty years. Among the major literary stimuli for this increase were the influential, if extraordinarily fragmented, phenomenon of the Gruppo 63 and the extremely self-conscious narratives produced by certain charter members of that group, such as Edoardo Sanguineti's oneiric *Capriccio italiano* (1963) and his pair of associative/combinative pastiche "games," *Il giuoco dell'oca* (1967) and *Il giuoco del Satyricon* (1970), and Nanni Balestrini's narrative collage, *Tristano* (1966). The works under consideration here (with the partial exception of Samonà's) also reflect the literary theories and practices of the authors associated with the French *nouveau roman* and, in descending order of importance, those of recent Latin American fiction writers and those of English-speaking authors working in the United States and elsewhere.

These three novelists have been selected both as significant in their own right and as instructively representative of current narrative interests and trends, with an eye to tracing the recent development of a set of fundamental literary phenomena: the moral relation between characters and their environments in terms of desire and will; the function of plot as a matter of ordered (or disordered) human destiny; the questions of literary representation and of literary parody (as a re-presentation of other literary discourse); and the interrelations of narrative fiction, truth, and aesthetic pleasure. These are some of the concerns that are shared by the literature of both modernism and postmodernism, though my discussion of these three novelists will eventually chart a movement away from modernist views regarding these issues and toward a more consistently postmodernist perspective. It should nonetheless be noted at the outset that this movement, from the knowledgeably transparent/opaque works of Samonà, to the polemically nonreferential tracts of Manganelli, to Eco's attempt at postmodernist extensions *and* recuperation, is by no means either linear or direct.

Carmelo Samonà. In the Grotto of the Psyche

Samonà, who is a professor of Spanish medieval and Renaissance literature at the University of Rome, started writing novels only late in life, after he had passed his fiftieth year. His two novels published to date, however, *Fratelli* (1978; *Brothers*) and *Il custode* (1983; *The Keeper*), both belie his inexperience as a novelist, since the prose of each is lucid as well as elegantly suggestive and in both the narrative artifice is at once delicate and finely wrought.[1] Both novels are short, which permits them to retain the intensity of their extremely narrow focus from beginning to end, in each case on the psychological rapport *a due* between two central characters.[2] The systematic restriction of this focus accounts to a large extent for Samonà's lack of genuine predecessors in the Italian tradition, with the possible exceptions of Tozzi and Svevo, and for the occasional references by critics to such seemingly similar European authors as Kafka and Beckett.[3] The most saliently self-conscious aspects of Samonà's work, as is perhaps suggested by the group of authors just mentioned, are aimed at language, including narrative language, in its function as the mediator, first, between helplessness and power and, second, between truth and falsity.[4]

In *Fratelli* the psychological and epistemological implications of language are of primary importance from the opening chapters. The story concerns the relationship of two brothers, one healthy, the other mentally ill.[5] The two of them live by themselves in a large apartment high above an unnamed city, through the rooms of which the narrator, the only family member to consent to care for his sick brother, guides his charge on journeys in a space that seems outside of time and society. In the narrator's descriptions of their interaction within the apartment and of their occasional forays into the world outside, he suggests the ways in which his supposedly dependent brother turns that apparent dependence into dominance over the healthy narrator. The question of the status and the force of individual will is thus paramount in the text, as is the question of narrative veracity, since the only access that the reader has to the deeds and the motivations of the schizophrenic brother is through the discourse of the narrator.

The first indication that imaginative imitation is crucial to the relationship and to the narrator's description of it occurs in the second chapter, when the narrator explains his position of exteriority in regard to his brother's experience: "Io posso, se lo desidero, *imitare* la malattia; lui è costretto a viverla" (9; "I can, if I want, *imitate* the illness; he is constrained to live it"). The narrator is free to mime the external effects of his brother's affliction and, as he says shortly thereafter, "to imagine" ("fantasticare") other lives and experiences different from his own; but his brother must follow the rules of the sickness that possesses him and those rules alone. At the same time, the narrator remains only partially capable of entering the internal world of his brother's illness and usually must be content to watch from without during his brother's "Grandi Viaggi," or "Great Journeys," as he calls his brother's experience of the illness. Together the brothers take "Piccoli Viaggi" ("Little Journeys") around the abandoned apartment that, at the beginning of the narration, often involve open parodies of such literary models as the flight of Icarus, the story of Pinocchio, and the various adventures of *I Promessi Sposi* and Verdi's opera *Don Carlos*. Eventually these fictional models encompass elements of the outside world, included within what the narrator refers to as "una intensa cornice teatrale" (37; "an intense theatrical frame"), leading to "una storia più ampia" ("a still larger story"). Once the healthy brother has proposed such imaginative activities, however, he is no longer really dominant, since he is then constrained to participate completely, following the desire of the sick brother for each of them to play his role to the hilt, much as an adult can play with young children—or in certain social situations even with other adults—only if, once the game is chosen, he or she submits to their understanding of the rules, in a willfully acquiescent suspension of disbelief: "Naturalmente sono costretto a simulare con lui una partecipazione completa, giacché egli accetta di *vivere la finzione* che gli propongo solo a condizione che io, *per primo*, ne rispetti fino in fondo le regole" (15, my italics; "Naturally, I am constrained to pretend total participation with him, since he accepts to *live the fiction* that I propose only on the condition that I, *first of all*, respect its rules completely").

In chapter 5, this consideration of the rules and restrictions of imitation and of ludic activity leads to another topic that is equally significant for the relationship between the two brothers, the difficulties of linguistic communication and of linguistic interpretation. As an example of the difficulties that the narrator experiences in his attempts to decipher his brother's language, and so to come closer to understanding the precise nature of his brother's illness, the narrator reproduces three sentences that his brother utters just as the narrator is about to go out of the apartment by himself: "Tu non hai paura: bravo fratello!" / "Correvo in un prato" / "Vattene via" (23; "You are not afraid: good for you, brother!" / "I was running in a field" / "Go away"). The narrator then goes through various possibilities of interpretation, initially for each sentence and then for the set as a whole. As he sees it, the overall meaning of his brother's utterances could be anything from the expression of a desire to go along, to the fear of abandonment, to an essay at inflicting punishment on the dominant narrator through the indirect accusation of guilt and even weakness. At this point the two brothers engage in a different sort of dialogue, one made up of glances, gestures, and other physical movements and approaches, all of which end up in what is very nearly a game between the two ("Giochiamo, quasi," 24; "We play, almost"). With this, the narrator gives up on the attempt to establish any single, unitary meaning for his brother's words, and a new cycle of games, journeys, and stories begins.

Although the narrator approaches the entire matter as though it were primarily a question of epistemology—that is, of interpretation and truth—it is clear that the exchange between the brothers also includes deep-seated elements of competition, jealousy, and guilt. Indeed, when the narrator eventually elaborates on his failure to construct a unified causal "logic" within his brother's fragmentary and seemingly inexplicable discourse (39), he describes his lack of success as a defeat in battle, as a distinct loss of authority "nella guerra fra i due linguaggi" (44; "in the war between the two languages"). The narrator's only recourse in the struggle with what he then terms "il nemico-fratello" (45; "the enemy-brother") is to separate himself from the other and thus "rompere la servitù dell'accoppiamento" (47; "break the servitude of the couple").

The psychological games of tension and exclusion increase as the narrative progresses. In the middle sections of the novel they are complicated by the entrance of an outsider (the "lady with the limping dog," who seems to communicate easily with the afflicted brother and who, along with the various textual references to the absent father, suggests at least *in nuce*, a symbolic family, replete perhaps with a secondary allusion to infirmity and, via the animal's "limping," to the Oedipal threat of castration).[6] However, the clearest indication of the sort of psychological violence to which these games lead occurs in the novel's climactic and most complex segment, chapter 20, in which the rapport of affection and conflict between the two brothers is again set within the general framework of language and, more specifically, within that of writing.

The narrator opens the chapter by explaining his daily procedure of recording the facts of his brother's behavior. His goal here as elsewhere—to understand the truth of his brother's illness—is not new in the text, but the medium of writing, and the effects that it entails for the subject as well as the object of the written word, give this section of the narrative an added dimension that is distinctly and disturbingly self-reflexive. The narrator describes the feelings of freedom and omnipotence in which, as a writer, he glories; and he mentions the one fear that afflicts him above all others, the one defect that any oral account and, indeed, all worldly activity outside of his writing—oddly enough, including his brother's interference—necessarily demonstrates: "incompiutezza" (92; "incompleteness"). Although in his life the narrator feels more and more subject to the inevitable process of time and aging, in his writing he can play with time and events as he wishes: "Scrivendo, posso tornare indietro per giorni e per settimane, distruggere con un solo tratto di penna un'epoca intera: o viceversa conservare il già scritto e metterlo al riparo, così, dalla minaccia di future smentite" (94; "Writing, I can turn back to days or weeks before, I can destroy with one stroke of the pen an entire epoch; or, vice versa, preserve what is already written and thereby protect it from the threat of future denials"). In short, his power, within the refuge of the written word, seems without limits.

Or almost. The problem, of course, is that his brother is not only the object of the narrator's description but also, within their physical and emotional relationship, the subject of his own actions and discourse. As subject, the brother is an agent capable of acting on his own, and he does so, both by spying on the narrator—whose writing, by turning him into an object in a form of fixity that resembles death (cf. 19), seems to displease him, to say the least—and by stealthily removing pages from the written "rendiconto" ("report"). This behavior further complicates the subject-object dichotomy—which had been implicit in the narrative from the beginning and which had come to a head earlier, in chapter 14, in the narrator's private/public act of betrayal and voyeurism—by adding to it the aura of internecine violence.

This violence quickly becomes explicit rather than merely suggested. When the narrator surprises his brother leaning over his desk, seemingly reading the pages he had written out, the narrator accuses him, as an intruder, of trying to ruin his work: "Da tempo ho capito che vuoi distruggere i frutti del mio lavoro con ogni mezzo" (98; "For a while now I've known that you have been trying to destroy the fruits of my labor by every means possible"). Although later on, the entire question of interest and responsibility becomes considerably murkier, for the moment the narrator believes that he has found conclusive proof of his brother's guilt (a sheet from the report stuffed in his brother's coat pocket). After a series of escalating exchanges, a fight ensues. This encounter, both "feared" and "desired" by the narrator, follows directly on the narrator's statement of his intention to split up their "bella famiglia" ("lovely family") and have his brother sent off to a hospital. The fight begins with the narrator attempting to stifle his brother's scream and his brother reacting "wildly" by biting the narrator's forearm. It ends with the two of them struggling together on the narrator's bed, bathed in sweat, the narrator's blood staining the bedsheets and his brother's shirt. Immediately thereafter the narrator denounces his brother's ingratitude ("Ho sacrificato per te i miei anni migliori"; "I've sacrificed the best years of my life for you"), and he then describes how his sick brother "slips off the bed" ("sgusciò dal mio letto"), leaving the apartment and staying away for three days, his longest absence ever.

The interaction between subject and object here demonstrates a variety of levels. The healthy brother feels that his sibling has intruded on the integrity and the privacy of his work. However, since the "work" itself is a report of his brother's illness, the ill brother also seems to feel intruded upon—indeed, violated not just in terms of work or any other activity but in terms of his whole being and existence. Within the closely delimited relationship, each aggressively challenges the subjectivity of the other by attempting to preserve the subjective integrity of the self. In this doubly sadomasochistic relationship, moreover, the effects of anguish and guilt are also intricate. Each brother could logically claim to be free from guilt, since the one brother's psychosis is an affliction rather than an offense and the narrator's taking on responsibility for his sibling seems nothing other than laudatory. But within the psychological framework of the relationship, once its boundaries have been tentatively established, the motivating forces of desire, guilt, and recrimination are nonetheless pervasive.

As the chapter concludes, the thematics of the self-other relationship continue to be cast in the imagery of psychological battle. When the ill brother returns, he exhibits, though exhausted and filthy, "la fierezza composta del *vincitore*" (102, my italics; "the confident pride of the *victor*"). However, the narrative quickly takes a surprising turn, in that it recasts what had previously been the self-other relation between the brothers, mediated by the Freudian background of the family and infused with the tincture of homosexual violence (the perspiration, the blood, the bed), and refocuses the rapport in terms of the specular relation of self to self. This shift occurs in a striking passage. As the narrator and his brother resume their fraternal activities, their games, and their exchanges of clothing, the narrator discovers that the jacket his brother had been wearing during what they later refer to with a smile as "la notte del rendiconto," or the "night of the report," had actually been *his* rather than his brother's. Since this was the jacket in which the narrator had found the incriminating page of his manuscript, the narrator's suppositions, underscored by linguistic repetition, arrive at an uncanny possibility: "Forse, frugando su di lui, avevo perquisito, senza rendermene conto, me stesso" (102; "Perhaps, rummaging through his pockets, I had been searching, without realizing it, myself").

The conclusion of the chapter thus opens up the novel to an allegorical interpretation in which the two brothers, in some combination like sanity and madness, reason and imagination, strength and weakness, or perhaps a mixture of all of these, would come together to form one complete picture of the human mentality. Although Samonà has rejected this sort of interpretation as too extreme for *Fratelli* (though admitting its appropriateness, at least in a certain measure, for *Il custode*),[7] the narrative itself, albeit briefly and indirectly, does suggest it. A possible solution to this and other questions regarding the narrative seems at first to be what the following chapter, which is the book's last, is heading towards. The relationship continues, but the narrator notes that both his brother's language and their competitive activities together (including that of their earlier "bed games" [107]), seem to have changed and to keep changing. He is certain, now, of at last being close to discovering the key to the true nature of his brother's affliction, and he is convinced that his discovery will naturally go hand in hand with his writing.

In the novel's final paragraph, the narrator repeats this avowal, recounting how his daily "readings" of his brother's "combinatory art" are finally leading to a gleam of truth, and from there, he believes, to full signification. But the narrative ends, and thus turns back on itself self-consciously *as* a narrative, with only the affirmation that this search for understanding continues. The powers of interpretation and the creative/destructive game of representational violence and representational exclusion that writing involves thus remain without completion. They do so, moreover, in a narrative the only end of which is now *itself* in its entirety, in its factitiousness both as the written word and as the authoritative report of its own—perhaps never-ending—narrative uncertainty and contingency.

Samonà's subsequent novel deals with many of these same themes, although in a sense the narrative mechanism of *Il custode* is reversed. The intense psychological focus recurs, as does the question of the force of the individual will within a relationship, but instead of a story narrated by the seemingly stronger partner, *Il custode* is narrated by the weaker, the object of his "keepers'" kidnapping. During the period of the novel's creation and publication, terrorist abduction was, of course, a topic of tremendous import in Italian social and political life. But because of *Il custode*'s unremittingly limited psychological focus, this phenomenon is portrayed as it affects the experience and perception of the individual and is therefore presented only indirectly as a social issue. This is not to say that the novel turns its back on contemporary social concerns, but only that, like *Fratelli*, it approaches the question of social power and social truth via the circumambulatory path of intense psychological representation.

In regard to literary self-reflection, the two most consistently important aspects of the novel have to do with linguistic and narrative self-consciousness: first, with the power of the word as the paramount medium of social interaction, and second, with the epistemological status of the narrator's perceptions of his surroundings and with the consequent veracity or error of his narration. The narrative opens with the narrator's statement that he is being held against his will in a place about which he knows nothing, in "una stanza anonima" ("an anonymous room") cut off from everything that had previously constituted his world. He knows nothing about the nature or the motives of his captors, and therefore neither does the reader. We do, however, come to know two things in these early chapters: that the narrator's relation to the terrorist band is channeled through one person alone, the one who brings his food, and that, owing in part to the narrator's ignorance and anxiety concerning his captors and in part to his sensory deprivation, the narrator's imagination becomes active indeed.

It is on the terrain of language that the narrator fights his battle with his keeper, at least at first. All his energy, his entire being, is devoted to the attempt to force his captors to engage him in speech and thus reconfirm both his humanity and the social world in which he longs to exist. His goal is stated succinctly at the conclusion of chapter 3: "un incontro aperto, frontale, che li obblighi, senza più reticenze all'uso della parola" ("an open encounter, face to face, that would obligate them, without further refusals, to speak"). However, to each and every attempt, whether he insists, connives, cajoles, or begs, he receives the same response: silence. Later on in the story, when the narrator becomes more obviously desperate and his behavior more aggressive, the reactions of his captors continue to be indifferent or, at best, ambiguous. Indeed, whether the response of the narrator's keeper (on whom his obsession has focused, to the exclusion of the others in the band) is actually one of sympathy or of punishment, or even a veiled plea for understanding, remains uncertain.

Intertwined with the thematic development of language as communication in *Il custode* is the topic of narrative veracity. What the narrator terms his "viaggi," whether into realms fertile and lush or barren and arid, are dreams and/or visions in which he regains, in a sense, control of his life through his imagination. But therein lies the problem, since, as he comments at the beginning of chapter 12, he is at one and the same time the "autore" ("author") of his imaginative creations and their "vittima" ("victim"; cf. 47–48). They do provide him with a kind of temporary escape, but they also pose another problem, one that, in a manner analogous to his relationship with his captors, is again framed in the thematics of will and dominance. The question is an intricate one, and it leads to a radical undercutting of the interpretative status of the narrator's own discourses. If his hallucinations have no immediate connection with reality, if they are fantasies cut from whole cloth, that still may not mean that the narrator is in charge of them. Perhaps some "angolo ribelle" ("rebellious corner") of his mind is at work producing images (such as the bracelet, the elements of the journeys, the reactions of the keeper himself) over which the narrator has no control. In other words, the problem is not so much one of external reality versus internal fantasizing as it is one of internal desire versus internal understanding. This fragmentation *within* the speaking subject therefore complicates not only the relationship between the narrator and the external world of his captivity but also his relationship to his own narration, which in this case, is what makes up the narrative.

This complication concerning the epistemological status of the narrator's discourse becomes clearer and more acute as the story approaches its climax. For a while it seems as though the narrative might actually continue to progress simply by oscillating, without conclusion, between the narrator's "viaggi" and his use of language, since when his linguistic concentration is most active his imaginative journeys are less frequent, and, so it seems, vice versa. But this is not what happens. Instead, the two sets of thematic concerns—the use of language and the status of narrative truth—come forcefully together in a series of scenes leading up to the story's conclusion, chapter 18, which does provide a climax of sorts.

One of these scenes occurs in chapter 15. Although the ambiguities of the narrator's various imaginative and real experiences—his dreams, his "viaggi," and his daily interactions with his keeper—do not coalesce under the unified rubric of potential hallucinations until the last two chapters, his uncertainties regarding all aspects of his perceptions have been fairly clear for some time. In chapter 15 the narrator attempts once again to force a response from his keeper, whose naked white arms have pushed the narrator's food toward him in a gesture that initially seems like a friendly embrace, then turns to one of threatening malice, and finally to one of open aggression. The narrator steps back quickly, suffused more with panic than disappointment, but still feeling the shameful "wound" of pleasure, as he blurts out, "Chi sei, il diavolo?" (95; "Who are you? The devil?"). Following this exchange of language for gestures the narrator openly requests help, saying he is afraid that he is going mad; but just afterwards, in the wake of the continued silence, he asserts the contrary, that he is not mad and that he has no need at all of the keeper's aid.

In terms of the narrative's minimal plot, this scene is especially notable as one of the story's psychological building blocks, since it prepares for the "grande incontro," or, roughly, "final showdown," between the narrator and his captors. But the thematics of the exchange, as well as their implications for interpretation, are also of central importance. The suggestion of an infernal presence, followed by an admission of insanity (albeit immediately retracted, as though in a lovers' quarrel; cf. 83), leaves the narrative open to an interpretation along strictly symbolic lines, in this case the psychological symbolism of schizophrenic madness as diabolic possession. This is by no means the only possibility offered by the text either at this stage or later, but from this point on the possibility that the narrative *as a whole* is more an allegory of a *single* mind gone awry than a study of the relation between *two* separate figures remains in force—and now much more openly and much more pertinently than had been the case in *Fratelli*.

The next two chapters trace the development of the narrator's sado-masochistic relation with his keeper in equally ambiguous fashion. They include details of a far more direct and thoroughgoing physical encounter (perhaps genuine, perhaps not) as well as various indications of the narrator's rapidly deteriorating physical condition. Through all this, the one thing that saves the narrator from oblivion, from complete loss of the world and of the self in it, is his continued ability to use language, what he terms "l'arma che impugno per continuare a essere io, e mantenere, finché posso, il controllo su ciò che vedo" (112; "the weapon that I hold in order to continue to be myself and to maintain control, as long as I can, over what I see").

In the concluding chapter, the use of language and its interpretation are again the paired topics of primary importance. As the chapter opens, the narrator, who is now close to losing all his objectivity, his mind at best "annebbiata" ("foggy"), prepares himself for the encounter that, he is sure, is soon to come. He awaits the event with the odd mixture of urgency and tranquillity that distinguishes his reaction to a fate that includes him yet remains outside his will, depending on him yet not decided by him, a destiny at once uncertain *and* predetermined. As he lies on his bunk listening to the voices of the men outside, whom he believes to be coming to some decision about his fate, all of a sudden, as though by tacit accord, all their talking stops. In the silence the door opens and a man enters, his whole figure open to the narrator's view. Curiously, the man seems less an invader than a prisoner in search of escape; but his true identity—be he a keeper, a fugitive, an insubstantial figment of the narrator's imagination, or even the figure of death itself—is not given. What is certain is that in the narrator's perception of what occurs after a moment of hesitation between the narrator and the other, the "nuovo venuto" ("new arrival") approaches the narrator and stops again before, having grasped the chair, "si mette al mio capezzale e mi parla" ("he places himself at my bedside and talks to me").

This concluding movement, right through to the text's last line, underscores the narrative's self-reflective concern for language as the principal instrument of social identity and social communication at the same time that it continues the dominant-dominated and subjective-objective play of interpretation as that play is embodied in discourse. The narrative of *Il custode*, in which language and narrative perspective do not so much reflect the world as constitute it, thus turns back on itself as a metaphorical representation both of linguistic communication's functioning and disfunctioning in social life and of discourse's inevitable epistemological uncertainty. In a society intimately familiar with the psychological symbolism and the actual experiences of terrorism and confinement, *Il custode* thus becomes a psychologically slanted and complex, but effective, discourse on the problems inherent in worldly discourse.

Giorgio Manganelli. The World of the Word: Fool's Truth

Manganelli has been publishing fiction for over two decades. Like Samonà, he was, for a time, a professor (of English) at the University of Rome. In the 1960s Manganelli was associated with the Gruppo 63, although his position regarding the relation between literature and society set him apart from many of the other writers in this group, perhaps most clearly from Edoardo Sanguineti. Sanguineti advocated a break with traditional narrative forms and traditional notions of representation for what can be construed as two basic reasons: first, in order to avoid repeating in literary form—and thereby acquiescing to—the institutional structures of bourgeois society; and second, in order to stimulate the public's awareness of psychological *and* ideological questions by radically altering not only accepted literary concepts but also literary practices.[8] Manganelli's view of the social ends of literature was, by contrast, remarkably different. In Manganelli's opinion, literature ought not to be viewed as being directly tied to social representation of any sort, since its discourse is not only *specific* (i.e., different from other forms of language and communication) but also *autonomous* (i.e., utterly separated from them).

Manganelli's position is set forth in a well-known essay of the mid-1960s, "La letteratura come menzogna," or "Literature as Falsehood."[9] In that essay, literature is described as a distinct and special realm, an artifice that creates the order of an entire universe, sufficient unto itself with no necessary recourse to the world outside either for its sense or its authenticity. In short, as Manganelli asserts in the essay's conclusion, fiction is a lie, but a "heroic" one, without need for justification beyond the imaginative powers of its own rites and hierarchies:

> E qui si raccoglie e salda la provocazione fantastica della letteratura, la sua eroica, mitologica malafede. Con le sue proposizioni "prive di senso," le affermazioni "non verificabili," inventa universi, fingi inesauribili cerimonie. Essa possiede e governa il nulla. Lo ordina secondo il catalogo dei disegni, dei segni, degli schemi. Ci provoca e sfida, offrendoci un illusionistico, araldico pelame di belva, un ordigno, un dado, una reliquia, la distratta ironia di uno stemma. (177)

> And here literature's imaginative provocation is met and solidified once and for all, its heroic, mythological bad faith. With its propositions that are "without sense" and its affirmations that are "unverifiable," it invents universes, makes up inexhaustible ceremonies. It possesses and governs nothingness, orders it according to the catalogue of patterns, signs, schemes. It provokes and challenges us, offering us the illusive, heraldic hide of a wild beast, a contrivance, a dado, a relic, the distracted irony of a coat of arms.

As distinct from the thought of Sanguineti and that of many other politically committed writers of the experimentalist *neoavanguardia*, Manganelli's refusal to conceive of literature as a repetition of the signs of the bourgeois world evinces a displeasure not so much with the subordination of literature to the bourgeoisie as with the subordination of literature to *any* facet of the external world. This insistence on the autonomy of literary creation, with its echoes of Kantian and Crocean aesthetics, distinguished Manganelli from certain of his most important Italian contemporaries as well as from other European writers influential in Italy in the 1960s and early 1970s, particularly the members of the *Tel Quel* group in Paris. Manganelli did have highly visible Italian colleagues who concurred in several of his more important postulates, such as Angelo Guglielmi and Nanni Balestrini (though in time Balestrini moved considerably away from his beliefs of the mid-1960s, as is evident in his later narratives of obvious social commitment, *Vogliamo tutto* [1971] and *La violenza illustrata* [1976]).[10] But what is of special interest in Manganelli's fiction is that it continues even today to demonstrate, in remarkably open fashion, these same fundamental beliefs in the autonomy and in the internally self-justifying integrity of the narrative artifact.

These beliefs are also apparent in the chatty and highly self-involved presence/absence games of Manganelli's *Hilarotragoedia* (1964; *Hilariotragedy*), and in his *Nuovo commento* (1972; *New Commentary*), with its obsessive concern for the reader and its attempt at a new type of literary "commentary" aiming towards infinite openness rather than interpretative closure. They remain in evidence throughout his series of genre experiments of the 1970s: in the parodies of the fairy tale, the epistolary novel, and the expository essay in *Agli dèi ulteriori* (1972; *To the Ulterior Gods*); in his monologue and dialogue novels of the mid-1970s; and in his extended meditation on the story of Pinocchio, *Pinocchio: Un libro parallelo* (1977; *Pinocchio: A Parallel Book*), in which one of the key questions throughout the text is just what *is* the status of a "parallel" book, given that it is a work at once creative yet dependent, new yet predetermined, arbitrary yet documented, outside the object of its commentary yet somehow inside it—in sum, free yet bound.

This constellation of questions—which concern the problems of origin, repetition, and progression viewed in terms of literary and worldly genealogy, presence, motion, and death—also recurs in Manganelli's more recent narratives. *Centuria* (1979; *Century*) is made up of one hundred short chapters, each of them a novel in embryo.[11] Although the notion of putting together one hundred tales seems to suggest at least some sort of numerical unity, perhaps in the manner of the *Decameron*, the operative mode here is not wholeness but fragmentation. At the same time, the obvious challenge to the reader to try to make an interpretative and formal aesthetic whole out of the stubbornly fragmentary text by means of intricate comparison and cross-reference (i.e., by means not only of reading but also of rereading and study) suggests the academic nature of Manganelli's exercise and of his audience, as is alluded to in the author's characteristically clever (and slyly mendacious) preface. In that preface, Manganelli describes the "ambition" of his book: "Dunque, ambisce ad essere un prodigio della scienza contemporanea alleata alla retorica, recente ritrovamento delle locali Università" (5; "Therefore its ambition is to be a prodigy of that contemporary science that is allied to rhetoric, a recent rediscovery of the local Universities").

The stories tend to be self-reflexive in clusters as the chapters progress, with the topics of writing and of reading (as indicated initially in the program overseen by the preface's "Supremo Lettore," or "Top Reader") more or less constantly in evidence. But near the end of the book the self-conscious effects of the narratives grow more pointed, thus restoring, on the level of the overall collection, some of the frame and the perspective of narrative destiny that had been regularly foreshortened within the separate chapters. Since the concluding chapter reflects, by implication, on all of the previous stories, it also adds an element of "narrativity," or the paradigmatic density of narrative interrelations, to what had heretofore been primarily a procedure of "seriality," or strictly linear progression. The chapter's result, therefore, is to provide at least a partial sense of unity to a work that up to then had seemed programmatically, even relentlessly fragmentary. *Centuria* thus plays on the literary conventions of the "romanzo fiume" of its subtitle even while remaining to a large extent outside of them.

This final chapter, which is a diminutive novel of novels all on its own, begins with a writer writing a book about a writer who writes two books about writers writing, one of whom writes "perché ama la verità" ("because he loves truth") and the other "perché ad essa è indifferente" ("because he is indifferent to it") (205). As the number of fictional writers and fictional products—or, in Manganelli's earlier term, fictional universes—multiplies, the question of the relation between fiction writing and worldly truth becomes more pressing. The power of literature's "lie" is demonstrated in a form of narrative determinism that, with Manganelli's typical dose of parodic humor, recalls the works of both Borges and Lewis Carroll. At first the events of the fictional writers' lives and the events of their written narratives merely parallel one another in an uncanny fashion; but soon the literary narratives themselves seem to dominate and indeed to determine the events of the writers' worlds. This occurs to such an extent that one character feels not that he has chosen the wrong occupation ("sbagliato mestiere") but that he has in fact chosen the wrong novel ("sbagliato romanzo"), and so he attempts, by means of letters of recommendation, "di farsi cambiare romanzo" ("to get to change novels"). As the number of writers and books about writers writing threatens to increase to astronomical proportions, a single writer common to all the eighty-six thousand novels written thus far begins to emerge, "un balbuziente maniacale e depresso" ("a maniacal and depressed stutterer"). But when this writer sets out to write his novel about a writer writing a novel, Manganelli's narrator relates a strange turn of events:

> Decide di non finirlo, e gli fissa un appuntamento [allo personaggio-scrittore] e lo uccide, determinando una reazione per cui muoiono i dodicimila, i cinquecentonove, i ventidue, i due, e l'unico autore iniziale, che ha così raggiunto l'obiettivo di sco-

prire, grazie ai suoi intermediari, l'unico scrittore necessario, la cui fine è la fine di tutti gli scrittori, compreso lui stesso, lo scrittore autore di tutti gli scrittori. (206)

He decides not to finish it, and he makes an appointment [with his character-writer] and kills him, thereby determining a reaction that causes the death of the twelve thousand, the five hundred and nine, the twenty-two, the two, and the single initial author, who has thus attained the objective of discovering, thanks to his intermediaries, the single necessary writer, whose end is the end of all the writers, himself included, the writer-author of all the writers.

The wondrous genealogies spun out by Manganelli's infernal literary machine finally close back in on themselves and dissolve, when the last "romanzo fiume" appears to self-destruct as the parody *of* parodies. But this is the case only in part, since even though the writer-characters inside Manganelli's literary "scatole cinesi" have vanished, *his* narrator and *his* narrative remain, the product of the one "author" (not just "writer") who really is the creatively necessary point of origin, the figure smiling behind the curtains, enjoying, albeit in silence, the hundred narratives' last laugh on the true/false world.

Manganelli's subsequent book, *Amore* (1981; *Love*), is equally as self-conscious as *Centuria,* though in a somewhat different manner.[12] The phenomena of origin as absence and of absence as the spur to desire and so both to creation and, paradoxically, to nothingness are again central topics, though now they are viewed in terms of specifically amatory desire. The jouissance *of* the text and the jouissance *in* the text thus come together in a manner that is at times wittily evocative of many of the major works in the Italian literary tradition of the love-death (from the epigram's opening bow to Guido Cavalcanti's "Donna mi prega" through repeated glances towards the works of Ariosto, D'Annunzio, and others); and it also brings to mind the thought of theorists of the affective processes of writing and reading as diverse as Gaston Bachelard and Roland Barthes.

That absence is seen not only as a precondition of desire but also as a *continuing* aspect of love's itinerary is reflected in several of the major myths underlying sections of the text, tales in which, moreover, desire encompasses struggle and on occasion violent subversion. These include the myths of Echo and Narcissus, Persephone, Hermaphroditus, and the

Medusa (all reset in the dark and enchanted wood of traditional Romance, replete with trees that bear messages). Indeed, the inability of the lovers to meet in harmony—either in the book or in the world—is described at the narrative's conclusion as the very condition of love: "Amore. . . . Mi manchi, mi manchi molto. Lo sai, dunque, che questa è la descrizione del nostro amore, che io non sia mai dove sei tu, e tu non sia mai dove sono io?" (119; "Love. . . . I miss you, I miss you so much. You know, of course, that this is the description of our love, that I may never be where you are, and you may never be where I am?").

Writing itself is involved in these same thematics of desire, contingency, and uncertainty, as is suggested in minor ways throughout the book (from the comments on the narrator's "delirio figurale," 49, or "figure-engendering delirium," to the restrictive severity or even the "terrorism" of style, 51) and more generally by the text's repeatedly stated fascination with the creation of messages as well as the creation of narrative figures in and through messages (70 et passim). *Amore* thus takes form as both a parody of the love treatise and a literary allegory of desire itself, one in which seduction is inextricably bound up with imitation and imitation with violence (39). But despite the involvement of the *romanzo/trattato* with the underlying circumstances of its creation and with the affective and logical conditions of its own existence, it is not until Manganelli's next book, *Discorso dell'ombra e dello stemma* (1982; *Discourse of the Shadow and the Coat of Arms*), that the relations between writing, representation, and truth are put in question in the most radical fashion of all of Manganelli's works so far.[13]

This book continues Manganelli's experiments with literary forms, mixing together between its covers principal components of three traditionally separate genres: the literary treatise, the literary dialogue, and the novel. Rather than confronting problems of literary genre head on, however, the narrator begins by describing the age in which there was *no* literature, a period that probably had everything necessary for literature (words, illnesses, love, hate, families, adultery, massacres, and so forth) but in which, nonetheless, literature had not yet been invented by our "pre–Agatha Christie" ancestors ("i nostri antenati," perhaps in sly evocation of Calvino). True, there existed professors, critics, reviewers, and editors, but there was no literature. There were even writers, who could do nothing but accumulate "l'angoscia che sarà l'inchiostro del domani" (29; "the anguish that will be the ink of tomorrow"), but still no literature. Everyone knew that what did not exist—which is to say, literature—was *useless*; but, like the text's allusion to Deucalion and Pyrrha tossing behind them the stones of a future race, the seeds of madness also gave birth, and so literature was born: "La demenza abbisogna di demenza: dunque di letteratura" (34; "Insanity needs insanity: and so literature"). In this formulation, therefore, literature is not a solution to a difficulty but rather a further problem for mankind, one that includes reading in addition to writing. As the narrator comments shortly thereafter, "La demenza, dunque, è la madre della scrittura e della lettura; ma non ne è la soluzione" (46; "Insanity, therefore, is the mother of writing and of reading; but it is not their solution"). There is, in short, *no* solution; and the remainder of *Discorso* sets out to suggest why not, giving Manganelli another opportunity to say what, in his view, literature is and is not.

He does so in a text packed with allusions to the literary examples that so often occur in his earlier works as well, from the realms of ancient myth, fable, and romance to the creations of his postmodern contemporaries (including Borges, Calvino, and Manuel Puig, among a host of others). However, Manganelli's point here is not to single out exemplary literary authors or even exemplary literary environments but instead to focus on literature itself, on literature not as a product but as a self-contained entity, with an origin so pristine as to be in effect anonymous, so that its only true authorial attribution can be to the gods, or, as *Il discorso* claims in a somewhat more erudite formula: "Iuppiter scribit" (76 et passim). Literature does mean, or "signify," but because it creates its own world, its meaning does not derive from its relation to the world outside. In other words, literature does not mean by any process of external reference. Literature's signifying elements, thus liberated from the illusion of their dependency on anything signified in the external universe of matter and sense, anything both worldly and prior, gain their importance and their particular value *because of* rather than *in spite of* their status as a lie, as an untruth that turns out to be both more engaging and more important than the supposed truth of the everyday world. This freedom from external reference includes freedom from the imitation of man, so that literature is by nature non-anthropomorphic (with the apparent exception of the representational novel, such as *Madame Bovary*, explained as a modern aberration from literature's true, ancient vocation—one in which, moreover, representation is in fact nothing but a doubly perverse illusion [71–75]).

Manganelli's battle cry ("non significare," 75; "do not signify") thus reaffirms his earlier axioms in regard to the nonreferential, nonmimetic nature of literary discourse. It is perhaps not surprising that, once cut off from its supposed dependence on the external world for validity and sense, literature then turns back on itself to find both its validity in its "falsehood" and its sense in its "nonsense" (75). It thus becomes the most self-involved, and, in a specifically literary way, the most self-conscious endeavor imaginable, as all of Manganelli's customary references, from the classic example of *Tristram Shandy* to the later Joyce to the example of his own book, regularly attest. Indeed the "discourse" of the "stemma" and the "ombra" is in fact a discourse *about* literary significance (though, again, not external signification), one in which the apparent symbolic clarity of the "stemma" (one of Manganelli's favorite images, occurring in the concluding paragraph of the 1967 essay quoted previously and scattered throughout his other writings) and the obvious uncertainty and ambiguity of the "ombra" turn out to be the same concept and even the same word, mutually certain in their mutual uncertainty and contradictory without the one negating the other, since in *literary* terms, they actually are one and the same (68 et passim). The "distratta ironia di uno stemma" (from 1967) thus joins with the murky uncertainty of the shadow and becomes what literature finally is anyway, what in *Centuria* is termed the "Allegoria dell'Incapacità di capire le Allegorie" (174; "Allegory of the Inability to Understand Allegories").

Even after referentiality and subjective unity have been banished from Manganelli's pages via these assertions of literary autonomy and literary impersonality, the narrator remains aware of a further possible objection to his position, and he takes steps to head it off, though with only partial success. The narration itself is constantly broken up by such typical postmodern techniques as serial presentation, the foreshortening and apparently joyous fragmentation of plot and perspective, and the consistent emphasis on discursive surface rather than depth. At the same time, however, there is still another aspect of the book, besides the recurrent thematic concerns mentioned earlier, that serves to *unify* its presentation. That aspect is the voice of the narrator, which, despite occasional variations, is characteristically chatty, irreverent, insistent, occasionally prodding, often (insincerely) self-deprecating: in short, strikingly human. Manganelli foresees the potential difficulty that this creates for his argument against any notion of the anthropomorphic nature of literature, and he takes pains, particularly at the work's conclusion, to point out that the book is narrated not by any normal person but by a particularly literary figure, one that fits in nicely with the concept of literature as purely ludic rather than referential activity, a Fool:

> Quello che troverete scritto in queste pagine non ha senso: è questo il loro pregio essenziale, giacché suppongo che ciò mi dica: tu non ha idee. . . . Dai tempi dei tempi non è mai stato possibile sapere ciò che segue alla morte, e parlare di letteratura; ora sappiamo che i due problemi sono strettamente imparentate. Sulla letteratura si può solo fare della letteratura. Infatti, i libri generano libri, le parole, parole. . . . Dopo aver scritto questa pagina—vedete che credo di esistere? Sì, questo libro è un sintomo di guarigione, non la guarigione. La pagina si è scritta; è quasi finita, e vorrei leggervi cose. . . . Qualcuno sta sottraendo la pagina; la pagina ha fretta. Non dimenticate: queste pagine vi vengono consegnate da un fool. State di buon animo. Della letteratura sulla letteratura. . . . Stiamo invecchiando. . . . Vi prego, restate seduti. Il tempo è meraviglioso, ma la notte è certa. Grazie. Grazie. (167–68)

What you will find written in these pages does not make sense: that is their essential merit, since I suppose that what that says to me is: you don't have ideas. . . . From time immemorial, it has never been possible to know what comes after death, or to talk about literature; now we know that the two problems are strictly interrelated. About literature one can only make more literature. In fact, books generate books, words, words. . . . After having written this page—you see I believe that I exist? Yes, this book is a symptom of recovery, not recovery itself. The page is written [*literally:* has written itself]; it is almost finished, and I would like to read you things. . . . Someone is taking the page; the page is in a hurry. Don't forget: these pages were written by a Fool. Cheer up. Literature about literature. . . . We are growing old. . . . Please, stay seated. The weather is marvelous, but night is certain. Thank you. Thank you.

The identification of the narrator as a Fool (what implications this identity might have for the identity of the reader are, perhaps fortunately, left unspecified) permits Manganelli to hedge his bets, to protect his own discourse from accusations of blatant anthropomorphism by stipulating that his narrator is not an existing "person" as such but rather a function of a literary performance—a performance that, all in all, is reminiscent not only of the theater but also of Manganelli's own playfully theatrical contribution to the first Gruppo 63 anthology.[14] It is true that the distinction between narrating persona and living person (like that between literature and nonliterature, death and life) remains even here, albeit implicitly, a relational notion. That is, despite the narrator's various claims that the key concepts of non-anthropomorphism can stand alone, that they can be understood just from the inside and just on their own terms, they actually have meaning only *in relation to* something like anthropomorphism (in the same way that the apparent randomness of literary life and death, the aging and death of the speaker who dies with the cessation of his own discourse, has meaning only in relation to the order and destiny of worldly life and death, suggested here by the certainty of the coming night). It is also true that the *Discorso*'s polemic shares this sort of relational dependency with various other postwar arguments for the special status of literature, from Elio Vittorini's disagreements with Palmiro Togliatti and Mario Alicata in the 1940s, to the statements of certain participants in the Gruppo 63, most notably those of Angelo Guglielmi, Nanni Balestrini, and Alfredo Giuliani, and continuing with truly impressive consistency throughout Manganelli's work.[15]

Yet at the same time, it is undeniable that Manganelli's version of literature's supremacy within its realm, of "letteratura sulla letteratura" and what in chapter 8 is termed the discourse of "il pazzo nel pozzo" ("the madman [reflected] in the well"), goes considerably further than those of the vast majority of his predecessors, critics and fiction writers alike. Manganelli's experiment takes literary discourse—which in Samonà, as well as in the Gaddian pastiche and in the early Calvino, remains at least in part a question of conflictual, worldly tensions, of the conflict of desire and will in a social environment—and moves that discourse significantly closer to the realm toward which so much of the literature of postmodernism strives, the realm of Narcissus, of pure, unadulterated desire. In the process, Manganelli's work calls into question not just the means or even the ends of literary representation but the entire notion of representation itself. If the results of this departure from traditional concepts of referentiality, causal logic, plot organization, stable perspective, subjective integrity, and narrative depth seem somehow unsatisfying, or indeed altogether too uncontrolled to sustain interest for very long—something like a game of basketball being played without the hoop—so be it. Such is without doubt the path Manganelli has traced, one of the major paths of Italian narrative of the last two decades and leading into the 1980s. However, as soon as we have said that, we must quickly reconsider, since just when

Manganelli's brand of literary discourse might seem poised to carry the day, what should present itself for consideration but that recent witness to the powers of cleverly ordered representation *and* self-representation, the one that bears "the name of the rose."

Umberto Eco.   Interpretation without End: The Word of the World

Il nome della rosa (*The Name of the Rose*), Eco's first and, to date, only novel, initially appeared in 1980, though interest in it was quickly rekindled by the extraordinary success of its various foreign translations and by the publication of the author's *Postille*, or "Endnotes," in 1983.[16] Eco's detective story is set in a northern Italian monastery in the early fourteenth century, during the period of the religious controversies that surrounded the pope's move to Avignon. The Holmesian duo of clerical troubleshooters—Guglielmo da Baskerville and his trusted amanuensis, Adso da Melk—are charged with solving a series of (perhaps diabolic, or even apocalyptic) crimes. Their investigation follows a trail that turns out to be as labyrinthian as the monastery's magnificent library, which in the end does appear to hold the clue to the crime's solution in the prize so jealously guarded by Jorge (the devilishly clever and humorless monk): the manuscript that supposedly contains the lost second book of Aristotle's *Poetics*, on comedy. The growing complexity of the mystery (which Guglielmo, in Gaddian fashion, designates at an early point as "un bel pasticcio," 113; "a fine mess," 105), with its ordered progression of seven crimes in seven days, all reported by the narrator with the authenticity of historical detail and all gauged by the system of canonical hours, constantly challenges not only the text's internal investigators but also the novel's readers to examine, review, and weigh—in short, to interpret—the meaning of the signs left by the various crimes. That this is indeed a process of the reading and deciphering of signs (one of the great obsessions common to both medieval and postmodern studies, as Eco well knows) is regularly reaffirmed by the text itself, in its repeated descriptions of human understanding cast explicitly in terms of writing and reading. This is not, however, just a question of understanding the meanings of separate signs but also of understanding the relations among and between them, all within the overarching enigmas of worldly order and disorder, of human motivation, divine intention, and free will (495–96; 492–93).

The form of the book *as* a book also repeats both the labyrinthian organization of its plot and the open appeal to interpretation. The book begins, even before the author's preface, with the pretextual announcement of its written condition: "Naturalmente, un manoscritto" ("Naturally, a manuscript"). The nature and provenance of the manuscript are then described in the preface, dated 5 January 1980. The author (in the guise of the text's translator) recounts the various rebirths of his manuscript and the ample reasons to doubt not only the extent of its fidelity to the events that it purports to relate but also its utility in the contemporary world. After all, what purpose would be served by the translation into modern Italian of "una oscura versione neogotica francese di una edizione latina secentesca di un'opera scritta in latino da un monaco tedesco [Adso] sul finire del trecento" (13–14; "an obscure, neo-Gothic French version of a seventeenth-century Latin edition of a work written in Latin by a German monk [Adso] toward the end of the fourteenth century," 4)? On the question of representational fidelity the author/translator comes to a quick decision: it is not only clear but also right that Adso's memoirs share the same ambiguities and mysteries as the events that they narrate (13; 3).

If the question of utility receives somewhat more space, in the end the author's answer is equally confident. To make a long story short, the import of the book for the present world of men and events makes not a whit of difference:

> Trascrivo senza preoccupazioni di attualità. Negli anni in cui scoprivo il testo dell'abate Vallet [i.e., 1968], circolava la persuasione che si dovesse scrivere solo impegnandosi sul presente, e per cambiare il mondo. A dieci e più anni di distanza è ora consolazione dell'uomo di lettere (restituito alla sua altissima dignità) che si possa scrivere per puro amor di scrittura. E così ora mi sento libero di raccontare, per semplice gusto fabulatorio, la storia di Adso da Melk, e provo conforto e consolazione nel ritrovarla . . . così gloriosamente priva di rapporto coi tempi nostri, intemporalmente estranea alle nostre speranze e alle nostre sicurezze.
>
> Perché essa è storia di libri, non di miserie quotidiane, e la sua lettura può inclinarci a recitare, col grande imitatore da Kempis: "In omnibus requiem quaesivi, et nusquam inveni nisi in angulo cum libro." (15)
>
> I transcribe my text with no concern for timeliness. In the years when I discovered the Abbé Vallet volume [i.e., 1968], there was

a widespread conviction that one should write only out of a commitment to the present, and in order to change the world. Now, after ten years and more, the man of letters (restored to his loftiest dignity) can, happily, once more write out of pure love of writing. And so I now feel free to tell, for sheer narrative pleasure, the story of Adso of Melk, and I feel comfort and consolation in finding it . . . so gloriously lacking in any relevance for our day, atemporally alien to our hopes and to our certainties.

For it is a tale of books, not of everyday miseries, and reading it can lead us to recite, with the great imitator à Kempis: "In omnibus requiem quaesivi, et nusquam inveni nisi in angulo cum libro." (5)

It is true that the author's deprecation of any and all theories of literature's direct social intervention is not to be taken at face value, that the half serious, half tongue-in-cheek tone of the preface (which begins with the events in Prague in 1968, and leads through Austria and subsequently to Paris before bouncing, perhaps in Borgesian hommage à la "Jorge da Burgos," to the booksellers of Buenos Aires) precludes divorcing the preface's concluding polemic from its context, in which it is in essence both a fanciful and timely way of putting the story *en route*. Still, it is also clear that the Manzonian question that set the author's train of doubts in motion in regard to redoing the "found" manuscript ("Anzitutto, quale stile adottare?"; "First of all, what style should I employ?") has a great deal more to do here with the creation of literary pleasure than with the communication—however indirect—of worldly meaning. So even though Eco's book concerns the interpretation of life's signs in the world, it does so only in its makeup as a literary "storia di libri" with yet another manuscript about books at its center, which is to say as an artifact that means only *as* art, as the word of the world, but only *as* that world exists in and through literary re-creation.

These concerns for the means and powers of language continue beyond the preface into the narrative's first paragraph, which opens with the beginning of the Gospel according to Saint John, and from there throughout the entire narrative. The references to, and on occasion discussions of, the deciphering of the monastery's elaborate puzzle of signs are, as I have mentioned, fairly constant. But more to the point for our present purposes are the numerous comments regarding books and the relation between books and their environment. On occasion this relation seems to be one in which texts lead not to the material world but into a maze of other texts, in the sort of infinite regress that Manganelli toys with, for example, at the conclusion of *Centuria*. As Guglielmo tells Adso at one point: "Spesso i libri parlano di altri libri. Spesso un libro innocuo è come un seme, che fiorirà in un libro pericoloso, o all'inverso, è il frutto dolce di una radice amara" (289, cf. 495; "Often books speak of other books. Often a harmless book is like a seed that will blossom into a dangerous book, or, the other way around, it is the sweet fruit of a bitter stem," 286, cf. 492). But usually the text's "enigmas" are viewed in a different light— one far more felicitous for the genre of the detective novel, if not for its parody—in which signs do lead to other signs but also, via the *interpretative* faculties of the actively decoding reader, to the material facts of the world. Guglielmo later says: "Il bene di un libro sta nell'essere letto. Un libro è fatto di segni che parlano di altri segni, *i quali a loro volta parlano delle cose*. Senza un occhio che lo legga, un libro reca segni che non producono concetti, e quindi è muto" (399, my italics; "The good of a book lies in its being read. A book is made up of signs that speak of other signs, *which in their turn speak of things*. Without an eye to read them, a book contains signs that produce no concepts, and therefore is mute," 396, my italics). Despite the obviously scholastic cast of Guglielmo's discourse, this last reply to Adso is on the whole straightforward. This sort of invitation and challenge to worldly interpretation through signs, all activated by the perceptive faculties of each individual reader, recurs in the text's chatty, self-consciously reader-oriented conclusion, as the narrative complements its Latinate introductory citation of à Kempis with an equally erudite— and considerably more ambiguous—ending: "Stat rosa pristina nomine, nomina nuda tenemus."

The general import, if not the precise meaning, of this sentence is discussed by Eco in his *Postille*. But before we consider that brief yet instructive document in greater detail, several comments are in order regarding the relation between Eco's novel and the other contemporary works that have been discussed up to now. First of all, in terms of our general discussion, both the fragmentation of narrative framing and the skewing of narrative perspective, each of which had become increasingly extreme from the novels of Samonà to the works of Manganelli, have been at least partly countered by Eco's book. *Il nome della rosa* is certainly no less self-conscious than its companions in recent Italian fiction; but it does restore both the interest in long-range plot (as a combination of human motivation and worldly events) and the concern for the anthropomorphic functions of fictional narrative that Manganelli's most radical texts had not so much put in doubt as polemically abandoned. Nonetheless, just as Manganelli's postmodernist departure from the traditional concerns of narrative fiction, of characters in relation to their worldly environments, is not as complete as it might first seem, so Eco's return to narrative tradition, even if construed in the mode of parody, is hardly an unconditional one.

Several of the more salient problems of the narrative are clarified in the course of the *Postille*. Eco begins his "notes" by explaining—or better, reaffirming—the ambiguities of the book's title. He does so by referring to both medieval and modern theories of signs and signification from Bernard of Morlay and Abelard (and eventually including Roger Bacon, Ockham, and others), with special reference to proper nouns, which appear to retain their power even after what they supposedly name has disappeared (if it ever existed at all; cf. the conclusion of the fifth day in the novel, 400–409; 397–407). The emphasis on semiotics as well as on the experience of reading that runs throughout the *Postille* reflects Eco's voluminous and distinguished expository writings on these topics, carried on in concert with his university career as a professor of literary studies. These two topics eventually lead him to considerations of genre and of parody: for example, is *Il nome della rosa* a historical novel? (yes and no); a *giallo*? (yes and no); and so forth.

But still more apposite, given the present context, are the comments concerning what might be termed the nature of the novel, both Eco's own book and the novel in general. Eco discusses several of the more polemical positions of the Italian avant-garde of the 1960s (particularly that of Renato Barilli, as expressed in an essay published in the collection of papers resulting from the 1965 meeting of the Gruppo 63 bearing the subtitle *Il romanzo sperimentale*).[17] Eco's intent is to place *Il nome della rosa* in its historical perspective in regard to the avant-garde in Europe and America (33–41; 59–72). He does this with specific relation to the concept of "intreccio" (plot) and to the pleasures of reading.

These are, of course, just two of the categories that we have been considering in regard to postmodern fiction, but they are central ones. Eco's argument is, all and all, clear-cut. In the 1960s, as Barilli had suggested, the very notion of plot or narrativity, with its consoling effect of drawing the reader uncritically into the action of the text and its final revelatory illumination in "material ecstasy," was regarded not only as traditional but also as regressive in both artistic and social terms. With the subsequent years, however, and the intervention of American (as well as

French) theorists of postmodernism, Eco describes the return of the plot and the rehabilitation of the pleasures of reading, but not in any naive or innocent sense. According to Eco, such sophisticated (i.e., non-innocent) effects as irony, metalanguage, and complexly interlaced textual citations serve the discourse of postmodernism by permitting it to encompass that of the previous era, of modernism, while reproducing modernism's typical effects in a critical and sometimes parodic vein. For Eco this explains why, in postmodernist fiction as distinct from most earlier Western narrative, extensive literary self-consciousness is not just a symptom or an effect but narrative's most characteristic quality. As we have seen, too, in relation to Calvino's latest works, these narratives do not so much *evince* literary self-consciousness in the form of secondary discourse as *embody* it first and foremost from beginning to end. In schematic fashion, then, *Il nome della rosa* can be described as both retaining many of the more traditional moral aspects of novels like Samonà's, encompassing questions of individuals' motivation and will in relation to their environment, and at the same time incorporating some of the more insistently postmodern effects of the works of Manganelli and others even while keeping the notion of *literary* plot alive. Eco's book does this, in a fashion analogous to that of Calvino's *Se una notte d'inverno un viaggiatore*, by including plot while eschewing closure, by regularly aiming toward worldly representation and interpretation while denying stable meaning, and by creating aesthetic pleasure even while placing the notion of pleasure itself under examination. This is not to say, of course, that *Il nome della rosa*'s project of Barthian "replenishment" actually achieves any or all of these ends—that decision, for better or worse, must remain for each individual reader to make on his or her own—but only that these are the aims expressed by Eco in his autodescription.[18]

The subject of literary pleasure leads us back, if by a somewhat circuitous path, to the circumstances of the book's production, promotion, and consumption. Although the *Postille* broaches this topic only indirectly, it is of such importance—and obviously of such moment to Eco himself—that its effects may be said to appear at virtually every turn. Eco wants to see his book (and wants his readers to see his book) within the canon of what can only be called a, though perhaps not the, great tradition. Within this tradition, as we have seen, Eco claims the position of an innovator rather than a follower; and, maybe rightly so given this view in the *Postille*, his chosen points of comparison across the Western world aim extraordinarily high: from Stendhal, Tolstoi, Dickens, Defoe, Manzoni, and Balzac, backward to Homer, Cervantes, Dante, Ariosto, and Rabelais, and forward to Mann, Joyce, and Borges. It is true that, particularly in the more contemporary references, the level occasionally descends to that of mere mortals (Borgese, Pratolini, Woody Allen, even "Snoopy"). But generally speaking, the aura that surrounds the *Postille* is nothing less than one of "Great Books."

If the effect on the public is to be measured by the novel's sales in the bookstore, the publication of the *Postille*, placed on top of the paperback edition *in vetrina* as part of the novel's continuing publicity campaign, seems to have served its purpose: not just renewed interest in *Il nome della rosa* but interest in what now appeared an authentic entrée to high culture, albeit mass-produced. The extent to which Eco can be charged with pandering to the bourgeoisie, with giving his audience the illusion of "passing" into the exclusive realm of consumer society's intellectual elite, remains open to dispute. But it does seem abundantly, if also disappointingly, clear that the cleverly anthropocentric focus of Eco's novel turns out to be aimed not just at the status of the individual subject as subject, but also, in terms of its author and its audience, on the subject as at once *homo ludens* and *homo oeconomicus*. Through the autoreflexive agency of the *Postille*, the most self-consciously literary and obsessively intertextual aspects of Eco's novel thus attain the disquietingly *non*disturbing status of a work that is intended to flatter rather than challenge (or even *épater*) the world of its own words' reception. In the end, by mixing the attributes of the popular and the academic novel more astutely—and, perhaps it should be said, more assiduously—than any of his confreres, Eco has managed not only to relocate the Benjaminian "aura" of the work of art but also, for good or ill, to make it conspicuously marketable. The result of this entire process thus seems not only a newly triumphant version of Eco but also of a new, and now thoroughly postmodern, Narcissus.

CONCLUSION

Who, How, and Why

One of the salient challenges encountered in treating literary self-consciousness from a historical perspective is that many of the accepted historical paradigms either do not work or work only by half. Despite standard critical formulae, there is no consistent "rise" in literary self-consciousness over the past two centuries of narrative writing in Italy. Even given the mid- and late-nineteenth-century realist "eclipse" of self-consciousness common to many critical descriptions of the subject (which in this context would include Verga, though, as we have seen, this would be appropriate only in part), the portrayal of a single line of steady growth in self-conscious knowledge and effects is obviously inadequate to describe the material covered here. Indeed, the description of an overall rise in self-consciousness is insufficient not only for literature in the modern period but also for the entire scope of Italian narrative from the early centuries on (i.e., how to explain the exceptionally clever layering of self-conscious effects in Bocaccio's *Decameron*, written against the backdrop of neophyte Florentine capitalism and the Black Death, with its delicately interlocking and often self-reflexive levels of narration, its elaborate interplay of frame story and novelle, and its open appeal to its readers in the remarkable prologue to the stories of the Fourth Day?). Furthermore, although one seemingly attractive solution to the problem of progressive development would be to break the topic up into narrative subgenres (the historical novel, the psychological novel, the expressionist novel, the experimental novel, and so forth), that choice itself, by emphasizing similarities at the expense of actual differences, risks obscuring genuine historical complexity in favor of highlighting unities that are ultimately secondary or, on occasion, illusory.

Because of these problems, it has been at once more useful and more accurate to view literary self-consciousness in the Italian tradition as a *mode* of discourse rather than as a *genre* of literary products. As we have seen, this mode is often operative even when it is not dominant, even when it is not so all-pervasive or all-important as to constitute a thoroughly self-conscious narrative. Once this view has been adopted, two consequences follow. First, literary self-consciousness takes on a genuine historical dimension, in which its relative significance and its changing focus can be traced through a rich variety of modern novels, from *I Promessi Sposi*'s supremely coy yet also deadly serious narrator, to Verga's polemically "objectivist" texts, through Dossi's pastiches and D'Annunzio's artist-heroes, and eventually—by way of Pirandello's developing oeuvre—into the literature of the twentieth century. This dimension gives a certain step-by-step consistency to a critical view of the phenomenon, although the approach necessarily remains layered rather than linear, one that deals with reactions as well as progressions, with literary anxieties as well as influences.

The second consequence has to do with the way in which literature is construed *within* a complex historical milieu. When the notion of literary *change* inside a definite frame has come into play, the relations between literature and its constantly shifting extraliterary environment, including social, economic, and political phenomena, become more clearly germane and at times considerably more pressing. Such relations are, of course, far from simple. Part of their complexity as far is literature is concerned is due to the difficulties inherent in the theory and in the practice of creative representation itself. In the course of this study, I have been dealing primarily with *literary* representation, although other kinds of representation (political and/or social) with analogous workings and contradictions have come to the fore now and then. The problems of fictional representation, including re-presentation of other literary discourse, run deep enough so that they affect both narrative and linguistic self-consciousness. For this reason, they are probably perpetual in narrative discourse rather than confined to any delimited historical period, though evaluations of them and responses to them differ within as well as across historical boundaries. Awareness of the basic difficulty—how to re-present in *fictional* terms something that *really* exists inside and, at least *in potentia*, outside of the work of art, even if only in terms of the reader's aesthetic experience—turns the literary narrative back on itself in an examination of both its narrative technique and its *status* as fiction, as the bound yet free, motivated yet arbitrary, slavish yet creative, and (somehow) true literary lie. In the process, questions of literary form and literary procedure inevitably get caught up in questions of epistemology as well as aesthetics, in questions of hermeneutics as well as rhetoric, and it is toward these central junctures that the effects of literary self-consciousness are regularly drawn.

These considerations repeatedly lead to another, perhaps even more basic one, not just the relation between the narrative and its own created world but that between literature and the world that it actually enters, the world of its creator *and* its public. The questions of worldly *praxis* in addition to those of literary interpretation and poetics have shown up in self-conscious fashion in almost every work that I have discussed, from Manzoni to Gadda, Morante, Calvino, and beyond, though usually in the guise of doubts and/or concerns about literature's influence on life rather than in the happier key of affirmation or in that of untroubled certainty. Although there is no one position on which all or even most of these authors, in and through their texts, would or could agree, this general topic is pertinent here in that it serves to return discussion to the last of our three initial concerns, not just who speaks and how, but also *why*.

Because of narrative's distinctive combination of creation and re-creation through representation, the question of causation, as it regards literary self-consciousness, diverges from related issues in other major literary genres such as lyric and drama. For narrative, the fundamental question may be formulated in this way: does literary self-consciousness create a disturbance in the text or does it provide a solution? Is self-consciousness in this context equivalent to self-knowledge, and if so, is the text's knowledge of itself as a literary artifact valued as good and beneficial or perceived as merely a source of frustration? In still other terminology, is the text to be considered the subject or the object of literary self-consciousness? Although the inquiry is cast here in terms of the text, it could also be aimed elsewhere, at the author, in the creation of the fiction, or at the reader, in the re-creating experience of reading. Recent criticism that has dealt in some fashion with self-consciousness has tended to come down on either one side of the argument or the other. Anglo-American New Criticism, for example, often evoking the effects of Romantic irony, tended to affirm the effects of closure in textual expressions of self-knowledge, whereas deconstructive criticism has usually seen self-consciousness as a way of opening up the text, at times to express, though not to resolve, its own inherent epistemological anxieties. In short—to borrow a line from Dante—

we scratch where it itches; but whether our reaction takes care of the problem or merely prolongs it (or, indeed, *constitutes* the problem) is not so easily determined. It is encouraging to note, however, that the difficulties intrinsic to this argument and the flexibility required to deal with them have on occasion been acknowledged both in the discourse of philosophy and in literary criticism.[1]

That neither side—self-consciousness understood either as a protective safety valve or as an open wound—is by itself entirely sufficient for any separate text or any group of texts suggests the critical intricacies of dealing with this issue. For critical methodology, what such intricacies mean is that, both in regard to individual works and to historical periods, the importance, the effects, *and* the sense of literary self-consciousness must first be examined on their own terms in the literary works themselves. However, since these terms, to repeat, are also intimately involved with extraliterary phenomena, literary history is obliged to include consideration of other areas of historical concern. The interlocking nature of these historical relations has particular import for evaluating the contemporary pervasiveness of self-consciousness in literature and in criticism, since any appeal to the progression of literary history alone to explain the recent craze for self-consciousness is far too limited, and in the end, needlessly so. While self-consciousness, including self-consciousness about the very voice of narration, is undeniably more pervasive and more extreme in the contemporary literature of postmodernism than in other periods—with such major Italian modernist forebears as Pirandello, Svevo, and Gadda, along with myriad less imposing figures from Alberto Savinio to Tommaso Landolfi—this literary phenomenon is also tied to an amalgam of extraliterary ones. Among these, to mention only the more obvious, are the increasing social alienation of the period of multinational capitalism, the ever-present threat of annihilation in the atomic age, and the constant questioning of social and cultural tradition itself in a rapidly changing world (including questions about the role of the university as a cultural institution and about the distinctions between serious and popular culture).

At the same time, the view of literary postmodernism outlined in the two previous chapters—seen as a way of recasting the cultural *and* social discourse of modernism in the postmodernist delights of the parodic, thoroughly *literary* pastiche, with the intent not of turning away from the world but of preserving literature itself in a new, less mystified literary *and* social era—is instructive in this context. This view not only helps to explain why specifically literary self-consciousness is currently at such a premium in the works of authors like Calvino, Manganelli, and Eco but also helps to reconstitute literature, and its relationship with the "subjects" of its world, via attention to the very phenomena of subjective fragmentation and interpretive uncertainty that had so harassed the literature of high modernism. Again, such a conception of the postmodernist delight in self-consciousness sees postmodernism's relation to modernism as a reaction against, as well as an extension of, the prior period. In terms of literary self-consciousness, it may appear that the difference between the two is strictly one of degree, but in fact it is also one of kind, since postmodernism aims not only at elaboration of the discourse of its predecessors but also at self-conscious refashioning and revitalization. Such current moral "replenishment," in its *resolution* of the opposing views of self-consciousness sketched earlier, as either the expressive closure of moral reaffirmation or the openness of unending doubt, may or may not be effective or lasting. Whether it will eventually turn out to be so, or whether it is merely a further illusion, a new variety of Zeno's *trucco buono,* is still, perforce, uncertain. At this point, one may hope that the answer will prove to be positive, for literature's "beautiful fables," for its audience, and for its critics; but this, then, is the point at which, for the present, criticism's analysis must cease—*E qui si tacque.*

Notes

Introduction. Literary Self-consciousness

1. Four further recent studies that have at least tangential implications for the reassessment of literary self-consciousness are Dorrit Cohn, *Transparent Minds: Narrative Modes for Presenting Consciousness in Fiction* (Princeton: Princeton University Press, 1978); Steven G. Kellman, *The Self-Begetting Novel* (New York: Columbia University Press, 1980); Michael Boyd, *The Reflexive Novel: Fiction as Critique* (Lewisburg, Pa.: Bucknell University Press, 1983); and Paul Jay, *Being in the Text: Self-Representations from Wordsworth to Roland Barthes* (Ithaca: Cornell University Press, 1984). Cohn's account of the devices and effects of the literary presentation of consciousness is a systematic treatment of narrative technique that takes her topic up to the point at which consideration of self-consciousness would logically come into play and provide the material for a full companion study (one that has not as yet, however, been written). Kellman's book, with Proust as its starting point, considers the "self-begetting," or author-centered, novel (which is also usually self-conscious) as a novelistic subgenre in which the "portrait" of the artist depicts his progress up to the time at which he is prepared to begin writing the story that then takes form as the novel itself. Boyd discusses Conrad, Faulkner, Virginia Woolf, Joyce, Beckett, Nabokov, and others in the context of fictional reflexivity. While Boyd's discussions of these authors are imaginative and often convincing, the book as a whole, unfortunately, adds little that is genuinely innovative to the question under consideration. Jay centers on nineteenth- and twentieth-century autobiographical expression in the relation between author and text.

2. Graff singles out one of Miller's earlier essays on classical realism to make his points: "The Fiction of Realism: *Sketches by Boz, Oliver Twist,* and Cruikshank's Illustrations," in *Dickens Centennial Essays,* ed. Ada Nisbet and Blake Nevius (Berkeley and Los Angeles: University of California Press, 1971), 85–

153. It is impossible in a brief note even to begin a bibliography of the essays and books in which Miller affirms the general outlines of his theoretical positions in regard to the nature of meaning and the illusions of referentiality. There is, however, a useful recent exchange on Miller's views: Vincent B. Leitch, "The Lateral Dance: The Deconstructive Criticism of J. Hillis Miller," and Miller's reply, "Theory and Practice: A Response to Vincent Leitch," both in *Critical Inquiry* 6, no. 4 (1980): 593–607, 609–19, and there is an informative interview by Robert Moynihan, "Interview with J. Hillis Miller," *Criticism* 24, no. 2 (1982): 99–125. In addition, in *The Yale Critics: Deconstruction in America*, ed. Jonathan Arac et al., Theory and History of Literature, 6 (Minneapolis: University of Minnesota Press, 1983), there is a useful essay by Donald Pease, "J. Hillis Miller: The Other Victorian at Yale," 66–89, and a bibliography of Miller's works (209–12).

3. Jonathan Culler, "Beyond Interpretation" (1976), revised in *The Pursuit of Signs: Semiotics, Literature, Deconstruction* (Ithaca: Cornell University Press, 1981), 15–16. For Miller's conception of what he terms the "linguistic moment" in realistic fiction, see his "Nature and the Linguistic Moment," in *Nature and the Victorian Imagination*, ed. U. C. Knoepflmacher and G. B. Tennyson (Berkeley and Los Angeles: University of California Press, 1977), 440–51. Miller has recently expanded this concept in a historical context, though with a focus on poetry rather than on narrative, in *The Linguistic Moment: From Wordsworth to Stevens* (Princeton: Princeton University Press, 1985).

4. See Graff, *Literature against Itself*, 175–78, esp. 177; and Culler, "Beyond Interpretation," p. 15. Culler is restating the argument that Miller makes in his review of Joseph Riddel's *The Inverted Bell* (1974), "Deconstructing the Deconstructors," *Diacritics* 5, no. 2 (1975): 30–31. See also Riddel's lively response to Miller, "A Miller's Tale," *Diacritics* 5, no. 3 (1975): 56–65. For a brief, trenchant statement of Graff's views on deconstruction in general see his review of *Deconstruction and Criticism*, by Harold Bloom et al. (1979), "Deconstruction as Dogma; or, 'Come Back to the Raft Ag'in, Strether, Honey,'" *Georgia Review* 34, no. 2 (1980): 404–21.

5. See Charles Altieri, *Act and Quality: A Theory of Literary Meaning and Human Understanding* (Amherst: University of Massachusetts Press, 1981). What is especially interesting in Altieri's book is not any single attribute of self-consciousness as such but rather the way in which Altieri conceives of and approaches his entire subject. As is true for his overall argument, which concerns the present state of literary culture and of the humanities as a whole, Altieri presents the fragments of the history of literary self-consciousness by means of the philosophical tradition of Hegelian dialectics, as read and evaluated by Jacques Derrida, as read and evaluated by Altieri through Wittgenstein (*Act and Quality*, 322–25). Though not a preeminent issue, self-consciousness is a significant one in this revisionist reading of Derrida and in Altieri's proposal to recon-

sider and resituate (by means of the notion of intensional logic) contemporary criticism and theory in their historical context.

6. See *The Phenomenology of Spirit*, trans. A. V. Miller, introd. J. N. Findlay (Oxford: Clarendon Press, 1979), and *On Art, Religion, Philosophy: Introductory Lectures to the Realm of Absolute Spirit*, ed. J. Glenn Gray (New York: Harper and Row, 1970).

7. Trotsky's early attack on the Formalists, "The Formalist School of Poetry," is included in *Literature and Revolution*, trans. Rose Strunsky (New York: International, 1925), 162–83.

8. See Jean Ricardou, *Problèmes du nouveau roman*, Collection "Tel Quel" (Paris: Seuil, 1967), *Pour une théorie du nouveau roman* (Paris: Seuil, 1971), esp. 171–207, *Le Nouveau Roman*, Écrivains de toujours (Paris: Seuil, 1973), 47–75, 109–12, and "La Population des miroirs: Problèmes de la similitude à partir d'un texte(s) d'Alain Robbe-Grillet," *Poétique* 22 (1975), rpt. in *Nouveaux Problèmes du roman*, Collection "Poétique" (Paris: Seuil, 1978), 140–78; Lucien Dällenbach, *Le Récit spéculaire: Essai sur la mise en abyme*, Collection "Poétique" (Paris: Seuil, 1977); Mieke Bal, *Narratologie: Essais sur la signification narrative dans quatre romans modernes* (Paris: Klincksieck, 1977), esp. 106–7; *Onze Études sur la mise en abyme*, ed. Fernand Hallyn, special issue of *Romanica Gandensia* 17 (1980); and *L'Autoreprésentation: Le Texte et ses miroirs*, special issue of *Texte* 1 (1980).

See also Bruce Morrissette's discussion of Gide's sense of this effect, "Un Héritage d'André Gide: La Duplication intérieure," *Comparative Literature Studies* 8, no. 2 (1971): 125–42, and Bal's enthusiastic review of Dällenbach's *Le Récit spéculaire*, "Mise en abyme et iconicité," *Littérature* 29 (February 1978): 116–28.

9. Dällenbach, *Le Récit spéculaire*, 140–48. Dällenbach's work makes clear why the usual structuralist conception of the mise en abyme as the hypodiegetic level mirroring and endlessly duplicating the diegetic level is insufficient to account either for the varieties of the operation's internal complexities or for its effects.

10. Gérard Genette, *Figures III*, Collection "Poétique" (Paris: Seuil, 1972), 245; Genette, *Narrative Discourse: An Essay in Method*, trans. Jane E. Lewin, introd. Jonathan Culler (Ithaca: Cornell University Press, 1980), 236.

11. Jorge Luis Borges, *Labyrinths: Selected Stories and Other Writings*, ed. Donald A. Yates and James E. Irby, introd. André Maurois (New York: New Directions, 1964), 196.

12. For Alter's later consideration of the subject of *Partial Magic*, see his "Mimesis and the Motive for Fiction," *TriQuarterly* 42 (Spring 1978): 228–49.

13. Alter's underestimation of the Victorians' awareness of the literary complexities both of worldly representation and of self-reflexivity is pointed out by George Levine in *The Realistic Imagination: English Fiction from Frankenstein to*

Lady Chatterly (Chicago: University of Chicago Press, 1981), 332, n. 18. Hutcheon sees Alter's lack of enthusiasm for nineteenth-century realism in *Partial Magic* as stemming from his "dualism of consciousness and the world," or, in literary terms, of "'art' and 'life,'" which effectively denies what Hutcheon terms the active "paradox" that "reading and writing belong to the processes of 'life' as much as they do to those of 'art'" (*Narcissistic Narrative*, 4–5). Miller's work also serves as a useful antidote to Alter's underestimation of the Victorians.

14. Two of the earliest American treatments dealing specifically with "metafiction" are by William H. Gass, "Philosophy and the Forms of Fiction," rpt. in *Fiction and the Figures of Life* (New York: Knopf, 1970), 3–26, and Robert Scholes, "Metafiction," *Iowa Review* 1 (Fall 1970): 100–115. Scholes's concept is elaborated, however schematically, in his *Fabulation and Metafiction* (Urbana: University of Illinois Press, 1979), and is also treated by Gustavo Pérez Firmat in his equally schematic review of Scholes's book, "Metafiction Again," *Taller Literario* 1 (1980): 30–38. These interests have now become much more common in criticism in English. See, for example, Inger Christensen's *The Meaning of Metafiction: A Critical Study of Selected Novels by Sterne, Nabokov, Barth, and Beckett* (Bergin and Oslo: Universitetsforlaget, 1981); Patricia Waugh's useful introduction and brief overview, incorporating recent psychological and sociological theories, *Metafiction: The Theory and Practice of Self-Conscious Fiction*, New Accents (London and New York: Methuen, 1984); June Schlueter's treatment of this topic in the modern theater, *Metafictional Characters in Modern Drama* (New York: Columbia University Press, 1979); and Margaret A. Rose's extension of her previous work on German verse in *Parody/Meta-fiction: An Analysis of Parody as a Critical Mirror to the Writing and Reception of Fiction* (London: Croom Helm, 1979). For current discussions of contemporary literary "narcissism," see Hutcheon's "Modes et formes du narcissisme littéraire," *Poétique* 29 (February 1977): 90–106; two books recently published in the University of Toronto Press's Romance Series (nos. 40 and 42, respectively): Valerie Raoul, *The French Fictional Journal: Fictional Narcissism /Narcissistic Fiction* (1980), and Brian T. Fitch, *The Narcissistic Text: A Reading of Camus' Fiction* (1982); and Allen Thiher, *Words in Reflection: Modern Language Theory and Postmodern Fiction* (Chicago: University of Chicago Press, 1984), esp. chs. 4–7.

15. It is worth noting that Hutcheon wrote the Introduction to the special issue of *Texte* (1980) entitled *L'Autoreprésentation* (see note 8 above).

16. Récanati adopts this distinction from Quine, who coined the term "referential opacity" to complement and revise (via Frege) Whitehead and Russell's concept of referential "transparency," as set forth in their *Principia Mathematica*, 2d ed. (Cambridge: Cambridge University Press, 1925), 1:665. See Willard Van Orman Quine, *Word and Object,* Studies in Communication (New York: Technology Press, Massachusetts Institute of Technology; London: John Wiley and Sons, 1960), 141–56, and *The Ways of Paradox and Other Essays*, rev. ed. (Cam-

bridge: Harvard University Press, 1976), 160–64, 174–76, and 188–91.

17. Rodolphe Gasché explains the relation between Austin's theory of performative utterances and the classical problem of the reflexivity of language in his review of de Man's *Allegories of Reading: Figural Language in Rousseau, Nietzsche, Rilke, and Proust* (1979), "'Setzung' and 'Übersetzung': Notes on Paul de Man," *Diacritics* 11, no. 4 (1981): 36–57, esp. 39–40. Despite mention of Récanati and of Benveniste's influential treatment of Austin, reprinted in *Problèmes de linguistique générale* (1966), Gasché's argument at least in this respect seems strained, since Austin not only neglects to "employ the philosophical terminology of reflexivity to describe his so-called revolution," as Gasché correctly states (39), but also seemed very little concerned with the traditional concepts and interests of reflexivity, which are present only in the most oblique fashion in his call to arms, *How to Do Things with Words*, 2d ed., ed. J. O. Urmson and Marina Sbisà (1962; Cambridge: Harvard University Press, 1975). Regardless of such theoretical and practical difficulties, this type of reading of Austin has attained an unquestionable stature in current French criticism, as evidenced by Shoshana Felman's extended treatment of Austinian linguistics and her willfully interpretive appropriation of its concepts in *Le Scandale du corps parlant: Don Juan avec Austin, ou la séduction en deux langues* (Paris: Seuil, 1980), in which Benveniste's treatment of Austin is also discussed.

It should be noted that most of the injustices done to Austin (and to ordinary language philosophy in general) by two decades of French attempts to read him in the tradition of the philosophy of reflection are corrected, if not canceled, by Récanati's most recent book, which perhaps fittingly has little to do with self-consciousness, *Les Énoncés performatifs*, Propositions (Paris: Minuit, 1981).

18. Two other discussions are at once distinctly original, wide-ranging, and useful: James Sloan Allen, "Self-Consciousness and the Modernist Temper," *Georgia Review* 33, no. 3 (1979): 601–20, and Christine Brooke-Rose, "Metafiction and Surfiction: A Simpler Formal Approach," in her *A Rhetoric of the Unreal: Studies in Narrative and Structure, Especially of the Fantastic* (Cambridge: Cambridge University Press, 1981), 364–89.

19. Barthes' comments on the topic of self-reflection in literature, and particularly on the nature of "metalanguage," also demonstrate a refreshing combination of theoretical dynamics and historical interests, though his historical paradigms are often less than convincing. See especially his short essay "Littérature et méta-language" (1959), rpt. in *Essais critiques*, Collection "Tel Quel" (Paris: Seuil, 1964), 106–7, translated as "Literature and Metalangage," in *Critical Essays*, trans. Richard Howard (Evanston, Ill.: Northwestern University Press, 1972), 97–98.

20. See Gans's *The Origin of Language: A Formal Theory of Representation* (Berkeley and Los Angeles: University of California Press, 1981). Gans posits linguistic consciousness itself (replacing Girard's notion of ritually purified col-

lective violence) as the communal event at the now lost origin of culture. Gans treats the development of human intelligence and representation as that of the progression through the various forms of utterances up to the level of the full sentence. Although his study's application to literature is unclear, his work, particularly in its concluding section, is nevertheless important for understanding modern society's "crisis" of self-consciousness, especially as that crisis is both manifested and examined in the humanities and in the social sciences today. That Gans's work is headed toward somewhat more sustained literary analysis is indicated by part 3 of his subsequent revision and continuation of his theories, *The End of Culture: Toward a Generative Anthropology* (Berkeley and Los Angeles: University of California Press, 1985), 177–300. This literary interest, however, is no longer focused on self-consciousness.

21. Robert C. Spires, in the introduction to his *Beyond the Metafictional Mode: Directions in the Modern Spanish Novel* (Lexington: University Press of Kentucky, 1984), 3–17, argues convincingly in favor of this distinction for the novel in Spain. (However, I find his conclusion [125–28] as regards elitism in art less than satisfying, and as regards the social function of the novel—or lack of it—wrongheaded.)

22. Mario Perniola, *Il metaromanzo*, I quaderni di Sigma (Genoa: Silva, 1966). It should be noted that Hutcheon treats Paolo Volponi's *La macchina mondiale* (1965) and the "Gruppo 63" in chapters 8 and 9 of *Narcissistic Narrative: The Metafictional Paradox* and that two of the essays in the special issue of *Romanica Gandensia* devoted to the mise en abyme (see note 8 above) deal with Italian narratives: Raoul Blomme, "A travers les miroirs de 'Gli Indifferenti,'" 54–65, and Évelyne Capiau-Laureys, "'La Coscienza di Zeno' di Italo Svevo: Discours spéculaire d'un roman psychanalytique," 67–81.

23. Millicent Joy Marcus's study of Boccaccio, *An Allegory of Form: Literary Self-Consciousness in the "Decameron,"* Stanford French and Italian Studies, 18 (Saratoga, Calif.: Anma Libri, 1979), is of related interest, as is Giuseppe Mazzotta's treatment of literary "self-reflexiveness" in the *Decameron*, "The Marginality of Literature" (1972) in his *The World at Play in Boccaccio's "Decameron"* (Princeton: Princeton University Press, 1986), 47–74. There is also a brief but suggestive discussion of the development of self-consciousness in Renaissance theories of art by Alfonso Procaccini, "Alberti and the 'Framing' of Perspective," *Journal of Aesthetics and Art Criticism* 30, no. 1 (1981): 29–39. For treatment of certain parallel aspects of self-consciousness in the English Renaissance, see Stephen Greenblatt, *Renaissance Self-Fashioning: From More to Shakespeare* (Chicago: University of Chicago Press, 1980).

It should perhaps be noted as well that the expression of self-consciousness in the vein of *modern* psychological self-questioning has a significant early example in Vittorio Alfieri's autobiographical *Vita*, published following his death in 1803.

24. The manuscript supposedly contained three texts, among which the translation of Sterne was the third. The first, Foscolo's satirical reply to his critics (actually published in 1815 as *Didymi clerici prophetae minimi hypercalypseos* [*Ipercalisse libro singolare di Didimo Chierico profeta minimo*]), kept up the Foscolo/Didimo relationship and contained the definitive version of the "Notizia intorno a Didimo Chierico." The second of the texts, entitled *Didymi clerici libri memoriales quinque,* was apparently to be Foscolo/Didimo's full "Confessions" but was never completed.

Chapter 1. Discourse in *I Promessi Sposi*

1. All references to Manzoni's works, cited by page numbers in the text, are to *Tutte le opere di Alessandro Manzoni,* ed. Alberto Chiari and Fausto Ghisalberti, I classici Mondadori, 7 vols. (Milan: Mondadori, 1954–70). The novel is contained in volume 2, tomes 1–3 (1954), tome 1, *I Promessi Sposi: Testo critico della edizione definitiva del 1840,* pp. 3–673; tome 2, *I Promessi Sposi: Storia milanese scoperta e rifatta da Alessandro Manzoni. Testo critico della prima edizione stampata nel 1825–27;* tome 3, *Fermo e Lucia: Prima composizione del 1821–1823,* pp. 1–669. Translations of *I Promessi Sposi* are from *The Betrothed,* trans. Archibald Colquhoun (New York: Dutton, 1951), which I have occasionally altered for accuracy. Page numbers are included in the text. The chapter epigraph, from *Fermo e Lucia,* is my translation.

2. This point is also made by Sergio Romagnoli in the course of his analysis of Renzo's linguistic education in "Lingua e società nei *Promessi Sposi,*" in *Atti del convegno manzoniano di Nimega (16–17–18 ottobre 1973),* ed. Carlo Ballerini, Istituto di lingua e di letteratura italiana dell'Università Cattolica di Nimega e Istituto Italiano di Cultura per i Paesi Bassi (Florence: Libreria Editrice Fiorentina, 1979), 126–59, now in Romagnoli's *Manzoni e i suoi colleghi,* Nuovi saggi (Florence: Sansoni, 1984), 35–64.

3. Giorgio De Rienzo, *L'avventura della parola nei "Promessi Sposi,"* L'ippogrifo, 21 (Rome: Bonacci, 1980), 42–43. De Rienzo, who sees the word as both the entry to and the embodiment of the "regno del possibile" (the worldly "realm of the possible"), goes on to characterize Don Rodrigo somewhat too grandiosely as "l'eroe negativo della parola" ("the negative hero of the word"). He eventually fills out this scheme through consideration of l'Innominato (the Unnamed), Fra Cristoforo, Don Abbondio, and Federigo Borromeo, as well as of Renzo's linguistic education and Lucia's silence. De Rienzo's perspective is limited by his continued emphasis on language as an act in itself, that is, apart from the other worldly gestures and attitudes that are essential to language's meaning and force. Despite this limitation, however, his book is a landmark in the study of linguistic self-consciousness in Manzoni's novel.

4. The term *Bildungsroman* is used by Giovanni Getto, who sees Renzo's

experience in Milan (ch. 14) as the key to his ongoing education, in *Letture manzoniane* (Florence: Sansoni, 1964), 241. See also Guido Baldi, "La ribellione di Renzo tra Eden e storia," in *Da Dante al Novecento: Studi critici offerti dagli scolari a Giovanni Getto nel suo ventesimo anno di insegnamento universitario* (Milan: Mursia, 1970), 489–512. For more recent treatments of this aspect of Renzo's story see Romagnoli, "Lingua e società nei *Promessi Sposi*"; Mary Ambrose, "Error and the Abuse of Language in the 'Promessi Sposi,'" *Modern Language Review* 72, no. 1 (1977): 62–72; Giorgio Ficara, "Renzo, l'allievo delle Muse," *Lettere italiane* 29, no. 1 (1977): 34–58; De Rienzo's chapter, "Renzo l'apprendista," in *L'avventura della parola nei "Promessi Sposi,"* 107–37; and Robert S. Dombroski, *L'apologia del vero: Letture ed interpretazione dei "Promessi Sposi,"* Guide di Cultura Contemporanea (Padua: Liviana, 1984), 35–66.

5. No one has reacted to this scene more appropriately than Attilio Momigliano, who, with exquisite sensibility, describes the innkeeper as Rembrandtesque and comments that the visual qualities of the portrayal of the crowd of drinkers bring to mind the paintings of Van Ostade, in *Alessandro Manzoni*, 5th ed., rev. (Milan and Messina: Principato, 1958), 267.

6. Renzo's words also echo Ferrer's earlier pronouncements to the crowd in chapter 13, as Clareece Godt points out in her extremely perceptive essay, "Multiple Perspective in *I Promessi Sposi*: The Uprisings in Milano," *Forum Italicum* 19, no. 2 (1985): 259–72.

7. The most useful treatments of this chapter are Luigi Russo's discussion of the historical roots of both the initial encounter scene and the eventual pardon in seventeenth-century tracts on chivalry, in *Personaggi dei "Promessi Sposi"* (1945; rpt. Bari: Laterza, 1965), 303–33 (but for Manzoni's general failings as a historian see also Fausto Nicolini, *Peste e untori nei "Promessi sposi" e nella realtà storica*, Biblioteca di cultura, 305 [Bari: Laterza, 1937]); and, on the psychological moral subtleties of Manzoni's portrayal of Lodovico/Cristoforo, Eurialo De Michelis, *La vergine e il drago: Nuovi studi su Manzoni*, Saggi, Letteratura e linguistica, n.s., 9 (Padua: Marsilio: 1968), 99–136.

8. The polemical nature of *I Promessi Sposi*, discussion of which began as soon as the novel was published, led Croce (in this instance borrowing his terminology from Giuseppe Citanna, with whom Croce exchanged opinions on Manzoni in Croce's journal *La critica* in the 1920s) to declare Manzoni's novel an "opera oratoria." See Benedetto Croce, *Alessandro Manzoni: Saggi e discussioni*, 4th ed., Biblioteca di Cultura moderna, 191 (Bari: Laterza, 1952), 105–11, 146, and Giuseppe Citanna, *Storia della letteratura italiana*, vol. 3, *Ottocento e Novecento*, 2d ed. (Milan: Garzanti, 1954), 40–63, esp. 59. For an important continuation of this once lively discussion, see Luigi Russo, "Alessandro Manzoni poëta an orator?" (1941), in *Ritratti e disegni storici*, 4th ser., *Dal Manzoni al De Sanctis e la letteratura dell 'Italia unita*, new ed., La civiltà europea (Florence: Sansoni, 1965), 109–47.

9. *Osservazioni sulla morale cattolica* (1855) in *Tutte le opere*, vol. 3, *Opere morali e filosofiche,* ed. Fausto Ghisalberti (1963). Manzoni's disagreement with the tenets of utilitarianism, which he saw as part of the Protestant view of the world, is explained in an appendix added to his revision of the 1819 text, entitled "Appendice al capitolo terzo: Del sistema che fonda la morale sull'utilità" (197–250). See also "Abozzo di un capitolo sull'utilitarismo," c. 1851–55 (251–62), Manzoni's sketch of a further discussion of the topic, which was, however, never completed.

10. In "Error and the Abuse of Language in the 'Promessi Sposi,'" Ambrose notes the "greater directness and trenchancy" of Fra Cristoforo's language in the published novel as compared to *Fermo e Lucia,* and she points out that in the revised versions of this passage Manzoni no longer felt obliged to explain that Fra Cristoforo's words were sincere and heartfelt rather than mere "arte" (71). This type of streamlining, moreover, is typical of Manzoni's revision, in which the self-conscious effects usually reside quietly but forcefully at the very center of the narrative rather than serving merely as rhetorical stylishness or descriptive elaboration. On the general topic of irony and metanarrative in *Fermo e Lucia,* see Antonio Illiano, "Tecnica e sintassi del racconto ironico in Manzoni: *Fermo e Lucia,*" *Italica* 61, no. 2 (1984): 85–95.

11. Jean-Pierre Barriçelli has noted that the effects of hierarchy, along with elaborate obstruction and closure, are even at work in Manzoni's composition of place (particularly in the novel's description of the path, the walls, and the cliffs and valleys of the opening paragraphs), in "Structure and Symbol in Manzoni's *I Promessi Sposi,*" *PMLA* 87, no. 3 (1972): 499–507.

12. Giorgio Ficara, "Le parole e la peste in Manzoni," *Lettere italiane* 33, no. 1 (1981): 3–37.

13. In regard to the chaos and reciprocal violence that the plague in literature (including *I Promessi Sposi*) both symbolizes and further incites, see René Girard, "The Plague in Literature and Myth," *Texas Studies in Literature and Language* 15, no. 5 (1974): 833–50, reprinted in *"To double business bound": Essays on Literature, Mimesis, and Anthropology* (Baltimore: Johns Hopkins University Press, 1978), 136–54. See also Robert S. Dombroski, "The Ideological Question in Manzoni," *Studies in Romanticism* 20, no. 4 (1981): 497–524, esp. 515–24, revised in his *L'apologia del vero,* 67–96, esp. 86–96; and Ficara, "Le parole e la peste in Manzoni."

14. Girard is succinctly explicit on this cluster of themes in "The Plague in Literature and Myth," 148–49. For his most recent treatment of this subject see *Le Bouc émissaire* (Paris: Grasset, 1982), esp. chs. 1–2, pp. 7–21, 23–36.

15. Girard discusses similar effects of hubristic pride and the communal doubling of sudden victimage in Artaud's work (treated by Girard in the context of Shakespeare and Dostoevsky) in "The Plague in Myth and Literature," 149.

16. In terms of the *symbolism* of narrative organization, this conversion and

shift also help save Lucia's honor, since one of the primary aspects in certain mythic representations of the scapegoat's role is sexual union with a beautiful maiden prior to his ritual expulsion or murder. The role of the scapegoat in modern literature, including this aspect of it, is discussed by John B. Vickery in *Myths and Texts: Strategies of Incorporation and Displacement* (Baton Rouge: Louisiana State University Press, 1983), 43–45, 102–47.

17. Salinari's important article on this topic (in which he takes his lead from Gramsci) was published in 1974 along with a response by Edoardo Sanguineti. See Carlo Salinari, "La struttura ideologica dei 'Promessi sposi,'" and Sanguineti, "Glosse a Salinari," *Critica marxista* 12, nos. 3–4 (1974): 183–200, 201–6. A longer version of Salinari's essay (which also served as the introduction to his edition of the novel) appeared in the posthumously published collection of his critical pieces, *Boccaccio Manzoni Pirandello*, ed. Nino Borsellino and Enrico Ghidetti, introd. Natalino Sapegno, Nuova biblioteca di cultura, 193 (Rome: Riuniti, 1979), 113–57. In the course of the subsequent critical debate on this topic in the mid-1970s, the most incisive as well as the most elaborate response was that of Sebastiano Timpanaro, in "Antileopardiani e neomoderati nella sinistra italiana," *Belfagor* 30, no. 2 (1975): 129–56, continued in *Belfagor* 30, no. 4 (1975): 395–428; 31, no. 1 (1976): 1–32; and 31, no. 2 (1976): 159–200; all four parts of this response were reprinted in *Antileopardiani e neomoderati nella sinistra italiana* (Pisa: ETS, 1982). See also Robert S. Dombroski, "The Seicento as Tragedy: 'Providence' and the 'Bourgeois' in *I Promessi Sposi*," *Modern Language Notes* 91, no. 1 (1976): 80–100, revised in *L'apologia del vero*, 5–33 (on Manzoni's depiction of bourgeois aspirations rather than historically completed accomplishments), and, for brief surveys and bibliographies of the various critical positions, Salvatore S. Nigro, *Manzoni*, Letteratura Italiana Laterza, 41 (Bari: Laterza, 1978), 210, and Dombroski, "Manzoni on the Italian Left," *Annali d'Italianistica* 3 (1985): 97–110. Most recently see Guido Baldi's masterful synthesis in *"I promessi sposi": Progetto di società e mito*, Strumenti per una nuova cultura (Milan: Mursia, 1985), 7–67 et passim.

18. Manzoni mentions Vico in the *Discorso sopra alcuni punti della storia longobardica in Italia* (1822; 1845), II, 4, in *Tutte le opere*, vol. 4, *Saggi storici e politici*, ed. Fausto Ghisalberti (1963), 25–44, in which he praises Vico for his wide-ranging imagination and for the breathtaking scope of his historical system. In Manzoni's view, Vico's approach serves, at least in a procedural sense, as a complement and potential corrective to Muratori's concern for single details. But despite the ever-present interest in the nature and workings of divine Providence in the *Scienza nuova*, Manzoni does not refer specifically to this aspect of Vico's thought.

19. The question of ideology, which in some fashion or other has occupied almost every critic on the left writing about Manzoni in the postwar period, has two repeatedly acknowledged touchstones, De Sanctis and Gramsci. For several

of the most important of these postwar studies, see Angelo Romanò, "Manzoni," *Officina*, no. 3 (September 1955), 87–91; Alberto Moravia, "Alessandro Manzoni o l'ipotesi di un realismo cattolico" (1960), in *L'uomo come fine e altri saggi*, 2d ed., Opere complete di Alberto Moravia, 15 (Milan: Bompiani, 1964), 303–43; Alberto Asor Rosa, *Scrittori e popolo: Il populismo nella letteratura italiana contemporanea*, 8th ed., Saggistica, 3 (Rome: Savelli, 1965), 36–39; Enzo Noè Girardi (writing in opposition to Moravia, with the end of situating Manzoni in terms of his predecessors rather than in terms of succeeding literature and philosophy), *Manzoni "reazionario": Cinque saggi sui Promessi Sposi*, Saggi e monografie di letteratura (Bologna: Cappelli, 1966); Natalino Sapegno, *Ritratto di Manzoni e altri saggi* (Bari: Laterza, 1966), 45–133; Gian Franco Venè, *Capitale e letteratura*, I Garzanti (1972; rpt. Milan: Garzanti, 1974), 74–93; Gianni Scalia, "Manzoni a sinistra," *Italianistica* 2, no. 1 (1973): 21–42; Salinari, "La struttura ideologica dei 'Promessi sposi'" (1974; 1979); Sanguineti, "Glosse a Salinari" (1974); Guido Guglielmi, *Ironia e negazione*, La ricerca letteraria, Serie critica, 24 (Turin: Einaudi, 1974); Timpanaro, "Antileopardiani e neomoderati nella sinistra italiana" (1975–76); Dombroski, "The Seicento as Tragedy: Providence and the 'Bourgeois' in *I Promessi Sposi*" (1976); Vittorio Spinazzola, "'I promessi sposi' e il mondo moderno," *Belfagor* 32, no. 3 (1977), reprinted as "Manzoni e il mondo moderno," in *Il libro per tutti: Saggio sui "Promessi sposi,"* Nuova biblioteca di cultura, 246 (Rome: Riuniti, 1983), 7–24; Arcangelo Leone de Castris, *L'impegno di Manzoni*, La civiltà europea (Florence: Sansoni, 1978); Dombroski, "The Ideological Question in Manzoni" (1981); and Sergio Zatti, "Effetti di compensazione nello stile e nell'ideologia dei 'Promessi Sposi,'" *Italianistica* 11, nos. 2–3 (1982): 213–26. The various earlier stages of ideological assessment can be traced through Giancarlo Vigorelli's huge critical anthology, *Manzoni pro e contro*, 3 vols. (Milan: Istituto di Propaganda Libraria, 1975–76). For Giorgio Bàrberi Squarotti's recent attempt to debunk Gramsci as a reader of *I Promessi sposi* (at the outset of Bàrberi Squarotti's endeavors to read the novel within a strict framework of Christian symbolism), see *Il romanzo contro la storia: Studi sui "Promessi Sposi,"* Letteratura e cultura dell'Italia unita, 12 (Milan: Vita e Pensiero, 1980), 9. In response see also Baldi, *"I promessi sposi"* (1985).

20. Claudio Varese points out the increasing complexity of Manzoni's economic theories and the concomitant attenuation of his earlier belief (deriving from Enlightenment thought) in human reason as adequate to redress all economic ills. Varese contrasts two explanations of economic phenomena in *Fermo e Lucia* with those in the published versions of the novel in his *Fermo e Lucia: Un'esperienza manzoniana interrotta*, Studi critici, 9 (Florence: La Nuova Italia, 1964), 96.

21. The employment of this figure for the worldly production of discourse and meaning also has a lengthy tradition in philosophical writing. See, for example, Socrates' comments in the *Theaetetus* 156 c–d, in *The Dialogues of Plato*,

ed., trans. B[enjamin] Jowett, 4th ed., 4 vols. (Oxford: Clarendon Press, 1953), vol. 3.

22. For helpful discussions of the role of Providence both in Manzoni's novel (almost all of which stem from Momigliano's seminal and often disputed characterization of the novel as the epic of Providence) and in Manzoni's religious thought, see Rocco Montano, *Manzoni o del lieto fine*, Criterion, 2 (Naples: Conte, 1958); Ferruccio Ulivi, *Manzoni: Storia e Provvidenza*, L'ippogrifo, 6 (Rome: Bonacci, 1974); Chiari, *Manzoni il credente*, "La corona d'argento," Letteratura italiana (Milan: Istituto di Propaganda Libraria, 1979); De Michelis, "Pessimismo mondano e ottimismo provvidenziale nei 'Promessi sposi,'" in *La vergine e il drago*, 7–33; Dombroski, "The Ideological Question in Manzoni"; and Carol Lazzaro-Weis, "The Providential Trap: Some Remarks on Fictional Strategies in *I promessi sposi*," *Stanford Italian Review* 4, no. 1 (1984): 93–106.

23. Olga Ragusa, "Imitation and Originality in Manzoni's Romantic Theory," *Le parole e le idee* 6, nos. 3–4 (1964): 219–28. On the development and complexity of Manzoni's aesthetic theories, in his own writings as well as in relation to competing theories of the period, see also Barbara Reynolds, *The Linguistic Writings of Alessandro Manzoni: A Textual and Chronological Reconstruction* (Cambridge: W. Heffer & Sons, 1950); Dante Isella, "Introduzione," in Alessandro Manzoni, *Postille al vocabolario della Crusca nell'edizione veronese*, ed. Dante Isella, Documenti di filologia, 7 (Milan: Ricciardi, 1964), vii–xviii; and Mario Puppo, *Poesia e verità: Interpretazioni manzoniane*, Biblioteca di cultura contemporanea, 137 (Messina and Florence: D'Anna, 1979). For brief commentaries on the close relation in Manzoni's thought between language and its practical use in society, see Maria Corti, "Uno scrittore in cerca della lingua," *L'approdo letterario* 10, no. 27 (1964): 3–20, esp. 12; and Vittorio Spinazzola, ed., *I promessi sposi*, 3d ed., I Garzanti, 382 (Milan: Garzanti, 1972), 11. On the relation between rhetoric and logic in Manzoni's aesthetic theories, and with particular attention to his *Storia della colonna infame*, see Angelo R. Pupino, *"Il vero solo è bello": Manzoni tra retorica e logica*, Saggi, 221 (Bologna: Il Mulino, 1982).

24. In regard to general questions of Manzoni's style as technique and meaning, see (on style and the mixture of narrative voices) Giuseppe De Robertis, *Primi studi manzoniani e altre cose*, Quaderni di letteratura e d'arte (Florence: Le Monnier, 1949), 3–110; (on style as both form and sense) Giovanni Nencioni, "Conversioni dei 'Promessi Sposi,'" *La rassegna della letteratura italiana* 60, no. 1 (1956): 53–68; (on linguistic parodies) Giorgio Petrocchi, *La tecnica manzoniana del dialogo*, Saggi di letteratura italiana, 10 (Florence: Le Monnier, 1959); (on rhetorical levels and stylistics) Giorgio Bàrberi Squarotti, *Teoria e prove dello stile di Manzoni*, I quaderni di Sigma (Milan: Silva, 1965); (on literary irony and social class) Guglielmi, *Ironia e negazione* (1974); and (on irony and metalanguage) Ezio Raimondi, *Il romanzo senza idillio: Saggio sui "Promessi Sposi"* (Turin:

Einaudi, 1974), 223–47, 250–307. Romano Amerio discusses Manzoni's views of the importance of both language's *use* in the world and its potential for *abuse* (as a key to human error) in his extensive commentary on *La morale cattolica, Osservazioni sulla morale cattolica*, ed. Romano Amerio, 3 vols. (Milan and Naples: Ricciardi, 1965), 3:106–17, 125–27.

25. Italo Calvino discusses the significance of these "biblioteche," in addition to questions of language and writing as worldly power, in "Il romanzo dei rapporti di forza," in Ballerini, *Atti del convegno manzoniano di Nimega*, 215–25, reprinted as "I *Promessi Sposi*: Il romanzo dei rapporti di forza," in *Una pietra sopra: Discorsi di letteratura e società*, Gli struzzi, 219 (Turin: Einaudi, 1980), 267–78.

26. The most important treatments of the effects and the implications of self-consciousness in *I Promessi Sposi*—all of which have been mentioned earlier in regard to specific issues—are Romagnoli, "Lingua e società nei *Promessi Sposi*" (1973); Calvino, "Il romanzo dei rapporti di forza" (1973); Raimondi, *Il romanzo senza idillio* (1974); Ambrose, "Error and the Abuse of Language in the 'Promessi Sposi'" (1977); Ficara, "Renzo, l'allievo delle Muse" (1977), and "Le parole e la peste in Manzoni" (1981); De Rienzo, *L'avventura della parola nei 'Promessi sposi'* (1980); and Spinazzola, *Il libro per tutti* (1983), esp. 229–76. There is also an earlier and extremely impressionistic (though lengthy) treatment of the topic: Giuseppe Sertoli, "Lettura metaromanzesca della prima pagina dei 'Promessi Sposi,'" *Il cristallo* 13, no. 3 (1971): 67–86. A recent structuralist reading of the novel points toward (though does not actually provide) another way of treating the "dédoublement" of the nineteenth-century narrator in relation to Manzoni's novel: Joanna Richardson, "Narrative Strategy in *I promessi sposi*," *Neophilologus* 68, no. 2 (1984): 214–24.

Chapter 2. Verga's "Rosso Malpelo"

1. In the introduction to "L'amante di Gramigna" ("Gramigna's Mistress"), Verga describes this illusion as one of the primary goals of his method: "L'opera d'arte sembrerà *essersi fatta da sé*" (Giovanni Verga, *Tutte le novelle*, edited with an introduction by Carla Riccardi, I Meridiani [Milan: Mondadori, 1979], 203; translated in *The She-Wolf and Other Stories*, ed. Giovanni Cecchetti, 2d ed. rev. [Berkeley and Los Angeles: University of California Press, 1973], 88). It is especially lamentable that the preface to *I Malavoglia* has regularly been omitted from the English translations. Cecchetti, however, has translated it himself and added it to his recent reedition of Raymond Rosenthal's fine 1964 translation, *The House by the Medlar Tree* (Berkeley and Los Angeles: University of California Press, 1983).

2. Since Luigi Russo first described the story as "il racconto più organico" ("the most organic story") of *Vita dei campi* (in his *Giovanni Verga* [1919; rpt.

Bari: Laterza, 1976], 95), many other writers have characterized the novella as Verga's most unified, most important, or simply as his best. The importance of the story is further indicated by Romano Luperini's dedication of an entire monograph to it, *Verga e le strutture narrative del realismo: Saggio su "Rosso Malpelo,"* Guide di cultura contemporanea, Sezione letteraria (Padua: Liviana, 1976).

3. "Ieli the Shepherd" and "The She-Wolf." The strongest link among the stories is usually asserted to be that between "Rosso Malpelo" and "Jeli," though at times this connection is described as one of contrast rather than of similarity.

In an interesting aside, Mario Petroni comments on the two stories as examples of the dark side of the normally harmless late *Ottocento*–early *Novecento* "fanciullo pestifero" ("little brat") genre of bourgeois children's literature—a genre including not only Collodi's *Pinocchio* but also works by such non-Italian authors as Twain, Robert Louis Stevenson, and Dickens—in *Effetto infanzia: Viaggio nell'immaginario,* "Controcampo," 26 (Rome: Armando, 1978), 73.

4. Verga, *Tutte le novelle,* ed. Riccardi, 173; *The She-Wolf and Other Stories,* ed. Cecchetti, 65; both hereafter cited by page numbers in the text. I have altered Cecchetti's English translation in one or two instances for the sake of accuracy regarding specific points of interpretation. The chapter epigraph is taken from an earlier edition of the novella, and the translation is mine.

The story first appeared in *Il Fanfulla,* 2 August and 9 August 1878. Riccardi follows the 1880 edition of *Vita dei campi* published by Treves (though introducing corrections of what she judges to be printer's errors and author's oversights) and includes variants from the deluxe edition of 1897 in the critical apparatus. In the notes following the text (pp. 1008–18), Riccardi offers an account of her editorial procedures and explains her disagreement with Cecchetti and others over which of the several editions is to be preferred. For another discussion, see her "Il problema filologico di 'Vita dei campi,'" *Studi di filologia italiana* 35 (1977): 301–36. Romano Luperini also treats the various editions of "Rosso Malpelo" in the first part of his *Verga e le strutture narrative del realismo,* 20–40, and he includes the entire 1878 *Il Fanfulla* redaction of the story in an appendix, 117–29.

5. This process of education, in which Malpelo demonstrates the force of willful action in relation to the internalization and then the repetition of the lessons he has learned from his experiences, has been noted by several of the story's most perceptive commentators, including Alberto Asor Rosa, "Il primo e l'ultimo uomo del mondo: Indagine sulle strutture narrative e sociologiche in 'Vita dei campi,'" (1968), in *Il caso Verga: Con scritti di A. Asor Rosa, V. Masiello, G. Petronio, R. Luperini, B. Biral,* ed. Alberto Asor Rosa, Problemi-Libri, 5 (Palermo: Palumbo, 1972), 74–76; Vittorio Spinazzola, "La verità dell'essere: *Nedda, Rosso Malpelo, La roba*" (1972), in *Verismo e positivismo,* I Garzanti-Argomenti, 17 (Milan: Garzanti, 1977), 56–59; Guido Baldi, "*Rosso Malpelo* tra

apologia indiretta e negazione" (1973), in *L'artificio della regressione: Tecnica narrativa e ideologia nel Verga verista*, Le forme del significato, 30 (Naples: Liguori, 1980), 61–65; Carlo Muscetta (in a series of university lectures on which notes were taken by C. Sciré and published by Luperini), in Luperini, "Giovanni Verga," *Il secondo Ottocento: Lo stato unitario e l'età del positivismo* in *La letteratura italiana: Storia e testi*, Grandi opere, vol. 18, tome 2, ch. 14 (Bari: Laterza, 1975), 230; Roberto Bigazzi, *Su Verga novelliere*, Saggi di varia umanità, n.s. 18 (Pisa: Nistri-Lischi, 1975), 44–48; Sergio Campailla, "Apparenza e realtà nelle strutture di 'Rosso Malpelo,'" in *Anatomie verghiane*, Letteratura italiana e comparata, 8 (Bologna: Pàtron, 1978), 193–95; and Giorgio Bàrberi Squarotti, "Il filosofo nella cava," in *Giovanni Verga: Le finzioni dietro il verismo*, Biblioteca di letteratura e storia, 11 (Palermo: Flaccovio, 1982), 91–148, esp. 108–16. Specifically on the relation between father and son, see Carlo A. Augieri, "La struttura della parentela come 'codice narrativo' in 'Vita dei campi,'" in C. A. Augieri et al., *Verga: L'ideologia, le strutture narrative, il "caso" critico*, ed. Romano Luperini, Edizioni Milella (Lecce: Milella, 1982), 49–59. The first of these studies, Asor Rosa's essay of 1968, has proven a seminal text for the subsequent social and literary revaluation of *Vita dei campi*.

6. Spinazzola characterizes these objects as "gli oggetti sacri del suo culto" in *Verismo e positivismo*, 63.

7: *Verismo e positivismo*, 57–58.

8. Campailla, "Apparenza e realtà nelle strutture di 'Rosso Malpelo,'" 193.

9. For an example of the connection with Judas in the mind of the populace, see Giuseppe Pitrè, *Proverbi siciliani*, ed. Aurelio Rigoli, introd. Giovanni Sprini, Biblioteca delle tradizioni popolari siciliane (Palermo: Il Vespro, 1978), 1:174–75.

10. Giovanni Cecchetti, "Il testo di 'Vita dei campi' e le correzioni verghiane" (1957), in *Il Verga maggiore: Sette studi*, Collana critica, 83 (Florence: La Nuova Italia, 1968), 58. Cecchetti's contribution to Verga studies in regard to the text of *Vita dei campi*, both in his careful readings and in his virtual rediscovery and detailed consideration of the 1897 edition, remains of fundamental importance. Campailla makes a point similar to Cecchetti's concerning the story's unity, though Campailla sees the details in the reference to the drama as too openly polemical in regard to Verga's presentation of class differences and economic motivations rather than as a question of the appropriateness of the reference for the representation of everyday life. See "Apparenza e realtà nelle strutture di 'Rosso Malpelo,'" 171–72. On the symbolic import of the ambience of the theater here and elsewhere in Verga's narratives, see Bàrberi Squarotti, "Il filosofo nella cava," 91–92, n. 1.

11. Giovanni Pirodda also discusses the importance of the myth of the lost miner in the context of the relation between man and beast, in *L'eclissi dell'au-*

tore: Tecnica ed esperimenti verghiani, Saggi, 7 (Cagliari: Editrice Democratica Sarda, 1976), 59–62, 77–79.

12. Russo refers to Malpelo's evil from the boy's perspective after the death of his father ("nequizia castigatrice d'altra nequizia"; "evil that castigates other evil"), although he extends this observation, rightly, to a notion of the correction of original sin that would pass beyond Malpelo's "vendetta" to include all society ("Per correggere quasi un peccato originale del mondo"; "To correct what is almost an original sin of the world"), in *Giovanni Verga*, 97. On Malpelo's psychological introjection of his role as scapegoat, see especially Luperini, *Verga e le strutture narrative del realismo*, 91–93.

13. On the difficulty of determining the temporal sequence of events within the story see Cecchetti, "Aspetti della prosa di 'Vita dei campi'" (1956), in *Il Verga maggiore*, 46. Pirodda, however, establishes the "'processo' narrativo" by considering the motivations expressed within the novella's skewed "logic" of presentation, in *L'eclissi dell'autore*, 65–68. Of course, Pirodda was not the first to do this: see also Russo, *Giovanni Verga*, 97.

14. The most precise and useful discussion of the novella's varying perspectives is Luperini's "Postilla su *Rosso Malpelo*," added to *L'orgoglio e la disperata rassegnazione: Natura e società, maschera e realtà nell'ultimo Verga*, Saggistica, 61 (Rome: Savelli, 1974), 79–82, and reprinted in part in *Verga e le strutture narrative del realismo*. Luperini responds to and expands upon Baldi's notion of three perspectives, as set forth in Baldi's 1973 article on the novella, "Ideologia e tecnica narrativa in 'Rosso Malpelo,'" *Lettere italiane* 25, no. 4, revised as "*Rosso Malpelo* tra apologia indiretta e negazione," in *L'artificio della regressione*.

15. The oddity of this "explanatory" series has regularly received commentary in recent studies. See, for example, Asor Rosa, "Il primo e l'ultimo uomo del mondo," 63; Spinazzola (who links the effect of this opening to an implicit appeal to the reader), "La verità dell'essere," 51; Baldi, "*Rosso Malpelo* tra apologia indiretta e negazione," 41–42; Luperini, "Postilla su Rosso Malpelo," 78; Muscetta, in Luperini, "Giovanni Verga," *Il secondo Ottocento*, 229; Campailla, "Apparenza e realtà nelle strutture di 'Rosso Malpelo,'" 162; and Giovanni Cecchetti, *Giovanni Verga*, TWAS, 489 (Boston: Twayne, 1978), 63.

16. Luperini, for example, in his "Postilla su *Rosso Malpelo*," 78, proceeds directly from the "perché . . . perché" of the first paragraph to the later explanation of why Malpelo's mother never caressed her son: "Il certo era che nemmeno sua madre aveva avuta mai una carezza da lui, e *quindi* non gliene faceva mai" (180; "One thing was certain: not even his mother had ever had a caress from him, and *so* she never gave him any," 73).

17. Luperini compares the details of the financial references in Verga's story to the information in the Franchetti-Sonnino parliamentary report in *Verga e le strutture narrative del realismo*, 3–19, esp. 11–12; he also discusses the relation between the report and certain parts of *I Malavoglia* in "Sulla costruzione dei

'Malavoglia': Nuove ipotesi di lavoro," in *Verga: L'ideologia, le strutture narrative, il "caso" critico*, 67–76.

For the report itself, see Leopoldo Franchetti and Sidney Sonnino, *Inchiesta in Sicilia*, introd. Enea Cavalieri, historical note by Zeffiro Ciuffoletti, Saggi Vallecchi, 15, 2 vols. (Florence: Vallecchi, 1974). Beyond its wealth of background information, the report is especially interesting in regard to "Rosso Malpelo" for its concluding section on child labor in the mines, entitled "Il lavoro dei fanciulli nelle zolfare siciliane," 2:269–79, from which Verga could get the details of children's salaries and treatment as well as the typical ages of the "carusi" (usually 8–11, sometimes beginning at 7 years old and perhaps earlier, though Franchetti and Sonnino could not actually confirm any age younger than 7). Verga almost certainly knew the report well, since, as Luperini notes, the preface to *I Malavoglia* repeats some of the sentiments *and* some of the language of the report's introduction (dated 20 December 1876), v–vi.

18. For overviews of this concern in terms of legislative interest and action (initiated in the late 1870s by Depretis), see Giulio Monteleone, "La legislazione sociale al Parlamento italiano: La legge del 1886 sul lavoro dei fanciulli," *Movimento operaio e socialista* 20, no. 4 (1974): 229–84, and Ciuffoletti, "Nota storica," in Franchetti and Sonnino, *Inchiesta in Sicilia*, 2:281–343. The Franchetti-Sonnino report also mentions contemporary legislation in Germany (2:278–79 n. 9). Along with the many political problems that such reforms faced, they also encountered, in the case of the mines, special opposition on practical grounds: because the underground galleries had been designed and constructed specifically with child labor in mind, they were too low for fully grown adults to move about in.

Significantly, Franchetti and Sonnino, in their description of child labor in the Sicilian mines, abandon the report's pretense to concern only for economic and social facts and consider the problem from an openly "humanitarian" perspective (2:269). The report describes the children's miserable and extremely hazardous working conditions as well as the damage occasionally done thereby to familial relations. In conclusion, the authors (who after the report's appearance, as Ciuffoletti notes, p. 335, were accused by some of "Gefühlsozialismus," or "sentimental socialism") propose a possible route to rectification by way of national legislation, while they lay the responsibility for the miners' conditions on a single group: the *padroni* (2:278–79).

19. In regard to the characteristics of the collective in the mine and the contrast between that group and the (ideal) familial nucleus, see Asor Rosa, "Il primo e l'ultimo uomo del mondo," 68–85.

20. On Verga's view of postunification history from the perspective of his region and of his class, see especially Muscetta, in Luperini, "Giovanni Verga," 231; Luperini, *Verga e le strutture narrative del realismo*, 82–86; and Campailla, "Apparenza e realtà nelle strutture di 'Rosso Malpelo,'" 201–4.

21. Luperini, *Verga e le strutture narrative*, 94; on this topic see also 72–73, 113.

Chapter 3. Dossi and D'Annunzio

1. Dossi himself discussed *umorismo* both as a literary and as a moral phenomenon throughout his diaries, published as *Note azzurre*, ed. Dante Isella, Classici, 10, 2 vols. (Milan: Adelphi, 1964).

2. References to Dossi's novels, cited by page number in the text, are to the following editions: *La vita di Alberto Pisani*, introd. Alberto Arbasino, Centopagine, 44 (rpt. of 1st ed. [1870]; Turin: Einaudi, 1976); and *La desinenza in A*, Afterword by Laura Barile (rpt. of 2d ed. [1884]; Milan: Garzanti, 1981). All translations are mine.

3. Francesca Tancini, "La parodia del romanzo ottocentesco nella *Vita di Alberto Pisani* di Carlo Dossi," *Giornale storico della letteratura italiana* 157, no. 499 (1980): 431–44.

4. Roberto Bigazzi, *I colori del vero: Vent'anni di narrativa, 1860–1880*, Saggi di varia umanità, 10 (Pisa: Nistri-Lischi, 1969), 190–92 (in which Bigazzi contrasts Dossi's conclusion with the similar conclusion of Igino Ugo Tarchetti's story "Bouvard" [1867]). Enrico Ghidetti also discusses the close relation between the scenes in these two narratives, but he unfortunately misses the *literary* point of Dossi's handling of this material; see his *Tarchetti e la scapigliatura lombarda*, Collana di saggi e studi di letteratura italiana, 3 (Naples: Libreria Scientifica, 1968), 206.

5. The similarity of certain aspects of Dossi's work to works of modern writers, in particular Gadda, has been discussed by a great number of Dossi's recent critics, among them Walter Pedullà, "Tre sperimentali richiamati in servizio: Nelle 'Note azzure' di Dossi idee 'giovani' di un secolo" (1965), in *La letteratura del benessere*, 2d rev. ed., L'analisi letteraria. Proposte e letture critiche, 6 (Rome: Bulzoni, 1973); Mirella Serri, *Carlo Dossi e il "racconto,"* Strumenti di ricerca, 6 (Rome: Bulzoni, 1975), 30, 76–77; and Elio Gioanola, *La Scapigliatura: Testi e commento*, Letteratura & Altro (Turin: Marietti, 1975), 179–80, and cf. 18. Much of this discussion stems from Gianfranco Contini's "Saggio introduttivo" to Gadda's *La cognizione del dolore* (Turin: Einaudi, 1963), 5–28, in which Contini paints Gadda's literary milieu with what might be termed a broad European brush.

6. The question of revolution of style or of content has drawn adherents to both sides, with Dante Isella's seminal work as a stylistic touchstone (*La lingua e lo stile di Carlo Dossi*, Documenti di filologia, 3 [Milan and Naples: Ricciardi, 1958]), and Gioanola attempting to bridge the gap, even while emphasizing style over content (*La Scapigliatura*, 179–80). See also Piero Nardi, *Scapigliatura: Da Giuseppe Rovani a Carlo Dossi* (Milan: Mondadori, 1968), 230, 246, et passim.

On the side of content see Francesco Spera, *Il principio dell'antiletteratura: Dossi—Faldella—Imbriani*, Le forme del significato, 17 (Naples: Liguori, 1976), 13–17 et passim (in which Spera discusses Dossi's utopian novel, *La colonia felice* [1874; *The Happy Colony*] as well as Dossi's other work); and Pedullà, "Tre sperimentali richiamati in servizio," 165. Gaetano Mariani tends to dissolve such questions of content versus style in the ideal world of literature itself, in his massive *Storia della Scapigliatura*, Aretusa, 25 (Caltanissetta and Rome: Sciascia, 1967), 519, 824–25.

7. Dossi's anticlericalism shows up in fascinating ways in the *Note azzurre*, in which he regularly inveighs against Pius IX (Giovanni Maria Mastai Ferretti), who held the pontificate from 1846 to 1878 and who, in 1870, the year of the appearance of *La vita di Alberto Pisani*, presided over both the declaration of papal infallibility and the final loss of the papal territories outside of the Vatican.

8. On the uniquely forceful if also reactionary ideological slant of D'Annunzio's major novels (encompassed in an engagingly lyrical structure), see Paolo Valesio, "The Lion and the Ass: The Case for D'Annunzio's Novels," *Yale Italian Studies* 1, no. 1 (1977): 67–82.

9. This is the sort of appeal to narcissism and power underlying Fascism later disparaged by Carlo Emilio Gadda in *Eros e Priapo: Da furore a cenere* (Milan: Garzanti, 1967).

10. Quotations from D'Annunzio's novels, cited by page numbers in the text, are from *Tutte le opere*, ed. Egidio Bianchetti, *Prose di romanzi* (Milan: Mondadori): *Trionfo della morte* in vol. 1 (1940), pp. 651–1049; *Il fuoco* in vol. 2 (1942), pp. 569–861. All translations are mine.

11. *Taccuini*, ed. Enrica Bianchetti and Roberto Forcella (Milan: Mondadori, 1965), 14, my italics.

12. For detailed treatment of this scene, as well as an extremely perceptive and cogent discussion of D'Annunzian imagery and thematics, see Ezio Raimondi, *Il silenzio della Gorgone*, La parola letteraria, 1 (Bologna: Zanichelli, 1980), 41–147, esp. 85–87. See also Jean-Claude Bouffard, "L'Artiste e ses doubles dans *Le Feu* de D'Annunzio et le *Dedalus* de Joyce," in *Le Double dans le romantisme anglo-américain*, introd. Christian La Cassagnère (Clermont-Ferrand: Association des Publications de la Faculté des Lettres et Sciences Humaines, 1984), 191–205, esp. 200–201.

13. Giorgio Luti, *La cenere dei sogni: Studi dannunziani* (Pisa: Nistri-Lischi, 1973), 138. (Luti is considering especially *Il fuoco* and *Forse che sì forse che no* [1910; *Perhaps So, Perhaps Not*]). A similar point in regard to *Il fuoco* is made by Jacques Goudet (though he sees this effect in a distinctly negative light—in common, it must be said, with many of the critics of D'Annunzio's prose who prefer definite narrative order to experiments with lyrical fluidity) in his *D'Annunzio romanziere*, Biblioteca di "Lettere italiane," 15 (Florence: Olschki, 1976), 227–45.

For Benedetto Croce's description see "Gabriele D'Annunzio" (1903), in *La letteratura della nuova Italia: Saggi critici*, 4 vols., Scritti di storia letteraria e politica, 6 (Bari: Laterza, 1915), 4:10. Salvatore Battaglia argues instructively against the limitations of Croce's position in "La testimonianza di Gabriele D'Annunzio" (1963), in *Testimonianze del Novecento letterario* (Naples: Liguori, 1972), 139–66, esp. 159–65.

14. *La vittoria dell'uomo* and the *Trionfo della vita* (*Triumph of Life*) were projected by D'Annunzio as the second and third novels in the "Romanzi del Melagrano" trilogy, but they were not written. Marziano Guglielminetti discusses some of the autobiographical elements of the D'Annunzio/Effrena relationship as writers in *Struttura e sintassi del romanzo italiano del primo Novecento*, I quaderni di Sigma, 1 (Milan: Silva, 1964), 145–60.

15. Emerico Giachery discusses the narcissistic fear of temporal progression in *Verga e D'Annunzio* (Milan: Silva, 1968), 320ff.

16. Carlo Salinari, *Miti e coscienza del decadentismo italiano: D'Annunzio, Pascoli, Fogazzaro, e Pirandello* (Milan: Feltrinelli, 1960), 105.

17. The tempting exhortation that both precedes and follows this passage and that runs throughout the middle section of the narrative ("Servire, servire!" 656, 684, et passim) is another of D'Annunzio's bows to Wagner, this time in the form of a quotation from *Parsifal*.

18. See Fredric Jameson, "*La Cousine Bette* and Allegorical Realism," *PMLA* 86, no. 2 (1971): 241–54. On D'Annunzio's affirmations of totality conceived of as "strategies," see Vittorio Roda, *La strategia della totalità: Saggio su Gabriele D'Annunzio*, Saggi, 20 (Bologna: M. Boni, 1978).

Chapter 4. Pirandello's *Il fu Mattia Pascal* and *Uno, nessuno e centomila*

1. Pirandello's major novels, in chronological order, are *Il fu Mattia Pascal* (1904; *The Late Mattia Pascal*), *Suo marito* (1911; *Her Husband*), *I vecchi e i giovani* (1913; *The Old and the Young*), *Quaderni di Serafino Gubbio operatore* (1915–16; *The Notebooks of Serafino Gubbio, Cameraman*, originally entitled *Si gira* . . . , or *Shoot!*), and *Uno, nessuno e centomila* (1925–26; *One, None, and a Hundred Thousand*).

2. Antonio Gramsci, *Quaderni del carcere: Edizione critica dell'Istituto Gramsci*, ed. Valentino Gerratana, NUE, 1, 4 vols. (Turin: Einaudi, 1975), 2:704–5, 3:1670–74. Gramsci felt that Pirandello's resolutely antimelodramatic "critical" attitude was even more significant for its expression of intellectual and moral modernity than it was for its artistic effects (2:1195–97). When Gramsci mentions verismo in this context he is not talking about Verga's narratives.

3. Although Pirandello's works demonstrate originality and urgency, these attributes did not ensure that they would avoid either logical mystifications or markedly regressive social functions even while they denounced the entrenched

beliefs and habits of the bourgeoisie of their time. For further discussion of this point, see Robert S. Dombroski, *Le totalità dell'artificio: Ideologia e forma nel romanzo di Pirandello*, Biblioteca di cultura (Padua: Liviana, 1978), 1–10. Dombroski argues in part against the progressivist position staked out for Pirandello by Arcangelo Leone de Castris in his overly sanguine essay, "Il romanzo di Pirandello, fra tradizione e avanguardia," in *Il "romanzo" di Pirandello*, ed. Enzo Lauretta (Palermo: Palumbo, 1976), 7–21, which in turn picks up Leone de Castris' argument from his earlier study, *Il decadentismo italiano: Svevo, Pirandello, D'Annunzio*, Ideologia e società (Bari: De Donato, 1974), 155–207.

4. All citations are from *Il fu Mattia Pascal*, in *Tutti i romanzi*, ed. Giovanni Macchia and Mario Costanzo, introd. Giovanni Macchia, I Meridiani, Opere di Luigi Pirandello, 2 vols. (Milan: Mondadori, 1973), 1:317–578; and, for the English translation, which on occasion I have altered slightly for accuracy, *The Late Mattia Pascal*, trans. William Weaver (Garden City, N.Y.: Doubleday, 1964). Page references are included in the text.

5. The editorial notes to the beginning of chapter 5 in the Italian edition (pp. 1010–12) point out that the text's present one-sentence denomination of the widow as a "witch" ("La strega non si sapeva dar pace," 353), replaces the first edition's lengthy introductory discourse on witchcraft and, at least by allusion, the editor believes, on theosophy (which would thus tie this segment of the narrative to the later discussions of theosophy and *lanterninosofia* in Paleari's household in Rome). Olga Ragusa treats these textual changes and the editor's discussion of them in the context of both *Il fu Mattia Pascal* and Pirandello's essay *L'umorismo* in her *Luigi Pirandello: An Approach to His Theatre*, Writers of Italy, 8 (Edinburgh: Edinburgh University Press, 1980), 28–30. The entire topic of parapsychology and theosophy in Pirandello's works, with particular attention to *Il fu Mattia Pascal*, is treated by Antonio Illiano in his *Metapsichica e letteratura in Pirandello*, introd. Graziella Corsinovi, Collana di saggi e documentazioni del Centro nazionale di studi pirandelliani, 2 (Florence: Vallecchi, 1982), esp. 31–45.

6. *L'umorismo*, in *Saggi, poesie scritti varii*, ed. Manlio Lo Vecchio-Musti, Opere di Luigi Pirandello, 6 (Milan: Mondadori, 1960), 15–160; trans. and introd. Antonio Illiano and Daniel P. Testa as *On Humor* (Chapel Hill: University of North Carolina Press, 1974). Some of the categories adopted in the essay recall the thought of Henri Bergson as well as that of Gabriel Séailles.

7. Giacomo Debenedetti singles out the essay's dedication in the course of his extensive discussion of the novel in *Il romanzo del Novecento: Quaderni inediti*, introd. Eugenio Montale, Saggi blu (Milan: Garzanti, 1976), 391, as do Marziano Guglielminetti in his *Struttura e sintassi del romanzo italiano del primo Novecento*, I quaderni di Sigma, 1 (Milan: Silva, 1964), 90; Leone de Castris in *Il decadentismo italiano*, 178; Edoardo Ferrario in his monograph, *L'occhio di Mat-*

tia Pascal: Poetica e estetica in Pirandello, Strumenti di ricerca, 21 (Rome: Bulzoni, 1978), 11; and Ragusa, *Luigi Pirandello*, 18.

8. It is perhaps the peculiarity of *both* parts of this requisite combination of predisposition and experience that accounts for the rarity of the resultant point of view. In the essay on umorismo Pirandello mentions a few literary precursors to this general perspective (Spanish, Anglo-Saxon, and German as well as Italian), but he repeatedly stresses the dearth of genuine umoristi preceding his work (*L'umorismo*, 104–8 et passim; *On Humor*, 91–94 et passim). Interestingly enough, in this regard Pirandello mentions "the poets of the *Scapigliatura lombarda*" and the Mantuan author Alberto Cantoni, often discussed in connection with the movement (and to whose work Pirandello dedicated an entire essay in 1905, rpt. in *Saggi, poesie scritti varii*, 363–87), but he does not mention Dossi.

9. The most systematic treatment of the theme and the effects of doubling in Pirandello's work, as well as in his biography and correspondence, is Jean-Michel Gardair's *Pirandello: Fantasmes et logiques du double*, Thèmes et textes (Paris: Larousse, 1972). For discussion of the narratives, see especially pp. 33–54.

10. *L'umorismo*, 150; *On Humor*, 136.

11. At least to Croce, such complexity seemed mere confusion. See his "Luigi Pirandello," in *La letteratura della nuova Italia*, Scritti di storia letteraria e politica, 33, Saggi critici, 6 (Bari: Laterza, 1940), ch. 63, pp. 359–77, esp. 362–63, in which Croce responds to Pirandello's comments in *L'umorismo* and discusses what he terms the "capostipite della sua nuova maniera, quel romanzo del *Fu Mattia Pascal*" ("founder of his new style, that novel of the *Late Mattia Pascal*"). In this general context, on the other hand, Roberto Salsano emphasizes the crucial embedding of not knowing *within* knowledge in Pirandello's thought (typical of classical skepticism) in his *Pirandello novelliere e Leopardi*, La Giara, Studi pirandelliani (Rome: Lucarini, 1980), 9.

12. The function of artistic and psychological self-reflexivity in *Il fu Mattia Pascal* is pointed out by Dombroski in *Le totalità dell'artificio* in the sense of "Il romanzo [che] diventa simbolo di se stesso, metaopera, che non rimanda ad altro che ai processi mentali che l'hanno creato," 54 ("The novel [that] becomes a symbol of itself, a metawork that does not lead to anything other than the mental processes that created it"). Dombroski links this effect to European modernism. In a different context Dombroski also notes the reflexivity of Pirandello's next novel, *Suo marito*, in which "l'oggetto della narrazione . . . è l'arte: più precisamente il rapporto tra natura, arte e produzione artistica" (83) ("the object of the narration . . . is art: more precisely, the relation between nature, art, and artistic production").

13. The problem of freedom in relation to the will of the individual is the topic of a recent discussion by Madeleine Cincotta (with reference to *Il fu Mattia Pascal* in a specifically Sartrean context), in "Existentialist Freedom in Luigi Pirandello," *Italian Quarterly* 22, no. 86 (1981): 57–67. This topic in Pirandello's

work has a huge critical bibliography, some of the most significant contributions to which include Leone de Castris, *Storia di Pirandello*, 2d ed., Biblioteca di cultura moderna, 571 (1962; Bari: Laterza, 1966); Franz Rauhut, *Der junge Pirandello; oder, Das Werden eines existentiellen Geistes* (Munich: Beck, 1964); Lucio Lugnani, *Pirandello: Letteratura e teatro* (Florence: La Nuova Italia, 1970); Claudio Vicentini, *L'estetica di Pirandello*, Saggi di estetica e di poetica (Milan: Mursia, 1970); Debenedetti, *Il romanzo del Novecento*, esp. 333–47; and Graziella Corsinovi, *Pirandello e l'espressionismo: Analogie culturali e anticipazioni espressive nella prima narrativa* (Genoa: Tilgher, 1979).

14. The close relationship between *Il fu Mattia Pascal* and *Uno, nessuno e centomila* has often been described, perhaps most incisively by Arminio Janner, who sees the later novel as being in the same line as *Il fu Mattia Pascal* and perceives that whereas *Il fu Mattia Pascal* treats the discovery of psychological relativism, in *Uno, nessuno e centomila* this topic becomes "il nocciolo, il senso stesso del libro" ("the core, the sense itself of the book"). See *Luigi Pirandello*, Collana critica, 44 (Florence: La Nuova Italia, 1948), 260. In this regard see also Corrado Donati, "La ricerca dell'identità da Pascal a Moscarda," in *La solitudine allo specchio*, La Giara, Studi pirandelliani (Rome: Lucarini, 1980), 47–79, for a discussion that takes into account more recent criticism and theory from Debenedetti to Lacan; and still more recently, Elio Gioanola's chapter, "La crisi dell'identità: dal *Fu Mattia Pascal* a *Uno, nessuno e centomila*," in *Pirandello e la follia*, Università, 6 (Genoa: Il Melangolo, 1983), 79–115.

15. The historical importance of the question of self-reflection and estrangement—not just for fiction writers but also for critics and critical movements of the period, such as Shklovsky and the Russian Formalists—is pointed out by Marziano Guglielminetti at the conclusion of an essay in which Guglielminetti attempts to reverse the emphasis of much of the contemporary criticism of Pirandello's work by situating Pirandello more precisely within his own historical and intellectual context (i.e., that of the 1920s and 1930s); see "Le vicende e i significativi di 'Uno, nessuno e centomila,'" in Lauretta, *Il "romanzo" di Pirandello*, 183–207. In this regard see also Glauco Cambon's brief but sensitive discussion of the withdrawal and gradual dissolution of the individual subject over the course of Pirandello's narratives, in "Pirandello as a Novelist," *Cesare Barbieri Courier* 9, no. 1 (1967): 16–19.

16. All references are to *Uno, nessuno e centomila*, in *Tutti i romanzi*, 2:737–902; and *One, None and a Hundred-thousand*, trans. Samuel Putnam (New York: Dutton, 1933), which I have altered for accuracy. Page numbers are included in the text.

17. Discussion of the pervasive effects of the imagery of mirroring in Pirandello's works began as early as Adriano Tilgher (see "Il teatro di Pirandello," in his *Studi sul teatro contemporaneo: Preceduti da un saggio su "L'arte come originalità e i problemi dell'arte,"* 2d ed. [Rome: Libreria di Scienze e lettere, 1923],

157–218) and has continued, through various shifts in critical approach, to the present day. In regard to this subject in *Uno, nessuno e centomila* see, for example: Renato Barilli, "La poetica dello specchio," in *La linea Svevo-Pirandello*, 3d ed., Civiltà letteraria del Novecento, Saggi, 18 (1972; Milan: Mursia, 1981), 211–15; Gian-Paolo Biasin, "Lo specchio di Moscarda" (1972) in *Malattie letterarie*, Nuovi saggi italiani (Milan: Bompiani, 1976), 125–55; English ed.: "Moscarda's Mirror," in *Literary Diseases: Theme and Metaphor in the Italian Novel* (Austin: University of Texas Press, 1975), 100–126; Douglas Radcliff-Umstead, "Destruction of the Marionette," in *The Mirror of Our Anguish: A Study of Luigi Pirandello's Narrative Writings* (Rutherford, N.J.: Fairleigh Dickinson University Press; London: Associated University Presses, 1978), 269–93 (especially for his Lacanian interpretation of madness and possession, 292); Dombroski, "Il soggetto puro," in *Le totalità dell'artificio*, 119–35; and Corrado Donati, *La solitudine allo specchio*. For the progression of this and other topics from Pirandello's novelle to the novel, see Mario Aste, *La narrativa di Luigi Pirandello: Dalle novelle al romanzo "Uno, nessuno e centomila,"* Studia Humanitatis (Madrid: Porrúa Turanzas, 1979).

18. Mario Baratto discusses the effects of this seemingly vicious regress—in which the Pirandellian individual rebels from the fixed form of his mask only to end up caught inside another mask—in an essay on the development of Pirandello's theatre, "Per una storia del teatro di Pirandello," in *Atti del Congresso internazionale di studi pirandelliani*, Venice, 1961, Pubblicazioni dell'Istituto di Studi pirandelliani, Rome, 2 (Florence: Le Monnier, 1967), 285–302.

19. The image of the nose's appearance as at once insignificant and crucial was one of Pirandello's favorites. It also occurs in part 2 of the essay *L'umorismo* (153; *On Humor*, 138) and again in the essay's last pages, with special reference to Sterne (159–60; 145).

20. In *Le totalità dell'artificio* (156) Dombroski discusses the progression of this search for solutions (and the concomitant mystifications) in a non-Crocean context. He sees Pirandello's development as passing through three major phases that parallel the increasingly obvious failure of bourgeois institutions in Italy and the rise of Fascism: first, "La fuga provvisoria dalla realtà sociale, posta come alternativa ma *non* accettata come tale" ("The provisional flight from social reality, posed as an alternative but *not* accepted as such"), dominant in Pirandello's work up to 1916, and so including *Il fu Mattia Pascal;* second, the resolve to live "'fuori della società,' e cioè fuori dai limiti imposti dalle comuni esigenze razionali" ("'outside of society,' that is, outside of the limits imposed by the common exigencies of rationality"), as occurs, for example, in *Enrico IV*, 1922, *Sei personaggi*, 1921 and at the end of *Uno, nessuno e centomila*; and, third, the acceptance of the overriding principle of the irrational, "concretizzatosi nel mito (*La Nuova Colonia*, [1928])" ("realized in myth [*The New Colony*]"), which corresponds to the consolidation of the Fascist party's power and "a livello storico-

individuale, l'adesione formale di Pirandello al fascismo" ("on the level of individual history, Pirandello's formal adherence to fascism"). This last point, even more obviously than the two previous ones, is open to serious question, since Pirandello's relationship with the Fascist party was never simple or unreserved. Furthermore, such a tripartite division of the progression of Pirandello's ideas "in cui si unisce coerentemente la dimensione arte-vita a quella mitico-collettiva" ("in which the dimensions of art-life and of myth-collective are coherently united") is far too schematic, as Dombroski himself admits ("l'esame . . . sia pure schematico" ["the examination . . . albeit schematic"]). Nevertheless, Dombroski's attempt to provide a reasonable overview of the social, political, and ideological implications of Pirandello's thought—following his series of detailed readings, which are both broadly based and convincing—is of notable value. In this regard see also Gian Franco Venè's seminal (and highly polemical) *Pirandello fascista: La coscienza borghese tra ribellione e rivoluzione*, rev. ed., Saggi Marsilio, no. 96 (1971; Venice: Marsilio, 1981); Roberto Alonge's tendentious and, at least on *Il fu Mattia Pascal* and *Uno, nessuno e centomila*, very brief comments in his *Pirandello tra realismo e mistificazione*, Il sagittario, 8 (Naples: Guida, 1972), 161, 275, et passim; Leone de Castris' more general view of the relations between Pirandello's work and both the problem of decadence and the crisis of the liberal state in *Il decadentismo italiano*; and Dombroski's recent amplification of his position, "Pirandello: Fascismo e ontologia pura," in his *L'esistenza ubbidiente: Letterati italiani sotto il fascismo*, Esperienze, 99 (Naples: Guida, 1984), 51–70.

21. This relation, in terms of both parallels and significant divergences, is treated from several perspectives in Renato Barilli et al., *Il romanzo di Pirandello e Svevo*, ed. Enzo Lauretta, Collona di saggi e documentazioni del Centro nazionale di studi pirandelliani, 8 (Florence: Vallecchi, 1984).

Chapter 5. The Self-consciousness of *Zeno*

1. All references to Svevo's works, cited hereafter by page numbers in the text, are to Italo Svevo, *Opera omnia*, ed. and introd. Bruno Maier, 4 vols., vol. 2, pts. 1 and 2, *Romanzi*, vol. 3, *Racconti, Saggi, Pagine sparse* (Milan: Dall'Oglio, 1970 and 1968), with translations of *La coscienza di Zeno* from *Confessions of Zeno*, trans. Beryl De Zoete (1930; New York: Random House, 1958), which I have altered for accuracy. Translations of *Una vita*, of *Senilità* (1927 ed.), and of Svevo's diary are mine.

2. Giacomo Debenedetti singles out the attitude of the "osservatore" ("observer"), common to many of Svevo's central characters, in "Svevo e Schmitz" (1929), in his *Saggi critici: Seconda serie* (Milan: Il Saggiatore, 1971), 56.

3. Mario Fusco discusses this concluding scene in terms of Emilio's failures both at novel writing and at life in *Italo Svevo: Conscience et réalité*, Bibliothèque des Idées (Paris: Gallimard, 1973), 240–42. For discussion of the import of the

story's conclusion in the context of the entire novel and of Svevo's aesthetic development, see Eduardo Saccone, "Un'educazione sentimentale?" (January 1967), in *Il poeta travestito: Otto scritti su Svevo*, Saggi critici, 4 (Pisa: Pacini, 1977), 133–200; for the idealized concluding image considered in Freudian terms, see Paula Robison, "*Senilità*: The Secret of Svevo's Weeping Madonna," *Italian Quarterly* 14, no. 55 (1971): 61–84; and for a recent treatment of desire and temporality that takes its lead from this scene, see Gian-Paolo Biasin, "Un Deo gratias qualunque: Svevo, il linguaggio, il sapere," *Italica* 61, no. 2 (1984): 134–46.

4. Linda Hutcheon, *Narcissistic Narrative: The Metafictional Paradox* (Waterloo, Ontario: Wilfrid Laurier University Press, 1980; rpt. New York and London: Methuen, 1984), 132. The immediate context of this remark is Hutcheon's discussion of the Gruppo 63 and more specifically of Alfredo Giuliani's *Il giovane Max* (1972).

5. John Freccero treats *La coscienza di Zeno* in terms of the genre of the confessional autobiography (from Augustine and Dante to Rousseau, Dostoevsky, and Svevo), in "Zeno's Last Cigarette," *Modern Language Notes* 77, no. 1 (1962): 3–23.

6. At the beginning of "Zeno's Last Cigarette," Freccero notes the connection in this passage between writing and falsity, though he links the two directly together rather than including the crucial intermediary of standard Italian (as opposed to dialect). For discussion of the place of Triestine dialect and cultural tradition in this context, see Mario Lavagetto, *L'impiegato Schmitz e altri saggi su Svevo*, La ricerca letteraria, Serie critica, 34 (Turin: Einaudi, 1975), 103–7.

7. Gian-Paolo Biasin discusses the entire novel in terms of the basic metaphor of disease in "L'ultima bomba di Zeno," ch. 3 of *Malattie letterarie*, Nuovi saggi italiani, 18 (Milan: Bompiani, 1976), 81–124; English ed.: "Zeno's Last Bomb," in *Literary Diseases: Theme and Metaphor in the Italian Novel* (Austin: University of Texas Press, 1975), 63–99.

8. The patently Freudian aspects of the scene—as well as Svevo's ambivalence regarding Freudian thought—is treated succinctly by Paula Robison, "Svevo: Secrets of the Confessional," *Literature and Psychology* 20, no. 3 (1970): 101–14, esp. 104.

9. Elio Gioanola gives an overview of various possible positions (including those of Saccone, Lavagetto, and others) in regard to Zeno's illness and offers his own psychoanalytic interpretation in *Un killer dolcissimo: Indagine psicanalitica sull'opera di Italo Svevo*, Università, 1 (Genoa: Il Melangolo, 1979). See also Michel David, *La psicoanalisi nella cultura italiana*, introd. Cesare L. Musatti (Turin: Boringhieri, 1966), 379–404; Anthony Wilden, "Death, Desire, and Repetition in Svevo's Zeno," *Modern Language Notes* 84, no. 1 (1969): 98–119; Eduardo Saccone, *Commento a "Zeno." Saggio sul testo di Svevo*, Saggi, 133 (Bologna: Il Mulino, 1973); Cesare Musatti, "Svevo e la psicanalisi," *Belfagor* 29

(March 1974): 129–41; Lavagetto, *L'impiegato Schmitz;* and Franco Petroni, *L'inconscio e le strutture formali: Saggi su Italo Svevo,* Guide di cultura contemporanea (Padua: Liviana, 1979), 63–100. Despite the novel's appeal to this sort of reading, the fascination that a psychoanalytic approach holds is not felt by all critics. Renato Barilli, for example, attacks this sort of reading in the revised edition of his *La linea Svevo-Pirandello,* 3d ed., Civiltà letteraria del Novecento, Saggi, 18 (Milan: Mursia, 1981). On the other hand, Francesco Paolo Botti, Giancarlo Mazzacurati, and Matteo Palumbo defend it vigorously in their collection of essays, *Il secondo Svevo,* Teorie e Oggetti, 15 (Naples: Liguori, 1982).

10. Gioanola treats Zeno's limping in *La coscienza di Zeno,* along with that of another of Svevo's characters in the short story "La buonissima madre," in *Un killer dolcissimo,* 122–25.

11. Freccero, "Zeno's Last Cigarette." On the relation of disease and temporality in Svevo's novel see the seminal essay by Alain Robbe-Grillet, "Zeno's Sick Conscience" (1954), in *For a New Novel: Essays on Fiction,* trans. Richard Howard (New York: Grove Press, 1965), 89–94.

12. Glauco Cambon discusses Zeno's characteristic psychic internalization as well as his affirmations regarding the creation of images in "Zeno come anti-Faust," *Il verri* 11 (1963): 69–76.

13. The temporal disruption of the narrative is considered in relation to the novel's "specularity" by Évelyne Capiau-Laureys, "'La Coscienza di Zeno' d'Italo Svevo: Discours spéculaire d'un roman psychanalytique," *Onze Études sur la mise en abyme,* ed. Fernand Hallyn, special issue of *Romanica Gandensia* 17 (1980): 67–81. On the multiple levels (temporal as well as epistemological) of the narrative, see also Fusco, *Italo Svevo,* 321.

14. On the importance of the present moment as the attempted denial of temporal progression for Svevo and his characters, see Debenedetti (in the context of his polemical contrast between Svevo and Proust), *Il romanzo del Novecento: Quaderni inediti,* introd. Eugenio Montale, Saggi blu (Milan: Garzanti, 1976), 553–58 (cf. the contrast between letters and photographs as the atemporally immediate and therefore frozen representation of life in the opening of *Una vita*).

15. Debenedetti points out the importance of alibis for all of Svevo's major characters in "Svevo e Schmitz," 56.

16. For an extensive discussion of Svevo's relation to this crisis see Giuseppe Antonio Camerino, *Italo Svevo e la crisi della mitteleuropa,* Saggi di letteratura italiana, 36 (Florence: Le Monnier, 1974). See also Giorgio Luti, *Italo Svevo e altri studi sulla letteratura italiana del primo Novecento,* Saggi, 18 (Milan: Lerici, 1961), 253–65 et passim; André Bouissy, "Les Fondements idéologiques de l'oeuvre d'Italo Svevo," *Revue des Études Italiennes,* n.s. 12, no. 3 (1966): 209–45; n.s. 12, no. 4 (1966): 350–73; n.s. 13, no. 1 (1967): 23–50; Bruno Porcelli, "L'evoluzione dell'ideologia e della narrativa sveviana," *Problemi* 17–18 (Septem-

ber–December 1969): 767–82; Norbert Jonard, *Italo Svevo e la crise de la bourgeoisie européenne,* Publications de l'Université de Dijon, 42 (Paris: Société Les Belles Lettres, 1969), 39–61, 167–229; Fusco, *Italo Svevo,* 118–23 (on Svevo's reaction to the liberation of Trieste); Arcangelo Leone de Castris, *Il decadentismo italiano: Svevo, Pirandello, D'Annunzio,* Ideologia e società (Bari: De Donato, 1974), 145–53; Giampaolo Borghello, "Per una collocazione storica di Svevo: Un'ipotesi di lavoro," in his *La coscienza borghese: Saggio sulla narrativa di Svevo,* Saggistica, 82 (Rome: Savelli, 1977), 247–70; and Giorgio Zampa, "Italo Svevo e la cultura asburgica," in *Italo Svevo oggi: Atti del convegno, Firenze, 3–4 febbraio 1979,* ed. Marco Marchi, Nuovedizioni (Florence: Vallecchi, 1980), 50–66.

17. *Racconti, Saggi, Pagine sparse,* 816 (2 October 1899), and 372. On the diary passage and its significance see especially Fusco, *Italo Svevo,* 484–91. Comments linking imagination, writing, and understanding as *activity* are scattered throughout Svevo's diaries. See, for example, pp. 818 (December 1902) and 831 (6 May 1927). In this regard, see also "Il vecchione" (pp. 133–42), the opening pages of Svevo's unfinished novel, written in 1928.

Chapter 6. Silone and Neorealism

1. The novel appeared first in 1936 in a German translation, *Brot und Wein* (Zurich: Oprecht, 1936; Europa Verlag, 1937). The Italian original, *Pane e vino,* was published in 1937 (Lugano: Nuove Edizioni di Capolago). A completely revised version, entitled *Vino e pane,* was published in Milan in 1955 as number 26 in Mondadori's series Grandi Narratori Italiani. Page numbers in the text refer to this revised version and to the English translation, *Bread and Wine,* trans. Harvey Fergusson II, afterword by Marc Slonim (1962; rpt. New York: New American Library, 1963), which I have occasionally altered to render the Italian more literally.

2. Peter/Paul is at times described—especially in the early chapters—not just as a priest but as a "saint." The imagery of these early chapters also links the character to Christ (waking in the "crèche"; betrayed by friends), though there are other figures with occasional Christ-like attributes as well (e.g. "Cristina" and the sacrificed and ritually mourned Luigi Murica). Because of Pietro/Paolo's combination of spiritual and material goals, R.W.B. Lewis is correct in including a discussion of the character as the central figure in his study *The Picaresque Saint: Representative Figures in Contemporary Fiction* (Philadelphia: Lippincott, 1959), 148–60. For a more detailed treatment of the Christian symbolism in the novel, see Franz Schneider, "Scriptural Symbolism in Silone's *Bread and Wine,*" *Italica* 44, no. 4 (1967): 387–99.

3. The importance that the role of priest holds for the populace, despite the feelings of "Don Paolo" himself, is discussed by Piero Aragno in his chapter,

"*Pane e vino,*" in *Il romanzo di Silone,* Il portico, 55 (Ravenna: Longo, 1975), 35–55, esp. 41.

4. There are several differences between this presentation of the scene and that in the original version of the novel (145ff.). The original is much more diffuse, and it puts even greater emphasis on the distinction between true and false. Silone's revised version opens the chapter with the discussion at the inn and frames the action of the chapter inside Don Paolo's *reading and writing,* thus giving the entire scene both clearer bounds and greater thematic unity. There is a general discussion of the nature of the changes that Silone made in revising the novel in Luce d'Eramo's landmark bibliographical and critical study, *L'opera di Ignazio Silone: Saggio critico e guida bibliografica* (Milan: Mondadori, 1971), 131–67.

5. There is, of course, a huge bibliography on this topic, extending from Plato to Genette. One of the most concise treatments of the various theoretical positions is Roman Jakobson's essay "Quest for the Essence of Language," in the special issue of *Diogenes* devoted to "Problems of Language," no. 5 (Fall 1965): 21–37. In regard to the problems and pitfalls of language as portrayed in Silone's novel, see also A. Kingsley Weatherhead, "Ignazio Silone: Community and the Failure of Language," *Modern Fiction Studies* 7, no. 2 (1961): 157–68.

6. The translation attributes this statement to Matalena, the innkeeper, but in both the Italian original and the revision it is attributed to Mascolo.

7. Silone's description of such groups' entrenched views of the world and of their relationships to it as individuals anticipates in several ways Althusser's Lacanian definition of ideology as "une 'représentation' du rapport imaginaire des individus a leurs conditions réelles d'existence" ("a 'representation' of the imaginary relationship of individuals to their real conditions of existence"). Again, for Silone and later for Althusser, the complex mixture of imaginary and real is what makes substantitve worldly change so difficult. See Louis Althusser, "Idéologie et appareils idéologiques d'état" (1969), in his *Positions (1964–1975)* (Paris: Editions Sociales, 1976), 101, translated as "Ideology and the State," in "*Lenin and Philosophy" and Other Essays,* trans. Ben Brewster (New York and London: Monthly Review Press, 1971), 162.

8. See "La lezione di Budapest" (1956), in Silone's *Uscita di sicurezza* (Florence: Vallecchi, 1965), 157: "La peggiore tirannia è quella delle parole." (Translated by Harvey Fergusson II as "The Lesson of Budapest," in *Emergency Exit,* World Perspectives, 39, ed. Ruth Nanda Anshen [New York: Harper and Row, 1968], 132.) See also Don Paolo's distinction between real divisions among men and artificial ones, many of which are just "malintesi verbali" (173; "verbal misunderstandings," 158); cf. the equally illusory "accordi di parole" (173; "verbal agreements," 158). Of course, this is not to say that all language is necessarily misleading or tyrannical: Don Paolo himself keeps a notebook during the novel.

9. The same distrust of official organization and power as perhaps inevitably

corrupt is evident in Silone's depiction of his experiences in the enlarged Executive of the Comintern in 1927 in Moscow, in section 9 of his essay "Uscita di sicurezza" (1949), in *Uscita di sicurezza*, 55–115, trans. Harvey Fergusson II as "Emergency Exit," in *Emergency Exit*, 41–99; also included in *The God That Failed*, ed. Richard Crossman (New York: Harper and Bros., 1949), 76–114. See also the discussions between Pietro Spina and Battipaglia, the Party functionary, in chapter 17 of *Vino e pane* (183–86; 170–72). As is clear from Uliva's words in chapter 17, any tyranny taking charge of the state will attempt *first* to control language.

10. This humanist credo remained fairly constant throughout Silone's notable changes in religious, social, and political opinion. See, for example, his comments in 1949 on the necessity of "faith" in the understanding and the practice of Socialism, in "Uscita di sicurezza," 115; "Emergency Exit," 99. The difficulties inherent in such a credo are discussed by Murray Krieger in his treatment of Silone in *The Tragic Vision: The Confrontation of Extremity*, vol. 1 of *Visions of Extremity in Modern Literature*, 2 vols. (1960; rpt. Baltimore: Johns Hopkins University Press, 1973), 72–85. Krieger uses Eric Mosbacher's translation of the 1937 text rather than the 1955 Italian revision, which may account in part for the condemnatory tone of his assessment of the aesthetic and social merit of the novel. For far more favorable, if briefer, treatments of Silone as an author of "favole morali" see Nicola Chiaromonte, "Silone, scrittore veridico," in Giovanni Cristini et al., *Dal villaggio all'Europa: Omaggio a Silone* (Rome: De Luca, 1971), 13–18, and one of the first—and still among the finest—sympathetically perceptive discussions of Silone's early novels, Geno Pampaloni, "L'opera narrativa di Ignazio Silone," *Il ponte* 5, no. 1 (1949): 49–58. See also Alessandro Scurani, "La lunga confessione di Silone," *Letture* 21, no. 1 (1966): 3–26, and Carmine Taricani, *Ignazio Silone: Sofferenza e rivoluzione*, "Sapienza," 1 (Genoa: Parola Viva, 1979).

11. The story of Pietro Spina is continued in a subsequent novel, *Il seme sotto la neve* (Zurich, 1941; Lugano, 1942; rev. eds. 1950 and 1961; *The Seed beneath the Snow*), but the problems of social roles and social change, as posed in *Vino e pane*, remain unresolved.

12. Italo Calvino, 1964 preface, *Il sentiero dei nidi di ragno*, rev. ed., I Coralli, 11 (Turin: Einaudi, 1964), 8, trans. William Weaver as "Preface," in *The Path to the Nest of Spiders*, trans. Archibald Colquhoun (1957; rpt. New York: Ecco Press, 1976), vi.

13. This does not mean, of course, that the neorealists were uninterested in issues of language and representation—far from it—but only that their intent, like the twentieth-century American models so important to many of them (Hemingway, Fitzgerald, Caldwell), was to portray social and economic reality in language that was as far as possible both symbolically effective *and* transparent. For a recent treatment of this issue in Vittorini's fiction and aesthetic theories,

see Joy Hambuechen Potter, "Conclusion: Style and Ideology in *Le due tensioni*," in her *Elio Vittorini*, TWAS, 518 (Boston: Twayne, 1979), 124–31. Nevertheless, the sort of literary self-consciousness that was a secondary effect in Verga's nineteenth-century verismo, for example, was at best a tertiary one for twentieth-century neorealist narratives.

14. The most obviously self-conscious narratives by the three major writers of the neorealist group—Vittorini, Pavese, and Moravia—fall either outside the period (such as Vittorini's later novels or Moravia's *La noia* [1960] and *L'attenzione* [1965]) or outside the genre of narrative proper (such as Pavese's highly self-involved and disturbingly ironic *Dialoghi con Leucò* [1947]). There are two brief but precise treatments in French of the effects of self-reflection in Moravia's fiction: Jacques Marx, "Autopsie d'un roman-miroir: *L'Attenzione* d'Alberto Moravia*," *Revue des Langues Vivantes* 42, no. 2 (1976): 165–78, and Raoul Blomme, "A travers les miroirs de 'Gli Indifferenti,'" *Onze Études sur la mise en abyme*, ed. Fernand Hallyn, special issue of *Romanica Gandensia* 17 (1980): 54–65.

Chapter 7. Lampedusa's *Il Gattopardo*

1. Citations in the text are from Giuseppe Tomasi di Lampedusa, *Opere*, Gli Astri (Milan: Feltrinelli, 1965), 7–321, translated by Archibald Colquhoun as *The Leopard* (New York: Pantheon, 1960). I have occasionally altered the English translation for accuracy.

In regard to the dispute over the text of the novel, which was published posthumously, see Antonio Dipace, *Questione delle varianti del "Gattopardo,"* Biblioteca dell'Argileto, 1 (Rome: Argileto, 1971), and the treatment by Giuseppe Paolo Samonà (who is not in complete agreement with Dipace), "Sulle varie redazioni del 'Gattopardo,'"in his masterful study, *Il Gattopardo, i Racconti, Lampedusa*, Biblioteca di cultura, 121 (Florence: La Nuova Italia, 1974), 209–56. The 1965 edition included in the *Opere*, which is followed here, is a reprint of the version originally published in 1958 in a series edited for Feltrinelli by Giorgio Bassani, Biblioteca di letteratura, I Contemporanei, 4. Another version, introduced by Lampedusa's adopted son, was published in 1969: *Il Gattopardo: Edizione conforme al manoscritto del 1957*, introd. Gioacchino Lanza Tomasi (Milan: Feltrinelli, 1969).

2. The term *méconnaissance* means a motivated misrecognition. It is this combination of semiconsciousness and error that makes it so difficult to translate. Jacques Lacan uses the term in a psychoanalytic sense. Along with his usage of it in his *Écrits* (Paris: Seuil, 1966), see the brief but confusing transcription of his presentation, "Of Structure as an Inmixing of an Otherness Prerequisite to Any Subject Whatever," in *The Structuralist Controversy: The Languages of Criticism and the Sciences of Man*, ed. Richard Macksey and Eugenio Donato (Baltimore: Johns Hopkins Press, 1970), 186–95, and *The Language of the Self: The Function*

of Language in Psychoanalysis, trans. and ed. Anthony Wilden (New York: Dell, 1968), xv, 3, 12, 49, 54, 102, 104. Louis Althusser has appropriated the term for social analysis in his discussions of Freud and Lacan included in *Positions (1964–75)* (Paris: Éditions Sociales, 1976), trans. Ben Brewster as *"Lenin and Philosophy" and Other Essays* (New York and London: Monthly Review Press, 1971).

3. Paul de Man, "The Rhetoric of Temporality," in *Interpretation: Theory and Practice,* ed. Charles S. Singleton (Baltimore: Johns Hopkins University Press, 1969), 203. In the course of the essay de Man deals specifically with Stendhal's *Chartreuse de Parme,* whose main character also furnishes certain parallels with Lampedusa's. In this regard, see Jeffrey Meyers, "The Influence of the *Chartreuse de Parme* on *Il Gattopardo,*" *Italica* 44, no. 3 (1967): 314–25, which also treats Lampedusa's "Lezioni su Stendhal" (1955, published in *Paragone* 9, no. 112 [1959]: 3–49, and subsequently as *Lezioni su Stendhal,* introd. Philippe Renard, La civiltà perfezionata [Palermo: Sellerio, 1977]); and Olga Ragusa, "Stendhal, Tomasi di Lampedusa, and the Novel," *Comparative Literature Studies* 10, no. 3 (1973): 195–228, which also discusses Louis Aragon's work on Lampedusa (1959, 1960).

4. For examples of this willful confusion between protagonist, narrator, and author, see especially Gian Carlo Ferretti, *Letteratura e ideologia: Bassani, Cassola, Pasolini* (Rome: Riuniti, 1964), 64, and Gianfranco Contini, *Letteratura dell'Italia unita, 1861–1968* (Florence: Sansoni, 1968), 887.

5. De Man, "The Rhetoric of Temporality," 226. In terms of Lampedusa's literary interests, it is also important to note the Stendhalian tone of the cited passages. For a general discussion of Lampedusa's background, literary and otherwise, see Andrea Vitello, *I Gattopardi di Donnafugata,* Collana di saggi e monografie, n.s. 12 (Palermo: Flaccovia, 1963).

6. This episode furnishes a further parallel to *The Chartreuse de Parme.*

7. The four rivers could also indicate the biblical creation ("adamitico," 79). For Dante's "aiuola," see *Paradiso,* cantos 22 and 27.

8. For a discussion of the development of symbol within *Il Gattopardo,* and especially of the "fall" of Bendicò at the narrative's end, see Jeffrey Meyers, "Symbol and Structure in *The Leopard,*" *Italian Quarterly* 9, nos. 34–35 (1965): 50–70, and Stanley G. Eskin, "Animal Imagery in *Il Gattopardo,*" *Italica* 39, no. 3 (1962): 193–94. See also Arthur Evans and Catherine Evans, "'Salina e Svelto': The Symbolism of Change in *Il Gattopardo,*" *Wisconsin Studies in Contemporary Literature* 4, no. 3 (1963): 298–304, and John Gilbert, "The Metamorphosis of the Gods," *Modern Language Notes* 81, no. 1 (1966): 22–32. There is also a very general treatment of metaphor in the novel in Sergio Zatti, *Tomasi di Lampedusa,* "Invito alla ricerca letteraria" (Bresso: Cetim, 1972), 32, 49–53.

9. Simonetta Salvestroni notes a similar process of "amarezza" and "rasserenamento," or "bitterness" and "brightening up," in her *Tomasi di Lampedusa,*

Il Castoro (Florence: La Nuova Italia, 1973), 68–69, as does Ferretti, though in much more general terms (*Letteratura e ideologia,* 64).

10. The basic theory of pleasure as the result of a reduction in anxiety was already present in *The Interpretation of Dreams* of 1900, though the fuller theory of the instinct to repeat did not occur until the later works, particularly *Beyond the Pleasure Principle* of 1920. See *The Standard Edition of the Complete Psychological Works of Sigmund Freud,* ed. and trans. James Strachey in collaboration with Anna Freud, 24 vols. (London: Hogarth Press, 1966–74), vols. 5 and 18.

11. Cf. Freud on the temporal play within the dreamer-dream relationship: "By picturing our wishes as fulfilled, dreams are after all leading us into the future. But this future, which the dreamer pictures as the present, has been moulded by his indestructible wish into the perfect likeness of the past" (Freud, *Standard Edition,* 5:660).

12. The tempering of debasement with continuation is also noted by Tom O'Neill, "Lampedusa and De Roberto," *Italica* 47, no. 2 (1970): 180, and, more generally, by Leonardo Sciascia, "Il Gattopardo," in *Pirandello e la Sicilia,* "Aretusa," 13 (Caltanisetta and Rome: Sciascia, 1961), 159. For a complementary discussion of the overall structural integrity of the novel see Richard Lansing, "The Structure of Meaning in Lampedusa's *Il Gattopardo,*" *PMLA* 93, no. 3 (1978): 409–22.

13. For suggestive parallels to this process, analyzed in more formally psychoanalytic terms, see Freud's two essays, "On the Universal Tendency to Debasement in the Sphere of Love" (1912), *Standard Edition,* vol. 11, and "Splitting of the Ego in the Process of Defence" (1938/1940), *Standard Edition,* vol. 23.

14. De Man, "The Rhetoric of Temporality," 208.

15. Among the many treatments of temporal order, death, and the process of dying in the novel, the most useful are Sebastiano Addamo, "Il sentimento del tempo e della morte nel Gattopardo," in his *Vittorini e la narrativa siciliana contemporanea,* "Lo smeraldo," 17 (Caltanisetta and Rome: Sciascia, 1962), 119–38; Richard F. Kuhns, "Modernity and Death: *The Leopard* by Giuseppe di Lampedusa," *Contemporary Psychoanalysis* 5, no. 2 (1969): 95–119; Mario Materassi, "'L'ordine, il disordine': Il paradigma della circolarità ne *Il Gattopardo,*" *Lingua e stile* 7, no. 3 (1972): 545–60; and Nunzio Zaga, "Realtà e desiderio nel 'Gattopardo,'" *Sicularum gymnasium,* n.s. 31, no. 1 (1978), 102–37.

16. See Burke, *A Grammar of Motives* (New York: Prentice-Hall, 1945), 512. See, by Ricardou, *Problèmes du nouveau roman,* Collection "Tel Quel" (Paris: Seuil, 1967), 171–90; *Pour une théorie du nouveau roman* (Paris: Seuil, 1971), 171–207; *Le Nouveau Roman,* Écrivains de toujours (Paris: Seuil, 1973), 47–75, 109–12; and *Nouveaux Problèmes du roman,* Collection "Poétique" (Paris: Seuil, 1978), 140–78. By Dällenbach, *Le Récit spéculaire. Essai sur la mise en abyme,* Collection "Poétique" (Paris: Seuil, 1977). David Nolan discusses the

self-reflexive effects of this conclusion in terms of Lampedusa's overall view of history, in "Lampedusa's *The Leopard,*" *Studies* (Dublin) 55 (1966): 403–14, esp. 411–12.

17. De Man, "The Rhetoric of Temporality," 226.

18. Jeffrey Meyers, "Symbol and Structure in *The Leopard,*" 69–70.

19. As a continuing example of this type of critical méconnaissance, see Contini's very brief treatment of the book's powers of entertainment as "una gradevolissima 'opera d'intrattenimento'" in *Letteratura dell'Italia unita,* 887.

The treatments of *Il Gattopardo* as "engaged" or not cover the spectrum of political and social analysis. For useful and more or less representative examples see Roberto De Monticelli's interview with Elio Vittorini (who condemns the book as ideologically decadent), "Vittorini confessa: Scrivo libri ma penso ad altro," *Il giorno,* 24 February 1959, 9; Carlo Salinari (who takes a position notably different from, though not exactly opposite, Vittorini's), "Il gattopardo," *Vie nuove* 10 January 1959, 46; and two writers who fall more or less between Vittorini and Salinari on the question of decadence and self-knowledge in Lampedusa's novel, Giorgio Pullini, "Il Gattopardo di Giuseppe Tomasi di Lampedusa," in his *Il romanzo italiano del dopoguerra (1940–1960) con bibliografia, 1940–1965,* 2d ed. (Padua: Marsilio, 1965), 419–23, and Arnaldo Bocelli, "Perché il successo del 'Gattopardo,'" *La stampa,* 2 January 1969, 13.

For a summary of the criticism of Lampedusa up to 1974, see Samonà, "Lampedusa e la critica," in *Il Gattopardo, i Racconti, Lampedusa,* 357–426. For an overview of the debate following the novel's appearance (including a bibliography of the most accessible articles, reviews, and letters), see my own "*Scrivere o fare . . . o altro:* Social Commitment and Ideologies of Representation in the Debates over Lampedusa's *Il Gattopardo* and Morante's *La Storia,*" *Italica* 61, no. 3 (1984): 220–51.

Chapter 8. Gadda's *La cognizione del dolore*

1. *Meditazione milanese,* ed. Gian Carlo Roscioni, Einaudi Letteratura, 34 (Turin: Einaudi, 1974), the concluding section of which is entitled "Il sentimento e l'autocoscienza," or "Sentiment and Self-Knowledge" (235–97).

2. References in the text are to *La cognizione del dolore,* introd. Gianfranco Contini (Turin: Einaudi, 1970), with the English from William Weaver's translation *Acquainted with Grief* (New York: Braziller, 1969), which on occasion I have altered for accuracy. I have retained Gadda's extensive use of periods (which do not indicate ellipsis) throughout the quotations.

3. Aspects of this key scene are also discussed in a similar vein by Pietro Pucci, "The Obscure Sickness," *Italian Quarterly* 11, no. 42 (1967): 43–62, published in Italian as "Il male oscuro," *Belfagor* 23, no. 1 (1968): 91–98; and Robert S. Dombroski, "Overcoming Oedipus: Self and Society in *La cognizione del do-*

lore," *Modern Language Notes* 99, no. 1 (1984): 125–43, esp. 134–36.

4. The importance of the story of Christ in Gadda's work is treated (in terms of its similarities to the work of Joyce in this regard) by Rinaldo Rinaldi, *La paralisi e lo spostamento: Lettura della "Cognizione del Dolore,"* Collana di critica letteraria, 1 (Leghorn: Bastogi, 1977), 66–69. Gadda's interest in the mother/son/absent father at the heart of Christianity showed up in a striking variety of contexts. Among these, see the conclusion of the essay "Anastomòsi" (1940), in *Le meraviglie d'Italia-Gli anni* (Turin: Einaudi, 1964), 268; the end of "Psicanalisi e letteratura" (1946), in *I viaggi la morte* (Milan: Garzanti, 1958), 60; and, less directly linked to the Virgin but even more openly tied to guilt and the continuing act of confession, the end of Gadda's interview with Dacia Maraini, *Prisma* 5 (May 1968): 14–19, rpt. in her *E tu chi eri? Interviste sull'infanzia* (Milan: Bompiani, 1973), 9–21. There is also a notably odd version of Christian sexuality, again involving a game of exclusion, at the end of chapter 3 of *La meccanica*, "I bianchi" (Milan: Garzanti, 1974), 110.

5. Gadda's anger at the hardships caused by the expenses of his father's house in the Brianza is well known. He discussed it openly in his 1968 interview with Dacia Maraini, in which he also mentions its direct connection with the situation described in *La cognizione del dolore* (10). Gadda's grief over the death of his brother, Enrico, a flyer killed just before the end of World War I, is movingly documented in the March 1919 pages of his *Giornale di guerra e di prigionia* (Turin: Einaudi, 1965), 358–61 et passim.

6. The narrative's patent appeal to interpretation in a psychoanalytic vein has been discussed by many critics, among them Michel David, *La psicoanalisi nella cultura italiana*, Preface by Cesare L. Musatti (Turin: Boringhieri, 1966), 458–66; Carlo De Matteis, "Oltraggio e riscatto, interpretazione della 'Cognizione del dolore' di C. E. Gadda," *L'approdo letterario* 17, n.s. 53 (March 1971): 33–70; Elio Gioanola, *L'uomo dei topazi: Saggio psicanalitico su C. E. Gadda*, Il melangolo, 2 (Genoa: Il Melangolo, 1977), esp. 91–218; Romano Luperini, "Nevrosi e crisi dell'identità sociale nella 'Cognizione del dolore,'" *Problemi*, no. 60 (January–April 1981), 66–73; and Dombroski, "Overcoming Oedipus," in which Dombroski extends his psychoanalytic interpretation to include broader issues of social history, and his recent expansion of his position, "Gadda: Fascismo e psicanalisi," in his *L'esistenza ubbidiente: Letterati italiani sotto il fascismo*, Esperienze, 99 (Naples: Guida, 1984), 91–114.

Also of interest in this regard are Gadda's own comments on the status of the individual ego scattered throughout his writings and especially in "Emilio e Narcisso" (1949) and "L'egoista" (1953), both in *I viaggi la morte*, 257–79, 281–96; "Psicanalisi e letteratura"; and his book-length indictment of Fascist ethics, narcissism, and sexuality, *Eros e Priapo: Da furore a cenere* (Milan: Garzanti, 1967).

7. "Mourning and Melancholia" (1917), in *The Standard Edition of the Complete Psychological Works of Sigmund Freud*, ed. and trans. James Strachey in collaboration with Anna Freud, 24 vols. (London: Hogarth Press, 1966–74), 14:243–58.

8. For recent discussions of this topic (all of which deal with the splitting of objects between love and hatred and all of which are indebted in one fashion or another to the work of Melanie Klein), see Herbert Rosenfeld, "A Clinical Approach to the Psychoanalytic Theory of the Life and Death Instincts: An Investigation into the Aggressive Aspects of Narcissism," *International Journal of Psycho-Analysis* 52, pt. 2 (1971): 169–78; Otto F. Kernberg, *Borderline Conditions and Pathological Narcissism*, Classical Psychoanalysis and Its Applications (New York: Aronson, 1975), 16–18; James S. Grotstein, "The Psychoanalytic Concept of the Borderline Organization," in *Advances in Psychotherapy of the Borderline Patient*, ed. Joseph LeBoit and Attilio Capponi (New York: Aronson, 1979), 149–83; and Peter Giovacchini, *Treatment of Primitive Mental States*, Classical Psychoanalysis and Its Applications (New York: Aronson, 1979), 201–393.

9. On the conclusion of the narrative and the various real and/or metaphorical possibilities for "solution" of the crime (along with information found among Gadda's notes after his death), see Gian Carlo Roscioni, "La conclusione della *Cognizione del dolore*," *Paragone* 20, no. 238 (1969): 86–99.

10. Gadda mentions the importance of Carducci in his early readings (read after Manzoni and before D'Annunzio) in "Intervista al microfono" (1950), in *I viaggi la morte*, 109–12. (Gadda's continuing lovers' quarrel with Manzoni, who sees the dark terror beneath the baroque surface of life but tries not to face it too directly, is recorded in Gadda's 1924 essay "Apologia manzoniana," rpt. in *Antologia di Solaria*, ed. Enzo Siciliano, introd. Alberto Carocci, Antologie, 2 [Milan: Lerici, 1958], 175–84.)

11. The conception of grief as the recognition of irrational chaos in battle with order has been discussed in a wide variety of contexts regarding Gadda's works. See, for example, Dombroski, *Introduzione allo studio di Carlo E. Gadda*, Saggi di cultura contemporanea, 8 (Florence: "Nuovedizioni" Vallecchi, 1974), 19 (Dombroski eventually extends the notion of disorder to include war itself [45]); Gian-Paolo Biasin, "La penna, la madre," ch. 5, of *Malattie letterarie*, Nuovi saggi italiani, 18 (Milan: Bompiani, 1976), 157–90; English ed.: "The Pen, the Mother," in *Literary Diseases: Theme and Metaphor in the Italian Novel* (Austin: University of Texas Press, 1975), 127–55, in which Biasin takes his lead from Gadda's "Anastomòsi"; Giorgio Bàrberi Squarotti, *Poesia e narrativa del secondo Novecento*, 2d ed., Civiltà letteraria del Novecento, Saggi, 2 (Milan: Mursia, 1967), 208–12, in which Bàrberi Squarotti denies the concept of mimesis of reality in Gadda's works and emphasizes the psychological effects that reside behind the baroque appearance of Gadda's fictional worlds; Renato Barilli, *La barriera del naturalismo: Studi sulla narrativa italiana contemporanea*, 3d ed., Civ-

iltà letteraria del Novecento, Saggi, 7 (Milan: Mursia, 1980), 121–50, in which Barilli sees Gadda as still interested in the mimetic representation of life and, therefore, as remaining within literary naturalism even while straining at its limits; Olga Ragusa, "Gadda, Pasolini, and Experimentalism: Form or Ideology," in her *Narrative and Drama: Essays in Modern Italian Literature from Verga to Pasolini*, De Proprietatibus Litterarum, Series Practica, 110 (The Hague: Mouton, 1976), 134–55, in which Ragusa argues for Gadda as an obviously complex modern novelist but one with a traditional view of man in relation to his environment and to others; Enrico Flores, *Accessioni gaddiane: Strutture, lingua e società in C. E. Gadda* (Naples: Loffredo, 1973), 132–41, in which Flores discusses rhetorical and other technical similarities between Gadda and Joyce; Guido Baldi, *Carlo Emilio Gadda*, Civiltà letteraria del Novecento, Profili, 24 (Milan: Mursia, 1972), 104–29, in which Baldi points out that Gadda's characteristically chaotic pastiche (also discussed in Contini's introduction to the novel, 7–28) includes as one of its effects that of critical distance and so, along with it, the possibility of critical evaluation; and Gian Carlo Roscioni's influential study, *La disarmonia prestabilita: Studio su Gadda*, Saggi, 453 (Turin: Einaudi, 1969).

12. This image plays a central role in *Alcibiades I* 132–33, in which the subject under discussion is the Delphic maxim "Know thyself" and in which the proto-Gaddian topics of the *relational* nature of human knowledge and of human identity, will, and possession are stressed (for Plato, as distinct from Gadda, with divine knowledge as the ultimate, stable goal).

13. Faulkner stated this belief in a 1956 interview with Jean Stein for the *Paris Review*, rpt. in *Writers at Work: The "Paris Review" Interviews*, ed. and introd. Malcolm Cowley (New York: Viking, 1958), 138–39.

14. Guido Guglielmi discussed the effects of "metalanguage" in Gadda's narrative in "Lingua e metalinguaggio di Gadda," in *Letteratura come sistema e come funzione*, La ricerca letteraria, Serie critica, 1 (Turin: Einaudi, 1967), 128–37. For subsequent treatments of this topic, see Jacqueline Risset, "Carlo Emilio Gadda ou la philosophie à l'envers," *Critique* 26, no. 282 (1970): 944–51, esp. 945; Romano Luperini, *Il Novecento*, 2 vols. (Turin: Loescher, 1981), 2:493 et passim; and Dombroski, "Overcoming Oedipus," 29–30, in which Dombroski notes that the effect of critical estrangement created by metalanguage in *La cognizione* (a notion also discussed by Luperini) serves as a means of critical revelation in terms of the book's characters and at the same time, through the mechanism of the pastiche, as a protective shield in terms of its author (130–43).

Chapter 9. Morante's *La Storia*

1. All references are to *La Storia. Romanzo*, Gli struzzi, 58 (Turin: Einaudi, 1974), the text and pagination of which are reproduced exactly in the hardback edition published by Einaudi in the series "I millenni" in 1976, with translations

from *History: A Novel*, trans. William Weaver (New York: Knopf, 1977), which I have altered here and there for accuracy. Page numbers are included in the text. (The widely available 1979 Avon Books paperback reprint of Weaver's translation reproduces the text published by Knopf but runs to 691 pages as opposed to the 562 of the original hardback; the 1984 Aventura-Vintage Library edition repeats the pagination of the Knopf hardback.)

2. Interestingly enough, Giacomo Debenedetti had already commented on these two aspects of Morante's world view—and their occasionally troubled union—in his review of *L'isola di Arturo*, in *Nuovi argomenti*, no. 26 (May–June 1957): 43–61. Morante herself discusses poetry's force and its functions in the world in her response to "9 domande sul romanzo," *Nuovi argomenti*, nos. 38–39 (May–August 1959): 17–38 (in regard to the artistic intermixing of the realistic and the fabulous), and in "Pro o contro la bomba atomica," *Europa letteraria* 6, no. 34 (1965): 31–42 (in regard to art's powers against worldly disintegration and alienation). There is also a recent book devoted to the mixture of irrationality and reason in Morante's oeuvre, Donatella Ravanello, *Scrittura e follia nei romanzi di Elsa Morante*, Ricerche, 68 (Venice: Marsilio, 1980).

3. See Marx's discussion of the various *antagonistic* forms of social relations in what he terms the "prehistoric stages" of human society (Asiatic, ancient, feudal, and modern bourgeois), in the preface to *A Contribution to the Critique of Political Economy*, trans. N. I. Stone (New York: International Library, 1904), 13. Morante's conception of History is similar, though not identical, to Marx's notion of the antagonisms caused by these forms of society as expressed in this preface.

4. For treatments of this debate, see Gian Carlo Ferretti, "Il dibattito sulla 'Storia' di Elsa Morante," *Belfagor* 30, no. 1 (1975): 93–98, and "Perché tante storie dopo la neoavanguardia," *Rinascita* 32, no. 19 (1975): 23–24; Ferdinando Camon, "Il test della 'Storia' (Letteratura di massa, Critica della critica)," *Nuovi argomenti*, n.s. 45–46 (May–August 1975): 186–239; Gianni Venturi, "Bibliografia," in *Elsa Morante*, Il castoro, 130 (Florence: La Nuova Italia, 1977), 137–39; Ivan Seidl, "Il caso Morante sei anni dopo," *Études Romanes de Brno* 12, no. 3 (1981): 21–35; and my own "*Scrivere o fare . . . o altro*: Social Commitment and Ideologies of Representation in the Debates over Lampedusa's *Il Gattopardo* and Morante's *La Storia*," *Italica* 61, no. 3 (1984): 220–51. See also the "minidebate" introduced by Angelo Raffaele Pupino in *La fiera letteraria* 50, nos. 40–41; and "Dibattiti / Il successo letterario," *L'espresso* 20, no. 35 (1974): 34–38, introduced by Valerio Riva and including responses by Alberto Moravia, Liala [Amalia Negretti], Giorgio Manganelli, Italo Calvino, and Angelo Guglielmi.

5. In "*Scrivere o fare . . . o altro*: Social Commitment and Ideologies of Representation."

6. Calvino discusses Morante's attempt to work towards a new use of pathos as a literary device for nonmystifying moral pedagogy in his response included in

L'espresso's "Dibattiti / Il successo letterario" ["Allora Hugo disse alla Morante . . ."], 37–38.

7. Published as "La censura in Spagna," *L'unità*, 15 May 1976, and "'La Storia' secondo Elsa Morante," *Corriere della sera*, 15 May 1976. Translations included in the text are mine. See also Morante's earlier presentation of her conception of History in her Introduction, "Il beato propagandista del paradiso," in *L'opera completa dell'Angelico*, ed. Umberto Baldini, Classici dell'Arte, 38 (Milan: Rizzoli, 1970), 5–10. It is instructive to note the progression in Morante's thinking about the worldly powers of poetry, from conceiving of it as an "atto di ottimismo," or "act of optimism," in "Pro o contro la bomba atomica" of 1965, to an "atto d'accusa," or "act of accusation," in her 1976 address.

Chapter 10. Calvino's Fictions

1. As a matter of authorial *intention*, Calvino himself sees literary self-consciousness becoming an important factor in his work with the novels of the trilogy in the 1950s. See our discussion in "An Interview with Italo Calvino," *Contemporary Literature* 26, no. 3 (1985): 245–53, in which Calvino also discusses the development of literary self-consciousness through his other works.

2. Olga Ragusa discusses Calvino's uncanny ability to keep abreast of current intellectual interests in his fiction in "Italo Calvino: The Repeated Conquest of Contemporaneity," *World Literature Today* 57, no. 2 (1983): 195–201.

3. All references are to *Il sentiero dei nidi di ragno*, rev. ed., I Coralli, 11 (Turin: Einaudi, 1964), and *The Path to the Nest of Spiders*, trans. Archibald Colquhoun (Boston: Beacon Press, 1957), both cited by page numbers in the text. I have occasionally altered Colquhoun's translation for accuracy. References to the translation of the 1964 preface (7–24 in the Italian) are to "Preface," trans. William Weaver, added to the reprint of Colquhoun's translation of the novel (New York: Ecco Press, 1976), v–xxv.

4. This review appeared in *L'unità*, 26 October 1947; rpt. in *Saggi letterari*, Opere di Cesare Pavese, 12 (Turin: Einaudi, 1968), 245–47. Pavese had written a note on the novel for Einaudi's circular, *Bolletino d'informazioni culturali*, no. 9 (17 October 1947).

5. *Saggi letterari*, 247 (my translation, my italics).

6. Giovanni Falaschi points out the fantastic quality of Lupo Rosso's heroism (as well as that of the character's ideological commitment) in his fine treatment of Calvino's early fiction in *La resistenza armata nella narrativa italiana*, Piccola Biblioteca Einaudi, 262 (Turin: Einaudi, 1976), 118.

7. Among the most apposite of these essays in this context are "Il midollo del Leone" (1955), "Natura e storia nel romanzo" (1958), "Il mare dell'oggettività" (1959), "Tre correnti del romanzo italiano d'oggi" (1959), "Dialogo di due scrittori in crisi" (1961), and "La sfida al labirinto" (1962), all of which are

included in the selection of Calvino's expository prose, *Una pietra sopra: Discorsi di letteratura e società*, Gli struzzi, 219 (Turin: Einaudi, 1980), and several of which are discussed by JoAnn Cannon with special attention to the questions of social and political meaning in fiction in her *Italo Calvino: Writer and Critic*, L'interprete, 27 (Ravenna: Longo, 1981), 26–32.

8. Teresa de Lauretis, "Narrative Discourse in Calvino: Praxis or Poiesis?" *PMLA* 90, no. 3 (1975): 414–25.

9. References, given in the text, are to *Le Cosmicomiche* (Turin: Einaudi, 1965), and *Cosmicomics*, trans. William Weaver (New York: Harcourt, Brace and World, 1968). I have sometimes altered the translation for accuracy.

10. The various versions of linguistic determinism and some of their proponents (Whorf, Sapir, Cassirer) are discussed and criticized by E. D. Hirsch, Jr., in *The Aims of Interpretation* (Chicago: University of Chicago Press, 1976), esp. 51, 53, and 161, nn. 1–2.

11. Even though scientific and historical determinisms are often treated by others as separate determinist systems, in the *Cosmicomiche* they are regularly mixed together as one.

12. For a discussion of Calvino's refusal to espouse any rational determinism in the *Cosmicomiche* while nonetheless retaining his interest in contemporary social issues, see Giovanni Falaschi, "Italo Calvino," *Belfagor* 27, no. 5 (1972): 530–58. Falaschi traces Calvino's stances in regard to social and literary polemics of the late 1940s through the 1960s. Calvino himself discusses the need to know and understand various determinist systems (biological, economic, psychological, anthropological) in order to avoid being caught in them and, in the final analysis, in order to pass beyond them, in the course of an interview with Ferdinando Camon, in Camon's *Il mestiere di scrittore: Conversazioni critiche* (Milan: Garzanti, 1973), 187.

13. Donald Heiney depicts the *Cosmicomiche* as "satirical science fiction," though he does not develop this idea further, in "Calvino and Borges: Some Implications of Fantasy," *Mundus Artium* 2, no. 1 (1968): 73. In a very general treatment, Kathryn Hume discusses the scientific and social theories that she feels Calvino "spoofs" in "Science and Imagination in Calvino's *Cosmicomiche*," *Mosaic* 15, no. 4 (1982): 47–58, esp. 48.

14. For useful treatments of related aspects of the *Cosmicomiche*, see Gian-Paolo Biasin, "Our Ancestor QFWFQ," *Italian Quarterly* 10, nos. 39–40 (1967): 92–98 (on the combination of scientific and lyrical effects) and his "$4/3 \, \Pi r^3$" (1980), in *Icone italiane*, Strumenti di ricerca, 34–35 (Rome: Bulzoni, 1983), 209–37, esp. 228, translated as *Italian Literary Icons*, Princeton Essays in Literature (Princeton: Princeton University Press, 1985), 166–90, esp. 185; Antonio Illiano, "Per una definizione della vena cosmogonica di Calvino: Appunti su *Le cosmicomiche e T con zero*," *Italica* 49, no. 3 (1972): 291–301 (on the mixture of the realistic and the fantastic as well as on the effects of alienation and parody);

Teresa de Lauretis, "Calvino e la dialettica dei massimi sistemi, " *Italica* 53, no. 1 (1976): 57–74 (esp. 67–71, on the mixture of expressivity and rule in creative acts); Cannon's chapter on *Le Cosmicomiche* and *T con zero* in *Italo Calvino: Writer and Critic*, 49–64; and Anca Vlasopolos, "Love and the Two Discourses in *Le cosmicomiche*," *Stanford Italian Review* 4, no. 1 (1984): 123–35 (on the relation between amorous desire and the literary sign).

15. The self-reflexiveness of the internal cross-referencing within the collection is important yet very subtle. The partial extinction and the surprising reappearance of "the dinosaurs" mentioned here furnish the subject matter for the collection's ninth story, "I Dinosauri." The self-consciously programmatic pairing of the third and fourth stories—in which the creator of language takes as his topic the creation of language—is also significant. After the general problems of signs are treated in "Un segno nello spazio," the specific phenomenon of mythic discourse is demonstrated in action in "Tutto in un punto" ("All at One Point," in which the power of the idealized yet forever lost Earth Mother, "la signora $Ph(i)Nk_o$," is both described and invoked by the narrator).

16. For a discussion of the reasons why the possibility of synonymy—or different linguistic forms carrying the same meaning—undermines the notion of linguistic determinism, see Hirsch, *The Aims of Interpretation*, 50–73.

17. This point is made in the course of Pedullà's discussion of the relations between Calvino and contemporary French thought in "Calvino alla corte di Lacan," *Il caffè* 19, nos. 5–6 (1972): 80.

18. This is Francesca Bernardini Napoletano's general contention in *I segni nuovi di Italo Calvino: Da "Le Cosmicomiche" a "Le città invisibili*," L'analisi letteraria, proposte e letture critiche, 17 (Rome: Bulzoni, 1977), 45. Cannon makes a similar assertion in her openly Derridean evaluation of the logical and linguistic implications of "Un segno nello spazio," in *Italo Calvino: Writer and Critic*, 55–58, 63–64, especially on the story's treatment of "the various deficiencies of language" (56). See also de Lauretis, "Calvino e la dialettica dei massimi sistemi," 67–71, and "Narrative Discourse in Calvino," 421.

19. Calvino's interest in cybernetics and its relation to narrative is also evident in two essays of 1967 and 1968, both included in *Una pietra sopra*, "Cibernetica e fantasmi: Appunti sulla narrativa come processo combinatorio," 164–81, and "La macchina spasmodica," 204–6.

20. See Calvino's 1960 introduction to *I nostri antenati: Il cavaliere inesistente, Il visconte dimezzato, Il barone rampante* (Turin: Einaudi, 1960), xv. Jill Margo Carlton discusses the self-reflexive aspects of *Il barone rampante*, as well as Lupo Rosso's "story telling" in *Il sentiero dei nidi di ragno* and the subjects of telling and reading in Calvino's early short fiction, in her "Genesis of *Il barone rampante*," *Italica* 61, no. 3 (1984): 195–206.

21. The importance of these debates for Calvino's fiction in the *Cosmicomiche* was pointed out by Benvenuto Terracini in a sensitive early review of the

collection (in *Archivio glottologico italiano* 51 [1966]: 94–97). While paying special attention to "Un segno nello spazio," Terracini situates Calvino's discussion in relation generally to current interest in structuralist linguistics and specifically to the theories of Saussure, Trubetzkoy, and Jakobson. Since the issues at stake in the postwar debates over literary theory and practice in Italy have regularly had to do with questions of referentiality, the social aspects of these discussions have consistently been of particular importance.

22. All references are to *Se una notte d'inverno un viaggiatore* (Turin: Einaudi, 1979), and *If on a Winter's Night a Traveler*, trans. William Weaver, A Helen and Kurt Wolff Book (New York: Harcourt Brace Jovanovich, 1981), cited by page numbers in the text. I have occasionally altered the translation slightly for accuracy.

23. For a discussion of this topic in regard to *Se una notte d'inverno un viaggiatore* (with special reference to the theories of Eco, Riffaterre, Iser, and John Barth), see Franco Ricci, "The Readers in Italo Calvino's Latest *Fabula*," *Forum Italicum* 16, nos. 1–2 (1982): 82–102. JoAnn Cannon also describes the nature and the significance of Calvino's games with the reader in her chapter on *Se una notte d'inverno* in *Italo Calvino: Writer and Critic*, 97–109. See also Linda C. Bradley,. "Calvino *engagé*: Reading as Resistance in *If on a Winter's Night a Traveler*," *Perpectives on Contemporary Literature* 10 (1984): 102–11, for a treatment of the novel that, however overly sanguine, contrasts Calvino's view of the *social* aspects of reading with Roland Barthes' concept of the *individual's* pleasure of the text; and Brian Edwards, "Deconstructing the Artist and the Art: Barth and Calvino at Play in the Funhouse of Language," *Canadian Review of Comparative Literature* 12, no. 2 (1985): 264–86.

24. Cannon, *Italo Calvino: Writer and Critic*, 100.

25. These distinctions between some of the aims and characteristics of literary modernism and those of postmodernism derive from several sources, including Carol P. James, "Seriality and Narrativity in Calvino's *Le città invisibili*," *Modern Language Notes* 97, no. 1 (1982): 144–61; David Hayman, "Double-Distancing: An Attribute of the 'Post-Modern' Avant-Garde," *NOVEL* 12, no. 1 (1978): 33–47 (which treats primarily the contemporary French novel); Craig Owens, "The Allegorical Impulse: Toward a Theory of Postmodernism," *October* 12 (Spring 1980): 67–86, and *October* 13 (Summer 1980): 59–80 (which treats primarily art and film as well as literature and literary theory); Linda Hutcheon, "A Poetics of Postmodernism?" *Diacritics* 13, no. 4 (1983): 33–42; and Patricia Waugh, *Metafiction: The Theory and Practice of Self-Conscious Fiction*, New Accents (London: Methuen, 1984), 21–61. See also Gianni Celati, "Il racconto di superficie," *Il verri*, ser. 5, no. 1 (1973): 93–114; and Ricci, "The Readers in Italo Calvino's Latest *Fabula*," 96, 101–2.

26. Calvino recently acknowledged his turning away from any "ultimate goals" regarding political or social issues—in a sense that goes much further than

his essays of the 1950s and early 1960s—in an interview with Constance Markey, "Italo Calvino: The Contemporary Fabulist," *Italian Quarterly* 23, no. 88 (1982): 77–85, esp. 84–85.

27. Both of these topics are discussed by Calvino in "An Interview with Italo Calvino," 248, 250–51.

Chapter 11. Samonà, Manganelli, Eco

1. All page references in the text are to the Einaudi editions of *Fratelli* and *Il custode*, published in Turin in 1978 and 1983, respectively. Translations are mine.

2. The image of the grotto or cave to describe the narratives' restricted focus is Samonà's own. See his discussion of the intentions of his narrative practice in our 1984 interview, "Incontro con Carmelo Samonà," *Modern Language Notes* 100, no. 1 (1985): 170.

3. For Samonà's thoughts regarding this lack of predecessors see "Incontro con Carmelo Samonà," 155–56.

4. Gian-Paolo Biasin discusses the importance of language, the appeal to a "metanarrative" reading, and the relation between literature and life in *Fratelli* in "Il laboratorio e il labirinto" (1980), revised in *Icone italiane*, Strumenti di ricerca, 34–35 (Rome: Bulzoni, 1983), 181–208, translated as "The Laboratory and the Labyrinth," in *Italian Literary Icons*, Princeton Essays in Literature (Princeton: Princeton University Press, 1985), 143–65.

5. For a psychoanalytical reading of *Fratelli* see Giovanni Hautmann, "La relazione psicotica in 'Fratelli' (di C. Samonà)" (1980), *Rivista di psicoanalisi*, no. 1 (1981), 48–71.

6. Hautmann, 63–65, provides a patently Freudian elaboration of this possibility and also discusses what he terms the "crisis" scene of chapter 20 in some detail. For discussion of the linguistic abilities of the "Donna" as superior to those of *both* brothers, see Biasin, "Il laboratorio e il labirinto," 201–4; "The Laboratory and the Labyrinth," 161–64.

7. In "Incontro con Carmelo Samonà," 158, 162.

8. These beliefs run throughout Sanguineti's writings and commentaries of the period. See especially the following: his incisive comments during the Gruppo 63 debates of 4 October 1963, in part summarized and in part reproduced in *Gruppo 63: La nuova letteratura, 34 scrittori, Palermo ottobre 1963*, ed. Nanni Balestrini and Alfredo Giuliani, Le Comete, 31, panorami, 4 (Milan: Feltrinelli, 1964), 379–85, 401–5; his interview with Ferdinando Camon (in which the most prominent companions and opponents are the less politically oriented Angelo Guglielmi and the broadly based phenomenologist Renato Barilli), in Camon's collection, *Il mestiere di poeta*, Saggi, 36 (Milan: Lerici, 1965), 215–39; and "Avanguardia, società, impegno" (1966) and "Il trattamento del materiale verbale nei testi della nuova avanguardia" (1964), in his *Ideologia e linguaggio*, new

augmented ed., Materiali, 4 (Milan: Feltrinelli, 1978), 67–83, 91–131.

9. In *La letteratura come menzogna*, Materiali, 11 (Milan: Feltrinelli, 1967), 171–77, cited by page number in the text. All translations of Manganelli's writing are mine.

10. The most incisive and coherent treatment of the various positions within the Gruppo 63 is still Gian Carlo Ferretti's "Il Gruppo '63 e l'area dello sperimentalismo," in his *La letteratura del rifiuto*, Civiltà letteraria del Novecento, Saggi, 12 (Milan: Mursia, 1968), 274–99. See also Maria Corti, *Il viaggio testuale*, Einaudi Paperbacks, 90 (Turin: Einaudi, 1978), 131–66, for a discussion of the similarities and differences between Manganelli and other novelists of the 1960s and 1970s; and Linda Hutcheon, *Narcissistic Narrative: The Metafictional Paradox*, Library of the *Canadian Review of Comparative Literature*, 5 (Waterloo, Ontario: Wilfrid Laurier University Press, 1980; rpt. London: Methuen, 1984), 104–17, for a discussion of the parallels and contrasts between these aspects of the Italian and French intellectual avant-gardes of the 1960s.

11. *Centuria: Cento piccoli romanzi fiume*, La Scala (Milan: Rizzoli, 1979). All references are to this edition, except for those to the author's preface, which (since the preface appears on the hardcover's dust jacket) are to the Biblioteca Universale Rizzoli paperback edition of 1980. Page numbers are included in the text.

12. *Amore*, La Scala (Milan: Rizzoli, 1981), cited by page numbers in the text.

13. *Discorso dell'ombra e dello stemma, o del lettore e dello scrittore considerati come dementi*, La Scala (Milan: Rizzoli, 1982), cited by page number in the text. Manganelli's recent *Dall'inferno* (1985; *From Hell*), a "story" in dialogues, continues the literary and theoretical interests of *Amore* and *Discorso dell'ombra e dello stemma*, though it evinces somewhat less literary self-consciousness than either of the two previous books.

14. "Iperipotesi," in Balestrini and Giuliani, *Gruppo 63*, 259–63.

15. The disagreements between Vittorini, Togliatti, and Alicata appeared in *Il Politecnico* and *Rinascita* in the middle and late 1940s. For Angelo Guglielmi's view of the avant-garde of the sixties see his "Avanguardia e sperimentalismo," in Balestrini and Giuliani, *Gruppo 63*, 15–24, also, with slight variations, in *Avanguardia e sperimentalismo*, Materiali, 1 (Milan: Feltrinelli, 1964), 53–62. The latter collection also contains other essays on this topic by Guglielmi, followed by relevant exchanges with Calvino, Moravia, Nicola Chiaromonte, and Sergio Quinzio (85–99). See also the distillation of Guglielmi's comments during the open debate in *Gruppo 63*, 376–79; and his essays in "Parte prima: Idee generali" and his "Conclusione," in his *Vero e falso*, Materiali, 17 (Milan: Feltrinelli, 1968), 9–44, 165–73. For the subsequent development of Guglielmi's position see his *La letteratura del risparmio*, Nuovi saggi italiani, 10 (Milan: Bompiani, 1973). Giuliani's views (specifically in regard to poetic language) are

contained in his original 1961 introduction and his 1965 preface to the new edition of the ground-breaking anthology, *I novissimi: Poesie per gli anni '60*, ed. Alfredo Giuliani, new rev. ed., Collezione di poesia, 19 (Turin: Einaudi, 1965), 5–14, 15–32. See also his comments in *Gruppo 63*, 372–76. For Balestrini's views see his brief comments in the second Gruppo 63 anthology, *Gruppo 63: Il romanzo sperimentale, Palermo 1965*, ed. Nanni Balestrini (Milan: Feltrinelli, 1966), 132–35. This anthology contains the comments and reactions of many of the best known of the 1960s *avanguardisti*, including Barilli, Sanguineti, Guglielmi, and Giuliani.

16. *Il nome della rosa* (Milan: Bompiani, 1980), in English as *The Name of the Rose*, trans. William Weaver, A Helen and Kurt Wolff Book (San Diego: Harcourt Brace Jovanovich, 1983). Page references to these editions are included in the text.

Postille a "Il nome della rosa" first appeared in *Alfabeta*, vol. 49 (June 1983), and was then published as a pamphlet (and sold together with the paperback edition of the novel) by Bompiani in 1984 and published as an appendix to the hardback edition in 1985. It has been translated by William Weaver as *Postscript to "The Name of the Rose,"* A Helen and Kurt Wolff Book (San Diego: Harcourt Brace Jovanovich, 1984). Page references in the text are to the 1984 Bompiani pamphlet and to the 1984 translation.

17. Eco is referring specifically to Barilli's opening address, published in Balestrini, *Gruppo 63: Il romanzo sperimentale*, 11–26. Barilli's essay continues the line of inquiry proposed in his contributions to the first Gruppo 63 anthology ("Le strutture del romanzo," 25–47; see also 388–94), which is again taken up in the first version (1964) of his *La barriera del naturalismo* (Milan: Mursia) and in its various revisions up to 1980. Eco's doubts about the social postulates and literary projects of the Gruppo 63 were apparent as early as his contribution to their first anthology, "La generazione di Nettuno," in Balestrini and Giuliani, *Gruppo 63*, 407–16. On this point see also Ferretti "Il Gruppo '63 e l'area dello sperimentalismo," 284–85.

18. For John Barth's view regarding the positive aspects of postmodernist fiction (with Calvino seen as being among its principal exemplars), see "The Literature of Replenishment: Postmodernist Fiction" (1979/1980), rpt. in *The Friday Book: Essays and Other Nonfiction* (New York: Putnam's, 1984), 193–206. Barth intended this essay as "a companion and corrective to" his earlier essay concerning what he terms "the aesthetic of high modernism" (193, 206), "The Literature of Exhaustion" (1967), rpt. in *The Friday Book*, 62–76.

Conclusion. Who, How, and Why

1. Two influential examples are by Alfred Tarski and Roland Barthes. In "The Semantic Concept of Truth and the Foundations of Semantics," *Philosophy*

and Phenomenological Research, vol. 4 (1944), rpt. in *Readings in Philosophical Analysis,* ed. Herbert Feigl and Wilfrid Sellars, The Century Philosophy Series (New York: Appleton-Century-Crofts, 1949), 52–84, Tarski outlines the status and mechanisms (later much-debated) of "meta-language" and "object-language" while pointing out the "only . . . relative sense" of these terms, since "meta-" and "object-" are constantly open to new and shifting relations with one another and with other discourse, which may take the meta-language as *its* object (and thus, in creating a multiplicity of levels, "we arrive at a whole hierarchy of languages," 60). In "Littérature and meta-langage," *Phantomas* (1959), rpt. in *Essais Critiques,* Collection "Tel Quel" (Paris: Seuil, 1964), 106–7; translated as "Literature and Metalanguage," in *Critical Essays,* trans. Richard Howard (Evanston: Northwestern University Press, 1972), 97–98, Barthes' comments are, as usual, extremely suggestive despite the reductiveness of his historical scheme (leading from Flaubert to Mallarmé, Proust, the Surrealists, and Robbe-Grillet before doubling back, via an argument with Sartre, to Racine, and then concluding with the condition of literature in postwar French society). In this regard, see also Douglas R. Hofstadter, *Gödel, Escher, Bach: An Eternal Golden Braid* (New York: Basic Books, 1979), and the concluding chapter of Bruce F. Kawin, *The Mind of the Novel: Reflexive Fiction and the Ineffable* (Princeton: Princeton University Press, 1982), 211–323.

Index

Abelard, Peter, 326
Addamo, Sebastiano, 376n.15
Adorno, T. W., 7
Agamemnon, 111
Aleardi, Aleardo, 205
Alfieri, Vittorio, 340n.23
Alicata, Mario, 321, 378n.15
Allen, James Sloan, 339n.18
Allen, Woody, 328
Alonge, Roberto, 359n.20
Alter, Robert, 9–12, 15, 16, 17, 337nn. 12, 13
Althusser, Louis, 363n.7, 366n.2
Altieri, Charles, 4, 336n.5
Alvaro, Corrado, 177
Ambrose, Mary, 342n.4, 343n.10, 347n.26
Amerio, Romano, 347n.24
Amphitrite, 200
Aragno, Piero, 362–63n.3
Aragon, Louis, 366n.3
Ariadne, 109, 110, 111
Ariosto, Ludovico, 105, 205, 269, 277, 316, 328
Aristotle, 322
Artaud, Antonin, 343n.15
Asor Rosa, Alberto, 345n.19, 348–49n.5, 350n.15, 351n.19
Aste, Mario, 358n.17
Atreidae, tomb of the, 108
Auerbach, Erich, 260
Augieri, Carlo A., 349n.5

Augustine, Saint, 360n.5
Austin, J. L., 13, 339n.17

Bachelard, Gaston, 316
Bacon, Roger, 326
Bakhtin, Mikhail, 81
Bal, Mieke, 8, 337n.8
Baldi, Guido, 342n.4, 344n.17, 345n.19, 348–49n.5, 350nn. 14, 15, 371n.11
Balestrini, Nanni, 229, 301, 313, 321, 379n.15
Balzac, Honoré de, 5, 11, 428
Baratto, Mario, 358n.18
Bàrberi Squarotti, Giorgio, 345n.19, 346n.24, 349nn. 5, 10, 370n.11
Barilli, Renato, 326, 358n.17, 359n.21, 361n.9, 370–71n.10, 377n.8, 379nn. 15, 17
Barricelli, Jean-Pierre, 343n.11
Barth, John, 18, 327, 376n.23, 379n.18
Barthelme, Donald, 18
Barthes, Roland, 10, 13, 287, 316, 339n.19, 376n.23, 379–80n.1
Bassani, Giorgio, 365n.1
Battaglia, Salvatore, 21, 354n.13
Beckett, Samuel, 5, 15, 302, 335n.1
Bellow, Saul, 1
Benjamin, Walter, 7, 10, 264, 328
Benn, Gottfried, 5, 7
Benveniste, Émile, 339n.17
Bergson, Henri, 135, 355n.6
Berlinguer, Enrico, 260

Bernardini Napoletano, Francesca, 375n.18
Bernard of Morlay, 326
Beyle, Marie-Henri [pseud. Stendhal], 16, 327, 366nn. 3, 5
Biasin, Gian-Paolo, 358n.17, 360nn. 3, 7, 370n.11, 374n.14, 377nn. 4, 6
Bigazzi, Roberto, 104, 349n.5, 352n.4
Bilenchi, Romano, 195
Blomme, Raoul, 340n.22, 365n.14
Bloom, Harold, 5, 336n.4
Boccaccio, Giovanni, 22–23, 328, 333
Bocelli, Arnaldo, 368n.19
Bontempelli, Massimo, 156
Borges, Jorge Luis, 2, 8–9, 15, 18, 117, 315, 318, 324, 337n.11
Borgese, Giuseppe Antonio, 328
Borghello, Giampaolo, 362n.16
Botti, Francesco Paolo, 361n.9
Bouffard, Jean-Claude, 353n.12
Bouissy, André, 361n.16
Boyd, Michael, 335n.1
Bradley, Linda C., 376n.23
Brancati, Vitaliano, 195
Brecht, Bertolt, 260, 264
Brentano, Franz, 13
Bronstein, Lev Davydovich [pseud. Leon Trotsky], 6, 337n.7
Brooke-Rose, Christine, 18, 339n.18
Brunhild, 111
Bruno, Giordano, 277
Bukharin, Nikolay Ivanovich, 6
Burke, Kenneth, 219, 376n.16

Caesar, Julius, 143–44, 223
Cain, 68, 83
Caldwell, Erskine, 364n.13
Calvino, Italo, 20, 117, 194–95, 266–300, 317, 318, 321, 327, 331, 333, 347nn. 25, 26, 364n.12, 372nn. 4, 6, 378n.15, 379n.18. Works: *Il castello dei destini incrociati*, 287; *Le città invisibili*, 287; *Le Cosmicomiche*, 266, 276–87, 374n.9; essays, 275, 373–74n.7; *I nostri antenati*, 276, 286, 375n.20; *Palomar*, 299; Preface to *Il sentiero dei nidi di ragno*, 194, 275, 364n.12, 373n.3; *Il sentiero dei nidi di ragno*, 266, 267–76, 373n.3; *Se una notte d'inverno un viaggiatore*, 266, 287–300, 327, 376n.22; *T con zero*, 276
Cambon, Glauco, 357n.15, 361n.12
Camerino, Antonio, 361n.16
Camon, Ferdinando, 372n.4, 374n.12, 377n.8
Campailla, Sergio, 80, 349nn. 5, 8, 10, 350n.15, 351n.20
Cannon, JoAnn, 293, 374n.7, 375nn. 14, 18, 376nn. 23, 24
Cantoni, Alberto, 356n.8
Capiau-Laureys, Évelyne, 340n.22, 361n.13
Capuana, Luigi, 68
Carducci, Giosuè, 233, 236, 370n.10
Carlton, Jill Margo, 375n.20
Carlyle, Thomas, 9
Carroll, Lewis. *See* Dodgson, Charles Lutwidge
Cassirer, Ernst, 374n.10
Castaneda, Carlos, 14
Cavalcanti, Guido, 316
Cecchetti, Giovanni, 83, 347n.1, 348n.4, 349n.10, 350nn. 13, 15
Celati, Gianni, 376n.25
Centaurs, the, 109–10
Cervantes, Miguel de, 10, 16, 18, 328; *Don Quixote*, 8–9, 11, 205, 217
Chiari, Alberto, 346n.22
Chiari, Pietro, 23
Chiaromonte, Nicola, 364n.10, 378n.15
Christensen, Inger, 338n.14
Christie, Agatha, 317
Christopher, Saint, 46
Cincotta, Madeleine, 356n.13
Citanna, Giuseppe, 342n.8
Ciuffoletti, Zeffiro, 351n.18
Clemens, Samuel [pseud. Mark Twain], 348n.3
Cohn, Dorrit, 335n.1
Collodi, Carlo. *See* Lorenzini, Carlo
Conrad, Joseph, 10, 335n.1
Contini, Gianfranco, 352n.5, 366n.4, 368n.19, 371n.11
Copernicus, Nicolaus, 125, 128
Coriolanus, 230

Corsinovi, Graziella, 357n.13
Corti, Maria, 346n.23, 378n.10
Crispi, Francesco, 99
Croce, Benedetto, 110, 342n.8, 354n.13, 356n.11
Cronus, 214–16
Culler, Jonathan, 3–4, 336nn. 3, 4
Cyrano de Bergerac, Savinien de, 277

Daedalus, 108
Dällenbach, Lucien, 8, 13, 16, 215, 337nn. 8, 9, 367n.16
Daly, Mary, 14
D'Annúnzio, Gabriele, 20, 25, 96, 98, 99, 101, 105, 106–15, 223, 264, 316, 330, 370n.10. Works: *Cento e cento e cento e cento pagine del libro segreto di Gabriele D'Annunzio tentato di morire*, 115; *Forse che sì forse che no*, 115; *Il fuoco*, 98, 106–15, 353n.10; *Notturno*, 115; novelle, 111, 115; *Il piacere*, 106, 115; *Taccuini*, 107, 353n.11; *Trionfo della morte*, 106, 111, 115, 353n.10; *Le vergini delle rocce*, 106
Dante, 22–23, 135, 205, 258, 328, 331, 260n.5, 366n.7
David, Michel, 360n.9, 369n.6
Debenedetti, Giacomo, 21, 355n.7, 357nn. 13, 14, 359n.2, 361nn. 14, 15, 372n.2
De Chirico, Andrea [pseud. Alberto Savinio], 332
Defoe, Daniel, 26, 327
de Lauretis, Teresa, 275–76, 374n.8, 375nn. 14, 18
de Man, Paul, 3, 202, 204, 213, 219, 339n.17, 366nn. 3, 5, 367n.14, 368n.17
De Matteis, Carlo, 369n.6
De Michelis, Eurialo, 342n.7, 346n.22
De Monticelli, Roberto, 368n.19
Depretis, Agostino, 351n.18
d'Eramo, Luce, 363n.4
De Rienzo, Giorgio, 32, 61, 341n.3, 342n.4, 347n.26
De Robertis, Giuseppe, 346n.24

Derrida, Jacques, 3, 4, 14, 336n.5, 375n.18
De Sanctis, Francesco, 344n.19
Descartes, René, 13, 226
Deucalion, 318
Devil, the, 55, 73, 310
Dickens, Charles, 269, 327, 348n.3
Diderot, Denis, 10, 18
Dioscuri, 233
Dipace, Antonio, 365
Dodgson, Charles Lutwidge [pseud. Lewis Carroll], 315
Dombroski, Robert S., 133, 342n.4, 343n.13, 344n.17, 345n.19, 346n.22, 355n.3, 356n.12, 358n.17, 358–59n.20, 368–69n.3, 369n.6, 370n.11, 371n.14
Donati, Corrado, 357n.14, 358n.17
Don Juan, 57
Dos Passos, John, 248
Dossi, Carlo, 20, 98, 99–106, 114, 233, 330, 356n.8. Works: *L'altrieri: Nero su bianco*, 100; *La colonia felice*, 353n.6; *La desinenza in A*, 100, 352n.2; *Note azzurre*, 105, 352n.1; *La vita di Alberto Pisani*, 100–106, 352n.2
Dostoevsky, Fëdor Mikhailovich, 16, 258, 343n.15, 360n.5
Duse, Eleonora, 108, 111

Echo, 316
Eco, Umberto, 20, 287, 301–2, 322–28, 333, 376n.23. Works: *Il nome della rosa*, 322–28, 379n.16; *Postille a "Il nome della rosa,"* 322, 325, 326–28, 379n.16
Edwards, Brian, 376n.23
Eros, 205
Eskin, Stanley G., 366n.8
Eurydice, 111
Evans, Arthur, 366n.8
Evans, Catherine, 366n.8

Falaschi, Giovanni, 373n.6, 374n.12
Faulkner, William, 15, 156, 173, 241, 335n.1, 373n.13
Felman, Shoshana, 339n.17
Fenoglio, Beppe, 195

Ferdinand II (king of the Two Sicilies), 197, 200
Ferrario, Edoardo, 355–56n.7
Ferretti, Gian Carlo, 366n.4, 367n.9, 372n.4, 378n.10
Ficara, Giorgio, 342n.4, 343n.12, 347n.26
Fielding, Henry, 10, 11
Fish, Stanley E., 287
Fitch, Brian T., 338n.14
Fitzgerald, F. Scott, 364n.13
Flaubert, Gustave, 91, 107, 380n.1
Flores, Enrico, 371n.11
Fogazzaro, Antonio, 106
Ford, Ford Madox, 10
Foscolo, Ugo, 23–25; "Notizia intorno a Didimo Chierico," 24–25, 105, 341n.24; *Ultime lettere di Jacopo Ortis*, 23–24, 26, 101
Fowles, John, 10
Franchetti, Leopoldo, 91, 96, 350–51n.17, 351n.18
Franco, Francisco, 263
Freccero, John, 169, 360nn. 5, 6, 361n.11
Frege, Gottlob, 338n.16
Freud, Sigmund, 15, 231–32, 366n.2, 367nn. 10, 11, 13, 370n.7, 377n.6
Frye, Northrop, 5
Fusco, Mario, 359n.3, 361n.13, 362nn. 16, 17
Futurists, 115, 154

Gadda, Carlo Emilio, 20, 100, 105, 117, 222–45, 246, 321, 322, 331, 332, 352n.5. Works: "Apologia manzoniana," 370n.10; *La cognizione del dolore*, 223–45, 368n.2; *Eros e Priapo: Da furore a cenere*, 243, 353n.9, 369n.6; *Giornale di guerra e di prigionia*, 369n.5; *La meccanica*, 222–23, 224, 369n.4; *Meditazione milanese*, 222, 236, 368n.1; *Le meraviglie d'Italia-Gli anni*, 369n.4; *Quer pasticciaccio brutto de via Merulana*, 223, 224, 237–38, 241, 322; *I viaggi la morte*, 369n.4
Gans, Eric, 17–18, 339–40n.20
García Márquez, Gabriel, 15, 18

Gardair, Jean-Michel, 356n.9
Garibaldi, Giuseppe, 205
Gasché, Rodolphe, 339n.17
Gass, William H., 11, 338n.14
Genette, Gérard, 8, 337n.10, 363n.5
Geppetto, 271
Getto, Giovanni, 341–42n.4
Ghidetti, Enrico, 352n.4
Giachery, Emerico, 354n.15
Giants, revolt of the, 212
Gide, André, 8, 11, 337n.8
Gilbert, John, 366n.8
Gioanola, Elio, 105, 352nn. 5, 6, 357n.14, 360n.9, 361n.10, 369n.6
Giorgione, 109
Giovacchini, Peter, 370n.8
Girard, René, 16–17, 54–55, 340n.20, 343nn. 13, 14, 15
Girardi, Enzo Noè, 345n.19
Giuliani, Alfredo, 321, 360n.4, 378–79n.15
Godt, Clareece, 342n.6
Goethe, Johann Wolfgang von, 6, 23, 26, 107
Gonin, Francesco, 63
Goudet, Jacques, 353n.13
Gozzi, Carlo, 233
Graff, Gerald, 2–4, 11, 17, 18, 20, 335n.2, 336n.4
Gramsci, Antonio, 116, 248, 263, 344n.19, 354n.2
Greenblatt, Stephen, 340n.23
Grotstein, James S., 370n.8
"Gruppo 63," 224, 229, 261, 301, 312, 321, 326, 340n.22, 360n.4, 377n.8, 378n.10, 378–79n.15, 379n.17
Guglielmi, Angelo, 229, 313, 321, 372n.4, 377n.8, 378–79n.15
Guglielmi, Guido, 345n.19, 346n.24, 371n.14
Guglielminetti, Marziano, 354n.14, 355n.7, 357n.15

Hartman, Geoffrey, 3
Hassan, Ihab, 11
Hautmann, Giovanni, 377nn. 5, 6
Hayman, David, 376n.25

Hegel, Georg Wilhelm Friedrich, 6–7, 14, 15, 337n.6
Heidegger, Martin, 14, 15
Heiney, Donald, 374n.13
Hemingway, Ernest, 364n.13
Hercules, 205, 211–12
Hermaphroditus, 316
Hernández, Miguel, 258
Hesperides, Garden of the, 205
Hirsch, E. D., Jr., 374n.10, 375n.16
Historical novel, 25, 26–27, 62–64, 68, 195, 196, 199, 219, 247–48, 259, 269, 326; play of past and present in, 59–62, 67, 220–21, 247–48, 260–65; and Romantic irony, 65–67; and *romanzo popolare*, 264
Hitchcock, Alfred, 223
Hitler, Adolf, 259
Hofstadter, Douglas R., 380n.1
Holland, Norman, 287
Homer, 328
Hugo, Victor, 8
Hume, Kathryn, 374n.13
Hutcheon, Linda, 9, 11–13, 14, 16, 17, 20, 161, 338nn. 13, 14, 15, 340n.22, 360n.4, 376n.25, 378n.10

Icarus, 111, 303
Illiano, Antonio, 343n.10, 355n.5, 374n.14
Isella, Dante, 346n.23, 352n.6
Iser, Wolfgang, 287, 376n.23
Isolde, 111

Jakobson, Roman, 5, 363n.5, 376n.21
James, Carol P., 376n.25
James, Henry, 91
Jameson, Fredric, 114, 354n.18
Janner, Arminio, 357n.14
Jauss, Hans Robert, 287
Jay, Paul, 335n.1
Jesus Christ, 46, 78, 84, 185, 193, 230, 261, 362n.2, 369n.4
Jonard, Norbert, 362n.16
Jove, 206, 211–15
Joyce, James, 5, 7, 15, 91, 223, 267, 319, 335n.1, 369n.4, 371n.11

Judas, 83, 349n.9
Jupiter, 214, 318

Kafka, Franz, 5, 7, 175, 302
Kant, Immanuel, 15, 61
Kawin, Bruce, 9, 14–17, 18, 380n.1
Kellman, Stephen G., 335n.1
Kernan, Alvin B., 1–2, 18
Kernberg, Otto F., 370n.8
Kipling, Rudyard, 269, 271
Klein, Melanie, 166, 370n.8
Krieger, Murray, 364n.10
Kuhns, Richard F., 367n.15
Künstlerroman, 98, 100, 102

Lacan, Jacques, 3, 14, 15, 116, 154, 357n.14, 363n.7, 365–66n.2
Laclos, Choderlos de, 26
Lampedusa, Giuseppe Tomasi di, 20, 196–221. Works: *Il Gattopardo*, 195, 196–221, 224, 262, 365n.1; *Lezioni su Stendhal*, 366n.3
Landolfi, Tommaso, 332
Lansing, Richard, 367n.12
Lavagetto, Mario, 360n.6, 360–61n.9
Lazzaro-Weis, Carol, 346n.22
Leibniz, Gottfried Wilhelm, 222
Leitch, Vincent B., 336n.2
Leone de Castris, Arcangelo, 345n.19, 355nn. 3, 7, 357n.13, 359n.20, 362n.16
Levine, George, 337n.13
Lewis, R. W. B., 362n.2
Liala. *See* Negretti, Amalia
Lorenzini, Carlo [pseud. Carlo Collodi], 348n.3
Lucian, 272
Lugnani, Lucio, 357n.13
Lukács, Georg, 2, 5–7, 260
Luperini, Romano, 91, 96, 348nn. 2, 4, 349n.5, 350nn. 12, 14, 15, 16, 350–51n.17, 351n.20, 352n.21, 369n.6, 371n.14
Luti, Giorgio, 110, 353n.13, 361n.16

Macchia, Giovanni, 355n.5
Mailer, Norman, 1

Mallarmé, Stéphane, 107, 380n.1
Manganelli, Giorgio, 20, 301–2, 312–22, 325–26, 327, 333, 372n.4. Works: *Agli dèi ulteriori*, 314; *Amore*, 316–17, 378n.12; *Centuria: Cento piccoli romanzi fiume*, 314–16, 319, 325, 378n.11; *Dall'inferno*, 378n.13; *Discorso dell'ombra e dello stemma, o del lettore e dello scrittore considerati come dementi*, 317–22, 378n.13; *Hilarotragoedia*, 314; "Iperipotesi," 378n.14; "La letteratura come menzogna," 312–13, 319, 378n.9; *Nuovo commento*, 314; *Pinocchio: Un libro parallelo*, 314
Mann, Thomas, 5, 7, 175
Manzoni, Alessandro, 20, 26–67, 69, 223, 233, 327, 331, 370n.10. Works: *Discorso sopra alcuni punti della storia longobardica in Italia*, 344n.18; *Fermo e Lucia*, 26, 27, 64, 65, 341n.1; *Osservazioni sulla morale cattolica*, 48, 343n.9; *I Promessi Sposi*, 21, 23, 25, 26–67, 69, 73–74, 96, 117, 134, 220, 256, 258, 262, 267, 303, 324, 330, 341n.1
Maraini, Dacia, 369nn. 4, 5
Marcus, Millicent Joy, 340n.23
Mariani, Gaetano, 353n.6
Markey, Constance, 377n.26
Marx, Jacques, 365n.14
Marx, Karl, 191, 255, 372n.3
Materassi, Mario, 367n.15
Maupassant, Guy de, 91
Mazzacurati, Giancarlo, 361n.9
Mazzotta, Giuseppe, 340n.23
Medusa, 317
Melville, Herman, 14
Memling, Hans, 8
Meyers, Jeffrey, 220, 366nn. 3, 8, 368n.18
Miller, J. Hillis, 3–4, 16, 335–36n.2, 336nn. 3, 4
Minotaur, 86, 95
Modernism, 2, 7, 10, 25, 117, 137, 155, 162, 176, 298, 302, 327, 332–33, 356n.12, 376n.25
Molière. *See* Poquelin, Jean-Baptiste
Momigliano, Attilio, 342n.5
Montano, Rocco, 346n.22

Monteleone, Giulio, 351n.18
Morante, Elsa, 20, 246–65, 331. Works: *Alibi* ("Sheherazade"), 264; *Aracoeli*, 247; "La censura in Spagna"["'La Storia' secondo Elsa Morante"], 373n.7; Introduction to *L'opera completa dell'Angelico*, 373n.7; *L'isola di Arturo*, 247, 259; *Il mondo salvato dai ragazzini*, 256; "9 domande sul romanzo," 372n.2; "Pro o contro la bomba atomica," 372n.2; *La Storia*, 21, 220, 246–65, 371–72n.1
Moravia, Alberto, *See* Pincherle, Alberto
Morrissette, Bruce, 337n.8
Moynihan, Robert, 336n.2
Musatti, Cesare, 360n.9
Muscetta, Carlo, 349n.5, 350n.15, 351n.20
Muses, the, 39–40
Musil, Robert, 175
Mussolini, Benito, 115, 259

Nabokov, Vladimir, 1, 10, 335n.1
Narcissus, 154, 212, 228, 241, 316, 321, 328
Nardi, Piero, 352n.6
Negretti, Amalia [pseud. Liala], 373n.4
Nencioni, Giovanni, 346n.24
Neorealists, 20, 194–95, 346n.12, 364–65n.13, 365n.14
Nicolini, Fausto, 342n.7
Nicomedes IV, king of Bithynia, 144
Nievo, Ippolito, 68, 269
Nigro, Salvatore S., 344n.17
Nolan, David, 367–68n.16
Nouvea roman, 18, 301

Ockham, William of, 326
Oedipus, 164, 169, 230
Old Man of Crete, 205
O'Neill, Tom, 367n.12
Orestes, 111, 143
Orpheus, 110, 111, 112
Ovid, 244
Owens, Craig, 376n.25

Palumbo, Matteo, 361n.9
Pampaloni, Geno, 364n.10

Parini, Giuseppe, 235
Pascal, Blaise, 128
Pascal, Théophile, 128
Paul, Jean. *See* Richter, Jean Paul Friedrich
Pavese, Cesare, 177, 195, 268–69, 365n.14, 373nn. 4, 5
Pease, Donald, 336n.2
Pedullà, Walter, 283, 352n.5, 353n.6, 375n.17
Peirce, Charles Sanders, 184, 283
Pérez Firmat, Gustavo, 338n.14
Perniola, Mario, 21, 340n.22
Persephone, 111, 316
Perseus, 108
Petrocchi, Giorgio, 346n.24
Petroni, Franco, 361n.9
Petroni, Mario, 348n.3
Picasso, Pablo, 2
Pincherle, Alberto [pseud. Alberto Moravia], 7, 177, 195, 345n.19, 365n.14, 372n.4, 378n.15
Pindar, 61, 109
Pinocchio, 271, 303, 314
Pinter, Harold, 2
Pirandello, Luigi, 20, 25, 96, 105, 112, 116–55, 156, 169, 173, 177, 330, 332. Works: *Enrico IV*, 125, 129, 154; *La favola del figlio cambiato*, 155; *Il fu Mattia Pascal*, 116–36, 137, 139, 147, 150, 152, 153, 155, 162, 355n.4; *I giganti della montagna*, 155; *Lazzaro*, 155; *Liolà*, 118, 119; *La nuova colonia*, 155; *Quaderni di Serafino Gubbio operatore*, 153; *Sei personaggi in cerca d'autore*, 358n.20; *L'umorismo*, 122, 128, 131, 132, 136, 355n.6; *Uno, nessuno e centomila*, 117–18, 136–55, 162, 242, 298, 357n.16
Pirodda, Giovanni, 349–50n.11, 350n.13
Pitrè, Giuseppe, 349n.9
Pius IX, 353n.7
Plato, 6, 233, 243, 249, 345n.21, 363n.5, 371n.12
Pope, Alexander, 15
Poquelin, Jean-Baptiste [pseud. Molière], 168
Porcelli, Bruno, 361–62n.16

Porta, Carlo, 100
Port-Royal, 13
Postmodernism, 1–2, 10, 11–13, 18, 161–62, 267, 298–300, 302, 321–22, 325–27, 328, 332–33, 376n.25
Potter, Joy Hambuechen, 365n.13
Pratolini, Vasco, 195, 328
Procaccini, Alfonso, 340n.23
Propp, Vladimir, 269
Proust, Marcel, 16, 335n.1, 361n.14, 380n.1
Psyche, 205
Pucci, Pietro, 368n.3
Puck, 245
Puig, Manuel, 318
Pulci, Luigi, 105
Pullini, Giorgio, 368n.13
Pupino, Angelo R., 346n.23, 372n.4
Puppo, Mario, 346n.23
Pynchon, Thomas, 2, 18
Pyramus, 244
Pyrrha, 318

Quine, Willard Van Orman, 13, 338–39n.16
Quinzio, Sergio, 378n.15

Rabelais, François, 328
Racine, Jean, 380n.1
Radcliff-Umstead, Douglas, 358n.17
Ragusa, Olga, 64, 346n.23, 355n.5, 356n.7, 366n.3, 371n.11, 373n.2
Raimondi, Ezio, 21, 346n.24, 347n.26, 353n.12
Raoul, Valerie, 338n.14
Rauhut, Franz, 357n.13
Ravanello, Donatella, 372n.2
Récanati, François, 13–14, 17, 20, 338n.16, 339n.17
Reynolds, Barbara, 346n.23
Ricardou, Jean, 8, 13, 219, 337n.8, 367n.16
Riccardi, Carla, 348n.4
Ricci, Franco, 376nn. 23, 25
Richardson, Joanna, 347n.26
Richardson, Samuel, 23, 26
Richter, Jean Paul Friedrich [pseud. Jean Paul], 233

Riddel, Joseph, 336n.4
Riffaterre, Michael, 287, 376n.23
Righetti, Carlo, 99, 100
Rinaldi, Rinaldo, 369n.4
Risset, Jacqueline, 371n.14
Riva, Valerio, 372n.4
Robbe-Grillet, Alain, 2, 8, 361n.11, 380n.1
Robison, Paula, 360nn. 3, 8
Roda, Vittorio, 354n.18
Romagnoli, Sergio, 341n.2, 342n.4, 347n.26
Romanò, Angelo, 345n.19
Roscioni, Gian Carlo, 370n.9, 371n.11
Rose, Margaret A., 338n.14
Rosenfeld, Herbert, 370n.8
Rossi, Ernesto, 83
Rousseau, Jean-Jacques, 23, 207, 360n.5
Rovani, Giuseppe, 99
Royce, Josiah, 8
Russell, Bertrand, 338n.16
Russian Formalists, 2–3, 5–6, 357n.15
Russo, Luigi, 342nn. 7, 8, 347–48n.2, 350nn. 12, 13

Saccone, Eduardo, 360nn. 3, 9
Salinari, Carlo, 59, 61, 112, 344n.17, 345n.19, 354n.16, 368n.19
Salsano, Roberto, 356n.11
Salvestroni, Simonetta, 366–67n.9
Samonà, Carmelo, 20, 301, 302–12, 321, 325, 327. Works: *Il custode*, 308–12, 377n.1; *Fratelli*, 302–8, 377n.1
Samonà, Giuseppe Paolo, 365n.1, 368n.19
Sanguineti, Edoardo, 229, 301, 312–13, 344n.17, 345n.19, 377–78n.8, 379n.15
Sapegno, Natalino, 345n.19
Sapir, Edward, 374n.10
Sartre, Jean-Paul, 7, 15, 356n.13, 380n.1
Saturn, 206, 211–15
Saussure, Ferdinand de, 376n.21
Savinio, Alberto. *See* De Chirico, Andrea
Scalia, Gianni, 345n.19
Scapigliatura, 68, 98, 99–100, 114, 356n.8
Schlueter, June, 338n.14
Schmitz, Ettore [pseud. Italo Svevo], 20, 96, 105, 156–76, 177, 244, 302, 332. Works: "Le confessioni del vegliardo," 176, 359n.1; *La coscienza di Zeno*, 155, 156, 161–76, 333, 359n.1; diary, 176, 359n.1; *Senilità*, 156, 157–61, 173, 359n.1; "Il vecchione," 359n.1, 362n.17; *Una vita*, 156–57, 173, 359n.1
Schneider, Franz, 362n.2
Scholes, Robert, 11, 338n.14
Sciascia, Leonardo, 367n.12
Scott, Sir Walter, 27
Scurani, Alessandro, 364n.10
Séailles, Gabriel, 355n.6
Seidl, Ivan, 372n.4
Self-consciousness, literary: in American criticism, 1–4, 5, 7, 9–17, 18; and causation, problem of, 23, 331–33; and current emphasis on reader and reading, 266–67, 287, 325, 326–28; definition of, 19–20; and distinction between genre and mode, 17–19, 246, 330; and Girardian mediation, 16–17, 24; historical nature of, 17–19, 21–23, 329–31, 332; in Italian criticism, 21; in Lukács, Georg, 5–7; and metafiction, current works on, 11, 338n.14; and *mise en abyme*, 8–9, 219, 293, 337n.8, 376n.24; in modernism and postmodernism, 2, 298–300, 302, 321–22, 325–28, 332–33, 376n.25; New Critical and deconstructive approaches contrasted, 331–32; and philosophy of language, 13–14; psychological self-consciousness compared to, 162; and realist aesthetics, 2, 68–69, 96, 177–78, 194–95, 247, 266, 365n.13; and Romantic irony, 67, 331; in Russian Formalists, 5–6; and social commitment, 264–65. *See also* Historical novel; *Künstlerroman*; Modernism; Postmodernism
Serri, Mirella, 352n.5
Sertoli, Giuseppe, 347n.26
Shakespeare, William, 41, 343n.15; *Hamlet*, 9, 83–84, 143, 226; *A Midsummer Night's Dream*, 245
Shklovsky, Viktor, 357n.15

Siegfried, 111
Silone, Ignazio. See Tranquilli, Secondo
Snoopy, 328
Snow White and the Seven Dwarfs, 269
Socrates, 345n.21
Soderini, G. V., 122
Sonnino, Sidney, 91, 96, 350–51n.17, 351n.18
Sophocles, 164
Spera, Francesco, 353n.6
Spinazzola, Vittorio, 78–79, 345n.19, 346n.23, 347n.26, 348n.5, 349nn. 6, 7, 350n.15
Spires, Robert C., 340n.21
Stein, Jean, 371n.13
Stendhal. See Beyle, Marie-Henri
Sterne, Laurence, 10, 18; *The Life and Opinions of Tristram Shandy, Gentleman*, 5, 11, 24, 267, 319; *A Sentimental Journey through France and Italy*, 24–25, 341n.24
Stevenson, Robert Louis, 269, 348n.3
Surrealists, 2, 380n.1
Svevo, Italo, See Schmitz, Ettore

Tancini, Francesca, 101, 352n.3
Tarchetti, Igino Ugo, 352n.4
Taricani, Carmine, 364n.10
Tarski, Alfred, 379–80n.1
Tel Quel group, 12, 313
Terracini, Benvenuto, 375–76n.21
Thackeray, William Makepeace, 11
Theseus, 109–10, 111
Thiher, Allen, 338n.14
Thisbe, 244
Thomas à Kempis, 325
Thousand and One Arabian Nights, 9, 298
Tilgher, Adriano, 357–58n.17
Timpanaro, Sebastiano, 344n.17, 345n.19
Tintoretto, 109
Tobin, Patricia Drechsel, 1–2, 18
Togliatti, Palmiro, 321, 378n.15
Tolstoi, Lev Nikolaevich, 91, 327
Tomasi di Lampedusa, Giuseppe. See Lampedusa, Giuseppe Tomasi di
Tozzi, Federigo, 177, 302
Tranquilli, Secondo [pseud. Ignazio Silone], 20, 177–94, 247, 264; representational procedures of, compared to neorealism, 177–78, 195. Works: *Il seme sotto la neve*, 364n.11; *Uscita di sicurezza*, 363n.8; *Vino e pane*, 177–94, 195, 362n.1
Tristan, 111
Trotsky, Leon. See Bronstein, Lev Davydovich
Trubetzkoy, Nicolay Sergeevich, 376n.21
Truffaut, François, 223
Twain, Mark. See Clemens, Samuel

Ulivi, Ferruccio, 346n.22
Ulysses, 111
Uranus, 214–15

Valesio, Paolo, 353n.8
Vallejo, César, 258
van Eyck, Jan, 8
Varese, Claudio, 345n.20
Velázquez, Diego, 8
Venè, Gian Franco, 345n.19, 359n.20
Venturi, Gianni, 372n.4
Venus, 202
Verdi, Giuseppe, 303
Verga, Giovanni, 20, 25, 68–97, 98–99, 112, 173, 247, 262, 329; and *verismo*, 21, 25, 68–69, 94, 96, 115, 177, 330, 354n.2, 365n.13. Works: "L'amante di Gramigna," 68–69, 347n.1; "Cavalleria rusticana," 82; "Jeli il pastore," 69; "La Lupa," 69, 74, 89, 94; *I Malavoglia*, 68, 69, 80, 82, 92, 347n.1; *Mastro-don Gesualdo*, 69, 93; "Rosso Malpelo," 68–97, 348n.4; *Vita dei campi*, 69, 76
Vicentini, Claudio, 357n.13
Vickery, John B., 344n.16
Vico, Giambattista, 60, 207, 251, 257, 262, 344n.18
Viganò, Renata, 195
Vigorelli, Giancarlo, 345n.19
Virgin Mary, 369n.4
Vitello, Andrea, 366n.5
Vittorini, Elio, 177, 194–95, 321, 364–65n.13, 365n.14, 368n.19, 378n.15
Vlasopolos, Anca, 375n.14

Volponi, Paolo, 340n.22
Vulcan, 205

Wagner, Richard, 107, 111, 113, 354n.17
Waugh, Patricia, 338n.14, 376n.25
Weatherhead, A. Kingsley, 363n.5
Whitehead, Alfred North, 338n.16
Whorf, Benjamin Lee, 374n.10
Wilde, Oscar, 107

Wilden, Anthony, 360n.9
Wittgenstein, Ludwig, 336n.5
Woolf, Virginia, 335n.1

Zaga, Nunzio, 367n.15
Zampa, Giorgio, 362n.16
Zatti, Sergio, 345n.19, 366n.8
Zeno of Elia, 169
Zeus, 214–16

DATE DUE			
ILL: 40201			
12/8/96			

HIGHSMITH 45-220